What is
Clinical Psychology?

Second Edition

Edited by

John Marzillier

and

John Hall

Department of Clinical Psychology
Warneford Hospital, Oxford

Oxford   New York   Tokyo
OXFORD UNIVERSITY PRESS
1992

Oxford University Press, Walton Street, Oxford OX2 6DP

Oxford New York Toronto
Delhi Bombay Calcutta Madras Karachi
Petaling Jaya Singapore Hong Kong Tokyo
Nairobi Dar es Salaam Cape Town
Melbourne Auckland
and associated companies in
Berlin Ibadan

Oxford is a trade mark of Oxford University Press

Published in the United States
by Oxford University Press, New York

First published 1987
Reprinted 1989, 1990

Library of Congress Cataloging in Publication Data
What is clinical psychology?/edited by John Marzillier and John Hall.—2nd ed.
Includes bibliographical references and index.
1. Clinical psychology. 2. Clinical psychologists.
I. Marzillier, John S. II. Hall, John. 1944 Apr. 9–
[DNLM: 1. Psychology, Clinical—Great Britain. WM 105 W555]
RC467.W53 1992 157–dc20 91–39084

ISBN 0–19–262169–6 (h/bk)
ISBN 0–19–262168–8 (p/bk)

Typeset by Joshua Associates Ltd, Oxford
Printed in Great Britain by
Bookcraft Ltd, Midsomer Norton, Avon

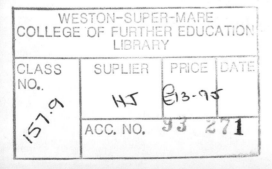

157.9

MARZILLIER, J. and   157.9
HALL, J. (Eds)

What is clinical psychology?   93 271

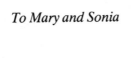

To Mary and Sonia

Preface to the Second Edition

Many people—friends, patients, professional colleagues—often ask us about our work as clinical psychologists. What exactly is a clinical psychologist? What do you do? How does your work differ from that of a psychiatrist or psychoanalyst? It was partly to answer these questions that this book was written.

We are aware that there are several 'good books' on clinical psychology, and some excellent ones. But they do not serve our need, for two reasons. First, the vast majority are American. Although there are many parallels between the practice of clinical psychology in America and that practised in Europe and elsewhere, there are also significant differences. To take one important example: in the UK clinical psychologists work in the National Health Service and are essentially public employees responding to the health care needs of the community. In the USA many clinical psychologists work in private practice and respond to market demands. This difference affects how the clinical psychologist works and what he or she does. Second, most of the books on clinical psychology are lengthy, detailed expositions of theory and practice. The reader needs to be prepared to take the time and the trouble to read through them. We wanted a book that was more readily accessible, or 'user friendly' as the current jargon goes. But above all we wanted the book to describe practice, to tell the reader what clinical psychologists actually do.

The book is divided into chapters describing the work of clinical psychologists in various settings and with different patient groups. This seemed the most sensible division as it closely accords with existing practice. There are clinical psychologists who work predominantly with children, others who work with older people, and others who work in psychiatric hospitals, for example. The book has also allowed us to invite a number of experienced practitioners to provide accounts of their work. There is overlap of course, though we have sought to minimize needless repetition, and we have in our final chapter brought out some common themes. The variety of settings and practices are significant since they illustrate how much clinical psychology has developed over the 25 years or so that we have both been working as clinical psychologists. We both began our work in psychiatry, carrying out psychometric assessments and some selected, mainly behavioural treatments. That was then the main role for clinical psychologists. Now, as this book illustrates, there is much more to the work of clinical psychologists, and the scope of their practice has vastly expanded. It is an exciting time to continue to write about our profession, and we have sought to capture the variety of ways that clinical psychology is practised.

Fifteen years before we wrote this preface, Don Bannister, a noted British clinical psychologist, wrote about the sort of professional who was needed in clinical psychology. He said, writing in visionary mood, it should be someone who could:

cope with a warring therapy group, excite a class of dead-tired nurses, investigate by test and/or conversation the dynamics of a family, devise a revealing and helpful attitude survey for a unit split by interprofessional differences, coax and bully a hospital committee into democratising its wards, introduce a machine teaching programme into a subnormality hospital, understand and counsel a virgin chronic patient on the joys of sex, act as a link man for a community anti-suicide programme and take a bunch of very old ladies for a really enjoyable trip to the zoo.

Trips to the zoo are relatively rare these days, but clinical psychologists appear to be involved in all these activities and more, as the various chapters of this book illustrate.

The book does not need to be read from beginning to end, although most readers will find it helpful to start with the first chapter. A glossary of key terms is included at the end of the book to explain the various technical terms used, although we have tried to keep these to a minimum. At the end of each chapter there is a short list of further reading on the material covered by each chapter: these titles have been chosen to be relatively accessible to the non-specialist reader.

We are grateful to the people who helped us in writing this book, especially those who commented on chapters: notably Sid Bloch, Hilary Edwards, Godfrey Fowler, Mike Hobbs, Joan Kirk, Ian McPherson, and Geoff Shepherd.

Oxford J.S.M.
January 1992 J.N.H.

Contents

Contributors

Paul Bennett
Lecturer, School of Psychology, University of Wales, Cardiff

Dr Ronald Blackburn
Director of Research and Honorary Consultant Clinical Psychologist, Ashworth Hospital Research Unit, Maghull, Liverpool

Professor Chris Cullen
SSMH Professor of Learning Difficulties, University of St Andrews, Scotland

Dr Dorothy Fielding
Head of Department of Clinical Psychology, St James's University Hospital (NHS Trust), Leeds

Dr Jeff Garland
Consultant Clinical Psychologist, Littlemore Hospital, Oxford

Dr John Hall
District Clinical Psychologist, Warneford Hospital, Oxford; Clinical Lecturer, University of Oxford; Consultant Adviser in Clinical Psychology to the Department of Health

Professor Ray Hodgson
Head of District Department of Clinical Psychology, Whitchurch Hospital, Cardiff; Honorary Professor, University of Wales, Cardiff

Dr John Marzillier
Consultant Clinical Psychologist, Warneford Hospital, Oxford; Clinical Lecturer, University of Oxford; Regional Tutor in Clinical Psychology, Oxford Regional Health Authority

Di Staples
Consultant Clinical Psychologist, Mary Marlborough Lodge, Nuffield Orthopaedic Centre, Oxford

Laurence Tennant
General Manager, Community Health Unit, Warwickshire Health Authority

Dr Louise Wallace
General Manager (Departmental services), East Birmingham Hospital

Dr Barbara Wilson
Senior Scientist, MRC Applied Psychology Research Unit, Cambridge

1

What is clinical psychology?

John Hall and John Marzillier

Clinical psychologists are health care professionals who work predominantly, though not exclusively, in the field of mental health. Among their main activities are: (a) *Psychological assessment*, that is the use of psychological methods and principles to gain better understanding of psychological attributes and problems. Intelligence tests and personality assessments such as the famous Rorschach 'ink-blot' test are well-known examples of psychological methods of assessment. But there are many others, as is illustrated in this book. (b) *Psychological treatment*, that is the use of psychological procedures and principles to help others to bring about change. There are many forms of psychological treatment, ranging from brief, practical procedures for overcoming specific fears to lengthy and complex treatments such as some forms of psychoanalysis. (c) *Psychological evaluation*, that is the use of psychological principles to evaluate the effectiveness of treatments or other forms of intervention. Clinical psychologists have been particularly involved in developing methods of evaluating psychotherapies and to a lesser extent physical forms of therapy.

Although these are the main activities of clinical psychologists, there are also others. Training of other professional staff, involvement in administration and advice, involvement in health service policies, and collaborative research are all activities that some clinical psychologists engage in as part of their work. This diversity is well illustrated in the subsequent chapters of this book.

WHAT IS PSYCHOLOGY?

The term psychology is derived from two Greek words: *psyche*, which means 'spirit' or 'mind', and *logos*, which means 'study'. 'The study of the mind' is therefore the literal, though not now the customary, meaning of psychology. Up to the end of the nineteenth century psychology did not exist as a separate academic discipline but was part of philosophy. Philosophers such as Locke, Descartes, Hume, and Berkeley addressed themselves to understanding mental processes via philosophical discourse and analysis. Descartes' famous dictum *Cogito, ergo sum* ('I think, therefore I am'), Locke's conception of the mind as a *tabula rasa* (blank state), Hume's careful elucidation of the principles of causation via mental association are all examples of a philosophical approach to understanding human behaviour. Psychology departed from philosophy in two fundamental ways. The first was the development of a *scientific* approach rather than a philosophical one. In 1879 Wilhelm Wundt opened the first psychological laboratory in Leipzig, Germany. There began a period of experimental study in which Wundt and his students sought to gain a scientific understanding of conscious experience by a systematic and carefully documented examination of their experiences and sensations when specific stimuli were presented, such as certain colours and sounds. This method of inquiry was known as introspectionism.

Although introspectionism proved a short-lived approach in psychology, mainly because of its reliance on idiosyncratic, personal accounts of experience, it embodied the experimental scientific tradition that has predominated in contemporary twentieth-century psychology.

The second departure of psychology from philosophy came in the extension of the subject matter beyond mental processes. In 1913 J. B. Watson, an American psychologist, had a profound effect on twentieth-century psychology with his call for psychology to be concerned not with internal mental processes, which he regarded as unverifiable and hence unscientific, but with observable behaviour. Behaviourism became the dominant creed of early twentieth-century psychology. Strongly emphasized was the need to place the science of psychology firmly on the bedrock of observed behaviour; experimental studies were conducted upon the behaviour of pigeons, rats, and other animals in the laboratory setting. B. F. Skinner pioneered the use of the famous Skinner box, in which rats pressed levers or pigeons pecked discs in response to various conditions of reward and punishment. These and many other laboratory experiments upon animal behaviour provided the basic psychology of conditioning and learning.

Psychology, therefore, had in the twentieth century moved from being a section of philosophy to becoming a scientific discipline in its own right. It had ceased to be the reasoned study of mental processes and become the experimental analysis of behaviour, animal and human. By this change psychology established links with other sciences such as biology, physiology, and biochemistry. The inter-relationship between psychology and these sciences could now be studied by examining the link between observed behaviour on the one hand and its biological basis on the other as, for example, in the relationship between brain waves and sleeping, or cardiovascular systems and emotions such as anxiety. Modern psychology is still rooted in this behavioural biological tradition.

The psychology of the present day is a flourishing and popular academic discipline which embraces a broad range of topics and activities. It requires knowledge of basic biological processes such as hunger, thirst, sex, sleeping, and waking, and of how these processes affect behaviour. Its central feature is the study of basic psycho-logical processes such as perception, learning, memory, language, thought, and emotion. Psychological study seeks to describe and understand these processes—for example, how memory processes work or in what ways people construct and organize their perceived world. The experimental method remains an important part of the psychological approach, although it is not the only method of inquiry. Developmental and social aspects of human behaviour are also vital features of modern psychology. Understanding human behaviour necessitates the study of its development and change from early infancy to old age. Developmental psychologists study, amongst many things, how children acquire and use language, the effects of early attachment and separation from parents, the pro-cesses and functions of play, and the effect of ageing on basic pro-cesses such as memory and thinking. Social psychologists study behaviour in its social context, which can be done experimentally in artificially created social encounters in the laboratory or naturally by observation and analysis of the individual in society. Finally, psy-chology merges into other academic disciplines, biological sciences (such as biology and physiology) on the one hand, and social sciences (such as sociology and anthropology) on the other.

In the example below the psychological approach is illustrated in the example of *pain*, which has an obvious biological and physio-logical basis in its relationship to tissue damage and the transmission of pain signals in certain nerve fibres to the brain. But it is not enough to describe pain in biological terms. Psychological factors play a significant part in our experience and expression of pain. The contribution that psychology has made in furthering our understanding of pain has led to one of the most influential theories of how pain is processed, the 'gate control' theory of Melzack and Wall (1988). Further, it has led to the development of new and promising treatments for chronic pain as well as effective methods of preparing individuals for necessary painful experiences such as surgery. It is the combination of basic research and theory and applied methods of assessment and treatment that characterizes the branch of psychology that is the subject of this book, clinical psychology.

THE PSYCHOLOGY OF PAIN

As we can all testify, pain is a response to injury or hurt. The more we are hurt the more likely we are to experience pain. Despite its unpleasantness pain has obvious survival value; it has the vital function of protecting us from serious injury. Thus a child's first contact with a hot stove will cause distress and pain but will rapidly lead to adaptive learning. Pain also sets limits on activity when a part of the body is injured. We learn to rest damaged ankles and knees rather than to continue to exercise them and injure them more.

Yet there are some intriguing facts about pain that cannot be explained solely in biological terms. Severe tissue damage, such as that produced by a deep wound, will in some people not produce any immediate pain despite the severity of the wound. Chronic and unremitting pain can occur in certain people long after the initial injuries have healed, the most dramatic example of which is 'phantom limb pain', pain localized in the place of an amputated arm or leg. The capacity for some people to undergo extremely painful experiences such as major surgery while hypnotized and not report or show any signs of pain has been well documented. The psychology of pain is concerned with understanding and influencing the psychological aspects of the experience of pain.

Psychological experimentation

Psychologists have contributed to our knowledge of pain in several ways. Firstly, by means of scientific experimentation they have clearly shown how psychological factors can affect when people will report pain (their pain threshold) and how much pain they will bear (their pain tolerance). The 'cold pressor test' is a laboratory test involving the immersion of a hand in ice-cold water. The use of this test has shown, for example, that people can learn to tolerate pain for longer periods of time by adopting deliberate strategies such as distraction. Other experimental studies have shown that if people believe they have control over the amount of painful stimulation they are receiving (for example painful electric shock), they can tolerate more pain (even if their perception of control is illusory).

Secondly, reliable measurements of the experience of pain have been developed. One of the best developed is the McGill–Melzack questionnaire (see Fig. 1.1), which presents a series of adjectives to describe the different sensations of pain experience. The adjectives can be categorized into three groups, namely those describing the sensory qualities of experience, those describing the affective qualities (for example tension, fear), and those that evaluate the intensity of the total pain experience. Studies of different types of pain using this questionnaire have indicated characteristic adjectives for different syndromes. For example, toothache tends to be described as throbbing, boring, and sharp, whereas menstrual pain is described as cramping and aching. Not only is a questionnaire such as this useful in gaining a better description of what painful experience consists of: it also helps in classifying different sorts of pain.

Thirdly, theoretical models of pain experience have been proposed, the best known of which is the 'gate control' theory. The theory proposes the existence of a neural mechanism, located in the dorsal horns of the spinal cord, which acts like a gate, modulating the flow of nerve impulses from peripheral fibres to the central nervous system. The 'gate' is also influenced by descending influences from the brain, representing the influence on pain of such psychological factors as attention, memory, and emotional states.

Finally, psychologists have developed a variety of treatment strategies for acute and chronic pain. These are described in more detail in Chapter 10. Relaxation, distraction, hypnosis, biofeedback, and planned behavioural programmes have shown promise in helping people cope more effectively with painful experiences.

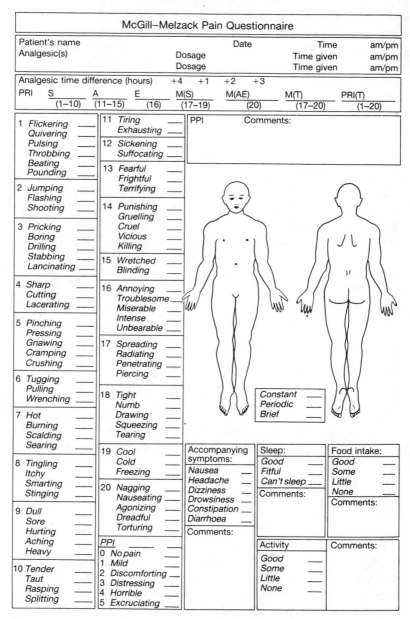

Fig. 1.1 The McGill–Melzack Pain Questionnaire. (Reprinted, with permission, from Melzack and Wall 1988.)

WHAT IS A CLINICAL PSYCHOLOGIST?

One of the commonest questions put to psychologists both by patients and professional staff is 'What is a clinical psychologist?' or 'In what way is a clinical psychologist different from a psychiatrist, a psychotherapist, or a social worker?'. In Table 1.1 we have listed some, though not all, of the health care professionals whose work may in some way overlap with or touch upon that of a clinical psychologist as they relate to each other in Britain (see Edwards (1987) for further details).

The main differences between clinical psychologists and other professionals occur (a) in training and (b) in the formal structure of their work. Psychiatrists, for example, receive their initial training in general medicine, which provides a solid basis of biological,

Table 1.1   Health care professionals

Profession	Training	Type of work
Clinical psychologist	First degree in psychology plus three years postgraduate training on University, Polytechnic, or Health Service Course	Psychological assessment and treatment, including psychotherapy (various). Specialist in cognitive–behaviour therapy. Research and evaluation
Psychiatrist	First degree in medicine plus three years postgraduate specialization in psychiatry	Psychiatric dianosis, pharmacological and physical forms of treatment, psychotherapy (various).
Psychotherapist	May take one of many specialist courses at various institutes or centres. Common for other professions (e.g. psychiatrist, psychologist) to take such courses after initial qualification. But need not be professionally qualified	Psychotherapy—type will depend on training and experience of individual

Table 1.1 Health care professionals (*cont.*)

Profession	Training	Type of work
Social worker	Two-year professional training, which may follow a first degree in sociology, social administration, or an unrelated degree	Social casework, and understanding of provision of social welfare benefits, housing, etc. Gives close support to individuals and families, which may include psychotherapy
Psychiatric nurse	Three-year training at School of Nursing	Direct nursing care of patients, both in hospital and in the community, including physical care and social support, and providing a pattern of daily living for patients
Occupational therapist	Three-year training	Provision of varied range of day activities, emphasizing rehabilitation, and creative activities, specifically aimed at improving patients' functioning
Counsellor	Variable. One to two-year courses in counselling	Psychotherapy/counselling for less disturbed individuals. Some specialist forms, *viz.* marriage guidance, careers

anatomical, and physiological knowledge of human functioning. By virtue of this training they have a particular expertise in physical and pharmacological treatments. Of all the professionals listed in Table 1.1, psychiatrists are the only ones with the right to practise medicine, i.e. prescribe psychotropic drugs or carry out surgical or physical treatments such as ECT. This right is protected in most countries by formal statute or registration.

Clinical psychology training involves specialized knowledge of psychological functioning and psychological methods, which provides particular expertise in carrying out psychological assessments such as psychometric tests, psychological treatments, and psychological methods of research and evaluation. In some countries the right to practice psychology is embodied into statute, usually by registering the title of 'psychologist'. In 1991 the implementation of Directive 89/48/EEC, under article 27 of the Treaty of Rome, requires all member states of the European Community to harmonize their training standards, to permit free movement of professions within the Community. This process of harmonization will undoubtedly lead to greater uniformity of practice between member states and probably to greater similarities in the protection of titles such as 'psychologist'.

The confusion between clinical psychologists and other professions therefore arises in part because of a real overlap between their respective activities. This is most evident in the case of psychotherapeutic skills, which are part of the activities of all the professions listed in Table 1.1. Clinical psychologists have specialized in some forms of psychotherapy, notably behavioural, cognitive and client-centred therapies (see Chapter 2 for a description of these approaches). And, to make matters worse, some clinical psychologists will *not* have trained in these methods but in other forms of therapy, or in fact may not practise psychotherapy at all! To the unsuspecting public the lack of a clear-cut description of clinical psychology, psychiatry, and other professions is not surprisingly a source of puzzlement and at times annoying confusion.

Towards a definition

Clinical psychologists tend to define their profession in terms of (a) the basic science of psychology and (b) its application to the understanding and resolution of human problems. The clinical psychologist is first and foremost and 'applied scientist' or 'scientist–practitioner' who seeks to use scientific knowledge to a beneficial end. Thus, in practising psychotherapy clinical psychologists are concerned to base their practices on what is scientifically known about problems such as depression, anxiety, schizophrenia, etc. and to use psychological principles that have been well established in experimental studies. They are also particularly concerned to develop and use only those psychological treatment methods that either have been shown to be effective or are in the process of validation. These attributes are well summarized in an American text on clinical psychology.

... clinical psychologists share several common attributes. They are *psychologists* because they have been trained to use the guidelines of knowledge of psychology in their professional work. They are *clinicians* because they 'attempt to understand people in their natural complexity and in their continuous adaptive transformations' ... They are *scientists* because they utilise the scientific method to achieve objectivity and precision in their professional work. Finally, they are *professionals* because they render important human services by helping individuals, social groups and communities to solve psychological problems and improve the quality of life. (Kendall and Norton-Ford 1982, p. 4)

The development of clinical psychology

Clinical psychology emerged as a recognizable profession at different times in different countries. In many countries clinical psychology does not exist as a distinct profession, and this is particularly the case when the academic discipline of psychology has only recently been established. In Britain clinical psychology was not formally recognized until after the Second World War and it then took until 1966 before a Division of Clinical Psychology was formed in the British Psychological Society. In the USA and the UK a significant impetus to the development of clinical psychology came from the two world wars. The need to recruit and select suitably qualified service personnel led to the development and use of psychological tests and other assessments. Psychologists were confronted with real-life problems and thereby required to apply their knowledge and skills. In the United States the psychological trauma caused by battle and injury resulted in psychologists becoming involved in treatment as well as assessment, and the wartime emergency hospitals in Britain became interested in similar problems.

The formation of the National Health Service in 1948 is an important landmark in the development of clinical psychology in Britain. The few clinical psychologists that existed were brought under the NHS umbrella, the vast majority working in psychiatric hospitals. In the USA clinical psychologists found fertile ground in the Veterans Administration Hospitals that were formed after the end of the Second World War.

The role for clinical psychologists in Britain from 1948 until the early 1960s was predominantly that of a laboratory scientist, carrying out psychometric and other types of tests. There was little direct therapeutic practice. The evolution of *behaviour therapy*—methods of treatment founded upon psychological principles and procedures—gave clinical psychology the entrée into therapy. By the end of the 1960s clinical psychologists had established themselves as clinical practitioners rather than laboratory scientists and had pioneered many successful new psychological treatments.

In Britain the profession has grown rapidly in proportional terms through the 1970s and 1980s, to become an independent profession with therapeutic functions and skills. A government report in 1977 encouraged the formation of larger departments of clinical psychology, rather than having groups of one or two psychologists based in individual hospitals. Since then clinical psychologists are now contributing to a growing range of clinical services outside the traditional areas of mental health and learning difficulties, such as the care of older people, substance abuse, and work with HIV/AIDS. During the 1980s the demand for clinical psychologists in Britain outstripped the supply of newly qualified clinical psychologists, so that in 1988 the British government commissioned a special reveiw of the function of clinical psychologists, leading to the publication of two significant reports, the MAS review, and the MPAG report. Taken together, these reports signal a way ahead via a consultancy model, involving clinical psychologists in working with others to enhance and support their psychological knowledge and skills (see Chapter 12).

Elsewhere in Europe similar developments have taken place. In most Northern European countries clinical psychology is both the largest field of specialization of psychology students—80 per cent in Germany—and the largest area of professional psychological practice—for example, over 60 per cent in the Nordic countries. The Netherlands are training too many clinical psychologists for their own needs, and a number of Dutch psychologists are now moving to work in Britain. In the USA too, PhDs in the health-service provider subfields of clinical, counselling, and school psychology now constitute 53 per cent of all new doctorates in psychology.

Training in clinical psychology falls into two stages. The first stage consists of the basic science, that is, the academic study of psychology in the form of an undergraduate degree. In most countries this is a three- or four-year course of study resulting in the award of a Bachelor of Science (BSc) or a Bachelor of Arts (BA) degree. The second stage consists of professional training in clinical psychology. The first degree is not a vocational or professional training in itself, although it may include a number of vocational courses or specialities.

International variations in professional training in clinical psychology

Professional training in clinical psychology varies considerably from country to country. A survey of 23 countries revealed a variation in total length of training (including first degree) from four years in Italy to nine years in the USA (Fichter and Wittchen 1980). Qualifications differ too. Several countries offer training to doctorate level; others (for example New Zealand, Britain) have Master's courses of two or three years' duration. Yet others have specialized Diploma courses or courses leading to a formal licence to practice. In the USA a Psy.D. qualification—emphasizing practitioner rather than research skills—has developed, often offered by independent graduate schools of psychology. This variability is a reflection of the stage of development achieved by clinical psychology in different countries. In the United States, where clinical psychology is a well-established profession, training is rigorous and lengthy, and courses are stringently monitored and accredited. However, in a number of European countries (Spain, for example) there is not as yet a specialist profession of clinical psychology. Psychology graduates will therefore obtain training by attending specialized courses in psychotherapy or by attending training courses in other countries. They may set up in practice as clinical psychologists, but there is as yet no professional career structure for them. Table 1.2 illustrates the similarities and differences in clinical psychology training between three countries. One major difference is that in some countries (for example Britain, Australia, New Zealand, the USA)

Table 1.2 Different patterns of clinical psychology training in three countries

Country	Description of clinical psychology training, qualifications, and duration
UK	First degree in psychology (three or four years). A small percentage of graduates go on to postgraduate training, usually after one or two years' relevant practical experience (e.g. as nursing assistant or assistant psychologist). Training is either on M.Sc. course or health service course, taking a total of three years. Training combines further academic study, supervised practical work, and clinical research. *Qualification*: **M.Sc. or M.Phil. in Clinical Psychology Diploma in Clinical Psychology** (British Psychological Society) *Duration*: 5–7 years
USA	First degree in psychology (four years). Graduates seek admission to four- or five-year doctorate programme in clinical psychology. Academic training is provided in general and clinical psychology. Students also carry out *practicum* placements, which are brief periods of supervised clinical work. The final year of training is an internship of one year in a hospital or similar centre. A doctoral dissertation in the form of an extended research project must be submitted. Some US programmes are only of two years' duration and lead to a Master's qualification. Some schools offer a Doctor of Psychology (PsyD) with greater emphasis on clinical work and training and less on research. *Qualification*: **MA or M.Sc. in Clinical Psychology Ph.D. Psy.D.** *Duration*: 6 years (Master's); 9 years (doctorate)
Norway	Clinical psychology training is part of a general psychology degree. After an initial introductory course, students take a psychological *embetsstudium* which is divided into two parts, each of $2\frac{1}{2}$ years. The first part is basic psychology and the second is practical training (academic and clinical). During the latter students carry out brief *practicum* placements as well as receiving formal tuition. All graduates are qualified to do clinical and psychotherapeutic work. The Norwegian Psychological Society accredits specialists in clinical psychology, who must have at least five years' practice in at least two institutions. *Qualification*: **Cand. Psychol.** *Duration*: $6\frac{1}{2}$ years

training is carried out on specific postgraduate courses which only a minority of psychology graduates enter, whereas in other countries (for example Norway, the Netherlands, West Germany) clinical psychology training is incorporated into the initial degree. In Norway, for example, it constitutes a second part of the Cand. Psychol. This means that many more clinical psychologists are produced in those countries where clinical psychology is 'embedded' into a general degree. However, it is likely that post-graduate courses, particularly to doctorate level, offer a more extensive and comprehensive training.

Another point of comparison concerns the extent to which academic teaching or clinical training are emphasized. The British courses generally offer clinical and academic training in parallel. In other countries, notably the USA, clinical supervision and academic teaching are kept separate by means of periods of 'practicum placements' and 'internships'. Another important area of variation is the range of clinical experience required during professional training. In the USA, where practice is dominated by private practice, a student may elect to gain a restricted range of experience in, say, clinical neuropsychology alone. In Europe, where employment by a publicly funded agency is more common, more emphasis is given to gaining experience with a range of client groups and settings.

There is thus considerable variation in the amount and content of clinical psychology training from country to country. This has meant that, as with other professions, clinical psychologists who wish to practise in countries other than those in which they received training need to obtain the relevant qualifications for the country in which they wish to practice. In the USA and Canada this usually entails formal examinations for the licence to practise as a psychologist. In Britain, there are procedures whereby foreign clinical psychologists may take the British Psychological Society's Diploma in Clinical Psychology and, depending upon the individual case, receive exemption from parts of it.

Professional training in Britain

There are two main routes to a qualification in clinical psychology training:

(a) Master's courses at Universities or Polytechnics, leading to a postgraduate M.Sc. or M.Phil. degree. Until recently these have been either two or three years in duration. The requirement that status as a Chartered Psychologist can be awarded only after three years experience or training following a first degree in psychology has pushed all courses towards a three-year programme. In some cases the final year is seen as an internship year along the lines of the US model.

(b) In-service training courses organized within the National Health Service by Regional or District Health Authorities. These are all three years in duration and lead to the Diploma in Clinical Psychology, a national examination organized through the auspices of the British Psychological Society.

Generally, university and polytechnic courses have tended to place greater emphasis on academic study, whereas health service courses have been stronger on professional training and clinical practice, although this difference has tended to become less obvious in recent years. All training courses, whether health service or University-based, combine further academic study of clinical psychology with supervised experience and training in clinical work. Table 1.3 illustrates the academic courses available on the Oxford Regional In-service Training Course.

Professional training is achieved through a combination of supervised clinical work on placements in hospitals, clinics, or departments and clinical skills training by means of workshops and courses. The British Psychological Society has specified that all trainees must have supervised experience of adult psychiatric patients both chronic and acute, adults and children with learning disabilities, children and adolescents with psychological problems, older people, and at least one specialist group (for example neuropsychology, delinquency). Placements vary from three to six months in duration and in most courses academic study is concurrent with clinical practice. In addition to academic study and clinical training trainees are required to carry out an applied research project which is written up and examined in the form of a dissertation. The acquisition of research skills is seen as a significant feature of clinical psychology training. Assessment of trainees is by a combination of academic course work, written examinations, ratings of clinical performance on placements, case reports of clinical work, and formal examination of the research dissertation.

A qualified clinical psychologist is expected to have acquired the

Table 1.3   Outline of the academic syllabus for the Oxford
Regional Training Course in Clinical Psychology

First year
(a) Preparatory training: 3 weeks of intensive workshops covering
interviewing skills, behavioural analysis and problem formulation,
psychometric assessment, professional issues, and preparation for clinical
placements

(b) Academic and clinical courses:
Cognitive–behavioural treatments, theory, research, and practice
Mental health services; Life-span development; Cultural and social context
Academic seminars; Psychiatric rehabilitation; Teaching methods
Introduction to psychotherapies; Psychological assessment; Therapeutic
     skills
Introduction to the systemic approach
Learning difficulties, theory, research, and practice
Children and young people, theory, research, and practice
Clinical seminars; Sensitivity group

Second year
Learning difficulties (cont.)
Children and young people (cont.)
Clinical gerontology; Clinical neuropsychology; Health psychology
Group psychotherapy; Family therapy; Professional issues
Drug and alcohol dependence
Research design and methods; Applied statistics
Clinical seminars; Revision seminars; Sensitivity group

Third year
Tutorial options (range of topics)
Research seminars; Clinical seminars
Management and organizational skills; supervision skills
Psychodynamic psychotherapy
Sensitivity group

Joint courses and workshops (all years)
Ethnic minorities; Post-traumatic stress disorder; Child neuropsychology
Physical disability; Forensic psychology; HIV/AIDS

---

necessary academic knowledge and professional skills to work as a clinical psychologist in the National Health Service, a position for which the award of the M.Sc. or the Diploma makes him or her eligible. However, it is recognized that further specialized experience and training is a necessary post-qualification requirement, particularly if a position entails working with a specialized population (for example the neuropsychologically impaired) or acquiring specialized skills (for example family therapy, psychosexual counselling). In Britain post-qualification courses are few and far between and as yet there is no formal structure for such training; but the need for such training and experience has been recognized.

WHAT DO CLINICAL PSYCHOLOGISTS DO?

Clinical psychologists are asked to assess and intervene in a wide range of problems where they are believed to have special expertise. The range of problems where psychologists probably have a distinctive and prime contribution cover psychological conditions such as phobias, obsessional and compulsive disorders, problems of disturbed and disruptive behaviour, deficits in everyday skills such as dressing and communicating with other people, discrepancies between ability and attainment, and disorders of mental processes such as memory. In all these cases the psychologist is trying to understand or change an essentially psychological problem of an individual, family, or group.

Secondly, a psychologist may be asked to help with the secondary consequences of a medical or physical problem, such as the sexual difficulties which may follow a spinal injury, when either a medical or other approach is appropriate for the primary problem. For some people, nothing can be done for the primary problem, but the individual still has a major and perhaps progressive handicap, as with some of the problems of old age.

Thirdly, a psychologist may be involved with an issue which does not primarily relate to identified patients, but affects the health care system as a whole. For example, many of the women who may potentially benefit most from advice on caring for their newborn baby find it difficult to understand some of the relatively sophisticated literature put out both by commercial firms and Government agencies. How can health literature be designed to maximize recall of its contents, and application of the recommended procedures? Many hospital staff may have to deal with extremely aggressive people from time to time, even though most of the time their work is routine and even dull. How can non-clinical staff such as laboratory technicians and secretaries be given some guidance or training in how to cope with this sort of infrequent event? In this third category of task, the psychologist is understanding and trying to change aspects of the health care system itself, or the way in which care is delivered, independent of the needs of individual patients.

A psychologist may respond to this array of problems in a number of ways. Firstly, by attempting to understand and define the problem as clearly as possible, perhaps making use of standardized psychological measures. Secondly, by intervening in the problem, with the specific intention of changing the problem in some specified ways. Thirdly, by evaluating what has been done to change the problem. Most of what clinical psychologists do is covered by these three categories of assessment, intervention, and evaluation. There are a number of other functions a psychologist may carry out; one of these major functions is to train or supervise others in the understanding and use of psychological methods, and this is covered in particular in Chapter 12, concerning work with other professions.

ASSESSING AND UNDERSTANDING PEOPLE

Probably one of the most common stereotypes of the psychologist is as 'tester'. Ever since Binet became interested in the attainments of Parisian schoolchildren before the First World War, formal psychometric testing of general ability, specific abilities, and of educational and occupational attainments has been viewed as one of the central professional tasks of a psychologist. Yet this attempt to assess the *maximum* performance of individuals, on apparently rather artificial tasks, is only one aspect of the modern psychologist's contribution to assessment.

Testing is an important type of assessment. Educational tests for children have come to be widely used both to see if there are any discrepancies between ability and educational attainment, and to predict the probable level of attainment of a child. Most ability or attainments tests for children and adults consist of a number of sub-tests, with all items carefully selected, arranged in order of successively greater difficulty, and with information painstakingly obtained on many hundreds of subjects for comparison.

Another major group of assessment procedures are those known as personality tests, which fall into two main subgroups. The first subgroup of personality measures are the 'projective' techniques. These all rest on the assumption that when an individual makes a response to a stimulus that is essentially ambiguous or unstructured, the detail and structure elicited tell us something about the individual's inner structure, or personality. These tests have continued to have a place in the hands of skilled practitioners: an example of such measures is the Thematic Apperception Test (TAT) cards. Second is the subgroup of 'objective' personality measures, which take the form of questionnaires completed by the patient. These questionnaires contain up to several hundred items covering different areas of functioning, such as getting on with other people or the tendency to dominate or be submissive to others. Some of the major work on these questionnaires has been done by personality theorists such as Cattell and Eysenck, who have thus given their names to some personality inventories. Some other related measures are not strictly personality tests, but give a clearer idea of how an individual views himself: the personality theory of George Kelly for example, has given rise to the 'Repertory Grid', a method of exploring an individual's view of his own world that can be represented graphically.

With both ability tests and personality tests, the psychologist's job is to administer the test on a one-to-one or group basis, carefully following the standard procedure. Many tests have 'norms' available, so that the performance of any individual can be compared with others. By contrast, some assessments are not 'norm-referenced' at all, but assess individuals against an explicit criterion of everyday performance. Criterion-referenced assessments of this type are very helpful in gauging the progress of the individual, when knowledge about other people is irrelevant. An example is given in section 2 of Table 1.4: a person's ability to organize his or her own daily routine can be assessed without reference to anyone else.

Apart from questionnaires used to assess personality in a global sense, many specific questionnaires are available, looking at tendencies such as conservatism, and at psychiatric or psycho-pathological dimensions such as depression. A wide range of checklists and rating scales exists, again mostly related to specific conditions or problems, and often completed by someone who knows the patient well, such as a family member. For example, there are several rating scales for use with people with learning difficulties which are completed by a nurse or care worker on the ward or hostel where the person lives. These typically have carefully graded items, so that an action such as 'doing up buttons' itself consists of several stages, viz. 'opposes button-hole to button' and 'inserts button into hole'. A psychologist will often be involved in training and supervising nurses and others in the use of this type of scale.

Another last category of assessment instruments consists of behavioural methods. These make use of direct observation of behaviour, often in a 'natural' setting, without the necessity of patients' even being aware that they are being assessed. They yield measures of the exact frequency or length of time of a piece of behaviour, such as an outburst of aggression, and may require the psychologist to be physically present in a ward or home for several hours. Physiological measures are not strictly behavioural measures, but have the same characteristic of producing a numerical index of functioning, relating to such physiological parameters as heart rate, blood flow, or skin resistance.

Psychological assessment instruments need to fulfil several different requirements. Most important of all, they should contribute unique information which will be helpful to the people intimately concerned with the care and treatment of patients. They need to be acceptable to the people who use them: not too complex in administration and scoring for the test user, not too threatening or demanding for the subject. Additionally, they should be psychometrically sound. This means that they should conform to technical standards of validity and reliability. The validity of a measure is the extent to which it measures what it says it measures. This means that the content of, for example, a reading test should be made up of words that are a reasonable sample of the sort of words that children of a particular country or locality use in practice. Validity is also evaluated by examining the relationship between the measure in question, and another measure of the attribute. Thus one index of the validity of a measure of depression would be the relative proportion of high scorers who present for treatment of depression, compared to the proportion of high scorers who do *not* present. Reliability is the extent to which a measure gives similar results under differing conditions of use. The administrator of a test or

Table 1.4 Major categories of psychological assessment

1. Self-description. Refers to those measures where the subject describes his own current feelings and behaviour, either in an open-ended way (as in interviews) or in a forced-choice way (as in personality questionnaires).

Example: personality questionnaire items:

Do you sometimes feel lonely?	Yes	No	Unsure
Are you easily upset when people criticize you?	Yes	No	Unsure

2. Ratings or judgements by others. Where a person other than the subject describes the subject's current emotions or behaviour, again either in an open-ended way or in a structured way (as in a standardized rating scale or checklist)

Example: a checklist item prepared for checking the early morning routine in a hostel, and requiring the observer to tick each item if that act has been performed:

wakes up when alarm rings
get out of bed (feet outside bedclothes) within 10 min. of alarm
washes unprompted before breakfast
chooses appropriate clothes unaided
dresses unaided
goes to dining-room unprompted

3. Life-history. Refers to the recording of *past* factual information about the subject, from whatever source, such as details of education, and of occupation.

4. Simulated real-life measurement. The subject is asked to demonstrate, or rehearse in practice, what is requested, in as real a way as possible.

Example: role-played test of social skills

5. Direct observation. Real-time recording of specific events or components of behaviour as they occur naturally.

Example: counting incidents of incontinence per day

6. Physiological. Refers to measures directly monitoring physiological functions of the subject's body, such as heart-rate or rate of sweating, by electronic sensors attached directly to the skin surface.

Example: EEG (electro-encephalogram) and EMG (electromyogram)

7. Performance tests. This category includes the classic concept of the 'test', and includes all assessment methods where the subject is asked to complete intellectual tasks by use of standard questions.

Example: cognitive or ability test items:

Pick out the word in the list below that does not go with the others
Brig   Yacht   Steamer   Schooner
Write in the next two numbers in this series
3   6   14   27   45   . . .   . . .

checklist may give it in slightly different ways, or pay attention to different characteristics of the patient's behaviour, so that different testers or raters give slightly different results. The similarity of results across two different sets of raters then gives an index of inter-rater reliability. The other important form of reliability is test–retest, or repeat reliability, indicating the similarity of results across two different occasions.

Clinical psychologists are shifting their interest in assessment from general measures of ability and personality to more specific measures of opinion, self-report, and behaviour that are more directly related to the patient's clinical problems and to their care and management. A comprehensive series of chapters on different aspects of assessment theory and practice is included in Peck and Shapiro (1990) and Table 1.4 illustrates the major categories of assessment method that have just been outlined.

INTERVENING IN PEOPLES' LIVES

The role of psychologist as therapist has developed rapidly over the last twenty years. Before this point only a small number of psychologists, mostly those practising as psychoanalysts or those working with children, spent the majority of their time in treatment. Since then, a range of psychological therapeutic methods have been introduced; many have been refined to such an extent that they have become the treatment of choice for some conditions.

Quite apart from those therapeutic techniques derived from psychodynamic, behavioural, or other theories, most encounters with patients involve the use of general therapeutic skills. These enable the patient to feel relaxed, to have confidence in his therapist, and to be able to recount events, experiences, and relationships which may normally make him feel embarrassed or stigmatized. Psychologists have examined the major attributes of the 'good' counsellor or therapist in constructing this basic therapeutic relationship, and drawn attention to the three key attributes of 'positive regard'—valuing the patient as an individual—'accurate empathy'—understanding the reality of the patient's experiences—and genuineness.

Those clinical psychologists who spend most of their time in psychotherapeutic work will probably enter advanced training with one of the established psychotherapy organizations, such as the

Institute of Group Analysis. Their clinical work may then be defined more by the nature of their therapeutic training and interests than by their initial training as a clinical psychologist. Psychotherapeutic approaches derive from the seminal work of Sigmund Freud, from the modifications to his theories of his early associates and later defectors such as Jung and Adler, and from later and contemporary workers such as Melanie Klein and Freud's own daughter, Anna Freud.

The therapeutic procedures which are currently most characteristic of clinical psychologists are those generally known as cognitive–behavioural methods. Depending on the client group and the problems with which individual clinical psychologists are presented, these approaches combine features of behaviour therapy, cognitive therapy, and often elements of group therapy and family therapy. Many clinical psychologists would describe their overall approach as eclectic, combining individual techniques as appropriate to the needs of the individual, rather than holding to one specified treatment approach. However, it is worth understanding the main features of both the behavioural and the cognitive approaches.

Behavioural methods of treatment require a psychologist first to engage in a behavioural analysis of the problem. A behavioural analysis, or 'functional analysis of behaviour', involves looking at the central problem, or 'Behaviour', in the light of its 'Antecedents'—those prior events or determinants such as time of day or place in the room where the behaviour occurs—and in the light of the 'Consequences'—those events following the occurrence of the behaviour in the actual environment.

Cognitive methods of treatment are based on the supposition that psychological problems may be seen in terms of a linkage between behavioural, cognitive—or affective—and physiological response-systems. These systems do not necessarily change together or at the same time, but the acceptance of these three systems paved the way to go beyond a simple unitary behavioural perspective, and to consider how patients evaluated their own problems. Bandura's work on observational learning drew attention to the way in which behaviour change was mediated by people's perception of how they performed. This in turn led to the development of self-instructional training—probably the first wholly cognitive approach to treatment. Probably the best example of cognitive approaches to treatment is the application to depression, where negative thinking is so obvious.

Apart from behavioural and cognitive methods of treatment, there are a number of other treatment methods that are based on psychological concepts. As physiological measurement techniques have become more reliable, and can now be used without any direct wiring between patient and recording apparatus, so they can be used to provide the patient with immediate feedback of his own physiological response, contributing to the developments of those treatment procedures collectively known as biofeedback techniques. Other treatment methods have been based on theories of memory, or on notions of the rational expression of emotion. For example, a prize-winning book by Rowe (1983) describes a psychological approach to the understanding and treatment of depression. The book draws on a wide range of concepts and models, but is very much informed by a personal-construct theory approach to understanding depression, followed by a cognitive theory guiding approaches to treatment. An example of the use of mixed approaches to both assessment and intervention is given by the case of Mrs Adams.

PSYCHOLOGICAL APPROACHES TO AN INDIVIDUAL PATIENT

Mrs Adams is a 46-year-old married woman, employed as an assistant in the technical library of a major industrial concern, who has had contacts with three different clinical psychologists over a 16-year period. Her case illustrates the changing role of the clinical psychologist over this period, the use and some limitations of standard assessment techniques, and the appropriateness of psychological treatment techniques.

Mrs Adams had failed to achieve well academically. Although she did well at school when younger, she scraped through her A levels and failed a degree-level qualification. Her life was more seriously affected by the sudden onset of diabetes at the age of 23. Her diabetes has been well controlled since then, although she has had hypoglycaemic episodes which have contributed to her persistent complaints that she is deteriorating mentally. Over the years she has had continuing contacts with physicians and with psychiatrists. She feels intellectually superior to her colleagues at work, including those who have obtained degrees, and constantly ruminates about the psychological implications of her diabetes. Her first contact with a clinical psychologist occurred at the age of 30, when a psychiatrist referred her to see if there was any evidence of diffuse brain damage. The psychologist reported a Verbal IQ of 141 and a Performance IQ of 110 but made no recommendations about treatment. Thirteen years later she was seen on referral from another psychiatrist by a second psychologist who repeated the same testing, obtaining a Verbal IQ of 144 and a Performance IQ of 106 and also gave some standard memory tests. The psychologist on this occasion discussed with Mrs Adams' ways of concentrating on her successes at re-membering things, and some guidelines on improving her memory were discussed. A psychotherapist felt she would benefit from psychotherapy, especially in view of her difficulty in maintaining adult relationships with others, but Mrs Adams did not take up this offer.

The third contact arose three years after the second, on referral from a physician who was seeing Mrs Adams for her diabetes, who was concerned both to reassure her yet again about her mental state, and about Mrs Adams' meticulous ways of coping with her job. Since Mrs Adams had already completed some of the standard tests twice, these were not presented again as complete tests, but some of the sub-tests from them were repeated, imbedded in other new specific tests of memory function. Yet again, there was no evidence of deterioration; indeeed some of the sub-tests showed remarkable consistency over the 16-year period. Since she continued to com-plain about the difficulties she was having at work, some time was spent with her, following the recommendations of Powell's (1981) text on '*Brain function therapy*'. This gave her some specific strategies for coping with her alleged memory problems. In addition, some time was spent with Mrs Adams examining the effect that her hypochondriacal beliefs about the consequences of her diabetes was having on the relationship with her colleagues at work, and with her spouse. Although she continued to reject the possibility of psycho-therapeutic help, there was some evidence that Mrs Adams was not so preoccupied with everyday lapses of memory, and had limited the expression of her ruminative thoughts so that people around her were behaving more positively towards her.

Many psychological techniques can be used with individuals or with groups. Controlled studies have shown that group application of some procedures, with carefully selected patients, can make more effective use of psychologists' time than seeing patients individually. The psychologist's task may then involve interviewing and assessing the patients, and supervising the conduct of the group. Many of these techniques can be used by the family member or prime carer looking after the patient, without the psychologist needed to intervene directly with the patient. This may be more time-consuming than seeing patients directly face-to-face, but can create more skilled parents or nurses, who can then use the principles and procedures they have learned at other times and with other patients.

HOW TO EVALUATE PSYCHOLOGICAL PRACTICE

There is no point in using psychological methods of treatment if they do not work. There are many examples of well-established therapeutic procedures being shown, on formal evaluation, to be of little or no value. Two of the most instructive examples for clinical psychologists working in the psychiatric field are insulin coma therapy, where a 20-year period elapsed between the introduction of the method and the final controlled outcome study, and prefrontal leucotomy, where an adequately controlled trial was never carried out. Psychological methods do not have the risk of irreversible side-effects of these two examples, but they may have some side-effects, and certainly their effectiveness should be established.

While methods of service evaluation can be highly formal, and rely on quantified measures, evaluation still implicitly involves making value judgements. An outcome to treatment may be evaluated differently by: the treating doctor, who will be influenced by professional expectation of outcome; by the manager, who will be influenced by the resources required for that treatment; and by the person treated, who will be influenced mainly by the impact on their own quality of life or, for example, freedom from pain. To whose opinion do we pay most attention? Similarly, people who know how to press for a specialist opinion, or who know how to make use of self-help literature, and who thus obtain professional help, may objectively be less handicapped by their condition than someone else who lacks the social skill and ability to obtain help. How happy are we that a 'good' treatment outcome has then been achieved by someone who is less handicapped, while a more seriously disabled person has received no treatment?

A common first step in evaluation is to show that the treatment under question is better than the routine treatment available as an alternative, or at least better than doing nothing. After that, evaluation usually takes the form of 'unpacking' the treatment package which is involved in all psychological procedures. For example, one approach to the treatment of chronic psychiatric patients involves a 'token economy', when the patient is given a token immediately after performing some desirable act. This token can then be spent on 'goodies', such as sweets, tobacco, or a magazine. However, observation of the moment when the token is given to the patient indicates that other things are going on at the same time. The patient is often praised verbally ('well done') and perhaps physically (a hand on the shoulder), informational feedback may be given ('you have got the token because . . .'), and the patient has an individual social encounter in the midst of an otherwise solitary day. Which of these events is the key therapeutic ingredient?

The example of evaluation of a token economy focuses on looking at the outcome of individuals or groups who have completed that treatment. However, there are other outcome criteria that can be used to evaluate the effectiveness of a treatment, such as the amount of resources that have to be devoted to a patient to achieve a given outcome. For example, if treatment A produced a given level of therapeutic response after 10 h of professional time, then it would be more efficient than treatment B if the latter required 20 h of professional time for the same level of response.

Even when resources are adequate, it is important to find out whether particular procedures are effective. In times of stringency, it is even more important to be able to show that a treatment regime meets stated objectives. Fig. 1.2 presents a model of a health care programme (from Holland 1983), and indicates the possibility of

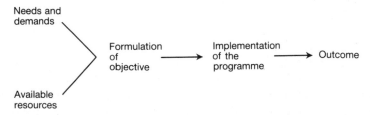

Fig. 1.2 A model of health care evaluation.

two types of evaluation of the programme. Process evaluation compares the proposed objectives and activities of a programme with the objectives and activities that are actually implemented and accomplished: it presupposes an operational plan of a programme, and makes it possible to pick up flaws in a programme before it has been completed. Outcome evaluation, on the other hand, is more difficult to perform than process evaluation, because there are often different levels of outcome, such as the patient's use of a treatment, or the impact of change in the patient upon the caring family. The particular contribution of psychologists to health care evaluation is twofold. Firstly, by translating overall service objectives into operational objectives, and secondly, by devising measures that may need to be used by relatively unsophisticated staff.

KEY PROFESSIONAL ISSUES

As a relatively recent health care profession, clinical psychology has had to find its own niche amidst the array of doctors, nurses, remedial therapists, social workers, and other workers helping people with medical and personal problems. Different countries have imposed different constraints upon the development of the profession, so that, for example, in France only doctors can practise psychotherapy, and in Britain patients seen by psychologists in the NHS normally have to be referred by a family doctor or other medical practitioner. Other professions are understandably concerned to know how clinical psychology fits into the health care system, and what assumptions they may make about this new professional group. There are three main issues which probably require some explanation at the outset.

Professional independence

Most health care professions have emerged and developed largely as the consequence of doctors identifying a practical task which needs to be performed, but which does not require a medical training to perform it. Bit by bit, these professions have become more independent of medical supervision, as indicated in Britain, for example, by doctors no longer acting as examiners of professional competence for nurses. None the less, there may still remain an argument that doctors possess an encompassing knowledge of other professions. By contrast, some of the newer health care professions owe their development to scientific disciplines which cannot be said to be encompassed by medicine. Speech Therapy and Medical Physics are examples of such professions. Like clinical psychology, they may owe part of their development to pressure and interest from medical colleagues; but those colleagues cannot claim an encompassing knowledge of the procedures used.

Another criterion of professional independence is the existence of a standard of training and clinical competence which permits independence of action. For most European countries the period of clinical experience required for qualification as a clinical psychologist is comparable to the clinical experience required of medical students, and similarly follows a degree-level preclinical qualification, suggesting that individuals entering clinical psychology are as likely to be able to practise independently as medically qualified people.

The expressed aspiration of a profession to achieve independence may not, of course, be consistent with the wishes of other colleagues, who far from wanting independence want close co-operation. In some forms of clinical practice, most notably perhaps child psychiatry, teamwork has been highly valued, so that team members value loyalty and commitment to their teams above commitment to members of their own professions. Co-operation with other colleagues is an essential part of the professional commitment of clinical psychologists, although the exact way in which this is worked out locally and in particular circumstances may need close examination.

Responsibility of clinical psychologists

In many health care professions, responsibility is closely bound up with the legal registration of the profession. In many countries the major health care professions have some form of registration procedure, which essentially prescribes minimum standards of training and competence, which may protect titles or functions of that profession, and which ultimately may lead to members of the profession being 'struck off' if they fail to meet standards of professional competence. For example, all the constituent states of Australia have a requirement for legal registration of clinical psychologists.

Apart from this form of legal responsibility, every practitioner also owes a legal duty of care towards the patients he sees. Quite apart from the specific implications of any registration procedure, an aggrieved patient may have recourse through the courts of law to correct alleged negligence or harm resulting from bad treatment. Professional bodies may also impose their own standards upon practitioners, independent of the standards imposed by courts.

It is consistent with a model of an independent profession to say that the psychologist's first responsibility is to his patient. The patient's needs and wishes should, from this point of view, dictate the psychologist's actions. On the other hand, when a psychologist is employed by a public agency there is no doubt that the policies of that agency may affect how a clinical service is delivered. The question of who is paying—whether patient or employer—alters basic assumptions about responsibility, and indeed in some schools of thought is believed to be an important component of the therapeutic relationship.

There is some ambivalence among British clinical psychologists about the advantages of becoming a fully fledged 'profession' with all the trappings of registration and defined responsibilities. Sensible of the evidence that professionalization may benefit the profession rather than the client, psychologists hesitated before plunging along this path. In Britain this hesitation has been supported by the fact that the major professional body for psychologists, the British Psychological Society, was originally a learned society. It still functions as a learned society, so that views of academic psychologists, and of applied psychologists who do not work in health care, have equal weight with those of clinical psychologists. The British Psychological Society has now established a process whereby psychologists can become chartered, and a register of Chartered Psychologists began in 1988.

The role of clinical psychology in the health care system

Most developed countries attempt some overall planning of health care. The separation of primary from secondary health care is vague in some European countries, so that in Belgium, as in other countries, the family doctor or general practitioner may often also practice as a specialist in a particular branch of medicine. In Britain there is a very clear separation between 'primary' services, and the specialized 'secondary' services, which has a marked effect on the work done by clinical psychologists.

Health care systems differ considerably in the extent to which there is central planning and funding of resources, the degree of choice available to the public, and the proportion of care provided by private or voluntary agencies. In practice, most Western countries have a degree of state control, via funding, of the majority of specialized health care facilities, so that, for example, in the Republic of Ireland services to mentally handicapped people are predominantly provided by religious orders, but are Government funded. The increase of 'socialized medicine' has had an important consequence, in that it has encouraged the planning of health care services on a population basis. If the size, age distribution, and morbidity of a population is known, then health facilities can be planned on some sort of rational plan and analysis of need. If, however, private practice develops in an uncoordinated way and forms a major component of the overall service, it is difficult to plan in this way.

As preventive medicine has been effective, and as antibiotics, corrective surgery in children, and better care of the aged have developed, so the health problems presented in the population have changed. As health care moves to a more preventive role, so issues of compliance with advice, and personal 'health care routines'—essentially psychological issues—will become more important. As a population ages and contains more people with chronic handicaps which no longer respond to medical intervention, so the emphasis of health care will need to change to emphasize coping with disability. It seems that further improvement in the health of a population will rely as much on change of lifestyle as on the ministrations of high technology medicine.

The role of clinical psychology in a health care system is thus determined by a number of factors. The capacity of clinical psychologists to contribute independently and responsibly is one major factor. The availability of psychological knowledge along the 'primary care'–'specalist' dimension further influences the number and nature of the problems seen, and by implication the demand for psychologists. The capacity of a health care system to identify need and to plan provision also implies planning the type and numbers of staff to make that provision. At present, there are growing expectations of clinical psychologists that they will be able to contribute to several points of the system. This book describes both what they are doing at present, and what developments lie ahead.

REFERENCES

Edwards, H. (1987). *Psychological problems. Who can help?* The British Psychological Society/Methuen, London.

Fichter, M. M. and Wittchen, H. U. (1980). Clinical psychology and psychotherapy. A survey of the present state of professionalization in 23 countries. *Am. Psychol.* **35**, 16–25.

Holland, W. W. (1983). *Evaluation of health care.* Oxford University Press.

Kendall, D. C. and Norton-Ford, J. D. (1982). *See* 'Further reading'.

Melzack, D. C. and Wall, P. (1988). *The challenge of pain* (revised edn). Penguin, Harmondsworth.

Peck, D. F. and Shapiro, C. M. (1990). Measuring human problems. Wiley, Chichester.

Powell, G. E. (1981). *Brain function therapy.* Gower, Aldershot.

Rowe, D. (1983). *Depression. The way out of your prison.* Routledge and Kegan Paul, London.

FURTHER READING

British Psychological Society (1988). The future of the psychological sciences: horizons and opportunities for British psychology. British Psychological Society, Leicester.

Kendall, P. C. and Norton-Ford, J. D. (1982). *Clinical psychology. Scientific and professional dimensions.* Wiley, New York.

Liddell, A. (ed.) (1983). *The practice of clinical psychology in Great Britain.* Wiley, London.

Tryon, G. S. (ed.) (1986). The professional practice of psychology. Ablex, Norwood NJ.

2

The psychological treatment of adults

John Marzillier

All clinical psychologists work to some extent with adults. Some provide a direct service to adult patients in the form of psychological assessment and treatment. Others work indirectly with adults; so, for example, those who work with children will also work closely with parents, teachers, and other professional staff. This chapter describes the therapeutic work of clinical psychologists, concentrating on the services that they provide to adult out-patients. The therapeutic work carried out by psychologists in psychiatric hospitals (in-patient work) is described separately in Chapter 3, and their role in general medicine is the subject of a further chapter (Chapter 10).

Psychological treatments take many forms and are characterized by various labels (for example, psychotherapy, behaviour therapy, psychoanalysis, etc.). There are many different 'schools' of psychotherapy, and practitioners differ in their allegiance to a particular theory as well as in their methods of treatment. Clinical psychologists have, on the whole, practised the briefer and more pragmatic types of treatment such as the cognitive and behavioural therapies. But some will also have received specialist training in other forms of psychotherapy, notably psychodynamic psychotherapy. Illustrations of the various therapeutic approaches are provided in the main body of the chapter.

THE SETTING

Clinical psychologists will most commonly see patients for treatment in some form of clinic. The site of the clinic will vary depending on the nature of the service as a whole. In Britain, for example, where clinical psychology has had a close historical asociation with psychiatry, many clinics are attached to psychiatric hospitals. But clinics may be set up elsewhere, for example in University psychology departments, general practices, and community mental health centres, or even over shop fronts in city centres. Where a private health service flourishes, as in the USA, psychologists will set up their clinics alongside those of other professions, and indeed compete for customers.

The word 'clinic' is used to describe the service, although its medical connotations sometimes make it an unpopular term. But in practice most clinical psychologists act like their medical colleagues. Patients are referred by others, most commonly the family doctor or a psychiatrist, are sent appointments, attend at a centre with a receptionist and a waiting area, and are usually given a fixed series of appointments until the 'treatment' has been completed. While the 'clinic' approach is still the commonest way of working, it is neither the most efficient nor the most responsive to the needs of the community. Psychologists often find themselves operating long waiting-lists, with the result that it is difficult to respond quickly to crises, and both patients and referrers turn elsewhere for help. A service that is based in the community, working closely with voluntary agencies and other professions, has been seen as a more viable alternative (see Chapter 11 for more details).

COMMON PSYCHOLOGICAL PROBLEMS

Clinical psychologists vary in the problems they treat and the types of treatments they provide. This variation arises partly from the differing theoretical orientation and experience of the psychologists, and partly from the different demands placed upon them in different settings. Some psychologists spend the bulk of their time in treating out-patients with emotional problems such as anxiety and depression. Others concentrate on applying their skills to the rehabilitation of chronic psychiatric patients in hospital. A few develop specialist therapeutic skills, usually as a result of further training courses in psychotherapy, or specialize in treating certain populations. Table 2.1 lists the problems for which psychological help is commonly sought.

This is not a recognized system of classification, since none exists, but simply a means of identifying and labelling common psychological problems. There is inevitably overlap between categories. For example, a person with a psychosexual problem may also be

Table 2.1 Common psychological problems seen by clinical psychologists for psychological treatment

---

  I. *Emotional problems*
   1. Fears and phobias
   2. Generalized anxiety
   3. Obsessions and compulsions
   4. Depression
   5. Other emotional disturbance, e.g. anger, guilt
 II. *Addictions and habit problems*
   1. Alcoholism and problem drinking
   2. Drug addiction
   3. Eating problems, e.g. anorexia, bulimia, obesity
   4. Miscellaneous, e.g. smoking, stuttering, gambling, tics
III. *Psychosexual problems*
   1. Sexual dysfunction, e.g. impotence, vaginismus
   2. Problems of sexual orientation
 IV. *Social and interpersonal problems*
   1. Loneliness, shyness, and social isolation
   2. Aggressive and antisocial behaviour
   3. Marital conflict
  V. *Psychosomatic and medical* (described in Chapter 10)
   1. 'Psychosomatic disorders', e.g. asthma, headache
   2. Cardiovascular disorders, e.g. hypertension, coronary heart disease
   3. Pain
   4. Chronic physical illness

---

depressed and experiencing marital difficulties. An alcoholic may behave aggressively towards his family and friends. The labels used in Table 2.1 are simply convenient means for the patient or the referring professional to identify the major problem for which help is sought. It is part of the job of the clinical psychologist to assess the case in greater depth to establish the nature of the problem and whether treatment can be provided. An example of how clinical psychologists practise psychological treatment is given in the case of Catherine and Henry. In this first case the process of assessment and treatment has been deliberately simplified in order to highlight the basic procedures and principles.

The treatment of a married couple with sexual problems

Catherine and Henry are a married couple in their early 30s with two children of school age. Henry approached his local GP complaining of impotence and lack of sexual satisfaction in his marriage. The GP suggested that he might benefit from seeing a specialist in the treatment of sexual problems and referred him to a psychosexual clinic run in a local Clinical Psychology Department. As is the normal practice of the clinic Henry and Catherine were both invited to attend the clinic for an initial assessment interview with a view to beginning a course of treatment.

In the initial interview the couple are seen together in the first instance. The problem that they present is one of impotence on Henry's part with the consequent breakdown of their sexual relationship. The first part of the interview is taken up with an account of the sexual problem, its origin, its nature, and how it affects their relationship. Some background information is also sought concerning their work, way of life, children, social activities, etc. Then Catherine and Henry are seen separately for a detailed interview of their sexual history and to explore their attitudes and feelings about the marriage. Each also fills in a questionnaire on their marital and sexual relationship. Finally, the couple are seen together again for a further discussion which focuses on possible treatments and their expectations concerning therapy. An agreement is reached that they will go away and talk together about the problem and the possibilities for treatment. A brief hand-out concerning psychosexual problems and their treatment is given to them to take away and read. Advice is given to refrain from sexual relations for the time being. Another appointment is made in a week's time, at which time a final decision on treatment will be made.

The next appointment begins with a general discussion arising out of their reactions to the first interview, the information in the hand-out and the talk they had between interviews. Catherine and Henry are eager to go ahead with treatment and the psychologist spends some time describing what would be involved both in terms of specific treatment procedures and the general requirements of therapy. It is explained that the treatment is based upon the work of the American researchers Masters and Johnston and in essence entails the relearning of their sexual relationship with the help of specific psychological procedures (see Hawton 1985). The possibility that Henry's impotence is caused by performance anxiety is raised and it is suggested that a gradual and undemanding programme of resuming sexual activity is a way of overcoming anxiety, allowing potency to return. The first of a series of practical exercises is presented to them and they are asked to implement the exercise at home. Appointments are made on a weekly basis, with the possibility of telephone contact between sessions if necessary. At first treatment progresses reasonably smoothly and Catherine and Henry gradually increase the intimacy of their sexual contact. However, Henry still has difficulty in maintaining potency and, after further discussions, is given some training in relaxation and advised not to be concerned with potency or sexual arousal, but to concentrate on remaining relaxed and on enjoying the intimacy of sexual contact. This results in successful sexual intercourse—the first time for many months—and leads to increased optimism and confidence on their part. Further satisfactory progress is made over the next few treatment sessions until treatment is formally ended after 12 weekly sessions. Catherine and Henry are seen for a final assessment and given a follow-up appointment in three months' time.

BASIC PRINCIPLES OF PSYCHOLOGICAL ASSESSMENT AND TREATMENT

The case of Catherine and Henry is a hypothetical case used to illustrate how psychological treatment can operate in an uncomplicated fashion. Few cases are perhaps as straightforward as this, but the basic principles are the same. Treatment is always preceded by a period of assessment whose prime purpose is to gather information concerning the nature of the problem so that the psychologist may arrive at an informed decision about treatment. The initial assessment also allows the patients and the psychologist to get to know each other and establish a relationship of mutual trust and confidence without which treatment is unlikely to succeed. The decision on treatment should be a mutual one, and therefore the patients must be informed about what the treatment involves and its likelihood of success. The active involvement of the patient in therapy is also something of importance, as treatment is regarded as a co-operative venture in which therapist and patient work together to achieve change. Treatment takes place over regular weekly out-patient sessions, although this will vary according to the type of problem treated. Some cases need to be seen intensively at first and others require a period of in-patient treatment. In some cases patients may be seen in groups and in others the psychologist works closely with other professionals, for example doctors, nurses, health visitors, and social workers. Finally, the effects of treatment are monitored by regular assessments and a final evaluation of the extent of improvement. Patients are often given one or more follow-up appointments to assess whether improvement is maintained.

Psychological treatment is not always as straightforward as this example suggests. For example, it is not always possible to define psychological problems simply or to use well-established treatment methods. An important part of psychological treatment is working with the patient to establish what exactly the problem is and working out an individually tailored way of treated it. In the hypothetical example, Henry's impotence could have been an expression of more fundamental marital difficulties and, if that were the case, the psychologist would need to shift his or her attention to that problem and consider whether he or she could provide help to resolve it. Psychologists differ too in how they conceptualize psychological problems, and this affects what treatment is offered. To some psychologists impotence may suggest unconscious conflicts about one's own sexuality, and treatment will be concerned with exploring such conflict in an attempt to make it conscious and resolve it.

COGNITIVE–BEHAVIOUR THERAPY

The case of Catherine and Henry can be seen as an example of behaviour therapy. This is a school of therapy which developed in the 1960s out of experimental studies of psychological principles in the laboratory, principles of learning in particular. The basic tenet of behaviour therapy is that emotional and other problems are learned and that by applying learning principles to their problems patients can learn to resolve them. It is now more common to describe this treatment approach as *cognitive–behaviour therapy* or CBT, to underline the importance of focusing on thoughts, images, beliefs, and other cognitions as well as behaviour. CBT can be seen as an amalgamation of the cognitive therapies developed by Beck and Ellis and the basic principles of the behavioural approach.

Cognitive–behavioural treatments tend to be brief—a few weeks or months at the most—and can in some instances be as short as four to six sessions. Their aim is to help the patient change his or her problem behaviour directly. Although a good therapeutic relationship can be important in cognitive–behaviour therapy it is not regarded as essential or as the main vehicle of change. The approach is best described as an educational and problem-solving one, with the therapist using his or her specialist knowledge to guide the patient towards a solution to his or her problems. Another characteristic of the cognitive–behavioural approach is the emphasis on the systematic assessment of change using scientifically derived assessment measures and carefully evaluated techniques (see Dryden and Golden 1986; Hawton *et al.* 1989).

Cognitive–behavioural treatments have proved to be particularly successful in helping people for whom anxiety is a major problem. Anxiety is commonly defined by subjective feelings of distress, often persistent and intense, in which there is a dread or apprehension about some unpleasant and uncertain future occurrence. There is little doubt that anxiety is in itself a normal experience which all of us encounter from time to time. The prospect of difficult examinations, a visit to the dentist, the vicissitudes of a difficult personal relationship, having to make a speech at a formal reception, are all examples where the experience of anxiety would be quite expected. In clinical practice, anxious patients seek help if their feelings of anxiety are so persistent and intense that they interfere with their daily lives or if they experience the sensations of anxiety without fully understanding what they are or why they occur.

Laboratory studies of the acquisition and treatment of fear have show that fears can be acquired as a result of conditioning and that they can be removed by deconditioning. Deconditioning, or 'desensitization', as the clinical method is known, involves two processes of change: a graduated approach to the feared object or situation, and the inhibition of the emotional state of anxiety by relaxation or a similar emotional state that is directly contrary to anxiety. These principles have been successfully applied in the clinical treatment of fears and anxiety, as the case of Jean illustrates.

The cognitive–behavioural treatment of an agoraphobic woman

Jean is a 33-year-old married woman with a young son of 7 years old. She is neatly dressed, pleasant-mannered and articulate, but rather reticent and soft-spoken. She complains of a fear of leaving her home on her own and of crowded places such as supermarkets in particular. Even at home on her own she experiences 'panics' and has to ring her husband frequently for support and help. She has very few friends and very little social life except for her mother, whom she tends to see most days. She can recall having experienced her fear and panic for several years, and has sought help now because she worries that her son may be experiencing similar anxieties; he has reported feeling nervous at school and on occasions has been reluctant to go.

Jean has a problem that is commonly called 'agoraphobia', which literally means (from the Greek) 'a fear of the market-place'. The main characteristics of agoraphobia are: (1) fear about leaving home or any place of safety on one's own; (2) a fear of crowded places; (3) a 'fear of fear' itself; and (4) avoidance of confined places, where escape is difficult. In this instance cognitive–behavioural treatment consists of: (a) a systematic programme of increasing exposure to the situations that provoke fear and anxiety; and (b) teaching Jean to become more confident in her ability to manage difficult situations on her own—i.e. restoring her confidence in herself.

In the first two sessions Jean and her therapist drew up a list of the most anxiety-provoking situations and worked out a graded programme of 25 steps ranging from '(1) Opening the door of her house and standing alone on the doorstep for 30 second's to '(25) Travelling by bus to the centre of town on a Saturday afternoon and visiting a supermarket'. Jean was also taught progressive muscular relaxation and given a rationale to the effect that her fear of going out had been acquired as a result of the panic that she had first experienced and was now being maintained mainly by her 'fear of fear', i.e. of the panic recurring. Successful treatment entailed her regaining confidence in her ability to be out on her own and to cope with symptoms of anxiety and panic.

There are two possible strategies that the therapist and Jean could have adopted at this point. The first is the graduated approach whereby the easiest situation in the hierarchy is tackled first until Jean can master it without undue anxiety. This may be done first in imagination and then in reality. Once Jean is confident in this situation, she progresses to the next, each time using relaxation to combat her feelings of anxiety. And so on until each situation in the hierarchy is successfully tackled. This method is known as 'systematic desensitization'.

The other method, known as 'flooding', entails tackling the most difficult situation first and persisting in it until Jean's anxiety decreases, a procedure which may take several hours. In Jean's case this meant visiting a crowded supermarket on a Saturday afternoon and spending the whole afternoon in the supermarket, resisting the urge to escape even if anxiety became intense. Although this is an unpleasant procedure, it can have a rapid and dramatic beneficial effect. In Jean's case, she realized that none of the awful things she feared actually happened, and her anxiety feelings eventually diminished so much that she was able to do her weekly shopping. The therapist and Jean repeated the treatment a couple of times, and each time it proved much easier for Jean. She was encouraged to tackle less difficult situations on her own, and thereby began the process of successfully counteracting her agoraphobia.

Jean's success in the behavioural programme helped to counteract her worries about possible catastrophe, since she could see how her 'panicky' symptoms were due to anxiety and that she could manage them herself. In addition, on the advice of the therapist she joined an assertiveness training group, in which she and other patients discussed and practised ways of being more assertive, i.e. standing up for themselves and taking an independent line. The group boosted Jean's confidence further and enabled her to deal more effectively with the demands of her family—her mother in particular. At the end of her treatment, she had not only become confident enough to go out alone but had also become a more outspoken and confident person who, as she put it, had learned that she was not there 'just to make up the numbers'.

Jean's case illustrates the way in which behavioural principles can be used in a practical and effective way to reduce anxiety and restore confidence. Many agoraphobic patients have been helped by cognitive–behaviour therapy, and research studies have confirmed the value of this approach (Mathews *et al.* 1981). This is not to ignore the fact that agoraphobia can be a complex condition in which factors other than anxiety on leaving home may play a part. Issues of dependency and lack of assertiveness may be evident, as they were in Jean's case. Marital and family relations can be disturbed. The more chronic cases do not respond well to treatment. However, the value of a pragmatic cognitive–behavioural approach for many patients has been established.

The cognitive–behavioural treatment of obsessional–compulsive disorders

Obsessional–compulsive disorders are characterized by the dual components of obsessions and compulsions. Obsessions are recurring, repetitive thoughts, images, or impulses which are experienced by the patient as intrusive, unwanted, and often abhorrent and senseless. They are often thoughts or images about doing harm, or harm being done to other people. One woman, for example, was beset with the image of stabbing her daughter through the heart with a knife. Occasionally, meaningless, repetitive, phrases are experienced (for example 'Put jam on it'). The intrusiveness and the unpleasant content of the obsessions cause considerable distress and anxiety.

Compulsions are stereotyped, repetitive behaviour, often ritualistic, evoked by a strong, subjective urge which the patient finds hard to resist. Quite often the behaviour is designed to forestall possible harm (for example washing hands thoroughly to avoid contamination) and its performance tends to lead to feelings of relief and the reduction of tension. Obsessions tend to lead to compulsions, although not in all cases. The commonest obsessions are repetitive thoughts of violence, contamination, and doubt (for example wondering whether the house is securely locked). Compulsions include repeated hand-washing, counting, and checking.

Obsessional disorders are tackled on three fronts. Firstly, the emotional component of the problem is directly tackled by means of anxiety-reduction methods. For example, a patient with obsessional anxieties about contamination by dirt may have his or her environment totally contaminated by the therapist in order to expose that person fully to obsessional stimuli and produce habituation of anxiety. Secondly, the behavioural components of the obsessional disorder, often expressed in terms of ritualistic behaviour designed to avoid or ward off anxiety, are directly tackled by a procedure known as 'response prevention'. As the name implies, the patient is encouraged not to carry out ritualistic behaviour in order that full exposure to the anxiety cues is achieved. Finally, patients are taught to distract themselves from upsetting thoughts and ruminations and, if possible, to dismiss them as irrational and unwanted.

The treatment of obsessional patients by these procedures is not easy to carry out, and is often facilitated by either admitting the patient to hospital and carrying out the treatment intensively with the help of other professional staff, as may be the case with the severer disorders, or carrying out the treatment in the patient's home environment, again on an intensive basis. Empirical research carried out both in England and in America has provided strong support for the effectiveness of a comprehensive behavioural approach of this sort. Rachman and Hodgson (1980) report a success rate of between 70 and 80 per cent for obsessional patients treated by this method and followed up for up to two years after the end of treatment.

Cognitive–behavioural treatments have been successfully used for many types of psychological problems, for example, addictive behaviours such as smoking and excessive drinking, psychosexual problems, relationship difficulties, eating disorders, and problems such as insomnia and excessive anger. The simplicity and directness of the approach are amongst its main assets.

COGNITIVE THERAPY

Cognitive therapy consists of methods of treatment which are specifically directed at the patient's cognitive or thinking processes. It is held that the emotional problems experienced by patients can be directly attributed to distortions in their thinking. These can take the form of the predominance of negative thoughts, thinking errors (for example over-generalization, polarized thinking) and irrational or maladaptive ideas and beliefs. In cognitive therapy patients are taught to recognize and counter their cognitive distortions and thereby reduce or manage their emotional distress. Like cognitive–behaviour therapy, cognitive therapy is a practical, problem-solving form of treatment which has been particularly used in the treatment of depression and anxiety. The therapist takes an educational approach, although the value of developing a good therapeutic relationship is also stressed. The use of cognitive therapy in the treatment of depression is described in detail below.

Cognitive therapy for depression

Depression is characterized by persistent and pervasive feelings of hopelessness and low mood, often accompanied by a number of somatic symptoms such as disturbed sleep, loss of energy, poor appetite, and psychomotor agitation or retardation. Depressed patients lose interest in normally pleasurable activities, find it difficult to concentrate or make decisions, and may experience intense feelings of guilt and self-reproach. Thoughts of death and suicide may be prominent. The experience of depression in mild or moderate forms is something many people have. Severe depression is experienced by a substantial number of people, perhaps as many as one in eight of the population.

Until recently antidepressant medication was the clear treatment of choice for depressed patients. Tricyclic drugs, the most commonly used antidepressants, have been shown to elevate mood and produce symptomatic improvement in a large proportion of depressed patients. For most doctors they remain the first choice in treatment. Medication, however, has several limitations. Not only can drugs produce toxic- and side-effects, but they can undermine the depressed patients' capacity to recover on their own. Any improvement may be attributed to medication rather than the patients' own resources. In this way medication can reinforce a patient's belief that he or she is hopeless and inhibit attempts to cope.

Cognitive therapy is a recently developed psychological treatment which aims to help depressed patients marshal their own resources to elevate mood, counteract depressive thinking, and produce positive changes in their behaviour and environment (Beck *et al.* 1979). It is practical and problem-solving, with the central aim of identifying and correcting the major distortions in thinking that are characteristic of depression.

Mrs Harris, for example, was severely depressed when referred for psychological help. She spent many hours of the day in bed, and had great difficulty in getting simple tasks around the house done. She was frequently tearful, and reproached herself for her inadequacy as a mother, housewife, offspring, and spouse. The first stage of therapy entailed asking her to keep a detailed record of her activities, and from this selecting the tasks that could be most easily mastered. She was seen twice a week at first and gradually, by means of structured planning and support, built up her activities. At the same time, she learned to attend to, monitor, and eventually challenge negative thinking. For example, she frequently had the thought 'I am hopeless. I cannot do anything right.' In therapy the accuracy of this thought was questioned; she was asked to find and list things that she in fact had done correctly. The thought was seen as an example of depressive thinking rather than a realistic appraisal of herself. She was helped to find a way of countering the thought, firstly by distraction and then by direct challenge. She learned that she could in fact achieve many tasks provided they were specific and small-scale. When Mrs Harris questioned the value of such achievement ('Anyone could do them. They are trivial'), therapy turned to a discussion of some of her basic assumptions and beliefs. It emerged that she had adopted a very rigid and perfectionist set of standards, which had been instilled into her from early childhood. Until her treatment Mrs Harris had not articulated these standards, and she was quite surprised at how extreme and rigid they were. It became clear to her that much of her depression was directly caused by her standards, which, because of their extreme nature, made it very difficult for her to succeed at anything. As therapy progressed she began to experiment with alternative ways of seeing herself and the world. Her depressed mood began rapidly to lift.

There is an increasing body of evidence to suggest that cognitive therapy is an effective method of treatment for depression. For example, in a controlled evaluation of cognitive therapy for depressed patients referred by general practitioners, Teasdale and colleagues (1984) found that cognitive therapy resulted in a clinically and statistically significant improved rate of recovery compared to the customary treatment from their GPs. Other studies in Europe and America have supported the value of this therapeutic approach (see Hawton *et al.* 1989).

PSYCHODYNAMIC PSYCHOTHERAPY

Anthony Storr, a leading British psychotherapist, described psychotherapy as

the art of alleviating personal difficulties through the agency of words and a personal, professional relationship (Storr 1979 p. vii)

In all therapies, including behaviour and cognitive therapy, the relationship between therapist and patient is important, since without a good relationship where there is an element of trust and respect there is unlikely to be the basis for meaningful change. In psychodynamic psychotherapy the therapist–patient relationship is the central core of the therapy and the main vehicle of change. The term 'psychodynamic' refers to the theoretical origins of this approach, in particular the ideas and practices of the psychoanalytic school. The focus in psychodynamic psychotherapy is not on producing symptomatic and behaviour change directly, but on establishing a therapeutic relationship in which the patient feels safe enough to reveal and explore emotionally charged and often upsetting material. This is a process of uncovering and of 'working through', with the therapist applying analytical skills to enable the patient to explore his intrapsychic world in an effective and productive way. There are many different 'schools' of psychodynamic psychotherapy, which reflect theoretical differences and divisions in the psychoanalytic movement. However, it has been suggested that the common factors in psychodynamic psychotherapy probably outweigh the differences between schools. An example of a psychotherapy case is given to illustrate this approach.

A psychotherapy case

Jack is a 38-year-old teacher, married with three children. He was referred to a clinical psychologist who specialized in psychodynamic psychotherapy by his GP because of frequent bouts of depression. Jack was ill at ease when he arrived, and initially quite reticent and defensive. He began by saying, 'I didn't really want to come here, you know. It was Sheila's idea . . . I don't want to waste your time.' He did not believe he had a 'problem' as such—just sometimes he got very unhappy. He did not know why. He was 'happily married' in a 'great job' with 'three lovely children'. As the interview progressed Jack relaxed and began to talk more freely about himself. He recounted some of the experiences of his childhood, which had been quite harsh at times. His family had been poor. His father had been frequently ill and off work, and there had been very little money around. He and his elder brother, Jim, had both done well at school; but, while Jim had gone on to University and eventually a successful job in engineering, Jack had left school at 16 against his parents' wishes. At first he had 'bummed around', taking various jobs before deciding upon teaching as a career. He entered a teaching training school, where he met Sheila. Shortly after he had qualified, they got married, and, after a couple of years in one school, he had got a job at his present school, where he had been for the past 14 years.

Jack said that there had been times during his childhood when he had felt very unhappy; but once he began on his career as a teacher, he had felt fine, very happy. It was only in the last year or so that he had felt very depressed, and he could not see why. He reiterated his statements about being really very happy with his family and in his work, but in a rather quiet and depressed tone of voice, so that the therapist gained a strong feeling of deep unhappiness and misery. The assessment interview continued, with the therapist asking Jack more about himself, his family, and his current life. Jack's unhappiness became more obvious; and at the end of the interview the therapist asked Jack whether he wished to embark on a course of psychotherapy, explaining that this entailed weekly therapy sessions of 50 minutes lasting for up to a year. She said that she felt that Jack was indeed very unhappy, and that psychotherapy was a way of exploring what the unhappiness was about; and that sometimes this could be a painful and difficult process, but in the end it could be of benefit. After a moment's hesitation, Jack agreed to 'give it a try'.

In an assessment interview such as this the therapist seeks to establish some form of psychological contact which will serve as the basis of the psychotherapeutic relationship. She or he also seeks to understand what it is that is troubling the patient, and perhaps already has some ideas about how to proceed. Jack's present unhappiness may well have an important relationship to his upbringing and the expectations of a bright young boy from a deprived background. But these are only tentative ideas. More will undoubtedly emerge as the therapy progresses. Jack too will have formed an impression of the therapist and have some thoughts about what therapy could offer. Sometimes these are unrealistic expectations and hopes, which are modified during treatment. Like any other relationship, a psychotherapeutic relationship entails a process of mutual adjustment and understanding.

It is not possible here to describe in detail the vicissitudes of Jack's therapy. Briefly, after a 'honeymoon period' of regular attendance, Jack became morose and withdrawn. He began missing sessions and arriving late. The therapist sought to explore what was happening in their relationship, thereby provoking considerable feelings of anger and hostility on Jack's part. A crisis point was reached when Jack might easily have terminated treatment. But the therapist worked hard to get through to Jack, accepting his anger without rebuff or recrimination and pushing Jack to examine why he should feel this way. Out of this emerged a picture of a younger brother who had felt neglected by his family and had harboured a deep resentment of his parents' apparent indifference to him in contrast to his elder brother. He had rebelled and left school and had eventually thrown himself into teaching partly perhaps as a way to provide others with the care and guidance he felt he had lacked. He had married a warm and openly affectionate woman who gave him the support and succour he felt he needed. He had immersed himself in bringing up his own family. However, lately, when his depression had returned, he had a powerful conviction that he had really achieved nothing worthwhile in his life and that he was a charlatan, someone who did not deserve the attention and interest of others. In therapy he had become withdrawn and angry at the therapist's constant attention, particularly as he had begun to develop warm and positive feelings towards her. His defence against such feelings was to withdraw; but when the therapist did not let him, he experienced powerful feelings of anger and hostility.

The experience of strong feelings towards the therapist, or 'transference', as it is known in psychodynamic terms, is regarded by many as a vital part of the therapeutic process. Jack's feeling towards the therapist can be seen as reflections of feelings experienced at other times and towards others, parents perhaps. It is the therapist's job to recognize these feelings and with the patient to 'work through' them in therapy. The patient may then begin to learn something about himself and how his current feelings are expressions of other thoughts and experiences of which he may have been unconscious. In Jack's case the therapist's acceptance of his anger and the open way she talked about their relationship proved a turning-point. He began to examine his past experiences, his childhood in particular, from a different perspective. He felt valued, almost for the first time, as a person in his own right. He saw how much he had striven hard either to meet the aspirations of his parents or to reject them. He ended therapy feeling an upsurge of morale and confidence and with the conviction that he had the capability to do well both at work and in his family.

A brief description such as this can only touch upon the complexities of a psychotherapeutic relationship. Patients vary, as do the problems they present and the ways in which they respond to treatment. Therapists too have different styles and theoretical orientations. The essential features that distinguish this approach from the behavioural and cognitive therapies described earlier lie in the focus on the therapist–patient relationship and on the analytic skills of the therapist in understanding and interpreting the feelings and problems of the patient. The practice of psychotherapy demands considerable personal skills from the therapist and the capacity to maintain a positive relationship with patients, sometimes under difficult and trying conditions. Not all clinical psychologists feel equipped to offer this form of treatment, and some are frankly antagonistic to it. Some schools of thought argue that those who practise psychotherapy should themselves have been in psychotherapy as an integral part of their training. Not all agree with this point of view. But certainly it is desirable that psychotherapists receive regular supervision from other experienced therapists.

THE ECLECTIC APPROACH

The differences between psychodynamic psychotherapy on the one hand and the cognitive–behavioural therapies on the other are not as definitive as might appear from the accounts of therapy given so far. Certainly there are real differences in theory; but theoretical differences relate only loosely to therapeutic practice. And some of the most obvious differences in practice can disappear as therapists of all persuasions converge towards an essentially similar pattern of treatment. One example is the trend towards brief psychotherapy amongst the psychodynamic therapists. Brief psychotherapy can be shorter in time than some of the cognitive–behavioural therapies, and although the approach is still essentially interpretative, with an emphasis on the therapist–patient relationship, the treatment is problem-focused and time-limited. A patient receiving brief psychodynamic psychotherapy will be encouraged to select a specific problem in therapy to work on just as he or she would be in cognitive–behavioural therapies.

Cognitive–analytic therapy (CAT) is one form of brief psychotherapy in which the pragmatics of the cognitive–behavioural therapies is combined with the insights and interpretations of the psychodynamic school (Ryle 1990). In CAT patients are encouraged to keep a diary and monitor their progress by means of rating scales; the approach is time-limited (usually 16 sessions) and problem-focused. These practical procedures are combined with a written psychodynamic formulation and interpretations of the transference issues that arise in the therapeutic relationship. Ryle and his colleagues stress the value of providing an integrated therapy applicable to an NHS psychotherapeutic service.

Many clinical psychologists now describe their therapeutic approach as 'eclectic'. By that they generally mean that they do not rigidly adhere to one treatment model, but are prepared to use a variety of models and techniques in helping a patient, i.e. they tailor the therapy very much to individual needs. Susan's treatment is a good example of this form of 'eclecticism'.

The treatment of a student with an eating disorder

Susan was a 21-year-old student in the final year of a history degree. She had become obsessed with food to such an extent that she found it impossible to concentrate on anything else. Her work had 'gone' and she had stopped seeing most of her friends. The GP who referred her for psychological treatment diagnosed her problem as *bulimia nervosa*, an eating disorder characterized by episodes of binge-eating and self-induced vomiting or purgative abuse, a constant preoccupation with food and eating, and a morbid fear of fatness. Susan was not markedly underweight, but appeared pale and drawn. She admitted that she binged two or three times a week, eating huge quantities of food and then deliberately vomiting. At other times she ate very little, and only a selection of carefully chosen 'good' foods which she believed were not fattening. Her mood was low and she felt unable to exercise any control over this part of her life.

A cognitive–behavioural treatment for *bulimia nervosa* has been described and evaluated (Fairburn 1985). It has three stages. Firstly, an intensive and supportive phase designed to disrupt the pattern of habitual overeating and vomiting. Susan was asked to keep detailed records of her food consumption and to identify meals in which she felt that she was in control and those in which she was not. She was advised to restrict her eating to three planned meals a day regardless of hunger. No attempt was made at this stage to check her vomiting or modify the type of food she was eating. The therapist gave Susan as much support as possible, seeing her initially two or three times a week, and provided her with corrective information about food, weight, and diet. As a result Susan gradually brought her eating more under control, and the episodes of bingeing and vomiting were markedly reduced. Her mood lifted and she began to take up her work again.

In the second phase Susan was seen on a weekly basis, and the focus shifted to the problems and stresses that had provoked the eating disorder. The therapist encouraged Susan to relax her rigid restrictions and try 'banned foods', as an experiment designed to demonstrate that this would not lead to a massive loss of control nor immediate weight gain. At this point Susan began to talk more generally about herself and in particular about her parents. The psychologist detected ambivalent feelings in Susan about her family. She described her father in highly idealized terms, yet it also appeared that he was rarely at home, and when he was he would shut himself away to work. Susan was often rather contemptuous about her mother's contribution to the family ('cook and housewife'). Yet it appeared that she was emotionally quite close to her. Susan also mentioned casually, in passing, an ex-boyfriend whom she had been very close to for most of her student life. These messages alerted the therapist to the role played by disturbed relationships in Susan's problems. Since the worst part of the eating disorder had been brought under reasonable control, the treatment focus could be shifted towards exploring Susan's feeling in relation to her family and her ex-boyfriend.

The final phase of Fairburn's approach focuses on the maintenance of change and preparation for possible relapse. In Susan's case, there was much less emphasis given to food as she regularly saw the psychologist over the next few months. Susan's trust for the therapist increased, she was able to admit for the first time how resentful and angry she felt towards her parents, her father in particular. The psychologist for her part was able to get Susan to see that such feelings were not abnormal and that Susan's worth as a person was not dependent on the approval of her parents or others. Susan's self-image had been narrowly restricted to her appearance; hence her excessive concern with food and eating. The treatment allowed her to see how other aspects of herself were valuable and important.

Susan's treatment illustrates how a practical cognitive–behavioural treatment can be successfully combined with a more psychodynamic approach. There was a clear need in the early stages of treatment for the therapist to provide practical help and emotional support. After that a variety of possibilities arises. A more specifically cognitive approach can be adopted, in which the patient's beliefs and attitudes about food and eating are directly tackled. This could be very much a part of Fairburn's approach; and for some patients this direct attack on their cognitions is of benefit. Alternatively, the patient's family could have been brought into treatment in the form of family therapy. The choice of strategy will depend very much on the type of patient and the nature of his or her problems, as well as on the particular experience and expertise of the therapist.

MARITAL OR COUPLE THERAPY

Most of the cases described so far have been examples of individual treatment where the therapeutic contact is between two individuals, patient and therapist. But, as the example of Catherine and Henry illustrated, sometimes patients can be seen in couples. In psychosexual counselling it is generally desirable to see both partners, where that is possible, since the problem is expressed in terms of sexual relationship. Moreover, the practical procedures that are part of sex therapy are obviously much more applicable to a couple than to a single individual.

Marital therapy is another example where both partners are almost always seen, for the same reasons as in sex therapy. The relationship is the crucial factor, and it is very difficult to work productively on a relationship when only one partner is present. In marital therapy, the psychologist's role is that of both facilitator and teacher. As a neutral outsider she or he can enable the couple to perceive and understand more clearly what the nature of their problem is, and by skilful guidance can hopefully help the couple resolve their difficulties and adopt a more productive way of relating to each other. Not all clinical psychologists will practise marital therapy, some preferring to refer patients to specialist organizations such as RELATE in the UK. On the other hand, there has been a particular interest in applying behavioural and social learning theory to marital therapy, and several practical psychological strategies have been devised (Jacobson and Margolin 1979). For example, where partners have a particular difficulty in communicating with each other, the psychologist can directly teach communication skills. This is done in relation to a practical problem in the marriage, and can be expanded to include problem-solving skills in general. Another approach is to examine the ways in which the couple seek to influence each other's behaviour. In some instances couples may be encouraged to make explicit contracts with each other which are written down, specifying the behaviours that they would like to see and what contingencies would follow (contingency contracting). By making the rules specific and explicit, the couple can learn the important skills of reciprocity and positive reinforcement.

FAMILY THERAPY

Another approach that differs from one-to-one treatment methods is family therapy. As the name implies, psychological problems are seen not so much as deficits or psychopathology within the individual, but rather as a product of the family and family relationships. Family therapy consists of bringing the whole family (or as many of the family as possible) into therapy and working with them in order to produce changes in the family structure and relations. This is sometimes generically known as a *systemic* way of working, underlining the need to look at a problem in relation to the system as a whole and not in isolation. This approach first began in relation to psychological problems in children and adolescents, where it clearly makes sense to see the child's problem in its context. For example, a child with nocturnal enuresis (bedwetting) might be providing a focus away from the parents' marital difficulties which are too difficult for the family to deal with directly, or an adolescent's anorexia (rigidly reduced eating) a response to implicit family demands to succeed at academic work at all costs by being too ill to work effectively.

A number of psychologists have begun to use family therapy approaches with adult patients. Members of the immediate family are invited to attend for therapy, and the family structure is explored. This is commonly done by means of a *genogram*, which is in effect the drawing up of a family tree, in the process of which family patterns, myths, and structures begin to emerge, and the problem, initially defined as the referred patient's, becomes more of a family one. Family therapists tend to work in a different style and format from most individual therapists. For example, it is common for therapists to work as a team, perhaps of three or four people, one of whom is the recognized therapist and the others advisers. The advisers watch the therapist and family working, perhaps from behind a one-way screen, and may interrupt the therapy to provide advice or suggest therapeutic strategies. The therapist will seek 'time out' from time to time to discuss progress (or the lack of it) with her advisers. Generally, family therapy is not a lengthy affair; it may be as short as 3 or 4 sessions, and can be spread out over a longer time-period (meetings every three weeks, for example). Most importantly, the systemic approach stresses the capacity of the family system to find and implement change itself; the therapists' role is to enable change by focusing on the family's strengths and allowing the family to gain a new perspective on its problems. Family therapy for adults is still in an early stage of development. However, the systemic approach has a broad application and can be used in individual, couples, and group therapy (see, for example, de Shazer 1988).

GROUP THERAPIES

Some people's psychological problems may best be dealt with in groups. This can be true when people share a common problem which requires a common treatment strategy. Agoraphobic patients, for example, with a fear of leaving the safety of their homes can be helped by means of a planned behavioural programme carried out in small groups of five to eight patients. The psychologist may set up a week's intensive treatment in which the group meets every day at the clinic and each day carries out a part of the behavioural programme, at first with the supervision of the psychologist and then on their own. Alternatively the group may meet weekly for a period of six weeks, with homework tasks set in between. Behavioural groups such as these can be very effective, particularly when the group is cohesive and mutually supportive. It is easier for some patients to take risks when others are in the same boat.

For some patients a group is part of the problem. People who are shy, unassertive, nervous of others or who lack 'social skills' may benefit from a group treatment since it allows them to learn how to overcome their difficulties and interact more effectively with others. Social skills training groups, for example, are ones in which people are directly taught various social skills, such as those used in holding conversations, making requests, forming friendships, or dealing with people in authority. Another related approach is assertiveness training, in which anxious and inhibited patients are taught how to stand up for themselves more effectively and to be more open and expressive in their feelings towards others.

Social skills and assertiveness training groups vary in size from as little as four patients to as large as ten or twelve, and often have two therapists. In most instances the period of training is deliberately circumscribed and a highly structured programme is followed. The content of the training varies from focusing on small and specific aspects of social interaction, for example, eye-contact in talking to other people or the use of gesture in conversation, to generalized and quite complex aspects of interpersonal relationships, for example, responding to criticism from other people, or breaking into a social group at a party. Training consists usually of modelling or demonstration by the therapist or others of appropriate social behaviour, repeated practice in the form of role play in the group or individually with the therapist, feedback on how successful the practice was, further repeated practice, and homework assignments for the patients to carry out outside the treatment.

Some forms of group therapy are much less didactic. Group psychotherapy, for example, can involve two therapists and eight or more patients meeting weekly for as long as 18 months. The focus of the group is on interpersonal learning, but by means of shared experiences rather than specific teaching. Typically, the therapists do not 'lead' the group, but seek to guide it forwards, creating a constructive and helping atmosphere in which personal problems can be freely discussed. The group itself becomes an important and valued entity, and is seen as the main vehicle of change (see Bloch and Crouch 1985). It may be that elements of both the skills training and the interpersonal learning groups can be combined to good effect. Practical role-playing exercises, for example, can often be a part of group psychotherapy, although their use is less for acquiring skills than for providing personal feedback.

HOW EFFECTIVE ARE PSYCHOLOGICAL TREATMENTS?

This question is not an easy one to answer. Firstly, there are many forms of psychological treatment, so that a general statement about their effectiveness is hard to make. In some quarters there is a widely held belief that all forms of psychotherapy are 'modestly effective', and no one treatment strategy is really superior to any other. But, optimistic as this verdict may be, it is undiscriminating and not very helpful. If all treatments are of equal validity, how does one decide which treatment to use? And is it plausible to maintain that *any* form of psychological treatment is of benefit? Surely some approaches are better than others.

A second difficulty in answering the question is the absence of good empirical knowledge about many treatments. Psychoanalysis, for example, the oldest form of psychological treatment, has had very little empirical research carried out into its effectiveness, and undoubtedly a main reason for this lies in the enormous complexity of the task. It is exceedingly difficult to translate the sophisticated theoretical terminology of psychoanalysis into practical data that can be scientifically measured and studied. The greater concreteness of behavioural and cognitive treatments has certainly helped researchers in designing and carrying out sound empirical research. It is easier to show that agoraphobic patients are able to go out more on their own after treatment than it is to show that their unconscious conflicts have been successfully resolved.

Thirdly, while people may show considerable improvement during treatment, it is sometimes difficult to distinguish the various factors that account for that improvement. The personality of the therapist, the personality of the client, the particular setting, the patient's desire to please the therapist, the reactivity of the measures used, the influence of extraneous variables, the passage of time, are all factors that can produce change. Research designs are becoming more sophisticated in the attempt to control for various factors, but it remains difficult to carry out complex outcome research successfully, and very few research trials of a good methodological standard have been carried out. Therefore many forms of psychological treatment remain of uncertain value. This does not mean that most treatments are ineffective; merely that there is insufficient knowledge to conclude definitely that a particular treatment works—a state of affairs that is not uncommon in other fields of clinical practice.

Clinical psychologists have shown a particular interest in treatment research, and have often been in the forefront of designing and carrying out research studies. The Sheffield Psychotherapy Project is a good example of a well designed research project into therapeutic outcome (Shapiro and Firth 1987). Two different psychotherapeutic approaches—prescriptive (similar to cognitive-behavioural) and exploratory (more akin to psychodynamic)—were compared using a cross-over design. That is, the same therapist gave both treatments to each patient, switching from one approach to the other after 8 weeks. The order of treatments was balanced so that half the patients began with prescriptive, and half with exploratory therapy. The design allowed the researchers to control for possible therapist effects (the same therapist gave both treatments) and to study possible order effects. In addition, only experienced therapists were used, and their faithfulness to the particular therapy was carefully assessed by the use of therapeutic manuals, weekly supervision, and audiotape recordings of all the sessions. Thorough assessments of change were made not only at the end of treatment and follow-up, but after each individual session, thereby providing considerable information on the process of change. Statistical analysis of the outcome showed that both therapies resulted in positive clinical benefit to the patients, with a small swing in favour of the prescriptive approach. Research designs that look more closely at the process of change, rather than only at outcome at the end of treatment, will provide much more useful information about effectiveness. We need to know not only that psychological treatment is of benefit, but how treatments work, which patients respond well and which badly, what therapists actually do that helps their patients, and many other important points. Treatment research in the 1990s has begun to address these issues.

SUMMARY

Clinical psychologists are specialists in psychological treatment and in particular have developed expertise in the short-term, pragmatic cognitive and behavioural methods. These methods have been described and illustrated with reference to phobic anxiety and depressive disorders. Some clinical psychologists go on to acquire further specialist training, which can take the form of a particular type of therapy (for example, sex therapy, marital therapy) or a particular theoretical orientation and practical skills. The psychodynamic approach has been described and illustrated with reference to a therapy case. Recently there has been a convergence of different schools of therapy, and many clinical psychologists describe themselves as 'eclectic', preferring to use a variety of methods and tailor these to the individual case. Finally, the effectiveness of psychological treatments has been examined in various research studies. Although many psychotherapists are optimistic about the results of their therapies, methodological shortcomings combined with the difficulties involved in carrying out good quality treatment research mean that our knowledge about the effectiveness of psychological treatments is still only at a rudimentary stage.

REFERENCES

Beck, A. T., Rush, A. J., Shaw, B. F., and Emery, G. (1979). *Cognitive therapy for depression*. The Guilford Press, New York.

Bloch, S. and Crouch, E. (1985). *Therapeutic factors in group psychotherapy*. Oxford University Press, Oxford.

Dryden, W. and Golden, W. (eds) (1986). *Cognitive–behavioural approaches to psychotherapy*. Harper & Row, London.

Fairburn, C. (1985). Cognitive behavioural treatment for bulimia. In *Handbook of psychotherapy for anorexia nervosa and bulimia* (ed. D. M. Garner and P. E. Garfinkel). The Guilford Press, New York.

Hawton, K. (1985). *Sex therapy. A practical guide*. Oxford University Press.

Hawton, K., Salkovskis, P., Kirk, J., and Clark, D. (1989). *Cognitive–behaviour therapy for psychiatric problems*. Oxford University Press.

Jacobson, N. S. and Margolin, G. M. (1979). *Marital therapy: strategies based on social learning and behaviour exchange principles*. Brunner/Mazel, New York.

Mathews, A., Gelder, M. G., and Johnston, D. W. (1981). *Agoraphobia. Nature and treatment*. Tavistock, London.

Rachman, S. and Hodgson, R. J. (1980). *Obsessions and compulsions*. Prentice-Hall, Englewood Cliffs, NJ.

Ryle, A. (1990). *Cognitive–analytic therapy: active participation in change*. Wiley, Chichester.

Shapiro, D. A. and Firth, J. (1987). Prescriptive v. exploratory psychotherapy. Outcomes of the Sheffield Psychotherapy Project. *Brit. J. Psychiat.* **151**, 790–9.

de Shazer, S. (1988). *Clues. Investigating solutions in brief therapy.* Norton, New York.

Storr, A. (1979). *The art of psychotherapy.* Heinemann, London.

Teasdale, J. D., Fennell, M. J. V., Hibbert, G. A., and Amies, P. L. (1984). Cognitive therapy for major depressive disorder in primary care. *Brit. J. Psychiat.* **144**, 400–6.

FURTHER READING

Aveline, M. and Dryden, W. (eds) (1988). *Group therapy in Britain.* The Open University Press, Milton Keynes.

Barlow, D. H. (1988). *Anxiety and its disorders: the nature and treatment of anxiety and panic.* The Guilford Press, New York.

Bloch, S. (ed.) (1986). *Introduction to psychotherapies* (2nd edn). Oxford University Press.

Rowe, D. (1983). *Depression. The way out of your prison.* Routledge and Kegan Paul, London.

3

Psychological work with longer-term problems
John Hall

Most adults with psychological problems are not permanently handicapped by their difficulties. They can continue to lead some sort of normal life, and can make most decisions relating to day-to-day living. A small but important proportion of the population are seriously handicapped by psychological difficulties, and some may not be able to continue living in ordinary domestic housing. This chapter is concerned mainly with people with major and seriously handicapping psychological difficulties, a proportion of whom live in some sort of institution.

A number of other chapters are concerned with the work of clinical psychologists with disabled people—people with a severe learning difficulty, or with a physical handicap. A proportion of those people will also live in some sort of institutional setting, so it is useful to consider some of the general attributes of 'institutions', irrespective of the specific medical or psychological difficulties those who live in them have.

WHAT IS AN INSTITUTION?

An institution is a living place where there are separate groups of staff, and inmates/residents/patients, and where the living conditions of the resident group are primarily determined by the staff group. Western European societies have traditionally provided a number of such institutions, most notably prisons, hospitals, and accommodation for the poor and 'needy'. Pungent criticism of institutional care by sociologists, and the indictment of official committee of enquiry reports at some psychiatric hospitals, have together combined to produce a situation where the need for institutional care has to be argued anew.

A psychologist should, of course, be asking, 'Why institutions anyway?' If the present institutions did *not* exist, would it be necessary to invent them? This section discusses the contribution of psychologists to institutions that currently exist, though that very contribution leads many psychologists to think that institutions, where the client need justifies institutional provision, should be as need-specific as possible. Providing an institutional solution to the needs of a patient when other solutions, maybe those open to 'normal' people, have not been explored, may serve to further remove them from normal services of support and service. Adopting this approach would no doubt lead to a new type of institutional provision, such as the hospital–hostels for younger chronic patients that are now being developed. By implication, such provision would also be in smaller units than at present, and very different total numbers of institutional places might be required.

Erving Goffmann (1961) is probably the best-known critic of institutional care. He coined the phrase 'total institution', which he defined as 'a place of residence and work where a large number of like-situated individuals, cut off from the wider society for an appreciable period of time, together lead an enclosed formally administered round of life'. Goffmann considered that *the* central feature of institutional life is a breakdown of barriers between three spheres of life: sleep, work, and play. This definition emphasizes a number of characteristics of the total institution, such as one organizational system embracing all aspects of the resident life and the homogeneity of the population of residents of any one institution. The total institution is at one end of a continuum, the other end of which is 'normal' self-determined life in domestic surroundings, with work and leisure carried out in different places.

What this definition makes clear is that institutional care is defined by a pattern of life, as much as by other features of the institution. Thus many people with severe psychological difficulties live in group homes run by charitable bodies, in hostels provided by public social welfare or social services departments, and in sheltered housing with resident workers. Whatever the label attached to these institutions, some of the practices encountered in Goffmann's total institutions *may* be encountered there. Handicapped people have traditionally been disadvantaged and indeed exploited, and some of the most handicapped people require a specially structured environment to enable them to acquire and maintain the skills they lack. This does not suggest they require institutional care, in the passive meaning of that word; but perhaps they do require a special place for living that cannot readily be provided in ordinary unstaffed domestic housing.

The discussion so far has concentrated, at least implicitly, on institutions for living. Goffmann's definition included reference to places of work: ordinary people usually go to work at a place other than their home, and those who work at home typically enjoy more autonomy in their pattern of work than those who are employed outside their home. A characteristic of many psychiatric institutions is that day activities are provided on the same site as the living facilities, and that the same group of staff supervise the residents in both settings, so the range of social relationships in which they are engaged is thereby narrowed. Providing day activities away from residential facilities then broadens the range of social relationships, quite apart from the extra social contact that results.

What if no institutional care is provided? In the last few years there has been major concern about the numbers of people with serious psychiatric illness who are homeless, or who have been placed within the penal system rather than the hospital. Nowhere has the rate and extent of de-institutionalization been higher than in the USA, where the numbers of 'street people' and 'bag ladies' are obvious; but similar folk are obvious on the streets of most major European cities. Night shelters may exist for some of the homeless, or in Britain they may be supported by local authorities in what is usually a poor standard of bed-and-breakfast accommodation. These settings have not been specifically set up to cope with people with long-term psychiatric problems, and often offer little or no special facilities for these people; hence the risk of relapse in such settings is high. It is a grim paradox that the lack of institutional provision for people with serious handicaps has been one of the greatest spurs to rethinking the whole issue of the best way to care.

Why do people live in institutions?

There is little doubt that the initial enthusiasm for asylum care in the nineteenth century was for genuinely humanitarian reasons, and the very title asylum implied the recognition of the need for a safe place to protect the incapacitated. In the run-down of large psychiatric hospitals that has been going on since the mid-1950s, surveys suggest that the specifically psychiatric nature of handicaps is often unclear in a substantial minority of the most chronic cases, although the application of modern diagnostic criteria retrospectively to these patients is admittedly fraught with theoretical difficulties.

However, the continuing accumulation of 'new chronic' patients suggests that even with the most vigorous pharmacological and social care, a small proportion of patients cannot be satisfactorily left unsupported. The most frequent disorder found is chronic schizophrenia, and it is significant that with increasing lengths of stay the proportion of patients who are so diagnosed increases to well above 50 per cent. Chronic schizophrenia thus forms the most serious psychiatric condition to continue to be found in psychiatric institutions. Other major diagnostic groups are chronic affective disorder—chronic depression or mania—and chronic personality and neurotic disorders. As these people become older, they are likely to have physical problems; and even among younger patients physical needs should not be overlooked. Thus most people who have lived continuously for any length of time—say 1 or 2 years or more—in a psychiatric institution will have had access to psychotherapy, social case-work skills, and other treatments, and in a sense are the 'failures' of acute psychiatric and psychological help.

Another reason why people may be living in a psychiatric institution is lack of an alternative place for them to go. There are several clinical groups, such as young adults with serious head injury, mildly mentally handicapped people with behaviour problems, and people with some progressive physical conditions, such as Huntington's chorea, which are small in number but whose members present considerable problems of community or family tolerance. The ability of a family to cope with these difficulties is strained by the constant vigilance required or sometimes by aggressive attacks, so that people who are strictly speaking not psychiatrically ill may be cared for on a long-term basis on a psychiatric hospital ward. Their needs are not primarily psychiatric, but are for a stable planned regime which will facilitate new learning, maintain existing skills, and accommodate disturbed and disruptive behaviour: this does not necessarily mean a hospital regime.

THE PROBLEMS TO BE FACED

A major concern in this chapter is to look at psychologically disabled people in the setting where they live. A psychological analysis of longer-term problems should therefore take account of the problems posed by the person, and of the problems posed by the environment.

Problems of the patient

The problems posed by the patient are the conventional focus for treatment in institutions; but they cannot be understood in isolation from the setting in which they occur. Psychologically, the problems of these patients are not defined primarily by their diagnosis. Thirty years ago the diagnosis of chronic schizophrenia may have carried with it a stereotypic view of the chronic patient. Paradoxically perhaps, the reduction in in-patient numbers over the last 30 years has meant that the extremely heterogeneous nature of the group is now clear. People with a chronic psychiatric disability form an extremely varied group by any standards. Quite apart from the primary problems arising from their psychiatric condition, chronic patients may have disabilities of other origins. They frequently have other pre-morbid handicaps, such as lower intellectual ability or poorer work records before they ever became ill. They also may have secondary handicaps arising from the way in which their families view and respond to them. Indeed the strictly psychiatric disabilities which remain may often not be the major focus of treatment for an individual.

From the point of view of an experimental psychologist, most chronic patients do have some common attributes. Many are slow, the slowness showing not only in experimental tasks, but in speech— meaning that enough time needs to be given for them to reply to questions—as well as in rate of output in jobs they do. Many may lack concentration, so they are relatively easily distracted from what they are doing, and easily influenced by peripheral stimulation. The more handicapped patients may have very low levels of motivation, as indicated by their poor response to those normal encouragements of praise, money, or tobacco, leading in the extreme to 'anhedonia'— the total absence of any apparent pleasure-seeking tendencies.

From the point of view of a clinical psychologist, the most obvious problem of these patients is lack of skill or motivation in a range of normal social behaviour. Some of these skills are related to looking after themselves—a lack of attention to personal hygiene, a lack of willingness to cook even simple meals for themselves. Other skills are related to getting on with other people—an unwillingness to initiate conversations with other people, a lack of persistence in some social game or activity, a lack of eye-contact with other people. It is these deficits of behaviour which constitute the overwhelming management problem of these patients.

By contrast, fewer patients show examples of bizarre or odd behaviour. Some patients may be seen as 'potentially' violent or aggressive, but are so controlled in one way or another that years may pass without a single violent episode. Yet undoubtedly some of them may behave in a very odd manner, such as the drum-majorette twirling of fingers and hands seen in some patients, and the peculiar forms of dress and self-adornment, such as the tin- and enamel-badge bedecked patient sometimes seen. Delusional ideas and hallucinatory experiences give conversations with some of these patients a profoundly unreal flavour. Even though such deviant and symptomatic behaviour is usually less frequent than behavioural deficits, it has a particular capacity to antagonize family and neighbours.

Last of all, it is important to acknowledge the need for medical care for many of these patients. Many of them are receiving maintenance medication, either of oral phenothiazine drugs, or of depot injections of neuroleptic drugs, which ensure that medication can be reliably administered without the individual patient's needing to remember a complex tablet-taking regime. For some patients in regular contact with their families, correct medication may be very important in preventing relapse; and it may be important for other patients. Second, chronic patients may need medical attention for ordinary physical ailments, especially since some of them may not spontaneously respond to pain and discomfort in their bodies, and thus physical problems may be well advanced before they are detected. Providing physical aids and prostheses, such as dentures and spectacles, can overcome some problems; but only if patients understand their value and are trained to make use of them.

Problems of the environment

The problems of the environment may be considered under two broad headings: the physical, and the social.

The physical problems of some of the larger older institutions are considerable. They are remote both from the neighbouring community, so reducing the chance of patients' using local shops, libraries, etc., and the community of origin of the patients, so that relatives face a time-consuming and expensive journey when and if they visit. The wards are large and barrack-like, making it difficult to provide much privacy. Some of the more modern units have the virtue of being smaller and more flexible in use, but may be designed on the same 'race-track' layout as a general hospital ward—not particularly suitable for psychiatric use. At a more micro-environmental level, storage space needs to be arranged so that recreational materials can be used readily, not just put in an inaccessible cupboard at the end of the ward. Chairs need to be arranged to encourage communication, not to line ward walls.

The social problems of the institution originate from two main sources: the staff, and the rules of the institution. Dr Albert Kushlick has suggested a notation for the role of different staff groups, based essentially on the amount of time that members of each staff group are in direct contact (DC) with the patients. Ward nurses and residential social workers are by his notation 'DC 12 hours'—they are in contact with the patient for all their waking life. Psychological studies of nurse–patient interaction indicate that the least well-trained direct-care staff spend more time interacting with patients than the more well-trained and senior staff, at least in part because of the ward-level administrative duties, which take the latter group away from the patients. Together these points mean that in many settings the staff who have the greatest potential to modify the patients' behaviour, psychologically speaking, are the least well-trained. This is not to deny the real interest shown in their patients by many such ward-level nurses, but to acknowledge their special needs, and to recognize the consequences of continued low staffing levels and sometimes poor morale. These staff may lack a coherent view of what rehabilitation is all about, may form a cohesive social group resistant to changes which threaten their status quo, and need both relevant training and continuing guidance and encouragement to give of their best, so that very careful design of both training courses and monitoring is required.

The rules of the institution form the other determinant of the institutional environment. One approach to assess the effect of these rules is to examine the 'restrictiveness' of a ward or unit, noting the amount of restriction on tobacco use, access of visitors, the time when lights have to be out, etc. (see Wykes 1982 for an example of psychological measures of restrictiveness). Some of these regulations are purely local to an individual hospital, while others have their origins in the practices of individual professions or of national guidance; but many tend to lead to a lack of individualized care.

The generic phrase 'rehabilitation' is often used to describe the range of activities undertaken to care for and treat chronic patients. However, one term is really inadequate to describe the range of procedures that have to be carried out with the extremely heterogeneous group of patients found in most institutional settings. The most handicapped group of patients may lack basic self-care skills, may be heavily dependent on care staff, and will most probably continue to spend most of their lives in a highly sheltered environment. Such a patient might be a 67-year-old woman who has been in hospital for the past 23 years. Admitted after her parents died, she never married or carried out a full-time job, and is not able to dress herself without help. She does not concentrate on games or other recreational activities, and positively avoids conversing with other residents or staff unless coerced to do so.

An intermediate group of patients may be able to use a wide range of community facilities, such as local shops, and can usefully be encouraged to use even more facilities, with suitable help. A group of 'new long-stay' or 'high contact' patients may still be in close contact with their families and may be seeking work, even though they have intermittent episodes of acute symptoms. An example of such a patient would be a 31-year-old man who failed to complete a college course of higher education, and who then drifted into casual hotel work. He can still keep such a job for a few weeks when demand for such work is higher over the summer, but has periodic psychotic episodes which gradually have become longer and longer. He then comes into hospital when his landlord realizes he cannot cope in his lodgings, despite the well-meaning support of his married sister who lives nearby. Hospitals vary in the extent to which old long-stay patients have left hospital, and in the range of hostel and group-home accommodation—and perhaps housing provided by voluntary Housing Association—associated with them. The task of the clinical psychologist will vary considerably, according to the mix of patients and the range of settings in which they live.

For many professional staff, the care of acutely ill people offers more professional gratification than the care of people with more chronic conditions. With the less severely ill, progress is usually more rapid; it is certainly easier to see the relationship between the use of particular treatments and specific benefit; and usually acute patients tend to be more articulate and verbal, so they are more rewarding to help. Whatever is meant by rehabilitation or intervention, it is important to define goals of work with chronic patients, and for all the staff involved to adjust to longer time-scales and slower rates of expected improvement. For example, some care staff remember past peccadilloes of the chronic patients they are working with, but find it hard to say what three things they would like a patient to be able to achieve over the next three months.

One psychological contribution to this field is the development of overall goals of services to handicapped people. Perhaps the concept of 'normalization', applied particularly with respect to mentally handicapped people, is the best known example of an overall service concept. This initially simple idea has been developed so that it carries with it the notion of availability of choice in different areas of living, the use of socially valued means of help with problems to counteract stigma, and the corollary of having to face reasonable risks. However, a number of other overall or superordinate objects of services have been suggested for work with chronic patients, which bear examination.

One such concept is the 'least restrictive environment'. Hospitals, according to this model, are the most restrictive type of environment because they cater for peoples' total needs over a 24-hour period. Even quite disabled people do not necessarily need total care in all areas of their life for 24 hours, and to that extent more of the person's life may be controlled in hospital than is necessary. By contrast, the services should seek to provide the least restrictive environment possible for an individual, based on an assessment of his continuing abilities and disabilities offering the 'minimum therapeutic dose' of assistance needed for each area of disability. A similar notion is that of the 'least segregated environment'. Segregation implies reduced contact with the neighbouring community, whether family, friends, or facilities such as shops and pubs. Segregation would then be reduced not only by the siting of an environment near main centres of population, but also by ensuring, in detail, that the environment was near a post office and a bus stop, and that members of the outside community really did come into the environment.

A rather different objective is that of 'personalization'. The concept of institutional neurosis views loss of personal events and personal possessions as one of seven contributory factors to this type of neurosis. The appropriate corrective action would accordingly be to restore personal events such as birthdays, and personal possessions, such as little trinkets and photographs, next to where the person sleeps. Personalization is also one component of 'resident-orientated' care, as opposed to the depersonalization seen in 'institutionally orientated' care.

A particular contribution which clinical psychologists can make is to offer some sort of conceptual clarification to their colleagues. Overall objectives like those outlined can be very helpful as a way of bringing cohesion to what could otherwise be a rag-bag of low-level subordinate goals, such as 'encouraging conversation' or 'going to the shops more'. An overall objective, accepted by all staff concerned, can help to develop a detailed programme of targets and a set of evaluation measures which are mutually consistent, and which can then provide an overall framework of treatment for staff and residents alike. More fundamentally, a psychologist may have to address the paradox of 'treating' chronic patients whom some staff may see as untreatable. Is there still a need for a concept of asylum? A psychologist working closely with direct-care staff is bound to encounter these issues, and can help them to think through the issues of handicap and disability, as well as issues of treatment.

Assessing and understanding chronic psychiatric disability

The first practical task of the psychologist may well be to contribute to an understanding of the range of needs that a 'rehabilitation' service may try to meet. This may lead to a distinctive type of assessment procedure, a large-scale survey of the clients in contact with a service, which has no parallel in work with more acute patients.

It is common for there to be relatively little information in long-stay patients' case notes, and what information there is often fails to indicate clearly the current problems of the patient, and how much he or she has changed over recent weeks or months. A detailed knowledge of the history of a patient, by contrast, can give an idea of past interests—to be hopefully re-awakened—and possibly of those circumstances that the patient has found particularly stressful. A systematic survey can then identify gross characteristics of the patients in standard form, including details of the patient's current behaviour in addition to other relevant information, such as the patient's current income—this may determine what activities he can afford—and degree of contact with relatives.

A large-scale survey of this sort may easily cover 200 or 300 patients in 10 or 15 settings, so the organizational aspects of a survey may require careful attention by a psychologist. A frequent consequence of such a survey is that patients are regrouped, so that any one unit contains patients more similar to each other than previously. This certainly assumes that staff are agreed about the main patient attributes—such as absence of physical and verbal aggression or level of self-care—which determine the groupings, and also requires some statistical sophistication, often supplied by a psychologist, to carry out such a grouping. Views differ on how to regroup, or indeed whether to regroup at all. One approach is to produce groups of patients as homogeneous as possible in their behaviour. This approach applied to the most handicapped or most over-active patients may produce a group of patients which would place unacceptable demands upon staff. If some patients have grown old together and show some evidence of friendship with each other, perhaps they should not be regrouped for the sake of homogeneity alone? Inevitably a psychologist involved in this type of exercise will need to be able to manipulate large numbers of variables, but also to retain some clinical sense of the needs of individuals while doing so—such as the need to produce groups of patients that the staff can cope with.

After such a general survey or regrouping, the assessment task of the psychologist becomes more refined and detailed. Now the task is to identify those attributes of the patients that are relevant to their future care. This may involve looking at some general area of functioning, such as the patient's ability to care for his own personal needs, and separately to assess skills in washing, dressing, shaving, sanitary care, cleaning teeth, toileting, feeding, etc. Abilities may need to be defined at several different levels of handicap, so some sort of rating technique may be required to produce a change-sensitive measure of each individual skill.

There is evidence that identifying specific therapeutic goals precisely, and communicating these goals clearly to both direct-care staff and to the patients themselves, is therapeutic. From a psychologist's point of view, this means that only a limited number of goals can be presented—so that staff and patients alike are not overwhelmed by too many goals—and the goals must be presented in a straightforward way.

Just as important as the initial specification of the goal is the regular checking or monitoring of the target that has been set, to see if change in indeed occurring. An interesting contribution to the way in which psychologists can help to evaluate change over a long period of time is the comparative study of Woods and Cullen (1983). They compared four studies, carried out with mentally handicapped and chronically mentally ill people, where behavioural data had been carefully collected over many months—up to five years for some patients. A summary table of the results (see Table 3.1) shows how little relation there was between what improvement had occurred and what improvement care staff *thought* had occurred. This illustrates the difficulty of maintaining staff behaviour over the very long periods of time inevitably involved with patients in institutions, and the possibility of complex relationships between staff and resident behaviour.

The focus of most assessment methods is the behaviour of the patient, both past and present, and looking at the remaining assets, as well as the deficits (or negative handicaps) and the deviations (or

Table 3.1 Effects of four behavioural programmes on residents and staff

Study	Resident behaviour	Staff perception	Staff behaviour
1. Toileting	Gradual improvement	No improvement	Sustained
2. Toileting	Gradual deterioration	No improvement	Sustained
3. Room management	Rapid improvement	Definite improvement	Not sustained
4. Token economy	Gradual improvement and maintained at stable level	Little or no improvement	Sustained

positively odd behaviour) of the patient. However, it may be important to assess the physical environment of the patient, as that environment may be setting limits to the patients' behaviour. Alternatively, it may be helpful to assess the social environment of the patients, typically the pattern of interaction of staff with the patients. All these assessment methods should be capable of being repeated from time to time to review patients, especially for those inoffensive and thus unnoticed patients who often compose the majority of the residents of a ward.

A peculiar difficulty in working with chronic patients is their reticence in expressing their own wishes in a way that is consistent. Often such patients may have difficulty in understanding questions, may be inarticulate in their replies, or may be easily influenced in their answers, so it is difficult to have confidence that you really have found out what *they* want. This can lead to ethical difficulties, since such patients, unlike many residents of mental handicap hospitals, have no relative or next-of-kin to whom you can turn when difficult decisions have to be made. This suggests more psychological attention should be paid to finding out how best to communicate with such patients.

For all these assessment decisions—categorizing, target-setting, or monitoring—there is a range of procedures available. In general, tests are not now widely used, and self-completion questionnaires are rarely used for more chronic patients, for the reasons just discussed. The two most frequently used types of assessment are ratings—either of ward behaviour or of interview behaviour—or behavioural assessment procedures.

Rating chronic psychiatric patients

Ratings require observers to record, in a standard way, their *opinion* of the relative strength of a particular attribute. Ratings of ward behaviour are usually completed by nurses, often on the basis of a few days' observation, and typically are high on general relevance. Conversely, ratings of interview behaviour may be more reliable, but may not be closely related to what the patient does outside the interview. A useful assessment instrument in this sort of setting should meet a number of criteria, including: (a) the possibility of its use in different types of setting, in particular in both hospital and community settings; (b) inclusion of items that differentiate between those patients who may be able to live independently, and those probably requiring some continuing degree of supervision; and (c) the possibility of detecting change in behaviour, even when change is limited in extent and occurs over a period of months.

With these aims in mind Baker and Hall (1988) have developed a behaviour rating scale, REHAB, for use by direct-care staff. There are a number of important features in this scale. The content of the items was chosen from research studies, to include items of problem behaviour that occurred most frequently, items considered by key staff groups to be most important, and those shown to be sensitive to treatment change. The individual items were designed to cover the full range of disability that can be shown with this client group, so that in the event a wide range of scores resulted, showing a good spread of scores. The whole scale was also worded and set out so that it could be easily read and understood by direct-care staff, such as nursing assistants, who may not have a high level of formal education. The scale was factor-analysed, in such a way that the factors that emerged were robust over the whole range of patients who were studied, so that the factors made practical sense both for the most handicapped and least handicapped patient. The scale was developed on nearly 1000 different patients, from three different centres, so the scale does not simply reflect conditions in one locality or hospital.

Some of the detailed investigations necessary to design properly a scale like this are of interest. It is obviously important that any standard instrument is used in a standard way, so a clear description is given of how to train raters, and copies of a special user's guide are issued with the scale. Most handicapped patients, irrespective of diagnosis, show two main types of behaviour problem. On the one hand they show deficits, or lack, of behaviour—they don't talk much, or they move slowly, for example. This type of behaviour may be assessed using a linear-graphic type of item, as shown below:

Item 8: 'How well did the patient get on with others on the ward or unit?'

Very poor relationship	Got on with	Got on well
with other patients	some patients	with other
Solitary and withdrawn		patients

On the other hand they show deviant, or bizarre behaviour—typically infrequent and unpredictable behaviour, such as shouting. This requires a different sort of item, mainly assessing the frequency with which such behaviour occurs.

Behavioural assessment procedures usually involve some timing or counting of events as they happen, with immediate recording using either a time measure or a direct count of the number of events, or use of a simple coding system to categorize events. There is currently a lot of psychological interest in the extent to which staff communicate with patients, and the extent to which patients keep their attention on therapeutic tasks. 'Time-sampling' is a frequently used behavioural assessment procedure in such 'staff–patient interaction' or 'engagement' studies. Time-sampling, in such a study, involves selecting a suitable system for observing each patient in turn, so for example, every 20 seconds a patient would be observed for 5 seconds exactly, and at the end of that 5-second period the patient's behaviour would be coded, using a set of behavioural categories. Adequate time must always be allowed for the appropriate category or categories to be selected and recorded, so the observer can then pick out the next patient in plenty of time, without being hurried. Using this schedule, a group of nine patients could be observed once in 3 minutes, or three times each in 9 minutes. Although there can be a problem of 'reactivity', which is the way in which a patient behaves differently because he knows he is being observed, an observer can be passive and non-responsive to patients, thus minimizing this problem. Since the rate of behavioural change with chronic patients is usually slow, it is possible to observe quite large groups of patients at a time, a task impossible with, for example, behaviourally disturbed children.

Psychological assessment has often been seen as the exclusive preserve of the psychologist. In long-term care settings, by contrast, the psychologist is very much concerned to work with other groups so that the assessment which *they* necessarily must make can be better understood and used. The psychologist is also concerned to work with others to clarify the goals of assessment, so that assessment decisions can be made as effectively as possible.

Psychological interventions with chronic patients

Historically, the treatment of chronic patients in institutions has been dominated by so-called 'social' models of treatment, and work-related approaches to treatment. Going back to Pinel and Tuke in the eighteenth and nineteenth centuries, 'moral' treatment approaches were the most influential, and indeed represented an often heroic attempt to combat exploitation and devaluing of the chronic patient. The place of work was central in most hospital regimes, culminating in the Industrial Therapy movement of the 1930s and 1960s.

The Second World War led to the development of more structured ideas of social treatment, particularly associated with the Therapeutic Community movement. This movement was strongly influenced by the work and ideas of Maxwell Jones, and therapeutic communities, whether hospital-wide or simply involving one ward, became quite common. The next major innovation, led by clinical psychologists, was the introduction of token economy programmes, based on an operant conditioning model and following the innovative work of Ayllon and Azrin. Although therapeutic community concepts and token economy concepts have been viewed as antithetical, a close examination of working practices in the two types of regime often shows surprising similarities. More recently other essentially psychological techniques of intervention have been used, such as social skills training, and problem-solving techniques (Hall 1989). It is perhaps a paradox that just as the numbers of long-term patients in psychiatric hospitals continue to fall, albeit more slowly than before, more psychological interest is being shown in how to treat such patients. The range of approaches and procedures available can be illustrated by briefly considering three of the main techniques or approaches.

The milieu approach

All therapeutic settings necessarily have some sort of milieu or atmosphere, but it may not be specifically recognized as a major tool in rehabilitation. Milieu approaches can be categorized under three main headings. Milieu Therapy is the general concept of the milieu as a mode of treatment, including theory and practice; a therapeutic milieu is a particular setting positively designed for the practice of social therapy, to produce desired change in those who enter it, and thus refers to a range of settings, such as hostels and workshops; a therapeutic community is a specific type of therapeutic milieu. The therapeutic community concept has been further subdivided into the general therapeutic community approach, and the therapeutic community 'proper'. This provides an essentially hierarchical classification; but an examination of therapeutic communities highlights some of the main features of this approach.

A fundamental feature of the milieu approach is its treatment of authority, so that authority on a ward is not exercised hierarchically, but diffused through the staff. Authority is often invested, at least partially, in regular ward meetings, which focus on immediate events and identify publicly the contribution of individual community members to those events. Responsibility is seen as being passed back to the patient for most areas of his life, including caring for himself and his immediate personal space, so no special efforts are made to spruce up patients on the ward so they look 'nice'. Reality-confrontation may be an important part of small groups within the ward, and the detailed analysis of events that thus occurs makes it difficult for conventional barriers of confidentiality to be maintained.

The contribution of a psychologist in this sort of milieu is likely to be similar to the contribution of members of other professions, for a large proportion of the time. The specific professional skills of the psychologist—and of the occupational therapist—may be called upon; but both will be asked to contribute to group meetings, and perhaps to lead staff feedback groups after main group meetings. Involvement in this sort of regime may both help a psychologist to develop group therapy skills, which might then be useful in, say, an addiction unit, and offer an opportunity to contribute other psychological skills, such as evaluating the effectiveness of the ward.

The token economy approach

Rewards have traditionally been given by hospitals to chronic patients—for example cigarettes doled out by ward and domestic staff. Such essentially casual systems of payment may conflict with the way in which any other money the patient has is distributed, and are not usually related to the main presenting problems of the patient. By contrast the token economy approach introduced on a wide scale the use of planned targets and systematic reinforcements to the large mental hospitals in the early 1970s.

The central physical feature of a token economy is some physically durable object, such as coloured plastic disc, or punched card, which has a distinct numerical value attached to it, and which acts as currency within the programme. The exact form of the token is essentially unimportant. However, a secondary benefit of token economy procedures is that an element of choice is restored to the patients: the patient has to choose how to spend his tokens, whereas before he made no choices in his day-to-day life. In a similar way, tokens can reintroduce the idea of cash values to a patient. Very often such patients may spend *all* the money they have in an extravaganza of tobacco early in the morning, and thereafter make no further use of money. Now, they are repeatedly confronted with token–economic decisions, which can be encouraged by using educational money as plastic money. A psychologist who is running a token economy, or other group behavioural programme, will have a number of different tasks to perform. Individual and group targets will have to be set and a careful system of charting introduced; care staff will have to be given specific training in how to dispense tokens; and some quite complex individual programmes will probably have to be carried out on a one-to-one basis. Only with investment of time can the foundations be laid for a realistic programme that will carry on for some time.

The social skills approach

A third treatment approach is that known generically as Social Skills Training (SST). A number of treatment packages have been described (Liberman 1988), many concentrating on the improvement of behavioural skills. The main features of this approach are the use of modelling (the demonstration of the relevant skills), rehearsal (repeated practice by the patient in a 'safe' setting), and feedback (detailed comment and criticism both by the therapist and by the use of audio- and videotape recordings).

This approach lends itself to group work, as it is usually fairly easy to find small groups of chronic patients with similar deficits in the area of social functioning. The psychologist's contribution to such a programme would involve a number of different components. The patients would need to be selected, and common goals identified. Probably other trainers would be needed, so nurses and other staff would have to be prepared for the task. The psychologist and others would have to contribute to the initial modelling of the deficient skills, so a certain degree of acting talent, and willingness to make a bit of a fool of yourself, might then be desirable professional qualities! As in all rehabilitative treatments, steps need to be taken to ensure that the results of the treatment generalize, or spread, to other novel situations. Thus one of the distinctive features of SST is the amount of therapeutic training that may take place actually in the supermarket, or at the bus-stop, or at the bar of the local coffee-shop or pub!

The place of work

As has already been discussed, work therapies have historically been an important way of structuring the daily activity of chronic patients. More recently, work as a form of therapy has become less common as a consequence of widespread unemployment's severely reducing the availability of work to those suffering from major psychiatric handicaps. At the same time, the role of work in offering a range of structured social relationships, and in requiring the individual to meet a range of expectations in the areas of skill, work-rate, and timekeeping, has become apparent.

This means that the role of the psychologist in contributing to the design of work regimes for people living in institutions is a complex one. Unless work is to be merely the performance of simple repetitive tasks, patients should be offered tasks which are within their competence and interest, but which also stretch them. Imaginative voluntary schemes have set up retail outlets and craft workshops where patients can be involved in a complete process of production and selling, where patients can be fitted into the right slot for them. The system of hospital reward payments and social security benefits in Britain is so complicated that considerable attention needs to be paid to incentive schemes for them to work. A number of countries have sheltered workshops, which may offer an offsite day activity for people who still have homes in hospital. Thus in Australia such workshops are operated by voluntary bodies with a gradually reducing state subsidy both for capital and staff costs, and with an incentive reward for every person who returns to outside employment.

Planning a group rehabilitation programme

Whatever the theoretical background to a therapeutic regime, a psychologist is likely to have a number of skills to contribute to planning and running the programme. The rehabilitation of the individual is obviously important (and is well illustrated in the appendix to Shepherd 1984), but group programmes require an additional ability to plan a system of care. Two types of settings represent the most common environments in which clinical psychologists are involved, working to produce a positive care environment.

A typical 'ward-in-a-house' attempts to combine the best features of hospital care, such as well-trained staff, with the best features of community-based care, such as small size and ready access to community facilities. An old house has been internally converted, so residents have to share bedrooms with a maximum of two other people, and the large kitchen is the hub of day activity in the house. There are 14 residents aged from 22 to 57. Most of the residents have been in hospital, some for as long as 6 years, but several have never been in-patients, although their families carried a significant burden in caring for them.

Alternatively, a typical hospital ward might consist of a 30-bedded mixed-sex ward, with two separate large dormitories and five single sleeping-rooms. There is a large day room with easy chairs and television, one small side room, and a spacious ward corridor (doubling as a dining area) leading to the main hospital corridor, off which open a few office rooms. There are 27 patients on the ward aged from 28 to 76, though 14 patients are aged over 60. All but five patients have been continuously in hospital for at least 8 years—one for 43 years; but two of the patients have been in hospital for less than a year, both previously having had several years' experience of 'revolving door' admissions to the hospital.

A psychologist becoming involved with either of these settings could start off with any one of a number of preparatory activities—first making sure she or he has the time to follow through all that will be involved. The literature on the psychologist's role as a 'change agent' will alert her or him to the need to promote group cohesion and group commitment to change amongst the staff involved. Visiting two or three other active rehabilitation units, and calling in two or three credible experts will enable staff to see that change is possible. A short but relevant staff training programme will help staff both to formulate objectives, and to begin to think of detailed procedures—such as a regular ward-based activity regime—they could introduce.

Assuming the original patients remain—and maybe one or two will be too old, or too mentally or physically handicapped—the assets and problems of each patient will need to be assessed. This may lead to the formation of three or four groups, each with relatively similar problems and each with an assigned trained staff member, each of which will have its own group programme. Resources of staff and equipment may well be limited, so it may be better to provide half an hour of structured activity each day—such as going through local papers to identify times of buses and films— rather than dilute the same amount of real learning over two hours. Doing regular assigned jobs can be helpful, as long as each resident does a job at the right level of difficulty, changes job at least every month or so, and perhaps always does the job with a companion or buddy. Success at these therapeutic tasks may then lead to a patient's moving to another programme aimed at his or her new abilities and needs.

Stitching together a programme in this way indicates the amount of overall planning and co-ordination required. Figure 3.1 indicates how this co-ordination can be viewed as an overall system, requiring psychological contributions to assessment and monitoring (the psychologist as psychometrician), promotion of group working among both staff and patients (the psychologist as group facilitator and

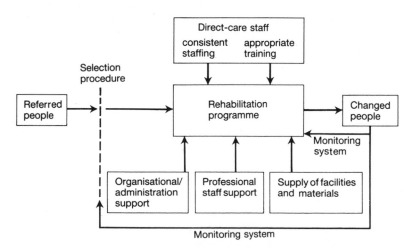

Fig. 3.1 Planning a group rehabilitation programme

therapist), fitting both staff and patients to the activities to which they are best suited (the psychologist as occupational adviser), and the design of individual therapeutic programmes (the psychologist as expert therapist).

Modern services for people with long-term psychiatric difficulties are likely to include a number of different elements, each organizationally and geographically separate, which replace the older style of monolithic hospital services on one site. This means that there is need for a broader type of co-ordination, which is usually called 'case management'. Case management refers to an approach to management which includes: comprehensive assessment of the needs of each individual; the planning of individual 'care packages'; making sure that the package of care matches up to the client's own wishes, and is practically delivered; monitoring the service actually provided; and adjusting the service provided in the light of that monitoring.

SUMMARY

Psychologists have a number of specific contributions to make to the care of patients in institutions. Most institutional residents have major chronic difficulties. Those difficulties can be conceptualized in psychological ways that help to frame treatment objectives, and may even lead to re-evaluating the type of institution in which that treatment should occur. Those difficulties need to be understood specifically and individually, and carefully chosen and applied psychological instruments can add to that understanding. Some of those difficulties can be overcome, if only partly and slowly. A major area of concern is the relative lack of evaluation of the effectiveness of the treatment available in institutional settings. Specific treatments have been evaluated, but the same attention has not been paid to the overall functioning of the institution. For example, there has been relatively little examination of the effectiveness of the major discharge policy adopted in Britain and most other European countries. Braun and colleagues (1981) give a detailed analysis of attempts at de-institutionalization in the USA and Europe: there is little factual evidence to support a complete abolition of institutional care. This does not mean that large, isolated, minimally resourced institutions should continue. It does mean that

82 *Psychological work with longer-term problems*

some small, accessible, adequately resourced institutions will continue to be needed, and that a wealth of psychological, sociological, and psychiatric guidance now exists to give no excuse for not providing a facilitating, co-ordinated, appropriate, and caring regime.

REFERENCES

Baker, R. D. and Hall, J. N. (1988). REHAB: a new assessment instrument for chronic psychiatric patients. *Schizophrenia Bulletin*, **14**, 97–111.
Braun, P., Kochansky, G., Shapiro, R., Greenberg, S., Gudeman, J. E., Johnson, S., and Shore, M. F. (1981). Overview: deinstitutionalisation of psychiatric patients, a critical review of outcome studies. *Am. J. Psychiat.* **138**, 736–49.
Goffman, E. (1961). *Asylums: essays on the social situations of mental patients and other inmates*. Anchor Books, New York.
Hall, J. N. (1989). Chronic psychiatric handicaps. In *Cognitive behaviour therapy for psychiatric problems* (ed. K. Hawton *et al.*), pp. 315–38. Oxford University Press.
Liberman, R. P. (ed.) (1988). *Psychiatric rehabilitation of chronic mental patients*. American Psychiatric Press, Washington.
Shepherd, G. (1984). *Institutional care and rehabilitation*. Longman, London.
Shepherd, G. (1990). Foreword: psychiatric rehabilitation for the 1990s. In *Theory and practice of psychiatric rehabilitation* (2nd edn), (ed. F. N. Watts *et al.*), pp. xiii–xlviii. Wiley, Chichester.
Woods, P. A. and Cullen, C. N. (1983). Determinants of staff behaviour in long-term care. *Behav. Psychother.*, **11**, 4–18.
Wykes, T. (1982). A hostel-ward for 'new' long-stay patients: an evaluative study of a 'ward in a house'. *Psychological medicine monograph*, Suppl. 2. Cambridge University Press, Cambridge.

FURTHER READING

Jones, K. and Fowles, A. J. (1984). *Ideas on institutions*. Routledge and Kegan Paul, London.
Watts, F. N., Bennett, D. H., and Shepherd, G. (eds) (1990). *Theory and practice of psychiatric rehabilitation* (2nd edn). Wiley, Chichester.

4

Working with children and young people
Dorothy Fielding

It has been estimated that, of a total of 1893 clinical psychologists in the National Health Service, some 292 (15 per cent) work full-time with children and adolescents.

Traditionally child clinical psychology services developed alongside those of child psychiatry. In those early days particular emphasis was given to the assessment role of the psychologist within the multidisciplinary team. Clinical psychologists would be asked to contribute to the work of the team by providing intellectual and educational assessments and making any comments about the child's personality or general adjustment that might aid in management.

In recent years, however, there have been substantial changes in the context in which child clinical psychologists work. A number of factors have contributed to these changes. In the first instance, reorganization of clinical psychology services into health district departments has given a wide range of professional workers access to psychological services. Secondly, legislative changes regarding the education and care of children, and the publication of a number of influential government reports have emphasized the advice-giving consultative and policy-making roles of clinical psychologists. Finally advances in research and clinical practice have widened the range of expertise of clinical psychologists, thus changing psychologists' perception of their own role. The following chapter reviews these developments in clinical practice by describing the settings in which child clinical psychologists now work and the contributions which they make to the health care of children and young people.

THE CHANGING HEALTH NEEDS OF CHILDREN AND YOUNG PEOPLE AND THE ROLE OF CHILD CLINICAL PSYCHOLOGISTS

Any discussion of services for children must take into account the changing patterns of health and disease amongst the child population. There is no doubt that over the last 50 years there have been dramatic improvements in the health of children and young people. Many of the crippling infectious diseases prevalent in the early part of this century have been eliminated and there have been impressive reductions in the mortality rate of young infants. Increased survival has been accompanied by improved growth. Children are taller and heavier than they were a generation ago. However, the factors that have brought about reduction in infant mortality and morbidity have also resulted in the saving of life of more low birthweight babies, and babies with inherited diseases and congenital conditions. More children therefore survive with chronic and handicapping conditions. With the declining importance of infectious diseases, chronic disorders (malformations, chronic illness, physical and mental handicaps) have become a major focus and concern for health care provision. These disorders call for a different approach on the part of professional staff working with them. For example, nursing staff may be involved in the treatment of these children's conditions over long periods of time. They may need to encourage them to participate in unpleasant medical procedures with distressing side-effects. They may be required to counsel very sick and dying children and their families. It has become increasingly clear that families and staff who care for chronically sick or severely handicapped youngsters are subject to considerable stresses. Increasingly paediatricians, nursing staff, and social workers are calling for psychological help with these difficult health problems of children.

Interview transcript—Psychological problems of a family with a chronically sick child

Alan is a 15-year-old boy who has been on dialysis since the age of $8\frac{1}{2}$ years. He has now obtained a transplant. His illness commenced not long after his birth, and he has a long medical history including many hospital admissions. He lives at home with his mother, father, and sister Sandra. The family has few social supports, and much of the responsibility for bringing up the family has fallen upon Alan's mother, as Alan's father's job has often taken him away from home. Alan's father and mother have disagreed about ways of treating their sick son. Alan's father has tried to take a more strict approach and Alan's mother a more lenient approach. The following transcript of an interview with mother and father illustrates some of the psychological problems arising in families who care for chronically sick youngsters.

These include marital problems and problems with their daughter (speech delays, complaints of pain, demanding behaviour). Finally, Alan's mother describes how near she has come towards harming her daughter.

Marital problems

Father: There was a period of time when we could have split up due to the pressures of this. I think there was one time that Irene thought that she couldn't rely on me to a certain extent.

Interviewer: In what way—

Mother: Bill at first would carry on and lead his life sort of thing. To me it should be—well if he was going to drink at least we should know where he was going.

Father: I disagree—on most occasions Irene—there was one or two occasions when I did slip up.

Interviewer: He'd leave it mostly to you and that upset you.

Mother: At times you get to a point when you feel it's all on you.

Father: There's ways in which Irene carries on, if I was that sort of person, I could get upset—you know I'm a man, but in our house there's two. In our house everything is done for Alan we don't have a social life—an active social life. I'd like to take Irene out. She'd say 'How about Alan?' It wasn't making the situation any better mollycoddling him.

Interviewer: Do you agree?

Mother: [nods] Got to the stage where Alan felt you shouldn't go out. No, he's got to learn—else he'll grow up thinking that you've got to do what he wants.

Interviewer: So, he was right. You've come round to that now.

Mother: I'll go out now, but I'll worry inside.

Reaction of other children in family

Interviewer: How did the situation affect Sandra?

Mother: You tend to feel guilty. Because Sandra was 18 months when Alan first went on the machine. So you either had to bring her with you so she had to spend a lot of time here [in the hospital] or you'd have to leave her.

Interviewer: Why did you feel guilty?

Mother: Because the time I'd been able to spend with Alan when he was little playing games and things—you couldn't do that with Sandie. We say she's old-headed.

Interviewer: [to father] What does Sandie say to you?

Father: She says, 'I don't like this house, everybody hates me.'

Interviewer: How do you cope with that?

Father: To be honest I say 'Don't be bloody ridiculous.' Then I'll leave her for 20 minutes and then fuss her.

Interviewer: Has it made her react in any other way? Has she thrown up any problems?

Mother: Her speech. [Sandie was late to talk and needed to visit a speech therapist.] You give her material things—but most important is time and affection—she doesn't get that.

Interviewer: Does she understand this?

Mother: She demands financial things. If you can't give them to her she says 'Well, Alan doesn't have to wait', then if Alan wants a roast dinner she'll say, 'I don't want that.' She'll rebel. Then she'd complain of pain and things.

Stress on parents

Father: At one time Irene's nerves went all to pieces.

Interviewer: [to mother] How did it affect you?

Mother: I thought that if I hit her then I really couldn't stop myself. I really would hurt her. I went to see the doctor about it but I was too embarrassed to tell him. It seemed as if everything was on top of me. He said 'You must know what's at the bottom of this'—but I couldn't say. He gave me some tablets—I threw them away, they didn't do me any good.

Improved standards of medical and nursing care and the development of new and effective treatments have obviously made considerable impact on the health of children. However, the decline of infectious diseases, already commented upon, has relied equally upon the development of better standards of living, for example reduction in overcrowding, improved diet, and smaller families. The epidemic diseases of today (for example, lung cancer, heart disease) are associated with particular styles of life (diet, smoking, lack of exercise). Many of these habits are built up in childhood and early adolescence, and it is increasingly recognized that future improvements in child health (and ultimately adult health) may depend as much upon changes in behaviour as upon changes in the technical aspects of medical practice. This has far-reaching implications for the role of psychologists within the health service. Increasingly child clinical psychologists are being asked to contribute to educational and preventive aspects of child health services.

One of the major concerns in child health is the large number of children with emotional or behavioural difficulties. One estimate suggests that in the course of one year some 5 to 10 per cent of children present with problems of sufficient severity to handicap them in everyday life. Clinical psychologists play an important role in the assessment and treatment of these disorders. Whilst clinical psychologists are often involved in the direct treatment of such problems in community and hospital settings, many psychologists have found that they can work equally or even more effectively by passing on some of their skills to other professionals such as teachers, health visitors, occupational therapists, or social workers. Much of their time is then spent working in a consultative role for these professions.

The health needs of youngsters are often intimately linked with the social and environmental circumstances in which they live. In the last 20 years there have been dramatic changes within society. The breakdown of the extended family and the rising divorce rate have led to an increasing number of single parents bringing up children in unsupported and isolated circumstances. Even where families are intact, young mothers may find themselves in neighbourhoods with few friends and little support. The high incidence of depression in the mothers of pre-school children is well documented. Under such circumstances normal childhood difficulties (for example, feeding, sleeping, and toileting problems) may loom large. Of the group of professional workers who are available for consultation by the parents of pre-school children, clinical psychologists, by virtue of their special training and expertise, are particularly able to give advice concerning the management of these frequently occurring childhood emotional and behavioural problems.

In extreme circumstances some parents may become locked into cycles of excessive punishment. Occasionally injury to the child results. Whilst the true prevalence of such violence is unknown, national data indicate that four children in every thousand are seriously 'at risk' of abuse. These reported cases obviously represent only a fraction of those who are maltreated. In recent years clinical psychologists working in health settings have begun to provide assistance to social service departments in both assessment and management of these problems of child abuse.

The rising unemployment figures have meant that many families suffer considerable financial hardship, with several family members out of work. The relationship between such social and economic changes and psychological well-being is neither simple nor clear-cut. However, some out-of-work youngsters with time on their hands will find themselves in the hands of the police as a result of petty crimes and excessive alcohol or drug use. In some parts of the country drug abuse and drug dependence amongst young people have reached epidemic proportions, causing health authorities to act swiftly in the setting up of new drug-dependency facilities. Psychologists working within adolescent health services are becoming increasingly involved in the in-patient and community care of youngsters with drug and alcohol dependency problems.

WORK SETTINGS OF CHILD CLINICAL PSYCHOLOGISTS

The preceding section has reviewed some of the health needs of children and young people and hinted at the settings in which psychologists work. Generally speaking children and young people do not seek help themselves—instead they are referred by adults who are close to them or who come into contact with them through their work. Whilst in some cases youngsters are referred by parents, in many instances it is other professional workers, for example teachers, paediatricians, clinical medical officers, health visitors, and social workers, who recognize that they are in need of psychological help. Children are therefore referred to clinical psychologists through the wide network of health, education, and social services. Table 4.1 describes some of the settings in which clinical

Table 4.1   Settings in which child clinical psychologists work and
examples of their work

Setting	Example
(a) *Health*	
(i) Community child welfare clinics Health centres GP practices	Liaison/consultation with health visitors Parents' groups for behavioural, sleeping, feeding problems of under-fives
(ii) Hospital Ante-natal clinics	Counselling of mothers with suspected handicapped child Counselling of adolescents deciding about termination of pregnancy
Intensive care neonatal units	Counselling for staff and parents
Paediatric assessment clinics	Assessment and remediation of development delays
Paediatric hospital wards	Preparation of parents/children for hospitalization Counselling of parents/staff dealing with terminally ill children
Casualty wards	Crisis counselling for adolescents who have taken overdoses
Psychiatric in-patient and out-patient units	Assessment and treatment with families of children showing emotional and behavioural problems Consultation/training of psychiatric child-care staff (in psychological procedures)
(b) *Social services*	
(i) Local authority nurseries	Advice to nursery nurses concerning problems of child abuse Assessment of development delays
(ii) Community homes	Consultation with staff concerning management of difficult behaviour problems Counselling foster parents
(c) *Voluntary organizations*	Drop-in clinics for adolescents with drug-taking or alcohol problems

psychologists work, giving some examples of the kinds of work that they do. Obviously not all child clinical psychologists are involved in all of these activities. The type of service provided within a district health authority will depend upon the availability or expertise of clinical psychologists who specialize in working with children. However the table reflects the range of activities that many clinical psychologists are engaged in.

ORGANIZATIONAL ASPECTS OF CHILD CLINICAL PSYCHOLOGY SERVICES

Historical accident and unevenness of health care provision have led to a situation where some health districts are well endowed with child clinical psychologists whilst others have few or even no clinical psychologists working exclusively with children. Nationally there is, therefore, great variation in the type and range of child clinical psychology services provided. Recent changes within the Health Service following the publication of the Government White Paper 'Working for Patients' have led to further diversification in the organizational framework for service provision.

In some small health districts, with a single unit providing all health care facilities, child psychologists may work within a child health section of a psychology department co-ordinated by an experienced head of section and providing a comprehensive service across a range of settings, for example acute hospital, community, and social services environments. In larger districts—for example, those with major teaching hospitals and serving populations in excess of 400 000—child psychological services may be large enough to be divided into specialized services, managed within different unit settings (for example, paediatric oncology, plastic surgery, or community services).

In addition to the direct provision of services child clinical psychologists will have representation on various health care planning committees. They may be called on to contribute to special working groups to set up specialist health projects (child protection services, drug-dependency clinics, etc.). An essential part of the role of clinical psychologists is collaboration with other professional workers in establishing policy and planning services for children.

Clinical psychologists are not the only group of psychologists working with children. All Local Education Authorities (LEAs) employ educational psychologists who provide a school psychological service. There are some 1500 educational psychologists working within LEAs in England and Wales and a further 300 working in Scotland. They act as advisors to LEAs and particularly to schools. Whilst both groups of psychologists have distinctive contributions to make to the health and educational needs of children, there is also a degree of overlap both in terms of clients and in terms of services provided. For this reason close collaboration between the two disciplines is frequently required. This is achieved either by the establishment of close personal contacts between individual professional workers or by local advisory groups on psychological services for children on which both educational and clinical psychologists are represented.

SOME GENERAL ISSUES CONCERNING WORK WITH
CHILDREN AND YOUNG PEOPLE

Before proceeding to a more detailed description of the ways in which clinical psychologists work with children and young people it is important to consider some general issues concerning the context in which childhood problems occur. These issues have implications for both assessment and treatment. Furthermore they may determine whether intervention is made at all in some cases.

Social context of problem behaviour

It is generally adults who refer children to psychological services. For this reason it is often worthwhile considering why a particular child is referred at a certain point in time. Why did this mother come to the GP at this time for help with her three-year-old son's temper tantrums? Why did the ward sister refer this particular eight-year-old who is fearful when blood samples are being taken? Why did this member of the child care staff feel that this fifteen-year-old was particularly difficult to handle? Of course, it may be that these problems were so severe that they caused special concern. However, this is clearly not always the case. Studies which have compared mothers attending clinics for help with a particular child's problem with mothers who are not attending a clinic yet have children with the same problem, have shown the 'clinic mothers' to be more anxious. Furthermore it appears that schools in quite similar areas with pupils from quite similar socio-economic backgrounds may have very different referring rates to educational psychology services. These simple examples illustrate the importance of the social context in which the childhood difficulty occurs, since this may determine whether help is sought at all. Moreover, the examples given above suggest that particular 'systems', be they families or institutions, play a part in creating and maintaining difficult psychological problems in children.

Developmental context

Development during childhood and adolescence is often rapid and sometimes uneven. Such change has implications for both assessment and treatment. Firstly, the significance of certain childhood problems may vary depending upon the age of the child. Table 4.2 displays a number of childhood behaviours which may cause parents, doctors, and other professional workers to seek psychological help. Surveys of the general population reveal that many of these problem behaviours occur quite frequently amongst a normal sample of children. Some behavioural problems are more frequent at certain ages. For example, bedwetting is so common amongst three-year-olds as to be considered normal. It is much less common in seven-year-olds, the age at which many paediatricians begin to consider children for treatment. Temper tantrums are very common in pre-school children but much less common in eight- and nine-year-olds. Such findings illustrate the importance of taking the age of the child into account when considering psychological intervention.

  The fact that developmental change may be rapid during various stages in childhood also carries implications for the stability of assessment information over time. For example, assessment of behaviour at one age (particularly at younger age-levels) may not be predictive of behaviour at a later age. Moreover, epidemiological studies which have followed normal groups of children over time indicate that many childhood problems are short-lived. Decisions concerning the mode and timing of the treatment intervention must be viewed in the light of existing knowledge concerning the natural remission rate of such problems.

Table 4.2 Common childhood problems for which psychological help may be sought

Somatic complaints (e.g. headaches, stomach-ache, etc.)
Fears and phobias
Obsessions
Temper tantrums
Fighting
Lying
Bullying
Destructive behaviour
Stealing
Distractibility
Over-activity
Poor concentration
Language delay
Reading retardation
Bedwetting
Soiling
Tics
Thumb-sucking, nail-biting
Overeating
Undereating
Sleep disturbance
School refusal
Autism
Childhood schizophrenia

Continuous influences on childhood development

Increasingly, research investigations of childhood development are emphasizing the importance of *continuous* influences on a child's development. Infants and children are remarkably adaptable. For example, adverse environmental conditions resulting from separation from parents and institutional care in infancy and early childhood do not inevitably produce severe long-term effects. If the child is later placed in the long-term care of a family that is warm and supportive, the effects of early deprivation may be considerably reduced. However, and equally important, children brought up in extremely deprived circumstances may be influenced little by remedial programmes that are brief and take little account of the later impoverished environment at home or at school. It is these and similar findings that have directed many clinical psychologists towards working directly with families and particularly parents rather than working individually with the distressed child or young person. In the case of children in care or children in a residential hospital unit many psychologists will work through the child-care or nursing staff who are with the child for much of the day. The aim is to produce maximal, long-term changes in the children's environment that will enable them to make healthy future adjustments.

WAYS OF WORKING

Orientation

A range of factors may influence the style of work of a clinical psychologist, for example the availability of residential facilities, the existence of community teams, the number of child clinical psychologists in a district health authority, or the people who make up the multi-disciplinary team. However, also important is the training and theoretical orientation of the clinical psychologist concerned. During their training clinical psychologists will be exposed to a variety of psychological approaches, for example dynamic psychotherapy, family therapy, and behaviour therapy. Their later clinical work will be influenced by the theoretical model they adopt following training. Not all of these approaches to child problems are equally effective with all client groups. Morever, some therapeutic procedures are under-researched in terms of their effectiveness.

In the following sections emphasis is placed upon those ways of working that have been subjected to empirical investigation. Problems of the child are viewed in a developmental and family context, and an emphasis is placed on those strategies that encourage children and their families to develop problem-solving skills.

Assessment and formulation

When a child is referred for specialized help assessment is obviously the first step that needs to be taken. The process of assessment involves the psychologist and co-workers in a number of tasks. The first of these involves *identification and specification of the problem* for which help is being sought. At first glance this might appear to be a simple task. However in any group, be it school, family, marriage, child-care establishment, or hospital ward, each member may well have a different perception of the problem. For example, in a family a mother may regard her difficult-to-manage son as suffering from a form of 'hyperactivity', which should be treated by management of his diet, whilst his father may believe that his son is disobedient and in need of strict discipline, and that his wife is too lenient with him. Since such factors may well influence the parents' handling of the problem and their reaction to future interventions, it is important that the psychologist obtain information from all those directly concerned with the child. Also, it is not uncommon for child-care workers, teachers, and parents to focus on the problem as if it resides solely in the child and is unaffected by their response to it. Accordingly, assessment of the problem is broadly conceived so that the focus is not solely on the child referred for treatment. In some cases where, for example, parental or staff expectations concerning the child are unrealistic, this may become the focus of intervention rather than the behaviour of the child concerned.

A second task of assessment involves *identification of factors influencing the occurrence of the problem*. This includes not only a detailed enquiry about early development, social and educational details, and a history of the current complaint, but also a thorough investigation of circumstances affecting the occurrence of the problem in the present. For example, it is necessary to consider the range of situations in which problems may occur (for example, home, school, playground, etc.). Surveys of the child population show that childhood problems are often situation-specific, so that problems may occur at home but not at school and vice versa. It is also important to note parents' or teachers' or care-staff's current ways of handling the child's difficulties. Enquiries into this area may elicit factors which may be encouraging the persistence of the problematic behaviour. Finally, assessment will also include *detailed analysis of the potential of the child and significant others* for coping with the problem. Parents often come to the clinic focusing upon the negative aspects of their child's behaviour and in doing so they may overlook important positive things that the child does. A recognition of these aspects of the child may raise their own self-esteem as parents and encourage their later participation in treatment.

For the clinical psychologist, assessment is therefore seen as an attempt to answer a series of interlinked questions about the child and family (school, child-care establishment, or hospital ward). What is the child doing or not doing that is considered problematic? What is the frequency/intensity of the problem behaviour? How does this child compare with other children of the same age-group? Where does the problem occur, with whom, and when? What events usually precede the problem behaviour and what follow it? What factors in early development may have contributed to the problem? What does the child or adolescent do that is not considered to be problematic?

Accordingly a range of variables (physical, biological, social, and environmental) are considered in relation to the child's problem. No prior assumptions are made about the relative importance of these variables. Instead their importance is determined by a careful analysis, based on a detailed observation and measurement. Such assessment may include the use of systematic interviews (with family, child, or parents alone) structured rating scales or be-havioural checklists (given to parents, child, or teachers/care staff) behavioural diaries (kept by the child or significant adult), or standardized psychometric tests, (intelligence test, reading test, etc.). In addition, detailed and systematic direct observation of the child's behaviour, the behaviour of other children (siblings/classmates), or significant adults (parents, teachers, ward staff) may be carried out.

Details obtained from the assessment allow the psychologist to prepare a detailed formulation of the problems. This formulation is basically a series of hypotheses capable of explaining:

(a) the development of the problem; and
(b) the persistence of the problem and the likely response to a particular treatment intervention.

An example of one such clinical formulation for a nine-year-old encopretic child is shown in Fig. 4.1.

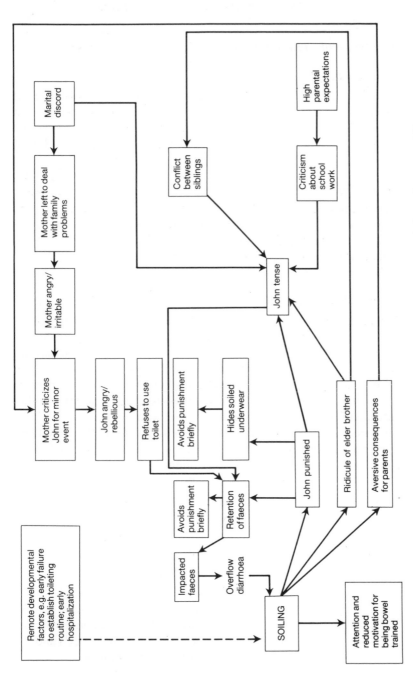

Fig. 4.1 Psychological formulation of events surrounding encopresis for a nine-year-old boy.

Treatment of a nine-year-old boy with soiling problems

Brief description of problem

John lived in the family home with his mother, father, brother Paul (aged 12), and sister Karen (aged 3). John had never been able to control his bowel motions, and the longest time he had removed free from soiling was a period of one week. He was referred to a clinical psychology department by a consultant paediatrician.

Assessment

Family interview;
Daily records of soiling and toilet-visiting;
Daily diary of other activities;
(including ratings of tension 1–10); and
ABC form of soiling.

Formulation of the problem

Detailed questioning of family members and examination of assessment records revealed a number of contributing factors (see Fig. 4.1). John received little praise or affection from his parents. Instead, most of the interaction between John and his parents took the form of arguments or criticism regarding his behaviour and in particular his soiling. Questioning of John's mother revealed a number of dissatisfactions regarding her relationship with her husband, which appeared to exacerbate her critical reaction to John. Both Paul and Karen received more praise and affection than John, which added to the conflict between John and his siblings.

Treatment programme

Treatment goals	*Therapeutic procedure*
1. *Encourage daily toilet visits*	*Written instructions given to John:*
	'Take Senokot before going to bed. In the morning have warm drink. 30 min later go to toilet. Tell mum you have been and complete your chart.'

Written instructions to parents:

'Praise John for visiting toilet. Help him to put a sticker on his chart if he has used the toilet and give extra praise.'

2. *Discourage retention of faeces and hiding of soiled underwear*

Give explanation using diagrams to parents and John how retained faeces can lead to overflow diarrhoea, which cannot be controlled.

Instructions to parents:

'Eradicate all criticism and punishment concerning soiling. Expect soiling at early stages of treatment.'

3. *Encourage effective communication/problem-solving regarding toileting*

Analogy of footballer in training used. John (like a footballer) has to complete programme (training) with parents (football coach) so that his muscles will be strong.

4. *Increase parental child-management skills*

Discussion of management of all children in family using examples from daily diary. Prevent 'scapegoating' of John.

5. *Increase communication between parents*

Encourage effective communication between parents regarding inequitable distribution of domestic chores.

6. *Monitoring of treatment*

Daily records of toileting, soiling, and other behavioural problems to examine treatment effectiveness (see Fig. 4.2).

The treatment of this young boy and his family was carried out by Mrs A. Devon while working with the author.

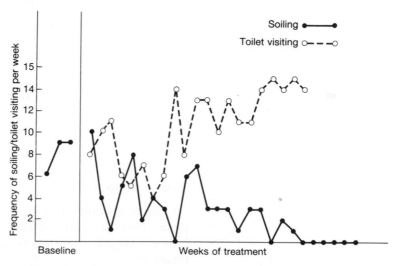

Fig. 4.2 Therapeutic progress of a nine-year-old encopretic boy.

Selecting treatment goals and planning treatment intervention

Once the problems have been precisely defined, the psychologist and others (parents, teachers, nursing staff, and the child, if old enough) make arrangements upon what course of action is to be followed. Although the child or adolescent has presented as a focus for treatment, the treatment goals may not include direct changes in the child's behaviour. For example, in the case of a mother seeking help for treatment of her three-year-old's essentially normal 'bed-wetting problem', possible goals for treatment could be a lowering of mother's expectations and anxiety. Treatment might then involve explanation of what bladder-control skills are considered normal for a child of this age, practical advice on how to encourage dry beds once they have occurred (lifting, praise, star charts, etc.), and explanation of what treatments are available if the problem persists. In the case of chronically ill children referred because of their excessive anxiety when undergoing painful hospital treatment, goals of intervention might be the construction of new methods of preparing children for hospital treatment (for example using specially constructed videos and explanatory leaflets geared to the child's level of intellectual development). Choice of treatment goals takes into account a wide range of variables including:

(a) age and developmental stage of the child;
(b) frequency, intensity and duration of the 'problem behaviour';
(c) potential value for the child of developing new behavioural skills;
(d) likelihood of successful results following an intervention; and
(e) important aspects of child's environment which may require change (for example behaviours of siblings, or significant adults).

Once treatment goals have been clarified decisions can be made concerning implementation of treatment. Intervention may be made at a number of different levels. At one level the psychologist may work directly with the child or adolescent, singly or in a group. At a second level, the psychologist may decide to work primarily with the adults who are responsible for the child (parents, teachers, child-care staff). This may involve the psychologist working with individual parents (teachers or hospital/child-care staff) who are experiencing difficulties in dealing with particular childhood problems, or with groups of adults.

Finally, the psychologist may decide to operate at a third level, that is with the institution or system (school, hospital, ward, or unit) making child referrals. This level may involve the psychologist working with the staff of the institution on policy and planning issues.

Each level of working carries with it particular advantages. For example, working directly with children and adolescents avoids some of the difficulties of working with uncooperative adults who are responsible for the youngster. Furthermore, individual therapy might be the most appropriate way of helping some young people, for example an adolescent who is not happy to discuss certain problems with his parents, or a youngster whose difficulties are relatively inaccessible to others (for example, negative thoughts, low self-esteem).

However, in certain circumstances a particular level may incur certain disadvantages. For example, when the child's home or school environment is maintaining the child's difficulties only limited change may be possible with individual therapy. In such a case it may be more appropriate and productive to work directly with adults responsible for the child. Some examples of different ways of working are given in Table 4.3.

At whatever level the psychologist chooses to work, an essential part of any intervention is an appraisal of its effects. A clear specification of treatment goals allows successive measurements to be made throughout treatment in order to monitor the effectiveness of the intervention. In the case of the nine-year-old encopretic boy described earlier, records of toilet visiting and soiled garments kept by the child and parents during treatment allowed them to examine the effects of their efforts (see Fig. 4.2). In the case of a new ward programme to prepare chronically ill children for painful treatment procedures a comparison of anxiety levels (measured on self-report and observer-rated anxiety scales) of all chidren entering treatment over a specified time-period both before and after the implementation of the new regime allowed its effectiveness to be ascertained. The following sections give some further illustration of the kinds of treatment interventions made by clinical psychologists in health care settings.

Helping children acquire skills

A frequent goal of many psychological interventions is to enable children and adolescents to improve existing skills or acquire new skills. For example, the psychologist may begin work with nursery staff to increase a pre-school child's language ability. The mother of a mentally handicapped child may be encouraged to teach her child to dress and feed himself correctly. The staffing in a community home may be helped to set up a group to teach adolescents interview skills, or a psychologist may work with nursing staff to construct a training programme to teach parents and haemophiliac youngsters skills which will enable them to take an active part in the management of their illness. Psychologists involved in such training schemes draw upon their knowledge of psychological theory and their understanding of clinical research, which has established the effectiveness of such treatment interventions. Such research emphasizes that skills should be broken down into *simple, well-defined steps* and that strategies such as *modelling, rehearsal,* and *corrective feedback and positive reinforcement* are important in establishing skills. Table 4.4 shows some of the basic steps employed in a training scheme to teach

Table 4.3 Examples of ways of working at different levels of therapeutic intervention

Level	Example
(a) *Working directly with children and adolescents*	
(i) Individual work	Counselling/behavioural programmes for adolescents with sexual difficulties, cognitive therapy for adolescents with low self-esteem/negative thoughts
(ii) Group work	Social skills groups for adolescents—decision-making groups for adolescents in residential unit/community home—'coping with illness' groups for chronically sick youngsters
(b) *Working with parents/teachers/ child-care staff (triadic model)*	
(i) Individual	Behavioural programme to be carried out by parents of a youngster with 'temper tantrums'
(ii) Group	Training group for local authority nursery staff dealing with pre-school children with language delays—group for parents with enuretic children using 'dry-bed programme'
(c) *Working with systems*	Planning treatment environments in conjunction with senior clinical staff on oncology ward dealing with children and adolescents—working with staff groups in community homes to discuss structure of unit, deployment of staff, etc.

Table 4.4   Sample items from a behavioural assessment instrument used in factor replacement therapy

---

Reconstitution behaviours
  1. Wash hands
  6. Double-ended needle—snap open
 10. Insert needle end into sterile water bottle
 14. Insert exposed needle into concentrate bottle
 15. Add sterile water to concentrate
 20. Sterile technique used throughout
Syringe-preparation behaviours
  2. Attach filter needle to syringe
  7. Insert filter needle attached to syringe into concentrate bottle
  9. Withdraw concentrate into syringe
 11. Remove air bubbles
 13. Twist filter needle off syringe
 20. Sterile technique used throughout
Infusion behaviours
  4. Scalp vein needle—bend wing ends
  6. Place tourniquet on hand or arm for venepuncture
  7. Select venepuncture site
  8. Swab skin surface with alcohol
 12. Pierce needle through skin
 13. Insert needle into vein
 14. Secure needle in vein
 15. Tape needle to skin
 16. Release tourniquet
 20. Attach scalp vein tubing to syringe
 22. Inject concentrate slowly
 27. Remove needle from skin
 28. Apply pressure over venepuncture site
 29. Place Band-Aid over venepuncture site
 36. Sterile technique used throughout

Source: Reprinted with permission from Varni (1983).

haemophiliac youngsters and their parents to carry out factor replacement therapy in the home (Varni 1983).

In this training programme, nursing staff were trained to build up skills gradually. First, youngsters and parents observed nurses carrying out (modelling) the first component of the skill: mixing the plasma concentrate. Parents and child then practised this part of the procedure themselves (rehearsal). Nurses prompted where extra help was needed and offered praise (positive reinforcement) where performance had reached the required level. Once this component of the skill was learnt parents and children moved on to the two other components of the skill: preparing the syringe and carrying out the injection. The final stage of injecting the concentrate was first practised on a dummy arm and then on an adult volunteer. Finally all aspects of the skill were combined.

Obviously, factor replacement therapy requires strict adherence to all procedures so that sterility is maintained and infection, damage to the veins, and spread of hepatitis to family members are avoided. Effectiveness of the new training regime was ascertained by comparing the adherence rates of parents trained under the scheme with parents who had been trained prior to the introduction of the new training method. At follow-up parents trained by new methods were found to adhere to 97 per cent of the component parts of the regime, whilst parents trained by the old methods showed only 65 per cent adherence. Similar training methods have been used to encourage asthmatic children to use inhalation equipment properly, to train children and parents to carry out home haemodialysis, and to teach diabetic children how to carry out their insulin injections correctly (Fielding 1985).

The skills taught above are obviously specialist skills not normally required by parents or youngsters. However, many children, because of depriving life circumstances, lack some of the crucial skills to cope with life in a satisfactory manner.

Some adolescents who are unable to cope withdraw from social contacts and become socially isolated. Others become depressed and some make suicide attempts. Surveys of suicide rates in the general population show that highest rates of attempted suicide occur in the age-range 15–20 years. This provides a major problem for health care provision. In contrast, some youngsters may respond to stress and frustration with violent and aggressive behaviour. Research suggests that many adolescent institutionalized offenders are deficient in terms of complex interpersonal skills and basic social skills when compared with youngsters of the same age and social background who have no criminal record.

Clinical psychologists working in different settings have approached these kinds of skill deficits in young people by instituting skills training programmes. These have been carried out in the context of youth clubs and local authority community homes and in clinic settings (Callias *et al*. 1987). Youngsters have been trained in a range of skills including basic conversational skills, dating skills, interview skills, and skills of communication within the family.

On the whole good short-term improvements have been achieved by such programmes. However, longer-term effects have proved more difficult to achieve, and research continues in order to establish methods of improving generalization of these procedures.

Helping children overcome fears

Fears and anxieties are common during childhood, and frequently disappear over time. However in certain cases they persist in providing serious disruptions in a young person's life. For example, it has been estimated that some 17 children per 1000 show serious phobic reactions to school and that 16 per cent of school-age children exhibit serious fear and avoidance-reaction to dental treatment. Non-attendance at school can obviously give rise to other important problems, such as educational underattainment and difficulties in peer relationships; whilst avoidance of dental treatment may have long-term implications for dental health.

In selecting an individualized treatment for a fearful or anxious child the psychologist will want to carry out a detailed analysis of the problem (Barrios and Hartman 1988). This will include a detailed description of the child's physiological, cognitive, and motor responses, as in the care of a child showing marked anxiety during a blood test. Physiological responses may include raised heart rate and respiration rate, while the child's cognitive response may include catastrophic and sometimes erroneous thoughts. In addition, the psychologist will want to examine the sorts of situations that elicit these responses and also the responses of other important adults in the situation. Depending on the initial analysis of the problem, treatment may involve explanation and reassurance, observation of a model participating in the feared situation, gradual exposure to the feared situation, praise and rewards for the child's efforts, or instruction to relevant adults in the appropriate way to react to fearful behaviour. In addition, children may be taught various relaxation and self-instructional skills to enable them to manage stressful situations.

In the case of an eleven-year-old boy suffering from panic and anxiety attacks at school, a combination of procedures was used following assessment of his problems (Ballard and Yule 1981). The boy's anxieties revolved around the belief that his mother might be killed in a car crash whilst he was at school. The school had previously dealt with his panics by allowing him to telephone home to check that his mother was there, while his mother was forced to remain at home during school hours. Treatment involved training the boy in relaxation skills and gradual exposure to situations where he was separated from his mother whilst she took her car for increasingly long journeys. Rapid progress in treatment was maintained over 10 weeks of treatment, and anxiety attacks had disappeared by the end of treatment. No problems were shown at 3-month and 15-month follow-ups.

Fears and anxieties may frequently arise in the context of medical treatment. For example, children may become distressed and fearful when admitted into hospital for surgical procedures. Furthermore, it may be necessary for children with certain chronic illnesses to undergo painful and distressing medical procedures. Patients with childhood cancer, for example, may be required to undergo painful diagnostic tests such as bone-marrow aspiration and lumbar punctures. The anxiety and distress produced in anticipation of aversive medical procedures may be so severe that children exhibit symptoms such as nausea, vomiting, insomnia, and nightmares prior to the procedures (Katz 1984). Recent psychological research has suggested that preparation procedures carried out before hospitalization and surgery can do much to reduce parental and child anxiety. Preparation may involve observation of a film of a child going into hospital, or home visits may be made by a paediatric nurse. Families may be shown visual aids that stimulate hospital procedures, and they may be given specially constructed educational pamphlets to explain how and when these procedures will be carried out. In addition children may be directly taught ways of coping with anxiety and pain. For example, the child may be taught relaxation or self-hypnotic procedures. Alternatively, distraction through play may be used. Psychologists working with children undergoing painful treatments have placed reliance on the child's ability to use imagery. For example, whilst relaxing and imagining a 'story book' scene children may be taught to imagine 'magic potions' or 'dimmer switches' which will enable them to reduce pain and increase relaxation. In addition specific therapeutic suggestions may be made to reinterpret the context of pain and anxiety. For example, during hydrotherapy for severe burns a child imagines he is swimming to his friends to save them from drowning.

These psychological strategies to alleviate pain and anxiety in sick children are at an early stage of development. However when viewed against some of the problems of medical management of pain (for example increasing dependence on large doses of analgesics) they must be seen as a worthy area for further investigation (Fielding 1985; Katz 1984).

Encouraging self-control and managing aggressive behaviour

Surveys indicate that from a third to a half of child referrals to psychologists by parents, teachers, and social workers are concerned with child and adolescent behaviour problems such as aggressiveness towards others (hitting, kicking, fighting), physical destructiveness, disobedience, and to a lesser extent problems such as stealing or starting fires. Developmental studies show that many children exhibit some of these behaviours at some time in their life, and that these problems are likely to decline with age. Follow-up studies of children with *severe* conduct problems show that if these problems go untreated they frequently persist into adult life.

Aggressive behaviour may occur in the context of the family, the hospital ward, the school, or the community home. Clinical psychologists may therefore be approached by a range of professional workers for help with such problems.

Examination of the families of aggressive children often shows distinct patterns of interactions. Observations show that many members of the family may be involved in coercive and aggressive behaviour. Moreover the perpetual conflict, anger, and negative attitudes lead to low self-esteem, anger, and helplessness in mothers of these problem children. It is within this context that child abuse may occur.

Such patterns of interaction within families have led psychologists to develop programmes of intervention which include parent training as an important component (Herbert 1987; Smith and Rachman 1984). Such programmes typically employ an initial intensive assessment phase involving all members of the family. Parent–child interactions in the home are observed and information obtained concerning the frequency of pro-social and coercive behaviour of the child. An analysis is made of important events leading up to and following disruptive behaviour.

In addition a study of the child's strengths and competencies is made. Parents are taught to define, track, and record aggressive and pro-social behaviour, and they may be required to attend a parent training group on child-management skills. Modelling and role-playing are the principal methods used, and sessions may consist of two-hourly weekly meetings over a period of 8–12 weeks. Training sessions may also be conducted in the home, with parenting skills modelled by therapists. Such training programmes have brought promising short-term results. Of 117 families referred to the Leicester Child Treatment Research Unit some 61 per cent were considered to have 'satisfactorily improved', 21 per cent 'moderately improved', and 18 per cent showed 'no change'. Using more specific outcome measures some American psychologists have shown significant decreases in aversive behaviour when measured during naturalistic observations. In these studies, decrease in symptom frequencies was also reported by parents.

Not all families treated require the same level of therapeutic work. In one therapy programme approximately one-third of families responded to quite simple interventions. However a further third required help resolving marital conflict and dealing with depression and additional problems in the family. Accordingly therapeutic time with each family ranged from 6 hours to 133 hours. Whilst complete follow-up data appear to be difficult to achieve, a number of studies now suggest that, in certain families at least, effects may be long-lasting.

Aggressive behaviour may also cause difficulties outside the family. Similar methods to those described above have also been adopted in residential settings.

Helping child survivors of abuse, trauma, and disaster

In the course of their work child clinical psychologists may also be asked to see children or young people who have witnessed or experienced extremely distressing and sometimes life-threatening events or situations. Such children may experience acute stress reactions, for example following a road traffic accident, a domestic fire, or sudden family bereavement. On other occasions the stressors may be chronic, such as those arising from prolonged marital discord and divorce, or in cases where there has been physical or sexual maltreatment of the child.

Much has still to be learned about the long-term consequences of such events or experiences for the child and the role of protective factors or processes which may mitigate long-term effects. A newly emerging research literature is beginning to provide a useful framework for clinical psychologists working in this area (Rolf *et al.* 1990).

Clinical psychologists working with child victims in the aftermath of national disasters have been asked to provide a range of services, including direct help for victims and their families and support for 'first-line' voluntary counsellors or health service workers, and to advise health authorities and social services in the planning of major accident procedures. The role of research and evaluation in this area is crucial.

Clinical psychologists working with child survivors of major shipping disasters have been surprised by the severity of children's distress as much as 12–15 months after the disaster. For example, when youngsters involved in the *Jupiter* disaster were assessed some 50 per cent of the 334 child survivors tested were found to be experiencing symptoms of post-traumatic stress disorder (Yule 1991). Common symptoms were sleep disturbances, intrusive thoughts, difficulties in concentration, and heightened alertness to danger. In addition many experienced fears, irritability, depression, and 'survivor guilt'.

Interestingly, in the course of this work, it was noted that children who had an internal attributional style in explaining what happened to them during the course of the disaster showed significantly greater levels of post-traumatic psychopathology one year later, illustrating the protective value of a more external attributional style for negative events. In addition, youngsters who accepted offers of psychological help on an individual or group basis following the disaster showed better adjustment five months after the disaster than those who had not received help.

Trauma may not always arise from events or situations external to the child's home situation. In some instances children may be caused considerable distress as a result of emotional or physical abuse from those who care for them. The term 'child abuse' covers a wide range of problems, including child neglect, non-organic failure-to-thrive, 'Munchausen syndrome by proxy', and physical, emotional, and sexual abuse. Child clinical psychologists working with abused children are part of a complex network of services concerned with the care and protection of abused youngsters (for example, community paediatrics, child and family psychiatry, social services, the NSPCC, and the police). Psychologists may assist in the provision of services aimed at prevention, identification, or rehabilitation. In addition clinical psychologists may undertake research to determine the effectiveness of these forms of provision.

The epidemiology, presentation, and consequences of these separate categories of mistreatment vary. Furthermore, although a number of social and demographic factors have been shown to increase the risk of abuse, no single pattern has emerged in the characteristics of those who abuse, and no single set of social circumstances have been linked to 'at-risk' families. Accordingly, strategies to prevent abuse are often broad-based and capable of addressing the wide range of problems encountered in this field of work.

In the case of child maltreatment a range of factors have been shown to place families at increased risk for abuse, including poor social support, high levels of family stress, limited parenting skills, and high rates of child behavioural problems.

Moreover there is evidence that at-risk families show low take-up of conventional health care services. Preventive clinical psychology services may therefore focus upon early identification of at-risk situations, 'accessible' and 'user friendly' services, and assistance for parents who are dealing with a range of difficult child behaviour problems. Enhanced social support networks in local communities in the form of befriending schemes may also be important (Cox *et al.* 1991).

Where child sexual abuse is strongly suspected or has been

previously disclosed social workers and police may jointly conduct evidential interviews with the child who has been abused. Such interviews need to be carried out with sensitivity and care. Some psychologists have been involved in the setting up of joint training schemes for social workers and police and evaluating the outcomes. Others have been involved in the preparation of children for later attendance in the courtroom.

Finally, clinical psychologists will also be involved in the broad spectrum of therapeutic or rehabilitative measures with victims of abuse and the families of abused youngsters.

Promoting health-related behaviours

An earlier section of this chapter alluded to the shift in emphasis in child health care provision from acute to chronic diseases. Moreover it was noted that many of the risk factors associated with major chronic diseases in adults (for example cardiovascular disease and cancer) had their origin in health-related behaviours such as dietary habits, exercise, and smoking. Such behaviours are frequently learned during childhood and adolescence. For example, the adoption of smoking habits typically occurs during adolescence. It has been estimated that one-third of all adolescents smoke. Furthermore, adolescents are more likely to smoke if one or more of their parents or older siblings smoke. An additional influence is the smoking habits of their friends and social contacts.

In recent years health care professionals have become increasingly interested in preventive aspects of health care. Prevention may be developed at three levels. *Primary prevention* refers to efforts designed to prevent the occurrence of a disease, while *secondary prevention* refers to early detection and treatment of the disease to prevent increased morbidity and mortality. Finally, *tertiary prevention* refers to rehabilitative efforts to prevent further morbidity, which may be associated with chronic disease and disability. This section comments upon the contribution of clinical psychologists to these three levels of preventive care.

Present levels of staffing in child clinical psychology services prevent a major contribution to the first level of primary prevention. However, given the growing problems of addictive behaviour amongst young people and the difficulties in providing adequate and effective treatment provision, preventive aspects of health care may assume much greater importance with child clinical psychology services in the future. The main impetus for *primary* prevention programmes for adolescents has come from the USA. Research has noted that although numerous health programmes have been instituted in schools, these have traditionally sought to promote behaviour change by emphasizing the harmful long-term effects of excessive smoking and drinking. Such studies, while frequently demonstrating changes in the knowledge and attitudes of young people, have shown little effect upon behaviour. Much more effective are those programmes which have encouraged adolescents to develop coping skills to resist social pressures to drink and smoke. For example, one such large-scale study selected popular high school youngsters to carry out a health programme within a school. These 'peer leaders' were specially trained to teach other people to recognize social influences (advertisements, television, friends) which might encourage young people to smoke. In addition they helped youngsters to practise ways of resisting such pressures. For example, a peer leader might encourage other youngsters to rehearse different ways of responding to friends who called them 'chicken' for not accepting a cigarette (for example 'I would be more of a chicken if I smoked just to impress you'). Early results of such skill training programmes have produced promising results as follow-up.

Clinical psychology services may also contribute to preventive medicine in their treatment of youngsters with severe eating disorders and alcohol or drug-related problems. Treatment may take place in a variety of settings, including paediatric out-patient clinics, health centres, and psychiatric out-patients and residential settings.

Finally, some clinical psychologists are beginning to examine methods of assisting paediatricians and nursing staff dealing with difficult chronic conditions of childhood and adolescence. Recent research suggests that psychological distress is a common feature of the families of chronically sick youngsters (Fielding 1985). Moreover, additional problems such as high rates of non-adherence to diet, exercise, and medical regimes, of crucial importance for health and survival, are frequently found. Clinical psychologists working with chronically sick youngsters are beginning to assess the effectiveness of therapeutic interventions to improve treatment adherence.

In the identification of important antecedents and consequences related to various health-related behaviours, behaviour using self- or parental monitoring is seen as an important first step. Where non-compliance is related to the aversiveness of the therapeutic regime, anxiety- and pain-management procedures described earlier may be appropriate. Where misunderstanding or lack of comprehension or recall is the issue, then care can be taken to provide preparatory verbal and written information that is specifically categorized and dispensed carefully over time.

Alternatively, if treatment results in major disruption in the child's or family's lifestyle then additional strategies, such as self-reinforcement, parental reinforcement, or contingency contracts may be used. In studies where such methods have been adopted there have been some promising results. For example, peer-group reinforcement has been found to be useful in groups of boys with haemophilia undergoing therapeutic exercise. Similar strategies have improved dietary adherence for youngsters on renal dialysis and regulation of urine glucose levels in diabetic children.

CONCLUDING COMMENT

The foregoing discussion has outlined some of the contributions that clinical psychologists are making to the health care of children and young people. In view of the many changes in this field, this chapter has given as much weight to these new developments as to those areas which have typically provided the routine day-to-day work of many child clinical psychology departments. In many parts of the country demand for child clinical psychology services far outstrips the current provision. In the present economic circumstances the vast increase in child clinical psychologists needed to meet these demands in unlikely. The future challenge for the practising child clinical psychologist is to find ways of applying important new clinical and research developments for the benefit of children and their parents, without detriment to current services. In this task the closest collaboration between psychologists and other child-care professionals is essential.

REFERENCES

Ballard, M. and Yule, W. (1981). A case of separation anxiety treated by *in vivo* systematic desensitisation. *Behav. Psychother.*, **9**, 105–10.
Barrios, B. and Hartmann, D. (1988). Fears and anxieties. In *Behavioural assessment of childhood disorders*, (2nd edn), (ed. E. Mash and L. Terdal), pp. 196–262. The Guilford Press, New York.
Callias, M., Frosh, S., and Michie, S. (1987). Group social skills training for young children in a clinic setting. *Behav. Psychother.*, **15**, 367–80.
Cox, A., Pound, A., Mills, M., Puckering C., and Owen, A. (1991). Evaluation of a home visiting and befriending scheme for young mothers: Newpin. *J. R. Soc. Med.*, **84**, 217–20.
Fielding, D. (1985). Chronic illness in children. In *New developments in clinical psychology* (ed. F. Watts), pp. 33–54. British Psychological Society, Leicester/Wiley, Chichester.
Herbert, M. (1987). *Behavioural assessment and treatment of problem children: a practice manual*, (2nd edn). Academic Press, London.
Katz, E. (1984). Psychological aspects of cancer in children, adolescents and their families. *Clin. Psychol. Rev.*, **4**, 525–42.
Rolf, J., Masters, A., Cicchetti, D., Neuchterlein, K., and Weintraub, S. (1990). *Risk and protective factors in the development of psychopathology*. Cambridge University Press, New York.
Smith, J. E. and Rachman, S. J. (1984). Non-accidental injury to children—II. A controlled evaluation of a behavioural management programme. *Behav. Res. Ther.*, **22**, 349–83.
Varni, J. W. (1983). *Clinical behavioural paediatrics*. Pergamon Press, New York.
Yule, W. (1991). Children in shipping disasters. *J. R. Soc. Med.*, **84**, 12–15.

FURTHER READING

Aldridge, J. (1988). Primary prevention in behavioural medicine with children. In *New developments in clinical psychology, Vol. 2* (ed. F. Watts), pp. 158–71. British Psychological Society, Leicester/Wiley, Chichester.
Elser, C. (1990). *Chronic childhood disease. An introduction to psychological theory and research*. Cambridge University Press.
Fielding, D. (1983). Adolescent services. In *The practice of clinical psychology in Great Britain* (ed. A. Liddell), pp. 129–50. Wiley, Chichester.

Herbert, M. (1991). *Clinical child psychology: theory and practice*. Wiley, Chichester.

Yule, W. (1983). Child health. In *The practice of clinical psychology in Great Britain* (ed. A. Liddell), pp. 151–69. Wiley, Chichester.

5

Working with people who have severe learning disabilities

Chris Cullen and Laurence Tennant

WHAT IS A LEARNING DISABILITY?

First a note on terminology. We have chosen the term 'learning disability' over the more common terms 'mental handicap' and 'learning difficulties'. We have done this not because we believe that labels in themselves can have major effects (although there is some debate on this), but because the term 'disability' allows us to acknowledge certain important distinctions between impairment, disability, and handicap. The World Health Organization recognizes that 'impairments' are what bring about a person's disability. For example, it is known that taking the drug thalidomide during pregnancy has led to children being born with physical impairments, such as improperly formed limbs. Such impairments often result in disabilities, which are sometimes severe. For example, having no arms makes it difficult to do certain things for yourself. The extent to which the disability becomes a handicap is dependent partly on societal reactions. If special aids—prostheses—are provided, the impaired person may be able to do much for themselves, and the handicap may be slight. However, if peers and those with whom they come into contact react to the disability by shunning the impaired person, the social handicap would be severe. Similarly, learning disabilities, which may be brought about by different impairments, sometimes originating in early damage within the brain, can become a handicap unless special help is provided. We suggest in this chapter that clinical psychologists are one of the groups of people who can provide that help. We will occasionally use the term 'mental handicap' when the context demands; but the term 'learning disability' is our favoured one.

People with learning disabilities, by definition, have difficulty in learning from early in their lives. This simple statement requires some elaboration before we can get a clear picture of the situation.

Most of us have some difficulty in learning some things; but a person with learning disabilities finds it difficult or even impossible to acquire some basic and important skills. These might even include self-care skills such as washing, dressing, or feeding oneself; and if this were the case, then the people affected might be described as having profound or severe learning disabilities, especially if they could not communicate at all with those around them or if they had very little awareness of their environment. People with less severe learning disabilities can be expected to learn to care for themselves in many respects, but may have problems with more advanced skills, such as handling money, using public transport and other local amenities, reading, writing, socializing, and so on.

It is relevant to consider why a person has difficulty in learning. A very young child cannot handle money and would have difficulty learning to do so before other relevant skills are acquired. Such a child would not, though, be said to have a learning disability. So there must be some reference to the person's having failed to learn to do things that others of his or her own age can do. Some people fail to demonstrate normal behaviour because they have suffered an injury that prevents them from doing so. Here the issues become contentious, and it is more difficult to be certain. If perfectly normal people have road traffic accidents that leave them incapable of speech, incontinent, and immobile, should they fall into our client group? Probably not, although methods of helping them might well be those used with people with learning disabilities. If a child is born with cerebral palsy, a disorder of the central nervous system, that may make it very difficult to acquire some basic skills such as walking or self-feeding—should that child be in our group? No, because he or she is almost certainly failing only because of a physical impairment. In fact, it is now realized that there are many people who have been labelled as learning-disabled in the past who actually have physical impairments which have prevented them from acquiring normal behaviour. Deafness is a good example. It has been estimated that there are significant numbers of people cared for in learning-disability services whose main problem has been that they did not develop normally because they were deaf or hard of hearing.

No mention has been made so far of *intelligence*. This is not because it is irrelevant, but to force attention on to the person's behaviour as one of the most important factors in deciding whether learning-disability services are relevant. There are some people who score poorly on intelligence tests, but who are totally independent, and could not sensibly be called learning-disabled. There are those who score within the normal range on intelligence tests, yet whose skill level is such that they can be helped by learning-disability services. Level of intelligence is only a rough guide.

SERVICE OPTIONS

People with learning disabilities need the same range of services, including general health care, as any other sector of the population. Beyond this, some may need specialist medical care. From a psychological perspective the major special needs are for:

- help with learning difficulties; and
- a range of facilities, such as residential and day-care settings, which will encourage as normal a life as possible.

People will have varying requirements for facilities and teaching at different stages in their lives. A severe learning disability is often identified at birth or in the first few years of life. It is possible to recognize certain impairments as the unborn child develops in the womb, but these account for only a small proportion of cases; more often specific causes remain unknown. The identification of a disability is the point at which psychological needs can first be addressed for the individual, and, importantly, for the parents and other family members. Families adjusting to this situation will require counselling and support in dealing with their own emotional reactions. They will later need advice and guidance in child management in relation to learning disability; and such support and specialist advice should continue at some level throughout the child's pre-school period.

Educational facilities for children with special needs, while imperfect, have progressed considerably in recent years. Special schools are often able to admit children at a very early age, and good schools have strong working links with the families they serve. Self-care, communication, and pre-academic skills are likely to be central to the educational and social care planning undertaken in the schools and within the community. The focus then is upon applying specialist knowledge of teaching methods to helping both child and family.

Since the introduction of the 1981 Education Act the goal of integration (called 'mainstreaming' in the United States) of children with learning disabilities into ordinary schools has been pursued with varying degrees of commitment within the UK. There are both moral imperatives and educational assumptions which underlie this. The moral imperatives are best described by a quote from the Warnock Report which paved the way for the 1981 Act: 'handicapped people should share the opportunities for self-fulfilment enjoyed by other people.'

The educational assumptions are that integrated education should lead to: a demise of pejorative labelling; increases in social benefits for children with learning disabilities; improvements in the partnership between parents and schools; more effective education; and benefits to peers who do not have learning disabilities. Unfortunately, there is not yet strong empirical evidence which allows us to believe that all the educational assumptions are justified (Danby and Cullen 1988). There is still a need for more research into these issues so that educational practices can be adjusted to meet the goals of the moral imperative—that children with learning disabilities have the rights to be educated with other children and for their education to be effective and beneficial.

When a child is clearly benefiting from being at school, education in Britain is often extended to the age of 19. Further specialized day training is usually offered within Adult Training Centres or Social Education Centres managed by Local Authorities, and some people with learning disabilities have opportunities to attend courses at Colleges of Further Education. However, the quality of day services in Britain varies considerably through the country, a point made in the 1985 House of Commons Social Services Committee Report on Community Care, and more recently by the Department of Health Social Services Inspectorate. Some areas have a reasonable network of day facilities, including special-care units for people with profound disabilities, sheltered workshops, and recreational facilities supported by Community Mental Handicap Teams. There is an increase in work opportunities for some people, where they might, for example, produce plants for sale at commercial rates. Other areas, unfortunately, still have poor and inadequate services.

The other kind of facility which may be required by people with learning disabilities and their families is residential care. In the early years the emotional and practical demands upon a family can be great, and a child with a disability requires a disproportionate amount of parental time and effort. Families may require a relief-care facility to give them a chance to relax or give time to other members of the family. This kind of support may be offered in a number of ways, including the use of foster-families, hostels, or small-group homes. Many professionals feel that it is particularly important that families are encouraged to use these facilities as the child grows older, both for the immediate relief they offer and because they afford an opportunity for parents to view their growing child in a normal way. Most non-disabled children leave home at some time and live away from their parents, and the use of short-term care not only provides relief but also enables families to prepare for the eventual separation of parent and child at the point at which this seems natural. Of course, the achievement of this objective requires appropriate facilities such as group homes and supported living arrangements, and this is an area in which an immediate growth in community resources must take place if a real alternative to hospital care is to be achieved. The Government White Paper, *Caring for people: community care in the next decade and beyond* (HMSO 1989) promises to set the occasion for a re-think on service provision—one which is expected to have positive benefits for all service users. It remains to be seen whether the promises will be realized, and in particular how the skills of the clinical psychologist (and other professionals) will be made available to people with learning disabilities.

In summary, the developmental needs of a person with learning disabilities are similar to those of any other individual, but differ in both time-scale (they change more slowly) and the extent of independence (they may require a more elaborate supporting environment than the average person). From the psychologist's point of view the individuals and their families are susceptible to the same range of needs as any family. In addition they may require special help, counselling, or guidance in relation to the learning difficulties experienced by the disabled person and in relation to emotional pressures which may result directly or indirectly from the disability. In practical terms, the points at which a clinical psychologist may help depend upon the nature of local services, and may range from a direct role in the teaching of a person with learning disabilities to a role in the planning and management of facilities.

THE ROLE OF THE CLINICAL PSYCHOLOGIST

A clinical psychologist working in a service for people with learning disabilities is almost always working in an actively multidisciplinary environment. This will include professionals such as teachers, social workers, and direct-care staff; doctors, nurses, health care assistants, and health visitors; administrators and planners; speech therapists, physiotherapists and occupational therapists; and, most importantly, parents. Each group has its own definable contribution, although there may be a good degree of overlap in the activity of the contact-oriented groups such as social workers, community nurses, and some clinical psychologists. This is particularly so in the area of general counselling, and recently in the teaching of behaviour-change procedures. The exact contribution of each professional tends to be determined by a combination of professional training, some statutory responsibilities, and local need.

There are two related but separate aspects of the psychologist's role. First is the application of the findings from research which are related to problems in learning disability. This could be a particular teaching procedure, such as errorless discrimination learning (see below); or it might be the implementation of a service-delivery plan. For example, the move to community care has come about *partly* as a result of research showing that large institutions tend to be places which result in clear disadvantages for people with learning disabilities. Clinical psychologists have been prominent in bringing this information to the attention of service-planners.

The second aspect of the psychologist's role is the application to everyday clinical practice of a systematic, scientific approach (cf. Dallos and Cullen 1990). The work of the clinical psychologist is guided by a *framework* which helps in the formulation and treatment of problems. This psychological analysis has the following characteristics:

1. assessment—the process of gathering information about a person;
2. interpretation—relating the observations to a broader theoretical framework;
3. intervention—putting into practice a treatment plan which follows from the interpretation; and

4. evaluation—monitoring change and, where necessary, reformulating the initial interpretation.

We will consider each of these in turn, giving some examples to act as illustrations.

Assessment and interpretation

Initially we must find out enough about the person to enable an individual plan to be drawn up. It is essential that the assessment should lead to some action—it is not sensible to initiate the assessment process without having some good reason (Cullen and Dickens 1990). The purpose of an assessment may simply be to say whether or not a person has a learning disability. This is essentially a screening function, and here it might be appropriate to use a test which compares the person with others of his or her own age. Such tests are called norm-referenced tests, and include the familiar intelligence and personality tests. While these procedures have a wide acceptance in society, their use by clinical psychologists working in learning disability has decreased steadily during the past two decades. The main reason (although there are others) is that the results do not help much in determining a plan of action. It is of little *practical* use to know that a person has an IQ of 57 or a Developmental Age of $2\frac{1}{2}$ years. (The habit of some of our senior judges in asking the *mental age* of a person with learning disability before making a judgement on their ability, say, to choose whether to be sterilized rests on an unfortunate but common misunderstanding. The (il)logic of the argument is that a woman with a mental age of 7 is 'really' like a seven-year-old girl, regardless of the fact that she might have a chronological age of 30 and many of the sexual/emotional needs and aspirations of any other adult woman.)

The alternative to norm-referenced assessments is to measure how much of a skill someone has. This allows a training procedure related to that measure to be devised. Most of the assessment now carried out in learning-disability settings is of this sort. There is a wide range of such assessments available, and some of them are related to norm-referenced tests, since they allow a computation of developmental age so that a comparison with other learning-disabled (and non-disabled) people can be made. Some of the most popular functional assessments in current use are the Progress Assessment Charts, the PIP Development Charts, the Adaptive

Behaviour Scale, the Behaviour Assessment Battery, the Vineland Adaptive Behaviour Scale, and the Everyday Living Skills Inventory.

All these allow the assessment of important skills. The items are usually ordered in increasing difficulty. The same broad skill areas are covered in each (for example self-care, communication, educational achievement, and socialization). Sometimes the items are linked together, forming a chain leading to a final goal. For example, 'visual fixation' precedes 'visual tracking' in the Behaviour Assessment Battery. Some of the assessments allow a measure of how much help a person must have—what type of prompt—before they can complete a task. This kind of information is very useful in designing treatment plans, since it helps to know what the minimum help has to be in order to get the person to succeed at the task. (More details on these and other assessment devices will be found in Cullen and Dicken 1990.)

For a complete assessment it is important not only to have a picture of what the person can do—referred to as *assets*—but also what behaviours the person has which are in *excess*. Consider the following situation. A child with a learning disability giggles and runs away whenever she is asked a question. This would not be noted on a typical assessment scale, but could be very important in understanding the child and subsequently helping her. A different kind of assessment procedure would then be undertaken, one aimed at finding out something about the causes of the behaviour. Someone in regular contact with the child, perhaps the mother, would be asked to keep a careful record of the following:

1. Antecedents—under what circumstances does the child run away? From which people? What locations? What kind of questions?
2. Behaviours—exactly what form does the behaviour have? Does she run far away, or does she run just out of reach? Does she look to see what reaction she is getting?
3. Consequences—what happens when she runs away? Does anyone chase her or remonstrate with her? Does it result in the question's being asked again?
4. Alternatives—what would it have been more appropriate for her to have done under those circumstances?

After a few days of collecting observations the following picture emerges. She runs away when she is not familiar with the person asking the question *or* when she is unlikely to know the answer. The usual effect is that she receives attention by being followed—in fact, she does not go far and seems to be waiting to be followed. She also manages to avoid answering the question, since it is usually not asked again.

This kind of exercise involves an assessment of the situation and an interpretation of the possible causes, or *functions*, of her behaviour. In this case it is reasonable to hypothesize that running away is partly an avoidance response—it serves the function of avoiding a situation in which she would fail. It also receives attention, and is quite effective at getting people to interact with her. This analysis leads to a programme which concentrates on the child's *deficits*, i.e. things she cannot (or does not) do. For example, she should be taught to say 'I don't know' if she cannot answer a question; she needs to learn ways of getting to know people with whom she is unfamiliar; and she needs to be taught to ask questions herself.

To summarize, an assessment should tell us about:

1. assets—those skills or patterns of behaviour in an individual's repertoire which are acceptable or useful and strong;
2. deficits—those skills or patterns of behaviour which are absent or weak and thought to be desirable or necessary; and
3. excesses—those patterns of behaviour which are strong, and unacceptable or disadvantageous to an individual.

There is a subtlety in this which may not be apparent. These ways of describing behaviour are culturally relative: what may be acceptable in one setting and can be described as an asset may not be in another setting, and may be thought of as an excess. We can still recall the occasion when a case conference was called to discuss the public disrobing problem of a young lady. She had the habit of dashing out of the house and stripping in the road. For many months she had been attending our self-help skills teaching programme where we were trying to teach her to undress before going to bed!

Another subtlety is that what may at first be considered an excess can be turned into an asset. Fleming (1984) reports the case of a man with a learning disability who had a history of ejecting clothes through a ward window and hiding them behind lockers. These were not his own clothes but those other residents had left lying around.

Rather than simply dealing with this as a problem to be removed, Fleming construed the situation in a different way. The man had a *useful* skill; he could recognize unattached and disordered items of clothing, collect them and transport them, with the effect of tidying the environment. The intervention, which depended on an imaginative assessment and interpretation of the situation, was to ask the man to collect any loose items of clothing and to take them to a large cupboard. This took place six times each day, and he received praise from staff for completion of the task. There was a decline in the number of items of clothing which were ejected through the window, and six weeks after the intervention ended, when staff were no longer asking him to take items to the cupboard, the man was reported to be independently collecting items and taking them to the cupboard. This is a good example of the approach we are advocating in this chapter—a constructional approach (cf. Cullen *et al.* 1981).

Assessment and interpretation, therefore, is not a mechanical exercise. It requires clinical judgement and experience. It is important to consider the *purposes* which are to be served. These might include:

(a) helping in the formulation of objectives for care plans;
(b) producing data which would allow progress to be evaluated; and
(c) discovering the critical functional relationships between key behaviours and the environment—the causes of behaviours.

These often require different methods. As noted above, formalized rating scales may help the clinician to describe current skills, and should lead to an outline plan for further investigation. However, more detailed observation and recording of activity will usually be required prior to the instigation of a training procedure in order to clarify the nature of the skills to be taught and to provide a baseline against which progress may be measured. This latter is particularly important in learning disability, since change is often slow, and can, therefore, be missed.

Observation and assessment of a young man at an Adult Training Centre

John came to the attention of the learning-disability service when his family moved into the locality. An initial contact through the Adult Training Centre was followed by a visit from one of the members of the Community Mental Handicap Team, in this case the clinical psychologist. As part of a general information-gathering exercise the psychologist reviewed a number of issues with the family, using a rating scale as a way of structuring the interview. The psychologist arrived at an outline picture of the family; the views of significant individuals concerning John's needs and also some idea of John's own view of his needs. It appeared that John was quite proficient in self-care, and in general life skills in association with home, and the psychologist was satisfied that opportunities for new learning at home were occurring. However, the parents indicated their concern (which supported a view offered by the Adult Training Centre manager) that their son was finding difficulty in communicating with his peers. Staff at the Training Centre had mentioned that on a small number of occasions John had been involved in minor fights, and were concerned that this should not develop into a major problem— they said that John was having problems in 'settling in'.

Information gained from the parents suggested that there was not a general social skills deficit. John coped well at his previous Training Centre, and had a number of well-established friendships. John himself seemed to be aware of a problem, but was unable to give a clear account of it. The next step was to ask staff at the Centre to undertake some simple recording of incidents, including basic behaviour–environment interactions. They were asked to complete an observation sheet with the following headings for each incident in which John was involved:

What did John do?
What happened immediately before the incident?
What happened after the incident?

At the same time a key member of staff was asked to record on a sampling basis the general interactive social behaviour shown by John during his working day.

When the observations were reviewed, two key factors emerged. Firstly, the incidents were often preceded by an interaction with a particular trainee at a time when John was required to share his tools with this person. The disagreement between them led to John shouting, which was quickly followed by an intervention from a member of staff, who resolved the situation. John's behaviour in this environment appeared to have been prompted by circumstances with which he was not familiar, nor was he effective in resolving the situation. It was noted in the more general observations that there were often times (usually at the change points in the daily timetable) when John found himself alone, perhaps because he had not yet learned what the next required activity was.

As a consequence of these observations of the frequency of behaviour and its environmental links, the Centre staff arrived at the view that John and his co-trainee required special attention at the point at which they needed to share tools; and, secondly, that just before each change point on the timetable a member of staff should ensure that either they themselves or a trainee explained the next activity to John. Recording continued, and showed a rapidly declining frequency of incidents.

A simple problem, perhaps; but allowing John to continue to 'settle in' without definite action might have strengthened the anti-social pattern. The initial interview provided background information, which continued to be useful and required regular updating. The specific observations identified deficits. John was not learning 'what followed what' in the timetable, but instead to wait to be taken to the next activity. The solution was to give him specific assistance which could be faded out gradually as he became more able. The observations also helped interpretation of the causes of behaviour—note the links between John's behaviour and the behaviour of staff. Finally, the observations allowed some evaluation. The interpretation was essentially the formulation of an hypothesis, and the intervention was in this sense experimental—the declining frequency gives confidence that the initial interpretation was accurate.

Supportive contact would continue with a family such as this, allowing regular reviews of target areas for progress, and perhaps some help in bringing about change. The focus of intervention may be at any time very specific, as in this case, or more broad and long-term. For example, we might encourage the family gradually to allow John more frequent opportunities to stay away from them, taking holidays with his new friends, or even preparing for a place in a group home. This kind of intervention would be directed both at John—allowing him to develop more independence—and at the family, in adjusting to this change. This family counselling would be very similar to that undertaken in other psychological specialties, and emphasizes the range of clinical activity undertaken by clinical psychologists with people who have learning disabilities.

Intervention

It is impossible to cover all the ways of changing behaviour which are available to the psychologist. Instead, we will discuss some of the basic principles and concepts which should be taken into account when designing an intervention. We will use the decision framework in Cullen *et al.* (1982) as a guide, which may conveniently be thought of as a flow diagram as in Fig. 5.1.

First, it must be decided whether the aim is to remove an excess or to remedy a deficit. Is the problem one of too much behaviour or not enough? This question is not as easy to answer as it first appears, because there is a complementarity between behavioural excesses and deficits. For example, if a person is engaging in a self-destructive activity, such as self-hitting, that might be construed as an excess behaviour to be removed, *or* as a behavioural deficit. Perhaps the person does not have any alternative way of occupying himself, or gaining attention, of dealing with frustration, and so on.

As a general rule, it is better to 'translate' a problem of excess behaviour into one of behavioural deficit if at all possible. Not only are there invariably ethical issues associated with removing behaviour (see below), but it is also difficult to achieve. So, if the problem can safely be ignored, it is advisable to do so, and to concentrate instead on building skills which will eventually displace it. If a child continually waves her fingers in front of her eyes, for example, she could be taught to do something more productive with her hands.

Sometimes, though thankfully only occasionally, an excess behaviour cannot be ignored, either because it interferes with attempts to teach new, adaptive repertoires, or because it is damaging to the person engaging in it or to others. Examples might be self-mutilation and aggressive behaviour. Here there is probably little alternative but to implement procedures which are specifically aimed at reducing or removing behaviour. There is currently a major debate on whether or not it is possible to help people using entirely *non-aversive* procedures, and there are clearly serious ethical considerations which have to be taken into account. We will not discuss this debate in detail; but see Cullen (1990) for a description of some of the relevant issues. Suffice it to say that non-aversive procedures, applied skilfully by competent staff, *can* deal with very challenging

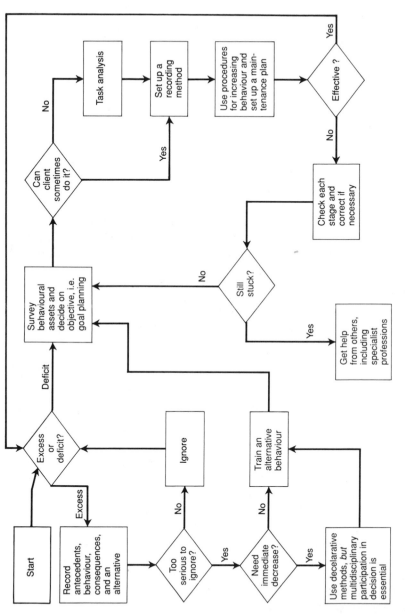

Fig. 5.1   A simple decision-making aid.

behaviour. However, there is still the possibility that, in some extreme circumstances, procedures which may be aversive in the short term (such as punishment) *might* be in the person's best long term interests. The decision to use such procedures *must* involve all those who have a reason to be involved, including the client or his or her representative; and the likely long-term benefits to the individual must be weighed against the short-term discomfort.

In 1982 the Association for the Advancement of Behaviour Therapy published a report on the treatment of self-injurious behaviour. This was compiled by a task force of some of the most eminent psychologists working in this field in the United States. Their recommendations included one that there should be a proper analysis of the causes of the behaviour and of the factors maintaining it before the institution of special procedures to remove it. In 1988 the Association for Behaviour Analysis also set up a task force of experts who produced a document on the 'right to effective behavioural treatment' (Van Houten *et al.* 1988). They produced a 6-point statement as follows:

An individual has a right to
1. . . . a therapeutic environment.
2. . . . services whose overriding goal is personal welfare.
3. . . . treatment by a competent behaviour analyst.
4. . . . programmes that teach functional skills.
5. . . . behavioural assessment and ongoing evaluation.
6. . . . the most effective treatment procedures available.

This sets the question of dealing with a person's behaviour in a wider context, and leads us to consider the ways and means at our disposal for establishing new behaviour.

There is an increasingly complex technology of teaching which is available to help people with learning disabilities. Some of the more recent advances rely on sophisticated computer technology, but all have common characteristics. The first of these is to break down the behaviour into small steps which can be tackled independently. How many components will depend on the current skill level of the person, since not everyone starts at the same point. Consider the (apparently) simple act of putting on a pair of shoes. Identifiable components include recognizing that there is a right and a left, putting the shoes on without the laces and tongue getting stuck in the shoe, and tying the laces. Each of these may then be broken down into its own constituents. Tying laces, for example, includes taking one end in each hand, crossing the separate ends and putting one end over and through to form a knot (this involves changing hands!), forming one loop, and then crossing the loose end over the loop, round it and pulling through to form the double bow—don't pull all of it or you finish with a single bow! We have no doubt that the literate person reading this who was previously unable to tie shoe-laces would be unlikely to learn from this description. What this shows, of course, is the complexity of tasks which most of us take for granted.

Having broken the task down into teachable components, each can then be taught separately—but in what order? Clearly, it does not make sense to start in the middle. Surprisingly, it is often best to start at the end, using a procedure known as *backward chaining* (because the elements are gradually linked together, starting from the last one). So, the person would be taught first to pull the two bows tight, everything else having been done by the trainer. She or he would be taught this by manual guidance and verbal encouragement, called by psychologists *physical and verbal prompts*. Upon comple-tion of this small step, the person would be given a reward. It might be that the reward would be something tangible such as a sweet or a hug; but more appropriate on this occasion would be the oppor-tunity to go somewhere interesting, in the same way as would any other person once they had fastened their shoelaces.

Once the step of pulling the two bows tight has been mastered, the person is ready to move on to the preceding component: pushing the loose end through to form the second bow. Having done this, prob-ably with some prompting at first, she or he can then *independently* pull the bows tight, hence completing the task. Two components having been mastered, the third from the end would be tackled, and so on until the person is carrying out the whole chain. In this way, many basic skills can be taught.

We have referred to the help or prompting which is given. As the person learns, this help should gradually be removed. Skilful *fading* of prompts can lead to learning which is totally errorless. If we are teaching a child to recognize which shoe to put on which foot, for example, we might paint two halves of a cat on the toes of the shoes, and teach the child that the picture of the cat is only complete with the shoes on the correct feet. Fairly soon, this visible cue will lead to the child always putting the shoes on the correct feet. Then, by putting on a layer of polish, the picture can be made less distinct; and, over time, it is faded out completely by further layers. Other cues, such as the shape of the shoe and the 'feel' on the feet become the ones which are important, as they are for competent dressers.

A certain degree of ingenuity is called for when things seem to go wrong with fading procedures. Some time ago we were involved in teaching people with learning disabilities to make a discrimination between simple words such as TOILET, DANGER, EXIT and so on. Based on errorless learning principles, the procedure was as follows. The 'target' word that was being taught was presented, with the alternatives from which it was to be chosen completely obliterated by several layers of tissue paper. On the instruction 'point to the word which says . . .' there was one visible word only for the person to point to. When this was being done reliably, with the word in any position relative to the other cards with their obliterated words, a layer of tissue was removed from each of these alternatives, so that they were slightly more visible. The person was still expected to point to the target word. Then another layer of tissue was removed, the procedure repeated, and so on. Eventually, all the alternative words were fully visible through a single layer of tissue, with the person still correctly pointing to the target word.

When the final layer of tissue was removed, to our surprise the person no longer pointed to the target word but pointed to any word on a completely chance basis. After some consideration, we realized that they had acquired a strategy which we had not foreseen. *They always pointed to the card without tissue*; and, for most of the time, in fact right up until the final trial, that strategy served very well; it was always correct and was rewarded. Only when there was no tissue paper present anywhere did the strategy fail. The answer? To start again, this time having the target card covered by a single layer of tissue, although still easily visible. It was not possible for the clue to success to be the absence of tissue paper. This time, the fading was successful, and our clients were able ultimately to point to the correct word in the presence of a number of alternatives, even when none of them had a covering of tissue paper.

The term for the important concept involved here is *stimulus control*. Its importance cannot be overstated, although there is insufficient space to discuss the topic in detail. Faulty stimulus control is the cause of many problems faced by psychologists in learning-disability settings. The person who urinates in public rather than in a toilet is under the control only of bladder cues rather than bladder cues plus various social cues. The person who talks to total strangers; the person who eats at the dining table with fingers rather than knife and fork; and so on. Each of these may be a stimulus-control problem. The task for the psychologist is to devise ways of bringing behaviour under appropriate stimulus control.

CHANGING SYSTEMS OF CARE

So far we have described aspects of the psychologist's role that involve face-to-face contact with clients. However, there are other considerations which have influenced how psychologists work. One of these is that there are too few psychologists to carry out all the one-to-one teaching required, and much of the work could be carried out by appropriately trained direct-care staff or parents. This has led in recent years to a burgeoning of staff-training workshops and home-teaching systems. Essentially, psychologists are operating through others, the people who are in most contact with the person with a learning disability.

Staff training has been the subject of evaluative research; but unfortunately, the outcome is not always encouraging. Most authors who review the field of staff training have found that, while it is possible to achieve short-term changes in staff skills and attitudes, they are rarely found to last, and staff do not usually change their practices when back in the workplace. Hence their learning-disabled clients do not benefit from the new procedures which the staff have learnt. Of in-service training for staff—usually conducted by psychologists—Ziarnik and Bernstein (1982) write:

It is our contention that the effectiveness of staff training has yet to be demonstrated because it is often incorrectly applied. That is, the assumption underlying the decision to provide staff training is that staff cannot perform the needed skills. That assumption is not always correct. Poor performance may be related to a variety of factors, only one of which is skill deficiency.

This is an interesting comment because it indicates that the failure of staff training to result in lasting changes in staff behaviour may be due to factors other than the training (cf. Cullen 1987). It is a consideration of these other factors which has led to some psychologists' moving away from face-to-face client teaching and from staff training. Often it is the very setting in which a person lives which is the main cause of the problem.

Consider, for example, the following case. A middle-aged woman was referred to the psychology department. The woman had spent much of her life in institutions, and was active and relatively able in self-care. Care staff requested help with persistent behavioural difficulties, the most evident of which was a tendency to take off her clothes. As part of an assessment of the situation, interactions between the woman and care staff were observed. This was done by having staff watch the woman for short periods of time during the day, choosing time-samples so that a representative picture of the whole day would eventually be formed. Table 5.1 shows the proportion of sample observations for each of the three interaction categories.

Table 5.1 Percentage of different types of interaction

Type of interaction	Percentage of total observations
Unattended	63.4
Engaged with staff in connection with problem behaviours	33.3
Engaged with staff in connection with acceptable behaviours	3.3

An intervention was then designed which had two major components:

1. An attempt to increase adaptive behaviour through brief periods of individual teaching planned to occur on a regular basis involving direct-care staff as far as their other commitments would allow.
2. A management procedure designed to affect the disrobing problem directly by removing her into her bedroom every time she removed her clothes inappropriately. This is a mild time-out procedure.

Both aspects of the programme were monitored with the support of clinical psychologists. The frequency of the use of time-out declined from an initial average of 14 incidents per day to approximately one per day by the 45th day of the procedure.

However, while the number of teaching sessions initially increased, a gradual decline took place between days 25 and 45. The frequency of sessions appeared to follow the frequency of problem behaviours. After day 45 both frequency of problem behaviours and that of teaching sessions rose again.

It seems as though pressures on staff in some way contributed to this phenomenon. Initially the woman may have been seen as extremely difficult and time-consuming for staff. A consequence of the programme was a reduction in problem behaviour, and hence less demand on staff time. Relative to others this woman became less of a problem and less often a subject of discussions between care staff and their senior managers. Other residents became more of a priority. The effect for the woman, as the problem reduced in frequency, was a reduction in the overall level of contact with staff. So, the frequency of problem behaviour then increased, as she returned to ways of behaving which had been successful in gaining staff attention. It seems likely that, in general terms, managers are most concerned about behaviours which are described as 'challenging'; that is, they may cause harm or indignity to people, or damage to property. Consequently, staff work hard to reduce these behaviours, and are forced into an orientation which produces cycles of behaviour problems. The task for the clinical psychologist is to reverse the tendency for staff to be most affected by behaviour problems and achieve a switch of emphasis to the maintenance of developmental gains. In this instance contacts between staff and the woman were almost invariably prompted by the behaviour problem. A procedure was designed which could effectively operate on this; but the residential system worked against long-term maintenance.

If it is the whole system which is at fault, the solution is to change it. Clinical psychologists are currently involved in different ways of trying to achieve this.

Influenced largely by Wolfensberger and his colleagues from the United States, many psychologists have advocated the principle of *normalization* as a means of solving the problems of people with learning disabilities. The basis of the approach is that it is largely the way in which society as a whole treats people with learning disabilities which is at the heart of the matter. The community has refused to accept learning-disabled people as equal members with equal rights and privileges, and has devalued them by either consigning them to segregated settings or by refusing them access to normal facilities and services. Change all that, and many of the problems will disappear. The argument is *not* that people with learning disabilities will somehow become 'normal' (in the sense of suddenly acquiring new repertoires) but that they will become 'equal', and will then be able to acquire new repertoires in a more supportive and conducive environment.

This is not the place to enter into a lengthy description of this topic. Suffice it to say that, for its proponents, normalization is a cohesive and comprehensive approach to service planning and design, with a sophisticated way of evaluating the effects of a service. There are those, though, who see normalization as a collection of slogans and statements, some of which are contradictory, and few of which are based on evidence that people with learning disabilities would benefit from the changes suggested (Mesibov 1990).

For those psychologists who see the need for a more pragmatic approach and who prefer to leave the business of changing society to others, the field of *organizational behaviour management* has become attractive. Here again the emphasis is on the whole system rather than the individual person. The essence of the approach is that the contingencies under which care staff operate have to be changed by appropriate management strategies if they are to engage in more appropriate client-related activities. These strategies have included giving instructions (both general and specific) and providing models for staff to copy. Special consequences such as written or verbal feedback from supervisors, monetary rewards, and the public posting of the results of care programmes have all been tried. The results of organizational behaviour management programmes have been variable, with most success seeming to come with procedures that incorporate more than one strategy. Ivancic and colleagues (1981), for example, combined a brief programme of in-service training (consisting mainly of direct instructions, modelling by trainers, and practice by the staff) with a system of prompting (i.e. publicly posted instructions, vocal instructions, and further modelling). They also included a feedback procedure, consisting of praise from supervisors and the public posting of results. All this resulted in an improvement in the staff's use of language-training activities with multi-disabled children during care routines.

Excursions into staff training and systems change are partly a result of the realization that a clinical psychologist, or indeed any member of staff, cannot expect to have a wide impact by working with individual clients. There have been other ways of tackling the problem. One is to work with groups of people with learning disabilities. A distinction should be made between procedures which are aimed at dealing with people *in* a group, for reasons of economy of staff time, and procedures for helping people to work *as* a group, the aim being to encourage co-operative social behaviour.

An example of the former is *room management*. This involves two elements. One staff member is designated as a room manager. It is his or her job to move around the group, praising clients who are busy with some activity, ensuring that everyone has access to materials, briefly prompting people who are not busy, and changing activities for those who have finished. A second staff member is designated as an individual helper, and his or her job is to spend a short (pre-determined) time with each person in turn doing individual training. The individual helper is also the person who answers the telephone, takes people to the toilet, deals with emergencies such as epileptic fits, and so on. Early studies on room management indicated that two staff could thus work with up to fifteen people with learning disabilities, and that the results in terms of levels of group engagement were very good. Unfortunately, the results tend to last only a few months; and, where they lasted considerably longer, it was found that the clients were busy but not learning very much. They were often still engaged on the same table-top tasks they were given many months previously.

Research on working with people *as* a group is still at an early stage, although there are some promising avenues to be explored. Cullen (1985) has reviewed some of the early work in this area.

Another way of maximizing the efforts of individual psychologists is by home teaching. In Britain since the mid-1970s there has been an increase in the number of home-teaching systems, especially for children with learning disabilities, based on the Portage approach. There are many such services operating, mainly in the densely populated areas of the country. This is somewhat paradoxical, because the value of home-teaching systems has been claimed to be for rural areas, where distance makes it more difficult for psychologists to have significant impact with a number of clients—Portage is a town in a rural part of the United States.

The defining characteristics of a Portage system are:

1. A home teacher visits a family and assesses the child. This home teacher, using teaching guidelines, shows the parents how to help their child to achieve a specific target. Visits are made regularly to monitor progress, set new targets, solve problems which arise, and so on. The home teacher may be someone already in contact with the family, perhaps a health visitor, or may be recruited specifically for the job. They will be given a basic training, lasting around one week.

2. Data on the child's progress are taken regularly to the supervisor, who is usually a psychologist. It is the psychologist who trains the home teacher, and who advises on problems which the home teacher cannot solve.

3. A management team, which is multidisciplinary, meets regularly to consider issues such as funding, the workloads of the home teachers, recruitment, etc.

Portage-type systems can be effective in disseminating a psychological influence. It is obviously a more useful way of using a scarce resource; but, as in all such systems, there is a price to be paid. The system itself has to be maintained, and so attention has to be given to those factors which are likely to threaten it. We touched on this issue above in our discussion of organizational behaviour management. In opting for a system which seems to make life easier for the psychologist (by easing the burden of too many direct client contacts) the problem has been changed into one of how to motivate home teachers, monitor their work, secure funding for the system, and so on. Also, whenever a psychological approach is disseminated it is likely to be diluted, and some of the subtleties may be lost. As we mentioned above when talking about stimulus control, it is likely to be just such subtleties that are important when helping handicapped people. However, the benefits of Portage home-teaching systems currently outweigh the disadvantages, so it is likely that their use will continue.

CONCLUSION

The picture of clinical psychology in learning-disability services is one of considerable diversity, ranging from direct work with clients to systems change and planning.

Overriding all is the simple fact that people with learning disabilities are *people*, who may sometimes have special needs which can be met in different ways, depending on their age and the nature of the services in their local community. The first characteristic of a psychological contribution is an analysis of the whole situation. This is accomplished by a variety of means, but leads to an intervention which is an experiment in the sense of being susceptible to continual modification in the light of changes for the disabled person. The interventions may be simple or complex, but they should be flexible.

In an attempt to help wider groups of clients, many psychologists have moved to work at a macro-level, designing and influencing systems. The knowledge base is not so secure here, and some activities—such as staff training and room management—are yielding disappointing results. But—as long as psychologists work at the macro-level with the same experimental rigour as they do at the micro-level—there is cause for optimism. It should be the central concern of psychologists that whatever is done for people with learning disabilities is done with good reason. The history of services shows that there is rarely a shortage of good intentions; but one of the roles for the psychologist should be to provide evidence to show which of the available options are likely to lead to the most benefit for clients. This should apply as much to service systems as to individual therapy.

REFERENCES

Cullen, C. (1985). Working with groups of mentally handicapped adults. In *New developments in clinical psychology*, (ed. F. N. Watts), pp. 84–95. The British Psychological Society, Leicester.

Cullen, C. (1987). Nurse training and institutional constraints. In *Staff training in mental handicap*, (ed. J. Hogg and P. Mittler), pp. 335–71. Croom Helm, London.

Cullen, C. (1990). The relation between ideology and clinical interventions for people with mental retardation. *Current Opinion in Psychiatry*, **3**(6), 1–4.

Cullen, C. and Dickens, P. (1990). People with mental handicaps. In *Measuring human problems*, (ed. D. F. Peck and C. M. Shapiro), pp. 303–16. Wiley, London.

Cullen, C., Hattersley, J., and Tennant, L. (1981). Establishing behaviour: the constructional approach. In *Applications of conditioning theory*, (ed. G. Davey), pp. 149–61. Methuen, London.

Cullen, C., Burton, M., and Thomas, M. (1982). A model for behaviour analysis in mental handicap. *Journal of Practical Approaches to Developmental Handicap*, **6**(1), 6–9.

Dallos, R. and Cullen, C. (1990). Clinical psychology. In *Introduction to psychology*, Vol. 2, (ed. I. Roth), pp. 724–70. Lawrence Erlbaum Associates (in association with the Open University), Hove.

Danby, J. and Cullen, C. (1988). Integration and mainstreaming: A review of the efficacy of mainstreaming and integration for mentally handicapped people. *Educational Psychology*, **8**, 177–95.

Fleming, I. (1984). The constructional approach to 'problem behaviour' in an institutionalised setting. *Behavioural Psychotherapy*, **12**, 349–55.

HMSO (1989). *Caring for people: community care in the next decade and beyond*. Her Majesty's Stationery Office, London.

Ivancic, M. T., Reid, D. H., Iwata, B. A., Faw, G. D., and Page, T. J. (1981). Evaluating a supervision programme for developing and maintaining therapeutic staff–resident interactions during institutional care routines. *Journal of Applied Behaviour Analysis*, **14**, 95–107.

Mesibov, G. R. (1990). Normalisation and its relevance today. *Journal of Autism and Developmental Disorders*, **20**, 79–90.

Van Houten, R., Axelrod, S., Bailey, J. S., Favell, J. E., Foxx, R. M., Iwata, B. A., and Lovaas, O. I. (1988). The right to effective behavioural treatment. *Behaviour Analyst*, **11**, 111–14. Also in *Journal of Applied Behaviour Analysis*, **21**, 381–4.

Ziarnik, J. P. and Bernstein, G. S. (1982). A critical examination of the effects of in-service training of staff performance. *Mental Retardation*, **20**, 109–44.

FURTHER READING

Brown, H. and Smith, H. (eds) *Normalisation: A reader for the 90's*. Routledge, London. (In press.)

Donnellan, A. M., LaVigna, D. W., Negri-Shoultz, N., and Fassbender, L. L. (1988). *Progress without punishment: effective approaches for learners with behaviour problems*. Teachers College Press, New York.

Reid, D. H., Parsons, M. B., and Green, C. W. (1989). *Staff management in human services: behavioural research and application*. Charles C. Thomas, Springfield, Ill.

Taylor, S. J., Biklen, D., and Knoll, J. (eds) (1987). *Community integration for people with severe disabilities*. Teachers College Press, New York.

Zigler, E. and Hodapp, R. M. (1986). *Understanding mental retardation*. Cambridge University Press.

6

Working with physically handicapped people

Barbara Wilson and Diana Staples

INTRODUCTION

The patients

Physical handicap may result from neurological dysfunction or from musculo-skeletal disorders. In the former group the handicap follows impairment in the central nervous system rather than from damage to the limbs themselves. This is sometimes difficult for patients to understand, and it is often the case that a person with hemiplegia following a stroke will believe that the affected limbs are actually damaged rather than appreciating that damage to that part of the brain which *controls* those limbs is causing them to malfunction. When the handicap results from a musculo-skeletal disorder then obviously the problems encountered in manoeuvring are directly caused by some dysfunction of the muscles, bones, or peripheral nerves.

It is possible for a patient to have both kinds of impairment. For example, a head-injured patient may have a physical problem resulting from severe brain-stem injury together with problems following directly from damage to one or more limbs. The patient's condition could be even further complicated by contractures or myositis ossificans (bony growths), which are sometimes caused by inappropriate treatment.

A further example of neurological and musculo-skeletal problems occurring together would be seen in a patient with cerebral vascular disease necessitating amputation of a limb. However, most people with physical handicap will have either neurological *or* musculo-skeletal disorders. Some common causes of physical handicap can be seen in Table 6.1.

Table 6.1 Types and causes of physical handicap

Type	Some common causes
Neurological dysfunction	Severe head injury
	Cerebral vascular accident (stroke)
	Degenerative diseases, e.g. multiple sclerosis, Parkinson's disease
	Cerebral and spinal tumours
	Trauma to spinal cord
	Infections, e.g. encephalitis
	Poisoning, e.g. carbon monoxide
Musculo-skeletal disorders	Rheumatoid arthritis
	Osteoarthritis
	Amputations
	Peripheral vascular disease
	Muscular dystrophy
	Congenital abnormalities

The settings

Clinical psychologists may be found in neurology and neurosurgical departments, in rehabilitation centres, and in orthopaedic and paediatric departments. Occasionally they are attached to Social Services departments such as those for the young chronic sick, and sometimes they work in young disabled units run by the Health Service. Not all of these departments will have the benefit of the services of a clinical psychologist. In some centres there is no contact at all with a psychologist; in others psychologists may be asked to see the occasional patient for assessment or treatment; others will have a regular part-time psychologist, and still others a full-time clinical psychologist.

The role of clinical psychologists working with physically handicapped people

There are several ways in which clinical psychologists can work with people who have physical handicaps. Firstly, they can assist patients in managing their disease or condition by providing information about (i) the disease itself, (ii) ways of pacing activities, (iii) the use of drugs, and (iv) ways of combatting deleterious effects of modern living whilst promoting healthy activities. Secondly, they can work alongside other therapists in teaching the use of aids, orthoses, and alternative methods of carrying out activities connected with daily living. Thirdly, psychologists can get involved in sexual counselling. Fourthly, vocational and educational guidance can be given by psychologists. Fifthly, anxiety and pain can be diminished by the application of management programmes, and psychological treatment may be available for dealing with depression.

When cognitive or behaviour problems accompany the physical handicap psychologists may well be called upon to reduce or remedy some of these. Finally, psychologists may spend part of their working lives attempting to modify the attitudes of various sections of society towards people with physical handicap, acting as their advocates.

ASSESSMENT

Assessments are carried out in order to answer questions. These questions should be related to each patient's needs and rehabilitation programme, and the psychologist must therefore be flexible in developing assessment and rehabilitation procedures. While the physically handicapped individual is usually the focus of assessment, the physical and social *environment* may also need to be assessed and possibly changed in order to maximize learning and independence. Sometimes assessment is needed for administrative purposes, in order to implement planning changes and staff levels.

There are several types of assessment procedure from which clinical psychologists can choose when they seek to match a particular form of assessment to a particular question. Standardized tests are the most widely known tool of psychological measurement: there are tests to measure overall intellectual function as well as specific tests to measure cognitive functions such as attention, perception, language, reasoning, problem-solving, memory, and learning.

Other forms of assessment involve direct or indirect observation of the patient in the natural setting of home or work, in a hospital or rehabilitation centre, or in simulated situations such as a mock office. Behavioural assessment involves analysis of the relationship between the patient's behaviour, and its antecedents and consequences. The antecedents and consequences may then be altered to produce behavioural change in the desired direction. Rating scales are also used in order that the patient, relatives, or staff may make *judgements* about specific observable behaviours and about inner states and feelings.

Assessment techniques need to have the technical features of all good measuring devices: they need to be valid, which means they must measure what they say they measure; they need to be reliable, which means they must measure the same thing on different occasions or when used by different observers; they need to be generalizable, and sensitive to change.

Neuropsychological assessment

Neuropsychology is the study of the relationship between the brain and behaviour. A neuropsychological assessment will examine abilities such as memory, language, perception, attention, reasoning, and planning. For patients with neurological damage a neuropsychological assessment can be particularly helpful in pinpointing specific problem areas that will require treatment. Sometimes it is also necessary to carry out a neuropsychological assessment of a patient with a musculo-skeletal disorder in order to obtain information about cognitive functioning. Such information may be used in several ways. One of the most frequent reasons for carrying out a neuropsychological assessment is to estimate a patient's level of general intellectual ability. This is often obtained by the administration of an intelligence test such as the Wechsler Adult Intelligence Scale or the revision of this scale (WAIS-R), both of which consist of 11 sub-tests. Each sub-test measures a different aspect of intelligence. Some tests are primarily concerned with language skills and others with visuo-spatial skills. Because several of the tests have to be completed within a certain period of time, patients with motor problems are sometimes at a disadvantage and may score poorly, owing to their impaired manipulative skills rather than any deficiencies in intelligence. However, with sensible interpretation of the scores and due recognition of the disadvantages experienced by such patients the test can supply important information.

In addition to assessing current levels of functioning it is often necessary to estimate premorbid intellectual ability, particularly for patients with neurological damage. If a head-injured patient, for example, scores in the average range on an intelligence test it will not be clear whether this represents any deterioration in intellectual skills. It is often possible to get some idea of what a patient's functioning was like before the injury by studying school records or assessment of professional qualifications where these are available. In cases where there are no qualifications or records the usual procedure is to estimate premorbid levels by comparing performance on tests known to be sensitive to brain damage with performance on tests known to be fairly resistant to brain damage. For instance, performance on some visuo-spatial tests is vulnerable to many kinds of cerebral disorder, whereas knowledge of the meaning of words is fairly resistant to brain damage unless the language area of the brain itself is involved. This type of estimation obviously has to be cautiously interpreted.

Another reason for carrying out a neuropsychological assessment is to determine which cognitive abilities are intact or relatively intact, and which are impaired. Thus a picture will be built up of a patient's intellectual strengths and weaknesses. This may be particularly important information when designing a treatment programme. If, for example, memory deficit is associated with widespread intellectual deterioration then amelioration procedures will be different from a case where no other cognitive impairment is present.

Sometimes psychologists are asked to determine whether a problem is due to an organic or an emotional cause. Some psychiatrists mistakenly believe, for example, that left hemiplegic stroke patients (with right-hemisphere damage) are depressed because they fail to show facial expression and look emotionally flat. However, problems with emotional expression are frequent after right cerebral damage, and are associated with other problems—particularly visuo-spatial ones—and with denial of or indifference to their physical and cognitive difficulties.

Psychologists may be asked to carry out an assessment in an attempt to find out which part of the brain is damaged. Frontal lobe damage will result in certain kinds of deficits, temporal lobe damage will produce others, and parietal lobe damage yet others. Such localization has to be performed cautiously, as other factors may be involved (for example, intracranial pressure may make specific diagnosis difficult). Localization of damage is a less common reason for assessment today because greater use is made of CT and other brain scans than formerly (although some kinds of neurological deficit, such as anoxia, cannot be detected by CT scan)—furthermore MRI scans may be difficult to obtain.

Assessments are also carried out in order to obtain a baseline against which to measure future recovery or deterioration. Again, caution must be exercised, as there may be a practice effect which leads to better performance on a test simply because the patient has performed the test on an earlier occasion. If alternative versions of the test are given to reduce the practice effect then the tester needs to know the comparability of the two forms of the test in order to avoid differences in levels of difficulty. Using neuropsychological tests as baselines has limitations because the tests are frequently insensitive to the measurement of improvement. It is often better to use a behavioural assessment (described below), which can be made more sensitive to small but real changes.

Neuropsychological assessments can answer certain questions well. For example then can tell us whether a person's score on a test is in the impaired range, how a person compares with others of the same age in the general population, and whether a pattern of results is typical of a particular syndrome. However, there are other questions which neuropsychological assessment cannot answer so well. For example, we know little about the relationship between performance on tests and performance in everyday life. We do not know what treatment to offer as a result of a neuropsychological assessment; neither do we know how patients are responding to any treatment while it is in progress. In order to answer these and similar questions it will be necessary to use other procedures, such as behavioural assessment.

Behavioural assessment

As mentioned earlier, behavioural assessment involves an analysis of the relationship between the antecedents and consequences of the behaviour under consideration. Rather than focusing on whatever caused the problem and the internal state of the patient, the main interest is in current factors in the treatment setting that can be used to alter behaviour. Physical and social determinants of behaviour must also be recognized, as these may place limitations on treatment. Gross anatomical damage or physiological malfunctioning will limit improvement in motor skills. On the other hand, observers should not be *too* ready to accept these limitations, because functioning can sometimes be changed under special conditions. For example, it has been possible to improve short-sightedness with specially designed treatment programmes (Collins and Gil 1983).

One of the characteristics of behavioural assessment is that it has a direct relationship with treatment, unlike neuropsychological assessment, described above. If the behavioural assessment has correctly identified those factors which elicit and maintain behaviour, then those factors can be manipulated so that the behaviour itself will change: such change is the goal of treatment. Thus any distinction between assessment and treatment would become artificial, and in practice the two are indistinguishable.

In order to measure behaviour it is first of all necessary to define exactly what one is going to measure. It is not possible to observe and record everything the patient says or does. If the observer decides to measure pain behaviour or aggression then it is important to be specific about what constitutes pain or aggression as far as the particular patient is concerned. Recording the number of times the patient complains about pain, or swears at staff, will perhaps be appropriate; but it might be necessary to achieve even greater specificity. For example, the therapist may need to decide whether a groan on the part of a patient represents a complaint, or whether the expletive, 'Damn you!' amounts to swearing. The answers to such questions will depend on specific circumstances, but everyone involved in the assessment and recording will need to know what to include and what to exclude. It is also essential that the behaviours in question should be observable or rateable, and clearly and unambiguously defined.

Behavioural assessment will establish the extent of the problem prior to treatment, and it will also indicate whether observing the behaviour actually *changes* the behaviour. (As can happen, for example, when a person whose eating habits are being observed and recorded actually eats less because they know they are being observed.) Another difficulty can arise if assessment and treatment are introduced together, because it will be impossible to know whether any changes result from the assessment, the treatment, or both. In order to know whether the treatment itself has changed the behaviour, the behaviour during treatment must be compared with the baseline level so that progress can be monitored. It is also important to observe and record the events or situation that precede and follow the behaviour in which we are interested, because it is usually these factors that are manipulated in a behavioural treatment programme. If, for example, a physiotherapist frequently lets a patient who complains of physiotherapy have a short rest (thus rewarding inappropriate behaviour) we need to know how often this occurs before changing the situation. We might then persuade the physiotherapist to allow the patient a short rest when a certain exercise has been *completed* (thus rewarding appropriate behaviour).

The main tool of behavioural assessment is direct observation of the patient in a natural or simulated situation. The most useful methods of sampling and recording this behaviour and the relevant stimuli involve counting and/or timing: the observer counts the number of times the response occurs during a given period. Indirect measures could involve counting the products of behaviour, such as number of footprints on a chalky surface in a gymnasium, the number of articles completed in the workshop, or the number of soiled incontinence pads used in a day. Timing methods such as interval recording, time-sampling, and duration recording are all methods of measuring which behaviours occur during a given observational period or specific times. They may also be used to measure the length of time for which a behaviour occurs.

The instruments used for recording include simple hand-held counters, wrist counters, stop-watches, and specially prepared recording sheets on which tally marks are made. It is also possible to use automated measurement and recording devices which are operated directly by the patient's own movements. Some subtle behaviour changes can only be detected when special instruments are used. An increasing number of devices for automatically measuring behavioural deficits have recently been constructed. Voice-operated relays have been used to measure changes in voice loudness. Instruments have been developed for automatically recording changes in muscle tension, posture, position of the head, dribbling, sphincter pressure, and urine flow.

Other devices that are not operated directly by the target behaviour have been developed to simplify the mechanics of data collection. For example, timing signals may be recorded on tape so that observers may observe without having to glance repeatedly at a stop-watch. Audio-visual tape recordings allow behavioural episodes to be preserved for rescoring at a later date, and electrical counters have been developed so that observers may obtain frequency counts. These instruments can save time and effort, yield data on extremely subtle events, and lead to greater inter-observer agreement.

Factors influencing behaviour may include place, time of day, the patient's own position, the behaviour of other people around the patient, and what are termed 'mutually exclusive' and 'concomitant' behaviours. Several instruments have been developed to record this kind of information, one such being Lieberman's Behaviour Observation Instrument, which enables a trained observer to observe and record four of these dimensions with a group of patients. For example, the 'mutually exclusive' dimension is composed of five behaviours: running, walking, standing, sitting, and lying. Obviously, only one of these can be coded during the observation interval. 'Concomitant behaviour' may include anything which has been previously clearly defined, such as talking, grimacing, crying, eating, reading, smoking, or laughing.

Other categories can be devised. For instance, therapist or family behaviour could be coded in such categories as instructing the patient, correcting the patient, praising the patient, instructing other patients, and engaging in non-treatment behaviours such as looking out of the window, writing notes, or talking on the telephone. Information obtained in this way is not only useful for developing treatment programmes but also in training staff and families to learn the skills to help their patients and relatives.

ASSESSMENT OF MEMORY FUNCTIONING IN A YOUNG
MAN FOLLOWING A SEVERE HEAD INJURY

Mark was a young man who sustained a severe head injury at the age of 25 years and was unconscious for several weeks. During the months following his accident he made a partial recovery, but he remained physically and intellectually handicapped. On leaving hospital he went to a rehabilitation centre, where he was referred to the clinical psychology department for help with his memory problems. Before any treatment could be implemented it was necessary to carry out a full assessment of his memory functioning. Both neuropsychological and behavioural methods were employed to obtain information on the strengths and weaknesses of Mark's memory.

(a) Neuropsychological measures

One of the first tests administered to Mark was Digit Span. In this task Mark had to repeat numbers read out by the psychologist. He was able to repeat back seven digits before making mistakes. This represents an average score, and indicated that Mark's immediate memory was normal. Many people, including those with extremely severe memory difficulties, have a normal immediate memory span.

Mark was then asked to listen carefully to a short story and then repeat back as much as he could remember. The story was about six lines long and contained 23 sections or ideas. Mark only managed to recall four sections accurately, a poor score for someone of his age and overall ability. Half an hour later and without any warning Mark was asked to recall the story again. This time he remembered none of it, and in fact he did not remember having been told a story at all. Most people would be able to remember nearly as much after half an hour as they had when first asked to recall the story.

Several other neuropsychological memory tests were administered to Mark. These assessed his immediate and delayed visual memory, his ability to recognize faces and words after a short delay, and his ability to learn new information. On all of these tasks Mark was very seriously impaired. Finally, he was given several tests of remote memory which tested his ability to remember events, faces, personalities, and incidents that had been parts of his experience prior to the accident. When people have been unconscious it is common for them to have retrograde amnesia, that is loss of memory for experiences that happened *before* the onset of coma. In addition to anterograde amnesia, Mark had retrograde amnesia which extended back some seven or eight years. Thus, he thought he was 18 years old and worked at a job he had held some eight years earlier. He did not remember changes of address during the eight-year gap, he did not know the current year or current Prime Minister, and was quite unaware of recent happenings in the news.

(b) Behavioural measures

The tests mentioned above provided considerable information on Mark's memory. However, they did not throw much light on how Mark's memory problems affected his everyday life. In order to do this, several behavioural assessment techniques were employed. The psychologist observed Mark in different settings, including physiotherapy, occupational therapy, and the ward, and in a memory group session that Mark attended. Some major problems became evident during these observations. Firstly, Mark was frequently lost: he could not remember his way from one department to another, and had to be helped or rescued by members of staff or other patients. Secondly, he could not remember either the names or the faces of anybody working at the centre. Thirdly, he failed to refer to his timetable or his notebook to find out where he was meant to be.

In addition to direct observation, Mark's parents were interviewed and asked to describe what they considered to be Mark's main problems. They were also given a rating scale to complete which compared Mark's memory before and after the accident. This rating scale was adapted from one devised by Kapur and Pearson (1983). Several memory functions were listed, including remembering to pass on a message and remembering the names of people Mark had known for a long time. For each of these functions Mark's parents had to decide whether their son was (a) as good as he was before his accident, (b) slightly worse, or (c) very much worse. The ratings provided an indication of the severity of Mark's everyday memory problems. Mark also filled in the rating scale; but it was noticeable that he tended to underestimate the extent of his difficulties. In common with many other head-injured people Mark experienced difficulty in remembering just how bad his memory had become. However, the information obtained from Mark did give an indication of his *own* insight into his memory problems.

Mark and his parents also completed a questionnaire about the methods he used to compensate for his memory impairment. This questionnaire was adapted from Harris (1980). It concentrated on questions about the use of aids such as notebooks and alarms. In fact Mark used very few methods to bypass or alleviate his memory difficulties, certainly fewer than most people *without* memory difficulties.

Mark's therapists were asked to complete checklists every day for two weeks. At the end of his twice-daily physiotherapy sessions his physiotherapist spent a few minutes going through the 19-item checklist, recording any memory failures noted during the session. The items included questions such as, 'Did he forget where he had put something?' and 'Did he forget what he was supposed to be doing?' Mark's occupational therapist also completed checklists at the end of her sessions. The information provided a detailed picture of the number, type, and extent of Mark's memory problems during his daily life.

Mark was also tested on the Rivermead Behavioural Memory Test (Wilson *et al.* 1985), a test designed to predict which people will experience everyday memory problems. The test combines some of the strengths of standardized tests with the strengths of behavioural measures. As well as being an assessment tool the RBMT also indicated the severity of Mark's memory impairment. Finally, the information gathered from all the assessment procedures was used to design Mark's memory therapy programme.

TREATMENT

Introduction

People with physical handicap may come into contact with clinical psychologists for several reasons. Occasionally psychologists will be involved in the treatment of the physical or motor difficulties which all of these patients will experience. For example, psychologists may supervise biofeedback procedures used to improve foot drop in stroke patients. When physiotherapists and psychologists work together they can sometimes be effective in improving motor control by combining their skills. Thus, the physiotherapist's knowledge of muscles, joints, and physical therapy techniques can be combined with the psychologist's expertise in evaluating treatment programmes and knowledge of ways to improve learning.

Apart from physical handicap, which may or may not require treatment, there are other problems that require the attention of the clinical psychologist. For example, sensory difficulties such as impaired vision or touch may involve psychological intervention as well as the treatment supplied by physiotherapists, speech therapists, and occupational therapists. Behaviour problems, such as yelling and tantrums, are fairly common amongst patients who have suffered severe head injury, and other groups of physically handicapped people may exhibit similar behaviour in certain circumstances. Psychologists are often expected to devise programmes that will help patients overcome these disorders of conduct.

Emotional difficulties may also accompany physical handicap, leaving the patient fearful, anxious, or depressed. A patient with brain-stem damage, for example, is particularly likely to show emotional lability, and will change from extreme tearfulness to loud laughter within minutes. Diseases of the basal ganglia, such as Huntington's chorea or progressive supranuclear palsy, are also likely to promote emotional disturbances.

Cognitive deficits involving memory, language, and perception are commonly associated with certain kinds of neurological damage, including head injury, stroke, and encephalitis. Psychologists are becoming increasingly involved in the treatment of these disorders.

Finally, physical handicap may be associated with personality disturbances. These may develop as a result of neurological impairment such as bilateral frontal lobe damage, or because of environmental factors such as over-protection or rejection by the patient's family.

Treatment of a physical problem

Mrs A. was a 72-year-old widow who had her right leg amputated after several unsuccessful operations for vascular insufficiency. She was admitted for preliminary assessment to see if she was suitable for provision of a prosthesis and walking training. She was in moderately good physical health, but had some mild memory problems and was extremely anxious. However, she seemed highly motivated to walk, which was necessary if she was to return to her own home, which was unsuitable for a wheelchair. Emotionally, she seemed adjusted to the loss of her leg: she was able to examine her stump, touch it, bandage it, and was not worried about the appearance of it. She was cheerful and said she felt great relief in not having the continual pain she had suffered prior to amputation, which she regarded as a positive treatment rather than a devastating loss. She experienced minimal phantom sensation and, on provision of the artificial limb, experienced slight discomfort from rubbing of the stump in the socket—which was later modified by the prosthetist. After four days of walking and training she was referred to the clinical psychologist for fear of falling and for needing constant reassurance, and because she seemed unable to manage her own medication.

The fear of falling was tackled first, and a hierarchy of fearful situations was drawn up by the psychologist and Mrs A. Following this, Mrs A. was taught relaxation techniques. She then practised the early items of the hierarchy, first by imagining them and then by carrying them through with the help of the physiotherapist. Mrs A. rapidly progressed up the hierarchy until she was able to walk up and down the parallel bars four times. At this stage the psychologist observed the physiotherapist and Mrs A. during three training sessions in order to assess Mrs A.'s constant requests for re-assurance. Because Mrs A. was by now less afraid of falling, the number of requests had decreased to some extent; but when she did ask, the therapist spent a lot of time encouraging Mrs A., putting her arm around Mrs A's shoulders and patting her on the arm. However, when Mrs A. was walking successfully the therapist would speak to and touch Mrs A. less often. When this was pointed out to the therapist she changed her behaviour and gave Mrs A. attention and praise for *success* in walking, and removed attention when Mrs A. complained or asked for help. In two weeks Mrs A. was successfully managing two lengths of the gymnasium using her frame, and by four weeks she had managed to transfer to two walking sticks, and could also manage to climb a short flight of stairs.

The problem of forgetting to take her medication was helped by the use of a commercially available pill dispenser. A friend agreed to fill the dispenser every week, and as it was left on the dining-room table, where she ate her meals, she was reminded to take the pills in the compartment appropriate for the time and the day of the week.

Treatment of a sensory problem

Gary was a 39-year-old divorced man who had been living alone, working as a self-employed businessman, when he received a spinal injury in a road traffic accident. He received six months treatment in a Spinal Unit and recovered sufficiently to be able to walk quite long distances with a frame. He managed all self-care activities except for his bowel routine. He was left with an incomplete sensory loss below the sixth cervical (C6) level, with diminished sensation over his trunk below the shoulder level, but with other areas of extreme sensitivity and intense pain. Because of increasing pain he did less and less, and for the last month before admission he sat in a darkened room doing nothing at all. He had attended a pain clinic and, among other things, had been offered brain surgery. He was unwilling to accept this, saying 'My brain is the only bit of me that functions well, I would rather leave it alone.'

On admission he appeared depressed and complained bitterly of his pain. Assessment suggested that Gary had three kinds of pain. The first was a total body pain which affected him from the shoulders down, and this he described as aching, gnawing, and constant. The second was around the ribs, and he described this as stabbing, sickening, and intermittent. The third pain, in his right leg, groin, and buttock, he described as searing, burning, sharp, and unbearable. Gary was able to distinguish the three pains quite clearly, and could relate the different pains to different stimuli. The stabbing pains which were intermittent around the rib area seemed to be related to muscle spasm in his left arm. The most intolerable pain, that in his left leg and groin, seemed to occur after a period when he felt hot or uncomfortable. The total body pain seemed to be most pronounced when he was inactive.

A programme was worked out for Gary by the physician, physiotherapist, and psychologist. The drug Lioresal was given for the muscle spasm, nerve stimulation techniques were administered by the physiotherapist to help relieve the leg and groin pain, and an increasing activity schedule in the gymnasium and assessment flat, together with progressive relaxation exercises was used to help alleviate some of the general body pain.

Further investigation into the most unpleasant leg pain, which had responded slightly to the nerve stimulation, revealed that heat made Gary's pain intolerable. Even imagining a hot place worsened the pain. However, Gary learned to make the pain more manageable by imagining himself immersed in cold water.

Four months after discharge Gary was still using this technique and the nerve stimulation. He was living independently in a specially adapted flat, and planning to take a course in computer studies.

Treatment of an emotional problem

Jenny was a severely disabled 24-year-old woman with spinal muscular atrophy. She was confined to a wheelchair and dependent on others for all her needs except for the mobility provided by the powered chair. She was referred to an assessment unit to see if she could live independently in special accommodation, and to find out whether she was capable of directing live-in care attendants.

When assessed by the clinical psychologist Jenny was found to be intelligent. Her problem was that she was unhappy and felt that people did not like her. She also felt worthless. Her thoughts were concentrated upon two main themes (a) that she was worthless and unpopular because she was in a wheelchair that was regarded as a nuisance by other people and (b) that her appearance was unattractive and people did not like her because of this. In fact Jenny was a very attractive person who had beautiful hair, a lovely smile, and good dress sense. She drove her electric chair with great skill, and it was no nuisance in most small houses. Jenny's false assumptions were challenged, brought out in the open and discussed. The fallacies were pointed out to her. She was encouraged to monitor her thought about her wheelchair: she was asked to bang her hand on the side and say, 'I am in a wheelchair, it is a very nice, neat chair, it looks good and I drive it very well, and it can get into even the smallest space and it is no trouble to anyone.' When she noticed she was thinking about being exceedingly thin and ugly she was to say to herself, 'I have kept myself beautifully slim, I look very good in these modern clothes, I have very nice hair, people look at me and think what an attractive girl.'

At first Jenny found this procedure difficult, and felt she would become conceited. However, it became easier, and after two weeks she indicated that she was almost begining to think the statements were true! She then watched the psychologist modelling a confident, assertive disabled person, with one of the nurses playing the part of a care attendant. Jenny learned how to ask for her essential needs, and to be satisfied without over-apologizing or appearing too demanding or bossy. When discharged from the unit she stated tht she felt much better about herself.

Treatment of a behaviour problem

Physically handicapped people, like any others, can have behaviour problems. In some cases these will be unrelated to the physical handicap, and just happen to coexist with it. In other cases the behaviour problems and the physical handicap may both be direct consequences of neurological damage. For example, a patient with a large frontal lobe tumour may have difficulties in exercising motor skills *and* display behaviour problems, both directly resulting from frontal lobe damage. In another group of patients the behaviour problems may be indirectly related to the physical handicap. Thus a severely head-injured person who is unable to walk may develop problematic behaviour as a means of obtaining the attention of others.

M.B. was a young man who had received a severe head injury in a car accident. He was very ataxic and unsteady on his feet, had considerable intellectual handicaps, and was very disruptive in his therapy sessions. His main behaviour problem was frequent calling out to his physiotherapist and occupational therapist. He appeared to want their attention all the time, and interrupted the therapy of other patients as well as his own. The therapists and psychologist worked out a programme to try and reduce M.B.'s calling out. In the baseline period the number of times he called for the therapist was recorded. In the treatment stage staff explained to M.B. that they wanted him to call out less often, that they were going to count how many times he called out each session, and that they were going to count how many times he shouted out. They also informed him that when he managed to go two days without calling out, the physiotherapist, the occupational therapist, and the psychologist would take him to the pub for lunch. M.B. apparently found the idea of the pub lunch a powerful reward, for he earned it very quickly. It was gradually made harder for him to earn the lunch, and staff also took turns accompanying him, so that one or two staff members went on each occasion. With occasional lapses, M.B. continued to work reasonably quietly.

Not all patients will respond to treatment so quickly; but behavioural approaches have been effective with a number of physically handicapped people. Several examples can be found in Ince (1976) and Wood (1987).

Treatment of a cognitive problem

Such problems include difficulties with thinking, perceiving, remembering, and reasoning. They should not be confused with problems relating to emotional or physical behaviour, or to personality problems. Cognitive deficits are particularly likely to follow neurological damage affecting the brain, but they can also follow other handicapping conditions too. For example, some kidney patients show mild intellectual impairments, probably resulting from insufficient oxygen getting to the brain. Congenital handicaps can also lead to cognitive deficits, usually following on from interrupted or inappropriate education. Remedial education may be appropriate when cognitive difficulties occur in childhod. Similar procedures can be used with adults. There is currently a growing interest in cognitive rehabilitation for those patients who have been intellectually normal and whose problems result from brain damage acquired in adulthood (Wilson and Moffat 1984; Sohlberg and Mateer 1989; and Wood and Fussey 1990).

D.C. was a soldier who was shot through the head at the age of 23. He spent the next two years undergoing several operations and intensive rehabilitation. At the end of this two-year period he remained severely intellectually impaired and totally unable to read. He had been a normal reader before the injury. He never accepted the conclusions of the experts who told him that he would never read again. Three years after the injury an attempt was made to teach D.C. to read six useful everyday words. He failed to learn any of them. Two years later, that is five years after his injury, D.C. was taught the sounds and names of letters of the alphabet. These were taught one at a time, and upper-case letters were taught first. Following this, letters were presented in random order and D.C. was required to say the sounds. The next step was to teach him which letters were vowels. Then two and three regular words were introduced, and finally irregular words were taught. The teaching method was simply practice, feedback, and teaching one thing at a time. D.C. failed to learn anything using the whole-word method, but quickly learned to read using the phonetic method. It took three weeks to teach the sounds and names of the letters, and within six months D.C. had progressed from reading no words at all to reading at the level of a nine-year-old. He continued to improve until reaching the reading age of 13 years, at which standard he has remained for several years.

Treatment of a personality problem

It is not always easy to decide which problems are emotional and which are due to behaviour or personality disorders. We tend to judge people's personalities from the way they behave, describing a person who laughs a great deal as having a cheerful personality and someone who shouts and complains as bad-tempered. Similarly, if a person is fearful or depressed we might consider that this shows emotional disturbance, or we might suggest that they have 'personality problems'. It is usual to regard emotion as connected with feelings: behaviour relating to conduct, and personality representing the characteristics or traits of an individual. Among physically handicapped people, 'personality problems' may be a direct consequence of neurological damage or they may represent a maladaptive response to a handi-capping condition.

If a person is referred for help with 'personality problems' the psychologist will almost certainly identify some specific problem behaviours for treatment, and will not consider the personality as an entity that is capable of being damaged and therefore treated. Let us consider, for example, the case of A.F., who suffered a stroke, after which he became excessively demanding and asked staff dozens of times each day when his wife would be collecting him. She came each day at 4.30 p.m., and was never late. Treatment in this case consisted of (a) self-monitoring, whereby A.F. counted the number of times he asked the staff when his wife would be coming to collect him, and (b) imaginal desensitization, whereby he imagined his wife arriving a few seconds later each day. His questions never ceased entirely; but over a period of three weeks they dropped from over 40 per day to an average of five per day.

BEHAVIOURAL APPROACH TO PRESSURE-RELIEF
EXERCISING FOR A PATIENT WITH SPINAL INJURY

P.W. was a 34-year-old man who fell from a tree and sustained spinal injuries which left him with a partial paraplegia. His sensation was impaired and he had no feeling at all in his buttocks. He spent long periods in a wheelchair, and received advice from physiotherapists, doctors, and nurses on the necessity of lifting his buttocks regularly in order to prevent pressure sores developing. Despite considerable efforts to persuade him to co-operate with the recommended skin care, he failed to look after himself and developed a sacral pressure sore. More advice, encouragement, and persuasion followed, but P.W. still failed to respond; and soon afterwards staff noticed a new pressure sore developing. At this time P.W. was referred to the clinical psychology department with a request to seek ways of gaining his co-operation in the care of his pressure areas.

Pressure sores are a common complication after spinal injury and are difficult to treat. The patient has reduced circulation in the pressure areas but feels no discomfort, and so has little motivation to help the circulation by moving or lifting the buttocks. When the patient does lift there is no immediate reinforcement, such as relief from discomfort. Although in the long term patients know that sores may develop and that these sores may prove to be life-threatening if gangrene sets in, the consequences are far removed from the actual behaviour required to avoid them. In these circumstances even the sores may fail to act as deterrents, and the positive consequences of lifting may be obscured because the healing process is so slow.

Several methods have been used to encourage lifting in spinal patients. Most of these consist of some form of pressure-sensitive pad with an alarm to signal when lifts should be made. From the published reports it is often difficult to judge treatment effectiveness, but one important factor would appear to be the provision of immediate consequences for lifting. In P.W.'s case the immediate consequence was verbal feedback on the number of lifts made in a given period, and praise if he lifted often enough. On the basis of previous studies we decided that one lift should occur every 10 minutes. A lift was defined as a movement which involved P.W.'s buttocks leaving the seat of the wheelchair for at least 4 seconds. P.W. pushed himself up from the chair with his arms, which were not affected by the spinal injury. It was necessary to have equipment which would record the number of lifts made. This consisted of a pressure-sensitive pad attached to the seat of the patient's wheelchair. The pad was placed in a bag behind the wheelchair. Each time pressure was relieved from the pad for 4 seconds the counter registered a lift.

Before starting treatment baselines were necessary in order to know how few lifts were being made and how much improvement occurred as a result of treatment. P.W. was observed on two occasions in each of four different places: the woodwork shop, in the dining-room during lunch break, in the canteen during coffee and tea breaks, and on the ward at the end of the day. The number of lifts made in all these places was recorded. During two of the baseline sessions two observers carried out the recording in order to test for reliability between different observers. The agreement was 100 per cent.

Following these baselines the equipment was introduced in the woodwork shop. The counter was set to zero, the pressure pad placed in the wheelchair, and P.W. was told that this would count the number of lifts made, so that he would know if he was lifting often enough. He was told that the equipment was only being used in one place, woodwork, in order to give him a chance to get used to it. At the end of the session P.W. was told how many lifts he had made and praised if the number was equal to (or more than) the minimum number required (six lifts per hour). During the next week the equipment and feedback procedure were introduced in the dining-room during the lunch break. In the third stage the pressure pad and counter were used during tea and coffee breaks, and finally the equipment was introduced in the ward.

The reason for staggering the feedback procedure was to help decide whether increased lifting was directly related to treatment or was due to something else such as general improvement owing to P.W.'s becoming more settled at the unit. If it was due to treatment then improvement should occur only after the introduction of the treatment. If, on the other hand, it was due to something else then lifting should improve throughout the period being monitored, and show no relationship to the introduction of the feedback procedure.

As there was a strong association between the use of the intervention strategy and the number of lifts it appears that the feedback itself was effective rather than some general improvement. This method of staggering the introduction of treatment is known as a 'multiple baseline across settings' design.

Although the number of lifts made following the introduction of treatment was variable it was always above the minimum number required. Once equipment was being used in all situations we reduced the number of feedback sessions by combining two sessions together. At the same time P.W. began to take over responsibility for the recording. Increasing the number of lifts was, of course, a means to an end. P.W. was encouraged to lift to allow healing of his pressure sores to take place and to prevent further ones from developing. We were therefore interested to know about the condition of the skin around the pressure areas. Steady improvement took place soon after treatment began. Three weeks later the pressure sores were almost healed, and four weeks after this P.W. was allowed to use the hydrotherapy pool, which had been impossible while his skin condition had remained poor.

P.W. was seen again 10 weeks after the end of the treatment programme. His skin was still in good condition, although he was not lifting regularly. However, by this time lifting was less important, as he was spending periods on crutches and out of his wheelchair.[1]

COUNSELLING PEOPLE WITH PHYSICAL HANDICAP

The term counselling has different meanings in different contexts and for different people. It may refer to the giving of advice and information, which is the usual interpretation for the counselling offered to patients by doctors, health visitors, and therapists. Disabled people are often in need of information about drug and diet regimes, or appropriate appliances or new ways to carry out every-day activities. In each case the patient has to follow instructions from a professional, and it is the latter's responsibility to ensure that the information is clearly and unambiguously presented. Unfortunately, we know that much of the information given by doctors is forgotten or ignored. This may be due to anxiety, impaired memory, or some other disability on the part of the patient; or it may be due to an unfamiliar repertoire of language adopted by the doctor.

Psychologists can often help design the most appropriate format for the giving of information. For example, they may know whether a patient's verbal comprehension skills are sufficient to understand the language being used, or they can advise on the most readable form of written instructions for a particular patient. For people with language and/or reading problems it may be best to pass on information by drawings or diagrams, or even pantomime. For people with perceptual problems, however, these methods might be totally confusing; and in these cases simple written lists may be the most suitable form of communication. An example of the latter situation occurred for a man who had a left hemiplegia following a right cerebral vascular accident. He was rendered incontinent because of difficulty in performing actions in correct sequence. In the lavatory he stood up, urinated, unzipped his trousers, zipped them up again, sat down, and wondered why he was wet. When the instructions were written down for him he learned the steps by heart and repeated these aloud: 'Stand up, unzip, pass water, zip up, sit down.' Eventually he was able to manage without saying the steps.

Counselling can also mean advocacy, whereby the disabled person is given advice as to what to do or where to go to minimize a

---

[1] This patient is also described in Carr and Wilson (1983).

handicap. Understanding the complete range of health, social, educational, and employment services is beyond the scope of many people. Knowing what state benefits or allowances a person is entitled to is extremely difficult for newly disabled people and their relatives. Professionals may be expert in their own fields, but very few of them know about all the resources available across all the services. Some clinical psychologists believe that they should make themselves knowledgeable and act as resource centres, thus being able in some degree to point each patient in the right direction in order to solve certain living problems. Before embarking on counselling they need to equip themselves with knowledge of the patient's condition, understand the genetics (if appropriate), the causes, and the likely prognosis. They also need to know the medical steps required in the management of the condition in order to achieve the most appropriate treatment. Those clinical psychologists who counsel patients in this manner will obtain useful guidance from the *Disability rights handbook* (Disability Alliance 1990) and the *Directory for the disabled* (Darnborough and Kinrade 1989), both of which will inform them of other services which may be helpful to their patients. These books will also help to create a dialogue which is structured to enable patients to make the best possible choices for themselves and their families. If patients have problems with bureaucracy when seeking access to certain services then the clinical psychologist should be prepared to give support, and, if necessary, write back-up letters to gain the co-operation of other helpful people and organizations. Counselling of this type is of course often offered by members of several professions.

Counselling may refer to sexual advice in circumstances where a person with a physical handicap and his or her partner find sexual activities increasingly difficult. Psychologists are frequently asked to help with such problems. It is first necessary to identify what is causing the problem. Sexual drive may be diminished because of general malaise, pain, or muscle spasm, or weak, paralysed, or contracted limbs. If any of these constitute the cause it will be necessary to consider changing or introducing the use of drugs, and prior consultation with the patient's medical practitioner will be important. However, many drugs, such as anti-depressants, drugs for diabetes, and pain-killers, can diminish sexual drive. Sometimes the drug can be changed or the timing can be modified. Other solutions could involve changing positions, supporting limbs on pillows, or using methods other than straightforward sexual intercourse. Encouragement of direct communication between the disabled person and his or her partner plays an important role in this type of counselling.

Another problem may be with the patient's sexual image. Some physically handicapped people may have a very poor opinion of their bodies and feel they are not desirable to their sexual partners; consequently they do not project themselves as sexual beings. Other people who have been disabled from childhood may never have been given adequate sex education, or they may have been treated as perpetual children. Psychologists can provide sex education and teach the skills involved in forming a sexual relationship. Difficulties in sexual relationships may result from reduced opportunities to express sexuality. Somebody with paralysed arms, for instance, will find difficulty in hugging a partner. Certain conditions may make sex painful, and other methods of expression should be explored, such as the use of sexual aids. Finally, there may be a psychosexual problem which is not related to the physical disability (such as can, of course, be found in other couples without physical disabilities). In such cases a programme of re-education and psychosexual treatment such as that offered in sexual clinics may provide a solution.

Finally, counselling people with physical disability may mean supporting those who are dying. How people respond to terminal conditions will depend to a considerable extent on the explanations given to them. It is essential that anyone attempting this kind of counselling recognizes that people facing terminal illness pass through certain stages, although not necessarily in logical sequence. The spouse and children of the dying person also go through a form of anticipatory grief, and may show all the signs of bereavement. They may need as much help as the dying person at certain stages during the terminal illness (see Stedeford 1984).

CONCLUSIONS

Attitudes to physically handicapped people

Despite the professed goodwill towards physically handicapped people that is articulated in most European countries today, negative attitudes remain. This is shown, for example, by the lack of positive action on the part of society to make it possible for physically handicapped people to take a full part in the community in which they live. Rehabilitation is often seen as the bottom of the hierarchy of medical specialisms, and one of the consequences of this is that services to the physically handicapped receive the worst cuts during periods when all public services are experiencing withdrawal of funds. Clinical psychologists should be prepared to use their skills to change the attitudes and behaviour of people in the health and social services, and in the general public, towards those who are physically handicapped. Similarly, disabled clients can be helped to change *their* negative attitudes and behaviour: they can be armed with information concerning their welfare rights, and be informed of the services available to them. The learned helplessness seen in some disabled people can be reduced or avoided by encouragement to become more active in self-help groups. Physically handicapped people must be made aware of the control *they* can exercise over the environment in which they live.

Working with other staff

It is evident from this chapter that psychologists working with physically handicapped people do so in close collaboration with other staff, particularly physiotherapists and occupational therapists, and to a lesser extent with nurses, speech therapists, and social workers. At times the skills and interests of the psychologist may overlap with those of other disciplines. Some psychologists, for instance, are interested in motor problems; others may concentrate on language or perceptual deficits; others may prefer work connected with counselling. However, psychologists, having been trained in a different tradition, have few of the skills that are possessed by those other professionals with whom they work: for example, they do not have the speech therapists' knowledge of cleft palates and swallowing mechanisms; they do not have the occupational therapists' ability to make aids for physically handicapped people; nor do they possess the social workers' skills in sorting through financial benefits and future placements. Although this list of specific skills acquired and practised by other professionals is enormous, nevertheless psychologists have a general training in learning theory and behavioural methods which can be put to good use in the field of physical handicap.

Most psychologists also have a commitment to evaluate the effectiveness of their intervention procedures through single-case experimental designs or larger research studies. A smaller number will also be interested in developing new assessment and treatment procedures for use with handicapped people. Rehabilitation of people with physical handicaps will continue to improve as long as the different disciplines combine their specific skills and strengths for the good of their patients.

REFERENCES

Carr, S. and Wilson, B. A. (1983). Promotion of pressure relief exercising in a spinal injury patient: a multiple baseline across settings design. *Behav. Psychother.*, **11**, 329–36.

Collins, F. L., Jr. and Gil, K. M. (1983). Behavioural approaches to visual disorders. In *Contributions to medical psychology* (ed. S. Rachman) Vol. III. Pergamon Press, Oxford.

Darnborough, A. and Kinrade, D. (1989). *Directory for the disabled.* Woodhead Faulkner with RADAR, Cambridge.

Disability Alliance (1990). *Disability rights handbook for 1991.* Disability Alliance, London.

Harris, J. E. (1980). Memory aids people use: two interview studies. *Memory Cognition*, **8**, 31–8.

Ince, L. P. (1976). *Behaviour modification in rehabilitation medicine.* C. C. Thomas, Springfield, Illinois.

Kapur, N. and Pearson, D. (1983). Memory symptoms and memory performance of neurological patients. *Br. J. Psychol.*, **74**, 409–15.

Sohlberg, M. M. and Mateer, C. A. (1989). *Introduction to cognitive rehabilitation: Theory and practice.* The Guilford Press, New York.

Stedeford, A. (1984). *Facing death. Patients, families and professionals.* Heinemann Medical Books, London.

Sunderland, A., Harris, J. E., and Gleave, J. (1984). Memory failures in everyday life after severe head injury. *J. Clin. Neuropsychol.*, **6**, 127–42.

Wilson, B. A., Cockburn, J., and Baddeley, A. D. B. (1985). *The Rivermead behavioural memory test manual.* Thames Valley Test Company, 7–9 The Green, Flempton, Bury St Edmunds, Suffolk, England.

Wilson, B. A. and Moffat, N. (eds) (1984). *The clinical management of memory problems.* Croom Helm, London.

Wood, R. Ll. (1987). *Brain injury rehabilitation.* Croom Helm, London.

Wood, R. Ll. and Fussey, I. (1990). *Cognitive rehabilitation in perspective.* Taylor and Francis, London.

FURTHER READING

Baddeley, A. D. B. (1984). *Your memory: a user's guide.* Penguin, Harmondsworth.

Brechin, A. and Liddiard, P. (1981). *Look at it this way: new perspectives in rehabilitation.* Hodder and Stoughton/Open University Press, Sevenoaks, Kent.

Crewe, N. M. and Zola, I. K. (1983). *Independent living for physically disabled people.* Jossey-Bass, San Francisco.

Fordyce, W. E. (1976). *Behavioural methods for chronic pain and illness.* C. V. Mosby, St Louis.

Ince, L. P. (1980). *Behavioural psychology in rehabilitation medicine.* Williams and Wilkins, Baltimore.

Nichols, K. (1984). *Psychological care in physical illness.* Croom Helm, London.

Wilson, B. A. (1987). *Rehabilitation of memory.* Guilford Press, New York.

7

Working with older people
Jeff Garland

Rewards include: increased respect for human endurance; learning about the complexity of life-span development (life has to be lived forwards, but it can only be understood backwards); and the sheer diversity of encounters (ageing along various dimensions at varying rates augments individuality). The experience, in general, of old world courtesy and consideration is refreshing; there are frequent *memento mori* reminders of the ever-present need to prepare through personal development for anticipated rigours of one's own late life; there is bracing concentration of mind for both client and therapist, aware that the next life-threatening crisis may be painfully near; and at every turn there are openings for advocacy to question paternalistic patterns of care.

It is of course open to question whether older people ultimately are well served by being a subject of speciality, with possible consequences of segregation from the mainstream of clinical psychology. In an ideal world the psychology of adult health care could extend beyond 65 without a qualm. However, for the foreseeable future, a specialist service has its uses in ensuring that concerns affecting older people and their carers are not neglected.

Certainly such a speciality never wants for clients. Some 14 per cent of the population of the United Kingdom are over 65, inhabitants of 'the country of the old' mapped by Blythe (1979). Much effort with the most severely impaired old people, particularly with the growing numbers aged over 85, needs to be expended on supporting professional and paraprofessional health and social care workers, supplementing volunteers, neighbours, friends, and family drawn from a wide age-span. Preventive care is not to be neglected, and the continued campaign to improve health for 'seniors' (people over 50) offers opportunities for psychology.

TYPES AND SETTINGS OF CARE PROVISION FOR
OLDER PEOPLE

Geriatrics

This is a title properly used to define an area of medical specialization with patients usually over 65—geriatric medicine—but sometimes is misused to label patients. In-patient provision usually includes acute beds in general hospitals for emergency admission; rehabilitation beds with fast or relatively slower turnover; and continuing care wards. 'Holiday' or short-term care beds are widely used to back up community care. Day attenders are catered for by day hospitals in many localities. Outreach may include out-patient clinics, domiciliary visits and home-based support from geriatricians, geriatric liaison nurses, occupational therapists and physiotherapists, social workers, and psychologists.

It may often be difficult to tell if the problems of a given patient are primarily physical, social, or psychological; but there are as yet relatively few areas of the United Kingdom that offer a unified approach, with primary health care, social services, geriatricians, and mental health professionals working together. In many localities progress has been made in shared assessment procedures and in review panels for joint decision-making. In many instances one or more members of a mental health service may be called in for consultation by a geriatrician, either in an *ad hoc* way or as part of an established liaison service organized for crisis prevention.

Psychogeriatrics

This term refers to old-age psychiatry specializing in patients aged 65 or over, although again it is sometimes inappropriately used to describe the patients themselves. Traditionally, a local service has had some or all of the following types of in-patient provision. Continuing care wards look after long-stay patients, often with a mix of chronic psychiatric patients grown old as 'graduates' of the hospital system, and patients admitted in later life with disorders related to ageing. Assessment units are for patients who, in theory if not always in practice, come for short-stay admission. In some cases wards may mix continuing care, medium-term care, and assessment. 'Floating beds' on a rota system may be available, so that, through planned periodic admission, relief is offered to a number of patients and their supporters; and 'holiday beds' offer short-stay admission responsive to immediate needs. Many such wards also serve a small number of day patients, usually attending for from one to five days each week; and, more rarely, a few have a limited number of night 'hostel' beds catering for individuals whose management is most problematic at night.

In many areas this pattern is changing, with pressure to close large hospitals subject to heavy capital charges, to move away from the provision of continuing care, and to develop small-scale localized services primed to give early community-based support.

Many old-age psychiatry services also operate day hospitals, catering for attenders coming from one to five days each week, and may also support day centres, often run by local branches of national societies concerned with old people. Other psychiatric services are likely to include out-patient clinics, domiciliary visits, and home-based support to patients and their families, friends, volunteers, and professional staff. These services tend to rely on a front line of community psychiatric nurses, linked with social workers, psychiatrists, occupational therapists, and psychologists.

Social services

Local authorities make provision for old people apart from that made by health authorities, and, given resolution of current funding difficulties, can be expected to extend their role.

Home care schemes enable the client to stay at home with varying degrees of support. Sheltered housing with a warden provides for those becoming frail but still largely able to cope unaided. Old People's Homes are for those deemed to need full-time residential care. In some authorities homes are designated for the elderly mentally frail; in others *de facto* segregation is imposed by reserving part of each home for 'confused' residents; or relative integration may prevail.

General practice

Those doctors responsible for health care in the community, the general practitioners, are in the UK paid extra for looking after older patients because of anticipated extra demands on time. While intensive screening of this age-group does not appear to be cost-effective, an increasing number of GPs have special clinics for the over-65s, and sometimes involve a clinical psychologist through direct referral.

Community hospitals

These are relatively small units for a local community with beds controlled and serviced by local GPs. They usually have a large proportion of older patients, who are either receiving day care, in-patient rehabilitation, or longer-term care. Such units supplement the geriatric provision of larger hospitals.

Voluntary societies

There are a number of national organizations with local groups or initiatives related to local needs of old people. Age Concern, Help the Aged, the Alzheimer's Disease Society, and the Parkinson's Disease Society are examples. The psychologist and colleagues from other disciplines are likely to be found in such settings from time to time, offering consultancy or working with individual clients referred by the agency or self-referred.

Private care

Provision of private residential or nursing-home care for older people in the UK has been growing rapidly, and part-time involvement by National Health Service staff in the running of such businesses appears to be increasing. State assistance to private enterprise is provided in some cases where, on completion of active treatment and in the absence of a health or social services unit able to accept transfer, the financial resources of a resident from an NHS facility may be 'topped up' to enable that individual to enter private care, freeing a bed. Private Homes may seek consultancy from psychologists and others on general issues affecting staff training, management of difficult residents, and improving quality of life.

TYPES OF PSYCHOLOGICAL PROBLEM

Physical, social, and psychological factors interact in older people to produce increased variability in behaviour and a wide range of reactions to ageing processes. Treatable physical causes should be dealt with at an early stage, and social needs should also be met as far as possible, leaving the psychologist free to home in on residual factors; but in practice this rarely happens. Continual awareness that psychological factors cannot be approached in isolation remains necessary.

In listing the major types of psychological problem experienced by older people, we must recognize that many of these can occur in clients from other age-groups. While older people do have their characteristic concerns, they are basically just people who happen to have been around longer than the rest of us.

There is no widely accepted system of classification of the psychological challenges of late life. The common behavioural distinction between 'deficit' and 'excess' categories, which can be subdivided, offers a starting point. Interview schedules, behaviour rating scales, and other psychological tests have been widely used in large-scale surveys without as yet yielding a taxonomy that can be applied readily.

This is hardly surprising when we consider the following selection culled from records of a series of 50 new clients over a three-month period of my practice. Three main headings are: primarily physical, relating to physical activity and needs; primarily social, concerning social functioning; and primarily psychological, relating to thoughts and feelings. Some of the problems quite clearly come under more than one category.

Primarily physical

The following issues relate to physical needs and action, but have social and psychological components, since the behaviour, thoughts, and feelings of the client and others are intimately related.

Maintenance of the activities of daily living, for example dressing or undressing, or performing domestic tasks, can be disrupted in late life, so that the client requires retraining or other assistance. Maintenance of health, together with necessary compliance with medical or other treatment, may by interfered with through inability or unwillingness to act reliably in, for instance, maintaining body temperature by appropriate dress and heating.

Sleep can be less satisfying in late life, with sleep dissatisfaction tending to increase after 50, sometimes involving an exacerbation of worry over lack of sleep, leading to reduced sleep, which leads to further worry. Apparent incontinence without a direct physical cause may occur through inability to recognize a toilet, or failure to reach a toilet in time because of reduced mobility, or for many other reasons.

Primarily social

The social network of an impaired older person may be put under severe strain in attempting to cope with the major personality changes which Gilleard (1984) describes. Needs for information, reassurance, access to services, and specific counselling and advice on the understanding and management of behaviour, offer an unfolding series of challenges.

Loneliness, under-reported by older people who understandably may be reluctant to admit what can be seen as social failure, can be linked with reduced mobility, loss of attractiveness, and lack of money. Excessive requests for attention, like indiscriminate approaches with persistent questioning, may function to force social interaction from others, who would pass by without comment if the attention-seeker were quiet, preferring to 'let sleeping dogs lie'. The stress of relocation and adaptation to institutional living (the destination of about 5 per cent of older people) represents a major social upheaval, especially when the move is rapid, and the client ambivalent and still in the throes of life crisis.

Primarily psychological

Forgetfulness and memory impairment become an increasing concern for many. Clients can link everyday forgetfulness with 'Alzheimer's' or 'senility', and may develop unduly drastic or complex attempts to cover up or to cope in other ways which impose more burden than the actual memory deficit. Confusion, disorientation, and progressive inability to think straight may succeed failing memory, but do not do so invariably. This type of problem may well be episodic and patchy, particularly in its early stages, so that use of relatively convincing coping strategies can alternate with lapses during which the client can be aware that something is badly 'wrong' without being able to correct what is happening.

Anxiety, whether diffuse or relatively specific, accompanies many of the problems listed here, and appears in many forms. Depression, one of the most frequent and serious psychological challenges of ageing, similarly may appear in a variety of forms and degrees of severity. Often linked with depression, but worth considering as a separate entity, is demoralization. Low self-esteem and morale and a pervasive feeling of loss of control over one's own life may to some extent reflect the low social value of ageing and the aged in our society. A preoccupation with bodily discomfort and the maintenance of physical functions, particularly excretion, is characteristic of some elderly clients, particularly those who are depressed. Often chronic pain is experienced; but the client's signals complaining of pain can become augmented, and may function not only as a response to bodily state, but also as a means of operating on others to gain reassurance. Reaction to actual or anticipated loss—of social status, of economic or physical indepenence, of family or friends through relocation or bereavement, of one's own life—is of increasing concern in later life, and is often linked with depression or demoralization.

CERTAINLY A CHALLENGE

This is the phrase usually breathed by the awed clinical psychologist new to this client group, becoming aware that the above list could be twice as long and still not be truly comprehensive. However, the summary of practice which follows indicates that our resources are growing in response to the challenge. It remains the case that relatively few clinical psychologists devote all or even most of their time to this speciality; but this imbalance is slowly being corrected as the positive contribution which can be made is recognized.

Describing the various tasks of a clinical psychologist concerned with older people, Gottesman (1977) points to the construction and administration of tests, particularly of competence in daily living, and to carrying out counselling and therapy. Behaviour modification programmes and therapeutic environments have to be developed and a positive part has to be taken within the multidisciplinary team in administering and managing these. The psychologist has to work with community services in encouraging co-operation and new approaches, and in monitoring the cost-effectiveness of services; and act in relation to administrators as interpreter of research findings, as advocate of the needs of individual clients, and as a change agent working for the improved delivery of community care.

Assessment

It is of particular importance to use, and encourage others to use, a scientific approach. For this client group 'assessment' is too often invoked as a catch-all term, justifying emergency admission at the behest of hard-pressed community services or the client's despairing supporters. In these circumstances 'assessment' is rarely planned or related to design of treatment: it represents at best a breathing space while the multidisciplinary team seeks inspiration or moves on to the next task in hand.

As Hussian (1984) points out, there has been a shortage of psychological assessment instruments that are relevant for older people, and that have ecological validity in sampling the experience and activities of daily living. Some encouraging advances have been made in the area of brief cognitive assessment with the Rivermead Behavioral Memory Battery and with MEAMS (the Middlesex Elderly Assessment of Mental State); but the user of a psychological assessment service, asking 'What will the results contribute to the management of this case?', still needs guidance. Appropriately, the specialist psychologist is increasingly likely to offer a user's manual for such a service, since data on techniques or tests for use with older people can be complex and conflicting.

An example of a useful brief test is CAPE (Clifton Assessment Procedures for the Elderly), which consists of a congitive assessment and a behaviour-rating scale. CAPE is unusual in translating scores into levels of dependency characteristic of ability to cope with different environments, from independent living at home through to continuing care in a psychogeriatric ward.

Neuropsychological assessment can make a valuable contribution to diagnosis, to prognosis, to design of therapy for individual deficits, and certainly to the morale of some clients and their supporters. It can be a relief to hear that an observed specific impairment in cognitive functioning is not an indication of 'going mad' or 'becoming senile'—that its causes can be understood and explained clearly, and that many other aspects of intellectual performance can be shown to be relatively normal. Tests such as the Revised Kendrick Battery have shown a way forward for attempts to establish the sometimes difficult differential diagnosis between dementia and depression in older people.

Many clinicians use criterion-referenced testing, evaluating the client's ability to meet a criterion specified in the test. For example, in the assessment of testamentary capacity, or the ability to make a valid will, an old person's estimated ability to manage her or his own affairs, and make an informed decision on disposal of assets may be evaluated most usefully by constructing a personalized multiple-choice assessment of information and orientation with content selected for relevance to the direct demonstration of competence. There has also been progress in the objective assessment of family burden and strain felt by supporters of mentally frail older people living in the community.

Direct observation of behaviour, and of levels of engagement or constructive activity in institutional settings, can quickly point to priorities for management. For example, a man was admitted to hospital from an Old People's Home as 'physically aggressive' and 'incontinent'. Nurses did immediate event-recording when taking him to the toilet, recording any physical aggression or incontinence. In 25 consecutive observations he was wet once, and there was no aggression. Comparative observation of toileting approaches in the Home and in hospital revealed a confident approach by the hospital staff, pre-empting the frequent refusals and related incontinence, with an aggressive response when this was pointed out, which had been reported by the more tentative Home staff. Developing more assured staff behaviour in the Home through nurses' guidance, rather than concentrating on the resident's attributes of 'aggression' or 'wilful' incontinence, became the focus of a successful intervention.

Frequency, duration, timing, or intensity of a problem behaviour can be established by observation, as a baseline against which change can be evaluated. For example, a woman who 'wandered' around a ward was reported by staff as doing this 'all the time'. Structured observation for three days, using time-sampling, taking in this case a 5-second observation hourly, revealed that this was not the case. She was walking about on 47 per cent of the observations; but settled behaviour coincided with activity initiated by staff, such as feeding, washing and conversation. Again, how others were able to influence her behaviour became a focus for action.

Observer ratings, self-rating scales, and the varied techniques of naturalistic observation are favoured by psychologists; but it can be difficult to involve care staff, many of whom have difficulty of fitting structured observation into their notion of 'the real work' of care, and feel uncomfortable with what looks like a passive role while their colleagues are being visibly active.

PRINCIPLES OF INTERVENTION

There are 10 guiding principles for psychological intervention important for any client group, but particularly valuable for this relatively neglected and disadvantaged population.

1. Emphasize early action, producing minimal disruption for the individual.
2. Maintain the client's independence as far as possible.
3. Consult fully with the client and principal carers and supporters.
4. Establish the client's needs, and what incentives will help to meet those needs.
5. Reflect on the advisability or nature of an action before starting.
6. Work through carers and supporters in general.
7. Encourage objective assessment throughout intervention.
8. Set out action in small, specific steps, which are clearly understood.
9. Review progress with participants periodically.
10. Evaluate outcome and follow-up where necessary.

These guidelines are flexible. Despite point 6, for example, the psychologist needs to retain direct involvement with some clients to keep therapeutic skills sharp and to maintain effectiveness as a consultant. For some 'difficult customers' that no one else wants there will be no alternative.

Reality orientation

Reality orientation (RO), the best-known training approach for 'confused' older people, has two main forms. 'Classroom' RO is conducted with a small group or less frequently one-to-one, and cues, prompts, and selectively reinforces successive approximations to improved orientation. Information is shared with clients, recognition and repetition of general or personal information is encouraged, sensory stimulation is given, the environment is clearly and attractively labelled, and trainers are active in drawing out responses and offering correction or praise. Twenty-four-hour reality orientation, or 24RO, extends this approach as a model for consistent practice around the clock.

RO is a philosophy of care rather than a specific treatment, and effectiveness has been difficult to evaluate. However, a specific aspect of RO, the use of directional signs to which residents' attention is persistently drawn by staff, has been shown to reduce 'wandering'; and clinical psychologists have been active in developing individual applications of RO.

Validation therapy

RO is not always the approach of first choice with a 'confused' client. Validation therapy focuses on sharing and understanding the experience of the client as a pre-requisite for re-orientation.

For example, Marjorie, a 68-year-old in a wheel-chair after successive strokes, distressed fellow-patients and staff on a geriatric ward by repeatedly calling out, 'I'm going to have a baby!' Lecturettes on gynaecology and many other well-meant attempts at RO had proved of no avail, as her calling out continued.

I found from case-notes that she had miscarried several times and had no children, and guessed that she might be reliving these experiences of distress and pain. Our dialogue confirmed this, and gradually we were able to progress through to her present predicament, and to exploring how the ward team would have to take the place of her lost children, looking after her the best way we could. It was natural, we agreed, for her to revert to her former experience of hospitalization, threat, and loss, and this did not make her the 'daft ha'p'orth' that she had felt herself to be.

Thanks to nurses who gave her the necessary support in maintaining this insight, Marjorie's subsequent help-seeking became more appropriate in expression, and less frequent: the cry 'I'm going to have a baby!' did not recur.

Counselling

Many clinical psychologists counsel demoralized clients with an integrative model based on the capacities and strengths which normally develop in the course of growing old to overcome the demoralization which can be produced by the losses of ageing. Successive levels of counselling input are: meeting the material needs of the immediate situation; offering support and promoting efforts to stabilize self-esteem and morale; assisting the client to feel more in control of her or his life situation; and building positive long-term changes in self-concept and self-esteem. For the client who is facing bereavement, or who is in terminal care, specialist counselling techniques may be added.

Reminiscence and life review

In reminiscence, small groups are encouraged to share memories, stimulated by newspaper files, sound archives, photographs, films, and other sources. Private as well as public recollections gradually emerge, and group members are prompted regularly to return to the present to compare 'things then' and 'things now', and to appreciate the many challenges they have faced.

Life review is a more personal one-to-one therapeutic exercise in collaboration with a therapist, evoking pattern and meaning in a unique experience of life, and relating past events to present state within a sense of integrity.

Improving intellectual functioning

Wisocki (1984) reminds us that we tend to exaggerate the effects of ageing, which are less severe, more specific, and more amenable to efforts to cope than we might suspect. For example, memory-training programmes have drawn with success on a variety of techniques. These include: progressively lengthening by gradual increments the period of time over which memory is required; the use of external aids such as sign-posts, colour-coding of doors, and the use of diaries or notebooks, alarms, or other cues to prompt recall; and the use of internal aids such as visual imagery to build face–name links or identify places needing association with items to be remembered. Clients with relatively early or mild impairment can be expected to benefit most from such approaches in out-patient 'memory clinics'; but their lasting effectiveness is uncertain.

Coping with anxiety and depression

Anxiety is common with older people, and is amenable to anxiety-management training, although response tends to be slower and more difficult to sustain, possibly because everyday life holds more anxiety-provoking stimuli for older people.

Depression in late life is a major problem, yet anti-depressants have a risk of serious side-effects with this age-group, and the relapse rate after ECT is high. Prospects for cognitive therapy, in which the client is helped to identify and alter depressive patterns of thinking, having recognized their influence on mood state, are therefore of particular interest.

Cognitive therapy in a context of life review

Cecily, an 81-year-old widow living alone, referred herself by letter, after reading a newspaper account of a talk, 'Take Umbrage', I gave at an Age Concern meeting. I had recommended assertive behaviour by older people frustrated by unresponsive health care services. Also I had outlined the psychology of doctor–patient communication, as indicating ways in which patients could make themselves understood.

Cecily had heart disease, cerebrovascular insufficiency, and arthritis. Recurrently depressed (tearful, negative, given to suicidal thoughts and gestures), she had been attending a psychiatric day hospital. Well-known at the health centre for her frequent consultations, she had shuttled among the partners.

With the agreement of her current doctor I visited her, to find her complaining that she was 'confused' about her medication. She produced a pile of 14 different drugs, with antidepressants, tranquillizers, and sedatives prominent, prescribed over the previous three years. After most of these had been removed and her medication reviewed, we began life review, as her main concern was that her life had become 'useless to anyone, without meaning'.

Periodically, using life review material, we moved into cognitive therapy, confronting:

1. Her enduring belief that she was inadequate and 'just not good enough', so that it was dangerous to allow herself to get too close to other people. She traced this back to when she was 10, had been in trouble at school for fighting the battles of smaller children, and her mother had begun to warn repeatedly, 'You'll never come to any good!'

2. Her son in Australia who had not written lately had abandoned her as unworthy! Reviewing this possibility, we discovered that she had ended her last letter with, 'Don't come to my funeral.' Had he read 'I wouldn't be seen dead with you'? Oh no, she had meant, 'Please come now, don't leave it until you come to my funeral!' She sent a more explicit letter, and communication restarted.

3. Her pattern of 2 a.m. 'depressive' thinking when she woke was to reproach God for not having allowed her to die in her sleep. To replace this we arranged a comfort routine—flask of tea by the bed, radio with all-night programme ready tuned, her book of prayers, and a photo of her granddaughter, 'my reason for living'.

4. Recording and reflecting on her current achievements: giving support to the granddaughter in coping with a chronic illness, befriending new attenders at her church, baby-sitting for neighbours. As anticipated, Cecily developed further strengths, 'so I can have something different to write', she told me, as I admired a jaunty beret she had just bought.

(After 12 sessions over 39 weeks, self-rating on Brink's depression scale moved from 23, indicative of clinical depression, to 7, within normal limits.)

Older people have been shown they can develop positive patterns of thinking and ability to cope in stressful situations, such as their admission to residential care. Introducing subvocal self-statements such as 'This place is home now and I'm going to make the most of it' are one component of such cognitive therapy. In community health care studies clients aged 60 to 80 have been shown to benefit from cognitive classes on 'coping with depression'.

Reducing preoccupation with discomfort

For older people it is vital for them to recognize when they are not healthy so that they can take appropriate action. While many report increased bodily discomfort or pain, only a minority become excessively preoccupied. This minority can be an extremely vocal one, suffering and causing others to suffer, and becoming the target of intensive investigations and treatments which rarely yield long-term relief. A psychological intervention involves systematically withdrawing attention for complaining, giving attention and other rewards for 'well' behaviour, and above all encouraging distracting activities. These may include relaxation and the use of mental imagery to view discomfort and pain as controllable.

Rehabilitation

Psychologists are often asked to design and implement programmes for chronic psychiatric patients who return to the community after several decades of institutionalization. These programmes include modules of training in the activities of daily living and in social skills.

It is increasingly common for psychologists to advise on incentive programmes for those older post-stroke patients commonly described as 'lacking motivation'.

The staffing of 'movers' groups is necessarily multidisciplinary, but often offers particular opportunities for a psychologist. These groups integrate rehabilitation effort by giving clients feedback on progress, using successful 'graduates' as models, and by sharing information on requirements of the community settings to which moves will be made.

Behavioural deficits and excesses

As Hussian notes, many interventions by clinical psychologists working with older people in residential care have been directed at overcoming a lack of normal activity. Significant increases in constructive activity have been achieved by behavioural management procedures in, for example, self-feeding and personal hygiene. The basic approaches are those used for all client groups in these settings, such as helping the client to link specific desirable behaviour with particular features of the environment (stimulus control) and selectively reinforcing such behaviour.

Behaviour management can also reduce excess or high-rate behaviour. Excessive complaining has already been mentioned: significant reductions have also been achieved in, for example, inappropriate urinating, and with unwanted sexual approaches. Some of the main issues emerging in behavioural intervention with the elderly are addressed below, since the clinical psychologist's participation is essentially as researcher, teacher, and consultant. In some respects—for example, in family therapy with the client and immediate supporters—the psychologist will be found to be directly intervening to meet social and psychological needs. In general, though, his role as a scarce resource may be found more productively in research, teaching, and consultancy.

CONSULTATION AND TEAMWORK

As clinical psychologists are generally in short supply for all client groups, the necessity of transferring psychological knowledge and skills to non-psychologists must be recognized. This is particularly true for work with older people, where even in a relatively well-staffed locality the number of psychologists will be very few.

Traditionally, though, the therapeutic process of developing knowledge and skills in the client (and, with family therapy, in immediate supporters), has been through direct intervention. This has been seen as the 'real work' of clinical practice, fundamental to job satisfaction.

Less gratification has been perceived in consulting and teaching, viewed as a process of transfer of knowledge and skills to professionals, paraprofessionals, volunteers, and supporters. The traditional stance has been rooted in a tendency to perceive consultation and teaching as being primarily enforced by a lack of psychologists, and to consider the process one-sidedly as a depleting putting-in of expertise. Increasingly, though, the profession has come to appreciate the intrinsic value of consultancy as a mode of working, and to understand that in a joint effort to achieve change the consultant is recharged by the human potential drawn out by a successful intervention at this level.

Team or network?

With older people, as with other client groups, the multi-disciplinary team is a generally recognized unit of clinical practice. In theory, such an entity should foster consultation and teaching, since shared problem-solving and collaborative effort is implied. In practice, the working of the 'team' may create difficulties for consultation: members may protect expertise rather than share it in a trans-disciplinary style; paraprofessionals from within the same agency may be seen as only marginal members; and, more importantly, the interests of clients and supporters are not represented directly within the team.

In clinical practice the crucial venue for consultation and teaching is a specific support network, consisting of the client and other individuals with responsibilities in the assessment, management, and continued care of the older person. The most important criterion for effectiveness of consultation then becomes the condition of the network. If it is fine-tuned and responsive to change in the client's situation, consulting within that network should be efficient. Knowledge and skills 'given away' in conventional training, rather than earned by shared effort within a care network, may be less likely to be integrated effectively as increased psychological-mindedness in the non-psychologist.

GERONTOLOGY

Clients need to be understood in the context of gerontology, the scientific study of the normal and pathological changes occurring with ageing. In the social and behavioural aspects of this science the psychologist should be equipped as an information resource. A client may ask: 'What can I do about my failing memory?' A supporter: 'If we build a "granny flat" would it help?' A therapist: 'Why do so many patients get "stuck" in our rehabilitation programme?' In some cases it may be desirable only to offer access to information, encouraging the enquirer to draw her or his own conclusions.

Within gerontology, the following themes are of particular clinical interest.

Support for supporters

It has been wisely said that families of impaired older people need to be supported by professionals, but not supplanted. Such support is provided by many agencies in face-to-face contact with families, ranging from small *ad hoc* groups of supporters to national organizations such as the Alzheimer's Disease Society. While there are a number of excellent community care projects, there is also much muddle because many sources of support are involved, and beliefs differ about 'what supporters really need'.

Supporters identify three main types of need: emotional support, ranging from the reassurance of contacts with 'someone who listens', to intensive regular counselling where a care network is under intense pressure from guilt, anger, and physical exhaustion; information about, and access to, resources such as attendance allowance, transport, aids, day care, or holiday relief; and advice on techniques in coping with disturbed feelings or behaviour.

It has been suggested that the supporters who complain loudest get more than their fair share of assistance; that abuse of older people by their supporters is more frequent than is generally supposed; and that precipitate support may undermine families' commitment.

The psychologist will be involved both in direct consultancy to enhance supporters' skills, and in indirect advice to them on how service and supporters' needs can be matched more closely, and in recommending how such issues as suspected abuse should be dealt with.

Assessment

The psychologist offers consultation to others who may wish to use, or adapt, psychological assessment. Advice may be required by community psychiatric nurses wishing to evaluate the level of burden on supporters, or by doctors dissatisfied with traditional brief 'mental state' examinations. Some specialized instruments—for example, neuropsychological evaluations—may be retained by the psychologist; but the case for retaining assessment as an exclusive function should be examined carefully, rather than be taken as for granted.

Behaviour management

Consultation is a recurring issue, particularly with care staff who may be unwittingly maintaining a client's undesirable behaviour by inconsistent responding.

Such was the case with Agnes, who had been physically attacking fellow-patients and staff in a geriatric ward. Observation showed carers were responding in at least nine different ways: scolding; ignoring; separating antagonists; distracting her attention; secluding her; forcing her to apologize to the victim; slapping her lightly on the wrist with the injunction 'see how you like it!'; avoiding the situation by leaving the room; and even sitting Agnes down for tea and sympathy and asking her reasons for attacking others (these, in the classic delinquent response, were usually given as 'I don't know', and 'I won't do it again'.) The only consistency in her management occurred when she was not attacking someone. Then, she was studiously ignored. Consultation in this case focused on reversing contingencies, with an agreed standard minimal response to aggression, and a variety of positive responses when she was otherwise engaged. (This led, in one week, to a 70 per cent reduction in her attacks.)

Consultation on behavioural problems of impaired older people can draw from a 'menu' of procedures from which selection can be made according to carers' resources. An example is provided here, for the understanding and management of food refusal, by Violet, a resident in an Old People's Home. Staff were extremely concerned because sustained weight loss had brought her down to 40 kg. In-patient investigation by a geriatrician had shed no light on any physical cause of her refusal: her GP and a psychiatrist agreed that she was not mentally ill; and she affirmed that she did not want to die, and kept promising that she would resume eating and drinking normally (her fluid intake was being maintained, although at a low level and with much persuasion.)

With Sarah, a CPN, and care staff at a one-hour meeting in the Home, these guidelines evolved:

MENU: UNDERSTANDING AND MANAGING
FOOD REFUSAL

1. Maintain daily monitoring of weight on chart Sarah has hung in staff lounge.

2. Our aim at first should be to reduce rate of weight loss. It might not be realistic to expect immediate weight gains: it is most important to slow and stop loss of weight.

3. It is better for the time being for Violet to eat apart from other residents. Their comments—whether friendly or critical—may distract her, rewarding her with attention for not eating.

4. It is better for Violet to have some prompting from you when food or drink is placed before her. Otherwise her concentration is likely to wander and she will tend to 'forget' what she should be doing.

5. Understandably you are anxious about her and frustrated by her repeated refusals. It is important not to let your anxiety or frustration show when you are prompting Violet, as her awareness of such feelings is likely to interfere with her appetite. Stay calm if you can—try to relax for a moment or two immediately before you begin prompting her.

6. Keep conversation about food or drink to a minimum. When you start, give just one reminder that she needs to eat and drink to stay alive and to stay at the Home. Repeated questioning about why she is reluctant to eat or drink or how you could tempt her appetite is unlikely to yield useful information, and may actually put her off.

7. When you are with her keep your prompts mainly physical (lightly lifting her chin, gently aiding her to raise a glass to her lips, etc.).

8. If she raises objections such as 'I don't like it', do not respond directly ('why not?' 'it's very nice', etc.). Talk about something else for a few moments, then say 'time for some more' and start her drinking or eating again.

9. Give her just a little food on her plate. A normal portion probably looks like a mountain to her. It is better to present her with literally three spoonfuls on her plate and have the plate cleared than to present her with a full plate and have her take just two spoonfuls.

10. A dietitian may assist us with recommendations on intake and how this should be presented (realistically, taking into account what your kitchen can manage).

11. Sarah or Jeff could if you wish meet Violet's son to discuss her management with him so that he is fully informed and gets a chance to express his feelings.

12. Sarah and Jeff are each to make some visits to share with you in assisting her to eat and drink and to record her reactions. We all

need to share ideas to see if we can identify useful approaches we can all use in a consistent way.

(Over 6 weeks the chart recorded a gain of 5 kg, and Violet began to eat and drink spontaneously without assistance.)

Adapting institutional care

While residents whose behaviour presents a major challenge may need to be helped in adapting to their environment, the institutional environment itself needs to be shaped, like a prosthesis, so that the resident can be as independent as possible within the constraints of institutional life. Psychological approaches to reshaping care take four interrelated forms: stimulation and activity programmes; planned changes to the physical environment; 24RO; and behavioural management that consistently shapes and rewards constructive behaviour, while limiting attention given to behaviour of a destructive or needlessly dependent nature. The significance of 'environmental docility' in impaired older people has been well documented by psychological research, indicating that as competence decreases external environment factors become progressively more important in determining behaviour.

Occasionally a psychologist can be directly involved in planning the design of a new residential setting. In general, however, change is hard-won.

For example, the demands of 24RO should not be underestimated. Working consistently to remind an impaired resident of reality and to maintain a positive attitude demands dedication.

Hazel, a care assistant, tried with me to build a more personal relationship with a resident by teaching her her name. Over several days the resident made 26 unsuccessful attempts, but No. 26 held promise: 'Something to do with nuts, dear? Brazil? ... No, Hazel!' Hazel sat slumped. Somehow, for her, it no longer seemed to matter that much. With enthusiasm born of relief I congratulated the resident and Hazel, rekindling some of Hazel's interest. As this kind of experience illustrates, reshaping residential care takes time.

Psychologists have noted that certain routines in care of older people, such as bed-making or drug rounds, need no prompting. Others, such as activity programmes or reality orientation, appear remarkably subject to extinction through neglect. It has been suggested that the former are more stable because they are more visible, so that neglect would be noticed, and that they are in any case secure as they are seen as the 'real work' of care. Perhaps they also involve less close personal contact with residents who are likely to be severely impaired, and whose response to contact is at best hesitant and limited.

Staff support

To work with this client group demands adaptive skills of a high order. There is a heavy demand for services, while resources tend to be scarce or ill-coordinated. Health care networks can be fragile and their structure complex, rarely admitting of straightforward solution. The 'burn-out' syndrome linked with high absenteeism and low morale is not unknown in teams serving older people; and it is not uncommon for a psychologist to consult with others to give or receive support.

RESEARCH

The clinical psychologist is likely to be involved in fundamental research in clinical gerontology and in action research evaluating service, as well as participating in the work of other members with advice, general support, and collaboration if required.

There is now a substantial body of research with older people. Effects of impaired memory and problem-solving are beginning to be well understood, and compensatory programmes have been developed. Action research effort is growing, although there is still a major need to evaluate a mass of findings.

To illustrate this point, it has been shown repeatedly that increased occupational therapy resources in continuing care bring a corresponding increase in the habitually very low level of constructive activity shown by most residents. When resources are withdrawn, activity reverts to its original level.

Important questions then arise. In cosmetic terms increased activity looks good, but can it be shown to benefit residents? If it does, how can we devise intermediate types of occupational activity, attractive enough to engage both residents and direct-care staff who would be required to supervise in the therapists' absence?

Psychological research into intervention with older people has been remarkably inconclusive in some respects. For example, reality orientation is a well-known procedure which has been widely researched. According to some studies it yields modest gains in intellectual functioning, and considerable benefits for the morale of carers, who are able to interact with more confidence, and report greater satisfaction with what they do. However, the rationale for RO is debatable, and it has been suggested that it is such a complex procedure that it is impossible to date to conduct adequate research, as no evaluation could implement RO comprehensively or consistently enough.

Another area of uncertainty relates to research on psychological management of apparent incontinence, that is incontinence where no primary physical cause can be found. Outcome studies have produced mixed results, and one factor in accounting for this is lack of care in screening subjects, so that some clients were included who could not have been expected to respond to psychological retraining.

However, standards of research into the effectiveness of behavioural treatments for older people are improving, and a substantial body of literature is evolving (for some useful reviews, see Carstensen and Edelstein 1987).

In terms of fundamental research in clinical gerontology, investigation of early psychological correlates of chronic brain failure, 'this epidemic of our time', is being pursued in Oxford and a number of UK centres; and a number of complementary investigations of provision and co-ordination of support for those who care for such clients are under way.

It is important for the clinical psychologist working with older people to maintain a research interest in the relatively healthy. For example, I am finding that an ongoing study of individuals over 65 active in the Oxford area in campaigning for improved economic, health, or social conditions for their peers is not only a useful resource for community practice, but also gives balance to my perspective on this age-group.

ADMINISTRATION AND POLICY-MAKING

Apart from internal administration of a specialist professional service, the psychologist is expected to contribute to broader planning. There are four major goals.

1. To move toward a unified health and social care provision which recognizes the identity of interest between the sectors already mentioned.

2. To establish a service data-base with objective assessment of clients' functioning, as a basis for classifying the categories of challenge.

3. To develop services' responsiveness to needs of clients and supporters. The Niskanen Effect—systematic bias in providing what suits the service rather than what clients necessarily require—is too frequent.

4. To support regular systematic audit of operationally defined care procedures. All too often, what is actually done in work with older people is left unresolved and unclear, and terms such as 'assessment' or 'support' conceal more than they reveal.

CONCLUSIONS

Work with older people is a distinctive speciality for a number of reasons: the universality of ageing, so that we face in clients our own potential future; the aversiveness of ageing for many of us; the relative frequency of premature termination of work through the client's death; the nature of the required knowledge base in social and behavioural gerontology; the need to master specialized assessment and treatment approaches; operation in age-segregated settings; the relatively high incidence of physical symptoms interacting with social and psychological problems; and a high frequency of iatrogenic complaints related to multiple treatments and idiosyncratic responding. Also, we must consider: the prevalence of work through carers rather than directly with clients; family dynamics complicated by parent–child role-reversal, and expectations of paternalistic care; clients with a prolonged investment in current coping strategies, with strong resistance to change; older people's healthy scepticism of the psychological—'there's nothing wrong with my mind'; and comparatively greater evidence of barriers to communication—cognitive impairment, fatigue, and sensory impairment.

Within this speciality, in which they have a relatively brief history of involvement, clinical psychologists have drawn attention to individual psychological needs, developed assessment procedures, devised therapeutic interventions to produce demonstrable change, and contributed to a substantial literature in clinical gerontology.

Our need now is to ground our contribution more securely within the psychology of adult development and ageing, making a lasting contribution to the understanding of the process of late life, and the complex and often conflicting systems which enmesh older people.

Gerontophobia, a relatively common complaint among health care professionals, is a suitable case for treatment. A treatment package may need to embrace not only *in vivo* exposure to a wide range of older people, but also the practical application of well-grounded theory as a form of cognitive therapy to probe and modify assumptions of service providers and users to fit fact rather than fancy.

Clinical gerontology, the scientific study of normal and abnormal changes in health care needs with ageing, is the core knowledge unifying many health-related disciplines. The relevance of clinical psychology for late life is measured by practitioners' effectiveness in developing and applying this body of knowledge.

REFERENCES

Blythe, R. (1979). *The view in winter. Reflections on old age.* Allen Lane, London.
Carstensen, L. L. and Edelstein, B. A. (eds) (1987). *Handbook of clinical gerontology.* Pergamon, New York.
Gilleard, C. J. (1984). Living with dementia. *Community care of the elderly mentally infirm.* Croom Helm, London.
Gottesman, L. E. (1977). Clinical psychology and aging: a role model. In *Geropsychology: a model for training and clinical service* (ed. W. D. Gentry) pp. 1–7. Ballinger, Cambridge, MA.
Hussian, R. A. (1984). Behavioral geriatrics. In *Progress in behavior modification* (ed. M. Hersen, R. M. Eisler, and P. M. Miller), Vol. 16, pp. 159–83. Academic Press, New York.
Wisocki, P. A. (1984). Behavioral approaches to gerontology. In *Progress in behavior modification* (ed. M. Hersen, R. M. Eisler, and P. M. Miller), Vol. 16, pp. 121–57. Academic Press, New York.

FURTHER READING

Birren, J. E. and Schaie, K. W. (eds) (1990). *Handbook of the psychology of ageing* (3rd edn). Van Nostrand Reinhold, New York.

Bond, J. and Coleman, P. (1990). *Ageing in society. An introduction to social gerontology*. Sage, London.

Hanley, I. and Hodge, J. (eds) (1984). *Psychological approaches to the care of the elderly*. Croom Helm, London.

Holden, U. P. and Woods, R. T. (1988). *Reality orientation. Psychological approaches to the 'confused' elderly* (2nd edn). Churchill Livingstone, Edinburgh.

Mace, N. L. and Rabins, P. V. (1985). *The 36-hour day. Caring at home for confused elderly people*. Hodder & Stoughton and Age Concern, London.

Woods, R. and Britton, P. (1985). *Clinical psychology with the elderly*. Croom Helm, London.

8

Working with offenders
Ronald Blackburn

INTRODUCTION

The role of all health care professionals is constrained by the organizational structures of care delivery. For clinical psychologists working with offenders, these constraints are compounded by the legal requirements of the criminal justice system, which dictate who receives psychological services, and where. Current services are therefore as much the outcome of social policies as of the expanding role of clinical psychologists, and an understanding of work in this area requires first some discussion of the interface between the penal system, health care, and the social services.

TREATMENT OF OFFENDERS AND THE PENAL SYSTEM

The penal system functions to protect society from those who violate the criminal law, and does so through penalties which exact retribution, deter would-be offenders, or incapacitate the most harmful. The extent to which it also takes the offender's welfare into account reflects changes in attitudes to crime in the late nineteenth century, which have provided the basis for current services. The most important concern mentally disordered offenders, juvenile offenders, and rehabilitation as a goal of the penal system.

Mentally disordered offenders

Legislation for detaining offenders who are excused legal punishment on the grounds of mental disorder originates from 1800. This led to the creation of the 'criminal lunatic asylum', and as the courts turned to physicians for advice on the mental state of offenders, forensic psychiatry developed as a medical speciality charged with overseeing the detention, care, and release of mentally ill or mentally retarded offenders. Procedures for diverting mentally disordered offenders from legal punishment to health care were thus already in place at the time of the inception of the NHS, and these were effectively consolidated by the 1959 Mental Health Act for England and Wales, and its 1983 revision (Scotland and Northern Ireland have slightly different, though comparable legislation).

The Act defines mental disorder as 'mental illness, arrested or incomplete development of mind, psychopathic disorder and any other disorder or disability of mind', and on medical evidence that an offender found guilty suffers from such disorder, disposal options available to the court include imprisonment or a fine, a probation order with conditions of in-patient or out-patient treatment, or a hospital order requiring compulsory detention in hospital. The Crown Court may additionally impose a 'restriction order', which prevents a detained patient from being discharged from hospital without the consent of the Home Secretary. However, the 1983 revision of the Act gave power to Mental Health Review Tribunals, which are independent judicial bodies, to discharge a restricted patient under certain conditions.

The majority of mentally disordered offenders dealt with under the Act are diverted to the NHS. Over 10 per cent of involuntary admissions to psychiatric or mental handicap hospitals are admitted under a hospital order, although these make up less than 1 per cent of offenders convicted of crimes other than motoring offences. Other offenders may also be dealt with as out-patients under a psychiatric probation order. Some offenders are therefore likely to be referred to clinical psychology departments in the course of ordinary NHS practice.

However, about 200 a year are admitted to the Special Hospitals. These are maximum security hospitals, which under the 1959 Act are for patients who 'require treatment under conditions of special security on account of their dangerous, violent or criminal propensities'. There are four such hospitals in Britain, these being Broadmoor, Rampton, Ashworth (created in 1990 as an amalgamation of the former Moss Side and Park Lane Hospitals), and the State Hospital in Scotland. Together, they house some 2100 patients, four-fifths of them male. About 70 per cent have committed serious crimes such as murder, arson, or sexual assault; but the hospitals also admit prisoners who become mentally disordered while in prison, and psychiatric patients who exhibit serious violence in other hospitals. Until 1989, the hospitals were administered directly by the Department of Health, but are now administered by a Special Health Authority. Clinical psychology departments were established in the hospitals in the 1950s, and these have developed in parallel with their NHS counterparts.

The treatment of mentally disordered offenders came under critical scrutiny during the 1970s, partly because of declining psychiatric facilities for patients requiring moderately secure containment, but also because research questioned the ability of clinicians to predict future dangerousness. One consequence was the report of the Butler Committee (Home Office/Department of Health and Social Security 1975), which influenced the 1983 revision of the Mental Health Act. One of its important recommendations was to set up Regional Secure Units (RSUs) in the English and Welsh regions to provide 'medium' secure facilities for disruptive NHS patients and mentally disordered offenders.

RSUs are now seen as a base from which a specialist service to the community can develop through liaison with the courts, the penal system, and community agencies, as well as the NHS and Special Hospitals. All secure units have established posts for clinical psychologists, resulting in a significant increase of psychological services for offenders. While the units are headed by forensic psychiatrists, and accept in-patients under the Mental Health Act, close working with agencies such as the probation service has allowed psychologists to provide out-patient services to offenders, such as sex offenders, who may not be disordered within the meaning of the Act, but whom the courts accept are suitable candidates for psychological treatment.

Juvenile offenders

Since the turn of the century, most countries have operated separate systems for juvenile and adult criminal justice. A 'juvenile' is someone under the age of 17, and disposals available to the court include care orders transferring responsibility to local authority social services, which may entail the child's remaining at home, being placed with foster parents, or residing in a community home. They also include supervision orders, similar to probation orders, which may require attendance at intermediate treatment schemes aimed to involve the child in recreational, educational, or social activities in the community. Regular involvement of clinical psychologists in the juvenile court appears to be infrequent; but child offenders in the care of social services may be referred to educational psychologists, or to NHS child clinical psychologists; and a few clinical psychologists have taken an interest in intermediate treatment.

As a result of a gap in the provision for dangerous juveniles, two Youth Treatment Centres were established in the 1970s, one at St Charles in Essex, the other at Glenthorne in Birmingham, to accommodate boys and girls exhibiting severly disruptive behaviour, or who have committed serious offences. While providing a range of educational, therapeutic, and rehabilitative services, they are non-medical institutions, although psychiatrists, clinical psychologists, and social workers provide consultancy services.

Rehabilitation of offenders

Although only a small minority of offenders is diverted from the penal system to mental health facilities, the treatment ethos has been extended to those who remain subject to legal penalties. Beginning with reforming efforts of eighteenth-century Quakers, legal punishment came to be seen as an opportunity to correct offenders, and the impetus to rehabilitate offenders was sustained by the development of psychology and sociology. Early psychoanalytic theories encouraged the view that many offenders not considered mentally disordered may none the less have personal adjustment problems. While more recent psychological theories view antisocial behaviour more in terms of failures of appropriate social learning than of intrapsychic conflict, the emphasis has remained on rehabilitation as a process of correcting individual deficits or problems.

During the 1970s, however, rehabilitation as a penal goal came under attack. In addition to questions about the ability of clinicians to forecast dangerous behaviour, research findings indicated that despite the range of therapeutic programmes provided for offenders, 'nothing works' in terms of reducing reoffending. However, more recent evidence has justified continued faith in rehabilitation (Gendreau and Ross 1987).

Nevertheless, rehabilitation has always been an uneasy bedfellow of the punitive goals of the penal system, and specialist therapeutic services have typically been available to only a limited extent. A few penal establishments in Britain have had visiting psychotherapists for some years, and a treatment prison run on therapeutic community lines was set up at Grendon Underwood in 1962. Since 1946, the English prison system has also had its own psychological service. However, the number of prison psychologists (currently about 100) is small relative to the prison population, and few of these are clinical psychologists. Much of the work of the service is therefore directed to the needs of prisons as social organizations, and includes training and support for prison officers, consultancy services for management and planning, and research into the functioning of prisons as well as the problems of offenders (McGurk *et al.* 1987).

PSYCHOLOGICAL PROBLEMS OF OFFENDERS

There are no firm figures on the extent of psychological difficulties among offenders; but a substantial number have problems ranging from serious mental disorder to more focal and less serious disabilities, which may none the less warrant attention to improve their chances of rehabilitation. Research shows that anxiety, low self-esteem, poor impulse control, and social skill deficits are common among prisoners, and British estimates suggest that about a third have problems associated with alcohol and drug abuse or personality disorder. This last shades into interpersonal problems of varying severity.

The problems of offenders dealt with under the Mental Health Act are defined in terms of psychiatric disorder. *Mental illness* is not defined, but generally covers the most serious mental disorders, such as schizophrenia, affective psychosis, or organic disorders; and the majority of patients in Special Hospitals and RSUs fall in this category. *Psychopathic disorder* is 'a persistent disorder or disability of mind, whether or not including significant impairment of intelligence, which results in abnormally aggressive or seriously irresponsible conduct on the part of the person concerned.' *Mental impairment* and *severe mental impairment* refer to 'a state of arrested or incomplete development of mind which includes significant impairment of intelligence and social functioning and is associated with abnormally aggressive or seriously irresponsible conduct on the part of the person concerned', and hence essentially covers mentally handicapped people who are also 'psychopathic'.

The psychological problems presented by mentally disordered offenders overlap with those found in the mental health system generally. Mentally ill and mentally impaired offenders, for example, present problems of motivational and social deficits typical of long-stay patients, although they often also exhibit socially unacceptable behaviour, such as aggression, which impedes their return to less restricted environments. Therapeutic goals are therefore to provide the necessary coping and interpersonal skills which will enable them to survive in their optimal environment, whether an open hospital, a hostel, or their own home.

About a quarter of patients in Special Hospitals, and a smaller proportion of those in RSUs, fall into the 'psychopathic disorder' category. This has always been a contentious category, not least because of its vague criteria, but also because of the doubts of many that 'psychopaths' are treatable. In practice, the category includes the more serious violent and sexual offenders who additionally show personality disorder. The term 'psychopath' has been much abused in Britain as a 'catch all' for a variety of socially problematic behaviours, and patients in the psychopathic disorder category are heterogeneous in personality and the problems they present (Blackburn 1988).

Personality disorders cover a variety of deviant traits, such as impulsivity, egocentricity, hostility, or emotional coldness, which are not amenable to medical treatment; and psychological interventions are seen as the treatment of choice. However, psychologists typically redefine such disorders in terms of interpersonal skill deficits and dysfunctional cognitive styles and belief systems relating to self or others. The following two case histories illustrate some of the problems of patients said to exhibit psychopathic disorder.

Martin was a man in his early thirties, who was a 'professional' burglar with a long criminal record, mainly for housebreaking, but including rape. When arrested for his most recent housebreaking attempt, he was found to be armed, and confessed to plans to kidnap the householder. Psychiatric examination revealed proneness to depression, and preoccupation with fantasies of kidnapping and terrorizing women, and he was admitted to an RSU. It emerged that he had long-standing relationship difficulties beginning with his mother, stepfather, and brother, and subsequently with a succession of girlfriends, who all terminated their relationship with Martin because of repeated conflict. He had developed intense resentment

of women, but also felt unable to trust anyone. He frequently interpreted casual remarks as a 'put down', and this induced feelings of
depression alternating with anger, which usually led to attempts to
humiliate the perpetrator. Most of his burglaries were, in fact, a
revenge on women he felt had 'put him down' in the course of his
regular work as a salesman (of burglar alarms!), and were frequently
followed by humiliating telephone calls to the victim. This behaviour
pattern emerged as a generalized interpersonal style within the unit.
He readily perceived remarks of staff and patients as a 'put down',
would brood about them, and become vindictive. This took the
forms of hurtful comments to those he saw as putting him down,
sometimes of physical attacks, and of querulous letters to senior
managers. He consequently generated widespread antagonism,
which served to exacerbate his hostile beliefs, depressed mood, and
angry outbursts.

Gary was a young man with several convictions for indecent
exposure (exhibitionism or 'flashing'), and minor thefts. His most
recent incidents of exposure, however, were accompanied by physical assaults on his female victims, and threats with a knife. Interviews
revealed violent fantasies of rape and killing females, depressed
mood, and a history of social avoidance. He also had considerable
sexual problems, including anxieties about social and sexual interactions with females, erectile failure when he attempted intercourse,
excessive masturbation, and frequent urges to expose himself. His
violent fantasies were traced to the termination by a girlfriend of a
brief adolescent affair, which he attributed to her becoming a 'prosti-
tute'—an interpretation resulting from her developing an interest in
wearing heavy make-up and provocative clothes. He felt intense
hatred towards women he perceived as 'prostitutes', and this occa-
sioned his recent assaults. In addition to feeling depressed, he was
also frequently tense and anxious, and felt a failure in most areas of
his life. He also had a long record of unemployment, partly due to his
lack of skills, but also to impulsively leaving his jobs, and was
inclined to get into financial difficulties because of heavy gambling
and drinking.

Both of these patients display antisocial behaviour associated with
more general problems of distorted interpersonal beliefs, mood disorder, and inappropriate social behaviour. However, Martin is intelligent, articulate, and overtly self-confident, and has a belligerent
style, whereas Gary is of limited ability and deficient in social skills,

and tends to be timid and avoidant. Where Martin's problems centre particularly on hostility and anger, Gary's are primarily focused on sexual difficulties and social anxiety, associated with an idiosyncratic view of women. In each case, psychological treatment needs to address multiple problems.

Who gets treatment?

The most seriously disturbed offenders tend to be diverted to health care facilities, but many end up in prison, and there is considerable overlap between the populations of prisons and those of secure psychiatric establishments. The decision as to which offenders get access to clinical psychological services depends partly on availability of staff, but also on filtering processes within the criminal justice and health care systems.

The first filter occurs at the court stage. Since the courts process over 2 million cases a year, evidence on psychological problems will be sought in only a fraction. Psychological involvement tends to depend on good working relationships with psychiatrists, solicitors, or probation officers who are receptive to psychological perspectives; but while the number of offenders referred directly to psychologists from the courts has increased with the development of regional forensic services, the numbers remain relatively small. The second filter occurs after an offender has been dealt with by the court, and involves the decision of psychiatrists, and occasionally probation officers or social workers, to refer to a psychologist. Patients admitted to secure health care facilities have the most ready access to psychologists, although this has not always been guaranteed, as a result of recruitment problems in these services.

At the end of 1990, just over 100 clinical psychologists were working regularly with offenders, four-fifths of them in RSUs or special hospitals. Overall this represents a tenfold increase over two decades, and about 4 per cent of national manpower. It will be apparent that services are most likely to be provided for those in secure facilities in the health care system, although some with less serious problems will receive services from prison psychologists.

ROLES OF PSYCHOLOGISTS

The kinds of service provided by clinical psychologists for offenders vary according to their work setting and the legal procedures through which they receive their clients. For example, psychologists attached to RSUs spend much of their time working with clients in the community, while those in security establishments work within the constraints of a closed setting, which may itself create problems for both inmates and staff.

Models of service delivery parallel those found in health care generally. Most commonly, the psychologist is a member of a ward or unit multidisciplinary team of staff responsible for the care of a group of patients. In the Special Hospitals, for example, the team usually consists of a consultant psychiatrist, a social worker, a psychologist, and a charge nurse, while teachers and occupational training staff may attend team meetings as appropriate. Psychologists working in secure settings also provide consultancy services for professionals outside the team. However, this calls for a similar range of assessment and treatment tasks, which are considered in more detail below.

In a team context, the psychologist does not receive referrals as such, but rather negotiates the kind of involvement most likely to be productive. This has the advantage that the more pressing psychological problems are defined by the psychologist, rather than a referring agent. Collaboration between disciplines is also more likely in a team system. For example, the psychologist may work with nursing members in devising and implementing a rehabilitation programme for a particular patient, or with the social worker or psychiatrist in running a therapy group. Similarly, team psychologists are more likely to participate in group decision-making about patients with whom they are only indirectly involved, and can contribute an alternative perspective on such issues as the granting of parole.

Advocacy

Clinical interventions normally terminate when client and therapist agree that therapeutic goals have been achieved. In secure psychiatric settings, however, legal powers of discharge rest with the consultant psychiatrist for patients detained under a hospital order, and with the Home Secretary or a Mental Health Review Tribunal for those detained under a restriction order. Psychologists who assume responsibility for a major part of a patient's treatment are therefore often obliged to take on the role of patient's advocate after treatment has ceased. The prime task then becomes to convince other team members, governmnent officials, or a Tribunal that sufficient change has occurred for discharge or transfer to less secure conditions to be appropriate.

Offenders whose crimes are morally repugnant or difficult to comprehend invite little public sympathy, and are viewed with caution not only by officials responsible for public safety, but also often by care staff. There may therefore be strong resistance to arguments that an offender is ready for discharge, even when these are buttressed by objective measures of change, since predictions of behaviour in the natural environment from behaviour within the confines of a secure institution can only be tenuous.

In functioning as an advocate, then, the psychologist must defend a psychological interpretation of the patient's behaviour, marshal evidence of change from clinical observations and psychological tests, and present this in written reports or verbal arguments at team meetings or Tribunal hearings. While these arguments are not always accepted, the following kind of success may be sufficient to prevent demoralization.

Peter was admitted to a Special Hospital following an attack on three youths with a knife. For some months prior to the attack, he had been unemployed, isolated, withdrawn, and unkempt in appearance. The attack appeared unmotivated, and schizophrenia was diagnosed. While several psychiatrists subsequently commented on the absence of psychotic symptoms, the label persisted, and his rather odd, withdrawn, and unco-operative behaviour in hospital was attributed to persisting psychosis. The team psychologist, who was asked to evaluate Peter's social interactional skills, found him initially anxious and unforthcoming, but gradually learned that prior to the offence he had become depressed and left his job because of the death of a workmate for which he blamed himself. On his occasional walks, he had been taunted by the three youths for his unkempt appearance, and after they attacked him on one occasion, he bought a knife for protection. The offence followed further taunting and fears that he was about to be assaulted again. His unco-operative behaviour in hospital reflected resentment at what he saw as punishment for justified self-defence. Psychological testing showed no evidence of psychotic symptoms or cognitive impairment, but clearly indicated that Peter was an anxious, introverted, rather hostile, but unaggressive and socially unskilled person. While some of the team remained convinced that Peter was psychotic and dangerous, the psychologist presented an alternative formulation, relating his offence behaviour to depression and limited coping skills, and his hospital behaviour to anxiety and resentment. After a few sessions of anxiety management, Peter became more relaxed and co-operative. The team subsequently accepted the psychological formulation, and recommended his transfer to less secure facilities.

Staff support and consultancy

Psychological treatment methods are of limited value for many mentally disordered offenders, particularly those who exhibit florid psychotic symptoms. For much of the time, the primary therapeutic needs of such patients are likely to be medication and nursing management. However, while many offenders present few problems of management within an institution, their offences may invite negative reactions from staff, and some may be disruptive and un-co-operative. High-security establishments also often dictate an emphasis on security and containment, and a mistrust of inmates, which conflicts with therapeutic goals. Staff who work directly with offenders may therefore find their work stressful because of conflicting aims and uncertainties in their dealings with patients, particularly in units containing a high proportion of disturbed individuals. Similar problems arise in high-security prisons.

One role for psychologists in such settings is to provide staff support. This most commonly takes the form of group sessions, in which staff are encouraged to examine the basis for their negative reactions to particular individuals and alternative explanations for inmate behaviour. Sessions may also focus on coping skills required for inmate management, including training in basic behavioural techniques.

Psychologists also provide consultancy services to support management. Some psychologists, for example, have developed particular skills in dealing with hostage-taking situations, and provide advice when such incidents arise. While these are rare in mental health settings, they have become more frequent in prisons during the past decade. They call for skills of negotiation and of monitoring the state of hostage-takers and their relationship with the hostage if the incident is to be terminated without harm to the latter.

Forensic psychology

Forensic psychology describes a particular legal role in which psychological findings are used to assist legal decision-making, and it is not synonymous with clinical work with offenders. Nevertheless, it is a role which some clinical psychologists exercise regularly. Lionel Haward is a clinical psychologist who has achieved recognition as an expert witness by providing evidence to the courts for many years. He believes that clinical psychologists are particularly well placed to develop the role of forensic psychologist more generally because of their research training, and that they may assist the courts in more than purely clinical matters. His own contribution has included evidence in obscenity trials as well as mercantile disputes (Haward 1981).

In criminal cases, the forensic role of the clinical psychologist may include the presentation of psychometric findings on the characteristics of an offender, an assessment of likely response to treatment, or the setting up and reporting of a psychological experiment to clarify a critical point of evidence. For example, in one case of dangerous driving, a police officer claimed to have noted the registration numbers of four motor cyclists who passed him in a town at dusk, allegedly driving at 60 miles per hour. Haward was asked by the defence to investigate the credibility of this perceptual feat, and had 100 observers attempt to identify four number-plates presented for a comparable duration under similar lighting conditions. Since only five subjects correctly identified one number, and none two, Haward concluded that it was highly improbable that the officer's claim was valid. However, the psychologist's evidence was not accepted on this occasion, since the prosecution called a children's psychiatrist, who, armed with a copy of a physiology textbook, testified that the eye could see moving images more easily than stationary ones!

The prediction of dangerousness is one aspect of forensic psychology in which those working in secure settings engage regularly, since the legal decision to release a mentally disordered offender from detention depends on such evidence. However, as was noted earlier, the capacity of clinicians to forecast future dangerousness has been shown to be limited. The evidence suggests that clinicians typically overpredict dangerousness, in so far as many of those predicted to be dangerous will not in fact reoffend. The problem lies not only in our limited knowledge of what determines dangerous behaviour, but also in the low frequency, or *base rate* of such behaviour, even in offender populations. When the base rate is low, a clinical judgement or a predictive index will be less accurate than the blanket prediction that everyone is non-dangerous.

The latter statistical solution is clearly unhelpful to courts or Tribunals, who look to psychologists and psychiatrists for forecasts of the future behaviour of an offender. Since such predictions have to be made, the search continues for improved objective predictors. However, a more promising approach is to improve on clinical judgements by utilizing findings from psychological research on decision-making. This has identified many of the biases which reduce the accuracy of everyday decisions, such as failure to take account of base rates. It is therefore possible to train professional decision-makers to make more accurate predictions by avoiding these biases.

CLINICAL ASSESSMENT OF OFFENDERS

As in other areas, emphasis has shifted from providing diagnostic and prognostic information from psychometric tests to more direct involvement in treatment. Nevertheless, broad-based assessment combining interviews, tests, and individualized measures, and providing reports for others continues to be important in work with offenders. Apart from identifying and monitoring specific problems which are the focus of psychological treatment, objective psychological measurement may contribute to the way in which other staff deal with a patient—for example, by providing explanation and understanding of an offender's behaviour, as in the case of Peter described above. Moreover, those responsible for decisions to release an offender frequently rely on objective evidence of how far problems contributing to dangerous behaviour have been resolved, even though direct psychological intervention may have been negligible.

Psychological assessment of offenders draws on a variety of procedures commonly used in mental health settings. These include standardized tests of intelligence, personality, cognitive functioning, and social attitudes, and also more specific, often unstandardized procedures to assess emotional reactions to particular situations, beliefs about the self and others, or social skills. Methods used more particularly in work with offenders are illustrated by approaches to the evaluation of aggressive and sexual problems.

Assaultive behaviour tends to be an attempt to control a situation which the aggressor finds threatening, and is now generally understood in terms of cognitive processes and interpersonal skills. For example, research with violent delinquents has shown that they readily jump to conclusions about the intentions of others, and fail to consider future consequences. They also frequently lack skills for resolving minor conflict, and minimize the harmful effects of their behaviour. Assaults occur most commonly when people believe, whether mistakenly or not, that their physical or psychological well-being is intentionally threatened or thwarted by another person; when they are in the habit of resorting to coercion to obtain their ends; when they lack skills for resolving conflict by non-aggressive means; or when they fail to consider long-term consequences as a result of temporary situational factors, such as domestic stress or alcohol intoxication. The commission of an assault therefore invites questions about the immediate situation and how the offender perceived it, the relationship to the victim, and the offender's habitual interpersonal behaviour patterns. Answers suggested by the initial interview are explored and tested out by means of general and specific assessment procedures.

A general assessment of personality traits provides initial evidence of the personal characteristics which may contribute to assaultive acts. For example, not all criminal assaults are committed by habitually aggressive people. For *overcontrolled* people, who are typically unaggressive and have difficulty expressing feelings of anger, the assault may be a last resort when threat seems overwhelming. Peter is an example of such a person. Others may be *undercontrolled*, and resort to violence frequently as a result of easily aroused anger, and a lack of controls in the form of concern for others or future consequences. The writer has developed a standardized questionnaire, the SHAPS (Special Hospitals Assessment of Personality and Socialization) to assist in making this kind of distinction. It consists of 213 questions requiring 'yes' or 'no' answers (for example, 'Are the people who run things usually against you? Do you easily get impatient with people? Do you often get so annoyed when someone pushes ahead of you in a queue, that you speak to them about it?'). Answers are summed to yield scores on 10 scales (Lie, Anxiety, Extraversion, Hostility, Shyness, Depression, Tension, Psychopathic deviate, Impulsivity, Aggression). These are converted to standard scores to permit comparison with, for example, adult males in general. The more a score diverges from average, the more likely is the trait to be a dominant feature of the person's behaviour. Figure 8.1 shows the SHAPS profiles of Peter and Martin. It will be apparent that both have rather hostile, suspicious attitudes, and are prone to depressed mood and tension. However, Peter is shy and introverted, controlled (low impulsivity), and unaggressive; whereas Martin is socially confident and outgoing, prone to act on impulse, and aggressive in his dealings with others.

This kind of general picture indicates typical behavioural styles which may suggest personality disorder, and also identifies potential problem areas for treatment, but is simply a first step in assessment, which will usually include more specific tests, individualized measures, and observations from sources other than the offender's self-report. More individualized measures include structured

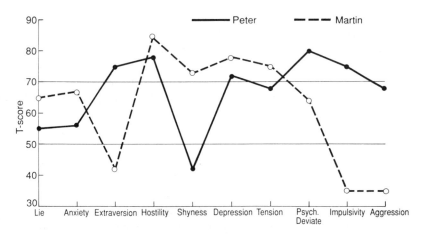

Fig. 8.1 Personality profiles on the SHAPS of two patients. A T-score greater than 70 is statistically abnormal relative to the normative sample mean of 50.

methods such as the Repertory Grid. This examines the dominant themes in people's interpretations of their interactions by means of comparisons of perceived similarities and differences in evaluations of significant people and events. Less structured are diary records or logs, in which the person notes incidents arousing anger and aggression, and the associated thoughts and coping attempts. Finally, assessment methods not relying on self-report include ward rating scales in which staff estimate the frequency of particular behaviours, such as 'gets involved in heated arguments' or 'boasts about his achievements', from which everyday styles of interaction can be assessed. Role-plays may also be set up in individual or group settings to examine how the person deals with provocation, and the kinds of interpretation and expectation elicited by such events.

The assessment of sex offenders is equally multifaceted, and requires attention to general interpersonal styles and expectations, beliefs about the victims of sexual assaults, knowledge of sexual matters, which is frequently deficient, fantasies used during masturbation, and specific skills in heterosexual interactions. Sex offenders often develop deviant preferences for children or vulnerable victims because they lack adequate skills of interacting and forming intimate relationships with adult females. These can again be assessed to some extent by diary records, role-plays, and specific self-reports.

One of the more central concerns in assessing sex offenders, however, is the strength of interest in particular kinds of sexual partner or practice. The most valid measure of this in males is penile tumescence to sexual depictions. In *penile plethysmography*, small erectile changes in the penis are measured by means of a thin mercury-filled rubber tube or a lightweight caliper-like device which encircles the penis, and which transmits a continuous electrical signal to a graphical recorder. Stimuli are presented under laboratory conditions, and may be slides portraying targets of possible interest, such as pictures of nude children, videotapes of varying types of sexual activity, or audiotaped descriptions. The procedure usually involves comparing tumescence to different stimuli, from which sexual preference can be determined.

Figure 8.2 presents a summary of such an assessment of a rapist with a history of sadistic behaviour towards prostitutes. The stimuli consisted of four two-minute videotaped portrayals (in this case, simulations by professional actors) of mutually consenting sexual

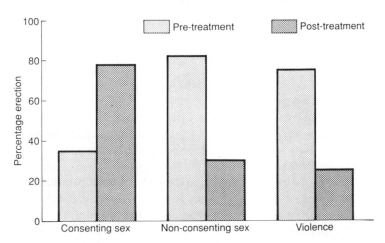

Fig. 8.2 Mean maximum erectile response of a rapist to three categories of stimulus material, pre- and post-treatment.

interaction, non-consenting coercive sex, and non-sexual violence to a female, these being presented in random order. The figure shows the maximum level of penile erection attained during these three stimulus categories, expressed as a percentage of full erection. As will be apparent, pre-treatment responses are predominantly to the more deviant, violent component of heterosexual interaction. Responses following two years of broad-based treatment, however show a significant reduction in these and a concomitant increase in sexual arousal to socially acceptable activity.

Penile plethysmography is clearly a sensitive procedure, which raises ethical issues about the often pornographic materials used; and psychologists in the Special Hospitals have therefore agreed a code of practice to cover the protection of the materials used, informed consent of patients who participate, and the conduct of staff who administer the assessment. The method also raises practical and technical issues which have been the subject of considerable research. For example, some patients can suppress their response by using distracting thoughts. While there are sometimes pressures on psychologists to use it as a 'lie detector' in cases where an offender claims to have lost his deviant interests, but verification is difficult to obtain, such use is contraindicated, as well as being ethically dubious. The procedure is most useful as one component of assessment in monitoring the treatment progress of well-motivated patients.

Offending behaviour is usually only indirectly the target of psychological treatment, although there are several reports in the literature, mainly from North America, of psychological clinics specializing in specific categories of offender, such as drunk drivers, minor sex offenders, or shoplifters. It has been found, for example, that shoplifting is commonly associated with distorted beliefs about the crime (for example, 'It won't harm anyone'; 'Shopkeepers deserve it'); and cognitive therapy groups have been set up in which these beliefs are challenged. However, clinical psychologists in Britain are more likely to deal with such problems when they are referred in a mental health context. Gudjonsson (1990), for example, reports dealing with 'compulsive' shoplifting on an out-patient basis, usually through psychiatric referral. In, this case, the targets are the depression, anxiety, and low self-esteem which the shoplifting behaviour functions to relieve.

Psychological interventions with offenders vary with the orientation of the psychologist, which may be behavioural, psychodynamic, or cognitive. However, cognitive–behavioural approaches have dominated recent developments, and will be emphasized here. Within this framework, intervention usually focuses on deviant belief systems and skill deficits. An early application of behavioural approaches, for example, was social skills training. Such training, using role-play, modelling, and feedback, usually in group settings, has differed little from that employed with other populations. However, its indiscriminate use with offenders has recently been criticized, particularly since there is little evidence that social skill deficits characterize all offenders, or that social incompetence is causally related to crime. There is also only limited evidence that the effects of institutional social skills programmes generalize to the natural environment, or reduce reoffending. While such training has not been abandoned, it is increasingly applied more selectively, usually as one component of a broad-based treatment.

Treatment of violent offenders

Violent offenders are not homogeneous, and hence do not respond to any single treatment approach. Among those who are aggressive with some frequency, aggression may serve different purposes. A distinction is commonly made between *instrumental* aggression, in which aggression secures some desirable goal (for example, in robbery), and *angry* aggression, which relieves a state of anger. For those who use aggression instrumentally, the problem is to change a style of behaviour which is maintained by rewarding consequences. In institutional settings, contingency management has been used to deal with repetitive aggression. Aggressive acts may be followed by loss of rewards or privileges, or by 'time out from reinforcement', i.e. brief removal from the opportunity to engage in rewarding activities. Alternative ways of attaining desired goals can also be taught. At least some aggressive offenders lack non-aggressive, assertive skills, and may generate conflict by their confrontational style. Social skills training focusing on conflict resolution has therefore been used in some programmes.

Recent approaches give greater weight to cognitive processes and the content of social beliefs. The ability to recognize interpersonal problems, generate alternative solutions, test these out, and act on the most appropriate has been found to be deficient in socially deviant populations, including aggressive delinquents. In problem-solving training, everyday problems posing a barrier to the attainment of a goal (for example, when someone wishes to watch a different TV channel) are examined in terms of the sequence of steps from problem recognition to resolution. Training consists of instructions and modelling, role-plays, and feedback, and may include the use of self-instructions. The aim is to generate a generalizable skill in which encounters with interpersonal problems will produce constructive resolutions rather than confrontation and aggression. Aggressive offenders also commonly hold distorted beliefs, such as that violence is legitimate, that it enhances one's image, or that victims suffer little. In group contexts, change has been achieved by having offenders develop and present arguments refuting these beliefs.

Most acts of serious violence probably involve angry aggression, although a proneness to experience excessive anger characterizes some overcontrolled offenders as well as the more habitually violent. *Anger management* is a treatment package originating in the work of an American psychologist, Raymond Novaco, which has become increasingly popular in work with offenders (Howells 1989). The programme may be conducted with individuals, though more commonly in groups, and aims at regulation and control of the experience of anger so that it can lead to constructive interpersonal outcomes. Attention is paid to four components thought to be significant in anger arousal: triggering events; cognitive appraisals of these events, including the person's self-statements (private speech); physiological arousal, which is experienced as tension; and behaviour when angry, which may include avoidance as well as aggression.

The programme proceeds through three stages. The first is cognitive preparation. The patient is introduced to the rationale of the programme, is given an instruction manual, and begins a diary record of anger experiences, both to facilitate awareness of the relation between anger and self-statements, and to monitor progress. Diary incidents form a basis for examining cognitions in subsequent sessions, when the conditions eliciting anger are reviewed, and distinctions made between justified and unjustified anger. At the skill-acquisition stage, the patient is taught how to reappraise anger-eliciting events in terms of possible alternative intentions on the part of the source of anger; to shift from a personal to a task orientation in confronting difficulties; and to employ self-instructions during an angry exchange. The self-instructions are statements which guide coping attempts ('I can handle this'; 'Resolve the problem, not the feeling'), and provide self-reinforcement ('I'm handling this situation well'). Relaxation training is given as a further self-control skill, and skills of assertion and negotiation are taught using modelling and role-play. The third stage is application practice, in which developing skills are applied and tested in graded simulated anger situations. This procedure is promising in dealing with the problems of violent offenders; but anger management in isolation is unlikely to be sufficient for serious offenders, who typically have multiple problems. This underscores the need for systematic individualized assessment.

Treatment of sexual deviation

Not all abnormal sexual behaviour is illegal, nor are all illegal sexual acts abnormal. Intervention is, however, ethically justified when there is a victim involved, and particularly when the offender is a recidivist. Most work is therefore conducted with rapists, child molesters, and exhibitionists. Psychological treatment is now typically broad-based, and targets include not only the deviant sexual act, but also the interpersonal difficulties and faulty cognition which often support it.

The central aims of behavioural treatments are to modify sexual preferences by enhancing non-deviant arousal and reducing deviant arousal. Procedures for enhancing arousal include masturbatory reconditioning, which involves associating orgasm with non-deviant sexual stimuli. The patient is required to switch his sexual fantasies during masturbation from his arousing deviant fantasies to socially acceptable fantasies as orgasm approaches. He carries this out as 'homework' over an extended period. Fading is a laboratory method with similar aims, in which pictures of adult females are superimposed on pictures of the preferred sexual stimulus when arousal level is high, as monitored by the plethysmograph.

Reduction of deviant arousal can be achieved by chemical suppression of male hormones, although this itself does not facilitate learning of non-deviant behaviour. More common has been the use of aversion therapy, in which portrayed or fantasied deviant acts are associated with brief electric shocks or foul odours. However, this procedure raises ethical concerns, particularly when applied to compulsorily detained offenders. Covert sensitization is an alternative approach to 'compulsive' problems, based on operant principles of punishment and negative reinforcement, which relies on the patient's imagining aversive effects of the behaviour to be eliminated, rather than on the physically unpleasant stimulation of aversion therapy.

Part of the treatment programme for Gary, one of the 'psychopathic' patients described earlier, aimed to deal with his indecent exposure, since his urges to expose himself persisted in hospital, and on a few occasions he exposed himself to female staff. In this case, covert sensitization began with a behavioural analysis of the sequence of antecedent events and thoughts leading to exposure, and its usual consequences, and tape recordings were made describing these events in incidents described by Gary. Certain consequences he identified as aversive (shame, physical pain, fear of arrest) were described on the tapes as occurring at critical points in the behaviour sequence. A final scenario described him exercising control over his urges early in the sequence, and the rewarding consequences of this. The tapes were played for an hour in 12 weekly sessions, and Gary also listened to them on his own between sessions. His self-monitoring of urges to expose himself revealed a decline from an average of two to three daily prior to treatment to less than one a month six months after treatment, and no further incidents occurred. While his urges were not completely eliminated, he described them as controllable and less powerful.

It should be noted that, in Gary's case, this procedure was only one component of treatment, which also included cognitive therapy for depression, hetero-social skills training, and counselling to deal with his stubborn, self-defeating behaviour. In general, modifying sexual preferences is unlikely to have a durable effect unless accompanied by modification of wider patterns of beliefs and social behaviour. Rape, for example, is frequently associated with anger and humiliation of the victim, and may serve more of an aggressive than a sexual function, expressing hostility towards women. Many rapists also subscribe to 'rape myths' about the desire of women to be subjugated. Additionally, a high proportion have difficulties in sexual performance, such as erectile failure or premature ejaculation, which occur in their normal sexual relations as well as during the rape. These problems are addressed by confronting attitudes towards females and sexual behaviour, by anxiety-reduction methods, and by treatment of sexual dysfunction where appropriate.

Social skills training directed towards hetero-social interactions is also a regular component of programmes for sex offenders. Exhibitionists in particular are often timid and unassertive, and lack simple skills of conversing with females, while child molesters may also experience social anxiety when interacting with adult women. Sex education programmes which focus on both basic sexual anatomy and psychological aspects of sexual experience have also been found to reduce heterosexual anxiety and to change beliefs about the acceptability of coerced sex to victims.

Psychological treatment of sex offenders, and indeed of offenders generally, is more analogous to remedial education than to medical treatment, and the notion of 'cure' as the goal is inappropriate. The most realistic goal is often to enable the offender to manage his problems without reoffending; and this may require periodic support over several years. In these terms, an occasional relapse as a result of unforeseeable stress does not necessarily represent treatment failure. Nevertheless, programmes which have been followed up have been found to reduce the rate of reoffending among those treated, compared with those not receiving treatment. Although this is not always dramatic, particularly in the case of rapists and exhibitionists, Perkins (1987) notes the cost benefits of treatment to both the justice system and potential victims for each reconviction prevented.

The effectiveness of treatment of offenders

Not all offenders have treatable emotional or social problems, but evidence suggests that psychological disabilities among apprehended offenders are more prevalent than in the population at large. Clinical services are therefore justified whether or not these problems are the cause of offending, and this applies as equally to those receiving legal punishment as to those diverted to the mental health system. In these terms, the effectiveness of treatment must be judged by clinical criteria of alleviating distress and disability, and not necessarily by effects on criminal behaviour.

Nevertheless, humane concerns for the well-being of offenders also include their future conflict with society, and the prevention and reduction of offending is both a legitimate and an expected goal of clinical psychological services to offenders. This has been clouded by widespread pessimism about the utility of these and other professional services aimed at the rehabilitation of offenders, because of the earlier evidence that 'nothing works'.

However, recent reviews of the rehabilitation of offenders suggest that this pessimism is unwarranted (Gendreau and Ross 1987). While by no means all psychological approaches to offenders have been systematically evaluated, controlled follow-up studies have shown that well-designed programmes can reduce recidivism by more than 50 per cent. These include relatively brief programmes for delinquents, as well as the more specialized programmes for disturbed offenders emphasized in this chapter. Most effective are programmes which focus on social–cognitive functioning, particularly those directed to empathy and role-taking skills, moral reasoning, and self-control methods, such as anger management.

Research is commonly cited as a major function of psychologists working with offenders, in keeping with the scientist–practitioner model which has guided the development of clinical psychology. This emphasizes training in research skills, and assumes that practitioners will both critically consume the products of research in the scientific literature and generate research relevant to methods of practice and knowledge of abnormal behaviour. The model has always been controversial, since surveys suggest that most psychologists do not carry out research after qualifying. Some have therefore characterized the model as the triumph of hope over experience!

The writer recently surveyed the research contribution of psychologists in the special hospitals over the three decades from the mid-1950s onwards, which proved to be extensive. This work represents 40 per cent of all publications from the special hospitals, and despite being one of the smallest professions there, psychologists produced more research than any other group. Three-quarters of the research was devoted to basic questions about mentally disordered offenders, notably cognition, personality, interpersonal behaviour, or psychophysiological characteristics of subgroups of violent and sex offenders and psychopaths. A search of publication citation indices revealed that although many studies attracted little attention, several were cited regularly over the years, and had thus become part of the body of knowledge about mentally disordered offenders. The scientist–practitioner model thus seems to exert a continuing and significant influence in this area.

CONCLUSIONS

This chapter has emphasized some of the more distinctive problems dealt with by clinicians working with offenders. However, crimes occur in social contexts which provide not only stress or temptation, but also encouragement for antisocial behaviour. Psychological treatments therefore need to look beyond the individual, and support the development of new cognitive and behavioural skills in the offender's natural environment. Increased opportunities for working with offenders in the community are thus likely to enhance the effectiveness of interventions.

Psychological services nevertheless represent only a part of the network of facilities provided for offenders, and given the small numbers of psychologists working in this area, it would be unrealistic to expect that the currently available services will have a major impact on 'the crime problem'. However, for every serious offence prevented, there is one less victim. This is, perhaps, an ample justification for psychological intervention.

REFERENCES

Blackburn, R. (1988). On moral judgements and personality disorders: the myth of psychopathic personality revisited. *Brit. J. Psychiat.*, **153**, 505–12.

Gendreau, P. and Ross, R. R. (1987). Revivification of rehabilitation: evidence from the 1980s. *Justice Quarterly*, **4**, 349–407.

Gudjonsson, G. H. (1990). Psychological treatment for the mentally ill offender. In *Clinical approaches to working with mentally disordered and sexual offenders. Issues in criminological and legal psychology*, No. 16 (ed. K. Howells and C. R. Hollin), pp. 15–21. British Psychological Society, Leicester.

Haward, L. R. C. (1981). *Forensic psychology*. Batsford, London.

Home Office/Department of Health and Social Security (1975). *Report of the committee on mentally abnormal offenders*. HMSO, London.

Howells, K. (1989). Anger management methods in relation to the prevention of violent behaviour. In *Human aggression: naturalistic approaches* (ed. J. Archer and K. Browne), pp. 153–81. Routledge, London.

McGurk, B. J., Thornton, D. M., and Williams, M. (eds) (1987). *Applying psychology to imprisonment*. HMSO, London.

Perkins, D. (1987). A psychological treatment program for sex offenders. In *Applying psychology to imprisonment* (ed. B. J. McGurk, D. M. Thornton, and M. Williams), pp. 191–207. HMSO, London.

FURTHER READING

Blackburn, R. *Psychology and criminal conduct: theory, research and practice*. Wiley, Chichester. (In press.)

Cooke, D. J., Baldwin, P. A., and Howison, J. (1990). *Psychology in prisons*. Routledge, London.

Howells, K. and Hollin, C. R. (eds) (1989). *Clinical approaches to violence*. Wiley, Chichester.

9

Working with alcohol and drug misusers

Ray Hodgson

In 1979 the Royal College of Psychiatrists produced a special report on Alcohol and Alcoholism in which they emphasized that: 'The scenes of our concern must embrace houses, streets, offices and factories, courts and prisons as well as consulting rooms, casualty departments and hospital wards. It must include the families and children, neighbours, workmates and the other road-users who are inevitably and repeatedly going to be involved.' This statement could be directed at all clinicians working in the alcohol and drug service, including clinical psychologists. In fact, clinical psychologists tend to perceive themselves as clinical and community psychologists, since a great deal of their work is directed towards community services and community interventions. Clinical psychologists are usually involved in community alcohol teams and community drug teams, if such teams exist in their district. They also co-operate with other sectors and organizations, including education, social services, the police, probation, and employers.

Some of this work will be described in the following pages; but the first priority must be to outline the psychological model of addiction that most clinical psychologists adopt.

CHANGES IN DEFINITIONS AND THEORIES

The simple disease model of alcoholism and drug addiction suggested a dichotomous categorization into normal drinkers or drug users on the one hand and alcoholics or addicts on the other. This 'all or none' model has now been overtaken by a rather more psychological approach, which emphasizes a continuum of dependence and views drug use as an acquired motivational state rather than a disease. This emerging psychological model embraces the following basic assumptions:

1. *Drinking and drug use is learned.* We learn about alcohol and drugs from parents, peers, books, films, and the broadcast

media. Some of the effects will be learned in this way. Others are learned through direct experience; and the likelihood that a person will have direct experience of heavy drinking or drug use will depend upon a wide range of psychosocial factors, including occupation, personality, subculture, price, and availability. Numerous direct experiences are involved, some of them powerful and others more subtle. Reducing and avoiding anxiety is one of the most frequently reported effects; and, among those who are becoming more dependent on drugs, quickly passing from an agitated state of withdrawal back to normality is a powerful reinforcing experience.

2. *Psychosocial processes are crucial.* In both social drinkers and those who are more severely dependent, it has been shown that expectations about the effects of drinking and not drinking are important predictors of behaviour (see Hodgson 1988). The excessive drinkers' expectations of positive effects from drinking predict drop-out from treatment. Furthermore, the expectation that alcohol reduces tension predicts relapse better than factors such as marital status, employment status, living environment, participation in aftercare programmes and social support. One crucial psychological construct is *perceived self-efficacy* or the perceived ability to cope with reduced drug consumption. In a recent study it was found that outcome expectancies (defined as the costs and benefits expected to result from a reduction in alcohol or drug consumption) did not predict consumption at follow-up, whereas self-efficacy expectations did. This finding suggests that an important treatment goal is to change self-efficacy expectations.

During the last 20 years psychologists have initiated a rich vein of experimentation on the effects of expectations as opposed to the direct pharmacological effects of alcohol. The balanced placebo design has been widely used in these studies. Subjects are given either alochol or a soft drink. In the 'given soft drink' condition, subjects are either led to believe that they are consuming alcohol (placebo) or that they are consuming soft drink. Similarly, in the 'given alcohol' condition, subjects are led to believe that they are consuming soft drink (balanced placebo) or alcohol. This design permits the separation of the effects of alcohol consumption from the effects of a cognitive set or expectation. There is a large and growing body of research which demonstrates the effect of a cognitive set on a range of social behaviour including aggression, sexual arousal, and self-disclosure.

Relapse and recovery are also strongly influenced by social factors. The available evidence indicates that social networks, marital cohesion, and job satisfaction are particularly influential. Finally, within a psychological model great emphasis is placed upon the development of cognitive self-control skills and the way in which such skills can be impaired.

3. *Learning is influenced by physiological adaptive processes.* Tolerance occurs, following drug use, when the same dose begins to have a reduced effect and, therefore, a larger dose is needed to achieve the same effect. The development of tolerance and withdrawal symptoms is usually explained by invoking the concept of an adaptive response which counteracts the effect of the drug. For example, insulin produces low blood sugar, whereas the compensatory-adaptive process results in high blood sugar levels. There is now a great deal of support for the hypothesis that this adaptive process can be conditioned to external cues and expectancies. For example, some studies have looked at the effects of a placebo challenge. If an excessive drinker is led to expect alcohol but is actually given a placebo then a compensatory reduction in heart rate can be observed, rather than the drug effect which is an increase in heart rate. There can now be no doubt that adaptive processes are involved, and future debate will be about their exact contribution to dependence. At what point in a drink or drug user's career are these processes involved? Can they be reversed? To what extent are learning and conditioning involved?

AN INTEGRATED MODEL OF CHANGE

Clinical psychologists dealing with alcohol and drug misuse have been strongly influenced in recent years by the integrated model of change proposed by Prochaska and DiClemente (1986). Their model brings together three psychological domains. The first involves *stages of change*. The second covers the *processes of change*, and the third emphasizes the different *levels of change*. These three dimensions will be considered in some detail, before moving on to discuss ways of helping people to change.

Stages of change

It is often assumed that there are just two types of addict. There are those who are desperate to change, and those who have absolutely no intention of changing. According to this view the one group is given help, whereas the other group is confronted with the facts about drug misuse until they are sufficiently motivated to accept help. In fact, this view is not supported by the evidence. Motivation to change is complicated and fluctuating. Furthermore, confrontation is not usually the best method of encouraging change.

Prochaska and DiClimente (1986) have carefully researched the way in which changes occur and concluded that there are at least four stages. In the *precontemplation stage* the drug user does not intend to change in the near future. This could be because the perceived benefits of drug use still outweigh the perceived costs, often because the costs are played down through ignorance or denial. Drug users who try to change but fail sometimes slip back into this stage. The *contemplation stage* covers that period when the costs and benefits are being reappraised, and ability to cope with behavioural changes is being assessed. This stage can last a few minutes or a few years. In the *action stage* a pledge has been made, and positive steps are being taken. Finally, the *maintenance stage* begins a few months after successful change. In this stage vigilance is still relatively high, in an attempt to prevent relapse.

The following brief case-description illustrates these stages, as well as the fact that there is not usually an orderly progression from one stage to the next. Stable changes are only achieved after many unsuccessful attempts.

Mr T is a successful doctor who has had to struggle with a drink and drug problem at various stages throughout his career. He went to medical school during the sixties, and started to drink excessively whilst living in a hall of residence in the centre of London. Almost every night a group of friends had three or four pints in the pub, sometimes at 10 p.m., after studying during the first half of the evening. Heavy drinking in this situation was socially accepted, even though it caused regular arguments with his girlfriend and a noticeable lack of vim and vigour in the morning. Mr T was not even contemplating change. The immediate pleasures of a carefree evening in the pub by far outweighed the delayed negative consequences. During this period he was in the *precontemplation stage*. During the next six to ten years Mr T used a range of drugs as well as alcohol, and there were many times when un-

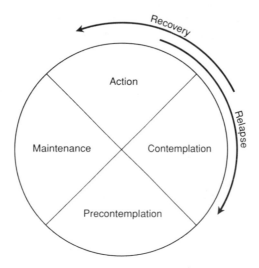

Fig. 9.1   Stages of change.

pleasant negative consequences forced Mr T to consider change. This *contemplation stage* would often last for days or weeks. Occasionally Mr T would be *ready for action* and would move into the *action stage*, when he set limits and planned alternative activities. More often than not he would, however, slip back from the *contemplation* or *action stage* into the *pre-contemplation stage*.

Whilst working as a junior doctor he continued to use drugs and drink heavily. He would often take a swig of whisky to get to sleep or to calm himself down. He recognized that he was risking his whole career; but his attempts to change always eventually failed, and he would then resist even contemplating change. He would slip back into the precontemplation stage, and remain there until he again reappraised the risks or discovered a new way of attempting to change. For most of the ten years after qualifying Mr T was in the precontemplation stage. Quite often he was contemplating change, sometimes he was ready for action and, occasionally, he moved into the action stage. At the time of writing he has been in the *maintenance stage* for several months. He now sticks to a few simple rules, and is aware that certain mood states (for example, tiredness), and certain situations (for example, travelling alone) are high-risk cues, and have to be given special attention.

One of the mistakes that is often made when attempting to help a problem drinker or drug misuser is to assume a readiness for action and discuss coping strategies prematurely. The ambivalence of wanting to change but not wanting to change is frequently experienced, and motivation can vary from day to day. Furthermore, a person in the contemplation stage needs a different approach from a person who is ready for action. In this chapter the approaches that clinical psychologists usually adopt will, therefore, be considered as they relate to stages of change (see, for example, Miller and Rollnick 1991).

The processes of change

As a drug user moves through the stages of change, whether slowly or rapidly, different *change processes* come into play. Consider, for example, the following brief case history of a young drug user who successfully changed.

At the age of 23, after five years of drug misuse, Elaine was deserted by her long-standing boyfriend. He could not cope with her mood swings and could not stand her drug-using friends. This event forced her to think a great deal about her future and, during the next six months, she made two important decisions. First, she moved out of central London, away from her friends and haunts. Second, she signed on for a full-time course in photography. At first she resolved not to go anywhere near her friends in central London; but, after a few months, she discovered that she could occasionally visit them without being tempted to get involved again in the drug scene. Elaine went on from strength to strength, even though, in her opinion, she could not have survived without the help of an Aunty who was always ready to talk and give her the support that she needed.

Elaine described many of the processes of change which have been identified by Prochaska and DiClimente. They have investigated the various processes involved in change, and conclude that those displayed in Table 9.1 are the ten most important:

Table 9.1 Processes of change

---

1. *Raising awareness*: This can be the result of a therapeutic intervention or, alternatively, a life event. Elaine was forced to face the fact that her drug misuse would almost certainly have a detrimental effect on her future social relationships.

2. *Self-re-evaluation*: Taking stock of one's current situation often precedes cognitive and behavioural changes. What are my talents and skills? What do I want to achieve?

3. *Social-environmental re-evaluation*: Elaine realized that she was locked into a social network of drug users and decided that, for her, a change of environment was called for.

4. *Self-liberation*: At some stage during change a feeling of freedom and confidence is experienced. Perceived self-efficacy, or ability to cope, is an important milestone and a predictor of future success.

5. *Social liberation*: When Elaine visited her friends in London she realized that she was now socially more skilled and was not compelled to use drugs when in the presence of her old friends.

6. *Counter-conditioning*: This process involves replacing drug use with other leisure or work activities—for example, an obsession with photography in Elaine's case. At another level it is the process of counteracting craving and temptation by replacing drug thoughts with other thoughts.

7. *Stimulus control*: Avoiding powerful drug cues or desensitizing them through cue exposure (see p. 237) is one component of the more behavioural approaches to treatment.

8. *Contingency management*: If abstaining from drugs (or sensible drinking) leads to immediate benefits then the new lifestyle will be reinforced. One year after moving out of London Elaine was sure that a life without drugs was more rewarding than her life as a drug user.

9. *Dramatic relief*: Catharsis and conversion sometimes occur during psychological treatment, during a religious experience, or after a drug-related catastrophe. Sometimes a dramatic change in attitudes occurs after a less obvious trauma (for example, an experience of impotence).

10. *Helping relationships*: Self-help groups, befriending schemes, and professional counselling are based upon the belief that it is easier to change with the help of a sympathetic friend or professional. Elaine considered this to be crucial in her case.

Prochaska and DiClimente present evidence that these processes are differentially linked to particular stages of change. Raising awareness and self-re-evaluation are dominant during a move into the contemplation stage. Self-liberation is a key process in moving from contemplation to action; whereas counter-conditioning, stimulus control, and contingency management are crucial during the action and maintenance stages. Psychological treatments must take these findings into account.

Levels of change

The third factor is the level or extent of change, whether produced by a psychological therapy or by natural psychological and social changes. One level is that of a circumscribed problem. For example, stopping smoking with the help of nicotine chewing-gum might leave untouched a whole range of psychological and social systems. The next level involves maladaptive thought patterns. The cognitive–behavioural treatment of depression would be working at this level. Interpersonal and family approaches consider even more extensive psychological systems; and it is suggested that the last level involves deep intrapersonal conflicts. One of the important decisions that a clinical psychologist has to make is the level and extent of change that is achievable.

The integrated model described above helps to put an addiction problem in perspective and enables the therapist to ask a number of relevant questions, the main ones being:

- What stage of change has this person reached?
- What change processes should be the focus of attention?
- What is the level and extent of change that is being considered?

HELPING ALCOHOL AND DRUG MISUSERS WHO ARE NOT READY FOR ACTION

Although clinical psychologists are able to apply a range of action-oriented treatments, these have to be introduced at the right time. A common mistake, which is made by therapists of all persuasions, is to tell substance misusers how to change when they are not yet ready to change. We would not try to force tennis lessons on to a child or an adult who had no intention of playing tennis—although, of course, we might exert an influence in more subtle ways. Many people with alcohol or drug problems will want help and will co-operate; but there will also be a number of clients who are resistant to any intervention. This applies especially to advice which is given at an early stage in the development of dependence. Here are two examples from a recent World Health Organization investigation which demonstrate how difficult it can be to engage a client's motivation and co-operation.

Example from Mexico

Mr P was a 38-year old man who worked as a security agent. He usually had some guns with him. Mr P lived with one woman, who had three girls, but they weren't married. He did not have a regular schedule at work; sometimes he worked at night, sometimes at noon. He was very reluctant to receive any advice, since 'all that stuff is useless and the information is only for young kids who do not know what they want'. He was very aggressive during the interview. Mr P did not change at all.

Example from Bulgaria

A 48-year old baker, married with two children had been drinking excessively for more than 20 years—mostly beer but sometimes brandy. During his first meeting with a health worker he was co-operative and didn't deny his drinking problem, but added 'I want to stop but I can't. Nobody can help me because I have no willpower. I am weak and I like drinking more than I like my wife and children. Friends forced me to stop, but I couldn't and I can't. That is all.' He still drinks too much, but now works on a farm. Otherwise, nothing has changed.

Of course, it has to be accepted that some people with drug and alcohol problems are going to resist all offers of help. Nevertheless, most people who are excessive users of alcohol or drugs are in the precontemplation or contemplation stages, and most of them do eventually try to change. This section is about ways of helping and influencing people who are not yet ready to radically change their patterns of substance misuse but are stuck in the precontemplation or contemplation stages.

Overview

The first point to make is that excessive drinkers and drug users might not be ready for action if the action means giving up alcohol or drugs, but might be ready for a range of other types of action. For example, they might be ready to learn about the known effects of drugs, and the psychology of addiction. *Motivational counselling* (Miller and Rollnick 1991) draws a client into this type of discussion in an attempt to restructure attitudes and beliefs. The therapist encourages the client to see connections between substance misuse and personal problems, and attempts to gently nudge the client from precontemplation to contemplation, and possibly to the action stage.

Clients might also be ready to discuss *harm limitation*. There are many methods of reducing the harmful consequences of drug misuse which might be acceptable since they do not involve giving up drugs altogether (for example, switching alcoholic beverages, needle exchange). Furthermore, a client might be ready to take action and accept help in dealing with a range of drug-related *psychosocial factors* such as social skills and anxiety. Finally, one important influence, which is under the control of the therapist, is the *therapeutic style*. It has been shown that therapists who adopt an empathic, non-confrontational approach are more successful than those who rely upon warnings, threats, and confrontations. This whole approach emphasizes motivation and stages of change rather than 'cures'. A service which is only interested in cures will drive away clients who are not ready to be cured, and will demoralize therapists who have nothing to offer the contemplators and pre-contemplators. On the other hand, a service which focuses upon motivational counselling, harm limitation, changing underlying psychosocial factors, and developing an empathic therapist style is good for the client and good for the therapist. Clients are less likely to drop out, and therapists are less likely to burn out.

Motivational counselling and therapeutic style

The core objective of motivational counselling is to restructure beliefs and expectancies about the costs and benefits of substance misuse. This is achieved by avoiding confrontation and instead adopting the following approach:

1. Creating a supportive empathic relationship which facilitates an accurate description of drug use, drug-related problems, and the expected consequences of behaviour change.
2. Giving the client clear feedback about the relationship between drug use and personal problems, as well as the psychosocial factors which appear to be influencing drug use. Helping the client to correct any cognitive distortions that make change difficult to contemplate (for example, 'I've tried to stop six times; there is no point in trying again').
3. Helping the client to consider possible alternatives to excessive drug use and then to make decisions.

Van Bilsen and van Emst (1989) were involved in a drug treatment service which changed in 1983 from a traditional out-patient methadone clinic to an approach which revolves around motivational interviewing. They describe in Table 9.2 (below) a number of major differences between the two approaches.

This psychological approach to drug users in the contemplation and precontemplation stages is spreading throughout the specialist alcohol and drug agencies, especially in the UK. Now is the time to direct resources towards well-designed evaluations of motivational interviewing, and especially of the effectiveness of this approach within primary health care and social work settings.

Psychosocial changes and harm reduction

Drug and alcohol abusers who are not ready to pledge themselves to total abstinence will often be willing to consider some psychosocial changes (for example, developing social skills) or some harm-limitation strategies. Psychological and social interventions will cover the whole range of problem areas, including the following (see, for example, Watts 1990):

Sleep difficulties	Social confidence/skills
Anxiety disorders	Obsessions and compulsions
Depression and boredom	Family and work relationships
Sexual/marital problems	Job-finding skills
Violence	Coping with frustration/craving

Harm reduction approaches might involve some moderation or drug substitution. Methadone maintenance, for example, helps the drug user to keep withdrawal symptoms at bay and avoid some of the harmful consequences which are associated with purchasing and injecting heroin (for example, infection, theft, and arrest). A brief period of supervised abstinence within a hospital or community setting can help to reduce harm by allowing the body to recover from many of the toxic effects of alcohol and drugs. A period of abstinence also facilitates self-re-evaluation and contemplation, as well as a general appraisal of physical health. Problem drinkers are sometimes happy to consider moderating their consumption or substituting a low alcohol beer on some occasions, even though total abstinence cannot be contemplated.

When moderation is not accepted there are still a range of possible

Table 9.2 Motivational interviewing versus a traditional approach

Motivational interviewing	Traditional approach
Denial/Telling lies	
• Denial and telling lies are seen as an interpersonal behaviour pattern (communication) influenced by the interviewer's behaviour.	• Denial and telling lies are seen as a personal trait of the heroin addict/junkie, requiring heavy confrontation by the interviewer.
• Lies and denial are met with reflections.	• Lies and denial are met with argument/correction.
Labelling	
• There is a general de-emphasis on labels. Confessions of being a junkie or being an irresponsible heroin addict are seen as irrelevant.	• There is a heavy emphasis on acceptance by patients that they are junkies or addicts. Self-labelling or confession is often an important part of group therapy.
• Objective evidence of impairment is presented in a low-key fashion, not imposing any conclusion on the client.	• Objective evidence of impairment is presented as a dire warning, as proof of a progressive disease and of the necessity of complete abstinence.
Individual responsibilty	
• Emphasis on personal choice regarding future use of heroin.	• Emphasis on the disease of addiction, which reduces personal choice.
• Goal of treatment is negotiated, based on data and preferences.	• The treatment goal is always total and lifelong abstinence.
• Controlled heroin use is a possible goal, though not optimal for all.	• Controlled heroin use is dismissed as impossible.
Internal attribution	
• Within limits the individual is seen as able to control and choose.	• The individual is seen as helpless and totally unable to control his/her own heroin use.
• The interviewer focuses on eliciting the client's own statement of concern regarding the heroin use.	• The interviewer presents his/her own tough assessment of the evidence to convince the client that he/she has a problem.

harm-reduction strategies. Needle-exchange schemes provide a good example. By providing drug users with a good supply of clean needles and discouraging needle-sharing there is less chance of infection, and thus the spread of AIDS will be curtailed in this high-risk group.

In some families the spouse and children are repeatedly exposed to harmful and sometimes dangerous situations. One harm-limitation strategy is to help them to solve some of the problems which occur during a period of excessive alcohol or drug use.

Psychosocial interventions and harm-reduction strategies can lead to health gain in the drug users and their families. They also keep the family in touch with services, so that problems can be monitored and any motivational changes can be acted upon. Attitudes towards drugs often change following a life event, marriage, the birth of a child, or simply reaching the age of 40.

Before moving on to psychological approaches which are appropriate to the action stage, the following case described by Baldwin (1991) illustrates the way in which a precontemplator was nudged into the action stage.

Ken is a 22-year old man who was referred by the district (magistrates') court for assessment for an Alcohol Education Course. At the time of referral, he was drinking three or four days each week, with an average intake of between 100 and 120 units during these sessions. Ken started the assessment interview by saying: 'I don't mind answering your questions, but I won't be going on the course, because I don't have a problem.' This was countered with 'It's not for me to tell you if you have a problem or not; it's up to you to decide that for yourself. Let's take a look at your drinking and see how you're doing just now.'

A detailed behavioural analysis was used to examine the functional relationship between Ken's drinking and offending. For each offence, Ken was asked about the preceding events. In particular, he was asked to focus on whether or not drinking had occurred prior to the offence. Further questions about whom he was with, doing what, where, and in what way produced this summary statement from the interview:

'Ken, what you seem to be saying is that you've been lifted five times before, and again last month. Each time you've been caught by the police, it's been after a long drinking session. Every time, you've been drinking for at least five hours; you've never been lifted before half-past ten, and always on a Friday or Saturday night. Gary has always been with you, and usually John as well. You've always been caught in the High Street, or in the Royal Terrace. Every time it's been because you've been making a noise in the street, or because you've damaged someone's property on the way home. What do YOU think? IS there a connection between your drinking habits and getting into trouble with the police?'

Despite a clear functional relationship between heavy drinking sessions and subsequent offending behaviours, Ken had not been aware of this. When asked, he had attributed his arrests and detention to a bias amongst police officers. This belief was also challenged, and Ken was asked to 'plot' his offences on a city map. His six offences formed a straight line between a city-centre pub and his flat.

Ken's lack of insight and distorted belief system were systematically challenged during the interview. His drink-related physical health and social problems were reattributed to alcohol consumption. Ken was assisted to view his problems as an *understandable pattern* rather than a *random set of unconnected events*. He subsequently decided to attend an Alcohol Education Course to help him with his drinking and offending behaviours.

ACTION STAGE: PSYCHOLOGICAL APPROACHES TO THERAPY AND BEHAVIOUR CHANGE

A psychological model of drug misuse places a great deal of emphasis upon the high-risk personal and social events which lead to temptation, as well as the more enduring psychological states and environmental situations which can influence the way in which a high-risk event is perceived. Consider the following example:

Lorna, a female heroin addict aged 27, left hospital on a Monday morning and survived for two weeks without even wanting to inject. The first weekend was a very lonely and depressing experience. Her feelings of helplessness were exactly those feelings that were usually associated with a desire to use drugs. She knew who to telephone to get a dose, nevertheless did not experience a strong craving. During the second weekend her ex-boyfriend moved in with her, and although he was a drug user she had a good weekend and was not tempted. The following week was a bad one, and resulted in a recurrence of her drug habit. She explained that on this occasion she felt very depressed and, furthermore, drugs were easily available. She could not resist the urge when she watched her boyfriend injecting.

These interactions between psychological processes, social environment, and drug availability are usually a major focus of a psychological analysis. The following are some of the examples of well-researched psychological treatments, although it should be noted that most of the research described in this section concerns alcohol dependence (see Hodgson 1988).

1. Coping skills training

In principle this approach is very simple. Just as a golfer carries around a bag of clubs designed to cope with different situations, so the addict has to devise or practise coping skills to deal with high-risk situations. The strategies can be attempts to avoid cues arising in the first place, or they can be methods of coping with unavoidable cues. In one study this approach was tested with hospitalized problem drinkers, although it should be emphasized that the method can also be used with problem drinkers or drug users in community settings. High-risk situations were considered under four headings, namely: frustration and anger, social pressure, negative emotional states, and intrapersonal temptation.

The intervention consisted of eight group sessions spread over a period of four weeks, during which specific situations were identified and ways of coping with them were discussed and rehearsed. This kind of practice led not only to an increased ability to think of coping strategies, but also to a decrease in the duration and severity of relapse episodes up to one year later.

Here are some examples of the cognitive and behavioural coping strategies that are commonly used:

Accepting craving: Sometimes it is difficult to do anything about craving, especially in social situations. One solution is to stop fighting, but recognize the fact that the craving will eventually subside. Sometimes seeing the craving as a bodily symptom, like 'flu, can help to put it in perspective. Sometimes seeing it as a storm that will pass over also helps. Whatever the image used, it has to counteract the thought that craving is an unstoppable biological process.

Social skills: In a social situation it is very easy to give in to social pressures, especially if coping strategies have not been rehearsed. It only takes a few seconds to say yes and start to inject. Saying no and providing a good reason must be rehearsed until it becomes second nature (for example, 'I'm trying to experiment to see what I'm like after 6 months without drugs'). Social skills training usually involves role-playing and real-life practice of difficult activities (for example, conversation, assertion).

Social contact: Sometimes just talking to a supportive friend can help to reduce craving. Alcoholics Anonymous recognize the power of social contact, and every member has a sponsor or buddy who can be contacted if urgently needed. Psychologists sometimes make use of a similar approach.

The aim of coping skills training is to develop a range of simple coping skills and to rehearse their use in specific tempting situations until they are readily available when needed. One analogy is that of an airline pilot practising ways of dealing with emergencies.

There is good evidence that this approach is useful and effective, even though there are also numerous occasions when addicts will say: 'I knew exactly what I ought to do but I didn't feel like doing it.'

2. Social and marital interventions

It has been argued that if the problem drinker or drug user is interacting well with his family and community, then sobriety will be reinforced and excessive drinking will be curtailed. Three trials of such a community reinforcement approach have now been completed by Nathan Azrin and his colleagues, and these suggest that increasing social and job-finding skills and improving marital relationships can have a strong beneficial effect. Although these trials involved fairly intensive work with severely dependent drinkers, many of the strategies can be used among the broad range of clients commonly encountered in community work. This community reinforcement approach is mainly behavioural or action-oriented. For example, their approach to marital counselling attempted to change day-to-day interactions in such a way that both partners benefited. Twelve specific problem areas were discussed, including money management, family relations, sex problems, children, social life, attention, neurotic tendencies, immaturity, grooming, ideological difficulties, general incompatibility, and dominance. The husband and wife together constructed a list of specific activities that each would agree to perform in order to please or help the other spouse. This list typically included preparing meals, listening to the partner with undivided attention, picking up the children from school, redistributing the finances, visiting relatives together, and spending a night out together. Absolute sobriety was requested of the husbands by all of the wives as part of this agreement. For unmarried patients living with their families, similar procedures were used. For those patients living alone, attempts were made to arrange a foster family who would regularly invite the patient to their house.

The social and job counselling procedures also focused upon

interactions and skills. Furthermore, a former tavern was converted into a self-supporting social club for the clients and provided a band, juke-box, card games, dances, picnics, snacks, bingo games, films, and other types of social activity. Alcoholic beverages were banned from this club, and any member who arrived at the club with any indication of having been drinking was turned away.

Changing family and community interactions is a major focus in the psychological treatment of many disorders (for example, schizophrenia), since there is a wealth of evidence that psychological disorders are influenced by the social context.

3. Cue exposure

It has been argued that experiencing a strong desire to use drugs or alcohol is not unlike the compulsive urge to wash or check described by people suffering from an obsessive–compulsive disorder. Indeed, there are so many similarities that it could be argued that methods which have been successfully used to treat obsessive–compulsive disorders might be successful in treating people suffering from drug dependence. One very powerful method, usually called cue exposure, involves repeated exposure to the cues that trigger or influence the compulsive behaviour.

The evidence relating to the effectiveness of cue exposure in the treatment of drug and alcohol dependence is very promising but still not conclusive. This is an important area crying out for further research. In one series of studies directed by the author severely dependent drinkers were given a priming dose of alcohol, in a safe environment, and then encouraged to resist consuming more of their favourite beverage. To briefly summarize this research programme, we were able to demonstrate that consuming alcohol did have a priming effect, but mainly in those who were severely dependent. We also produced evidence to support the view that this priming phenomenon is not simply related to expectancies, but is probably also a function of psychophysiological cues produced by the consumption of alcohol. After completing a number of individual case studies on cue-exposure treatment we decided to carry out a controlled study to test the hypothesis that repeated cue exposure would result in a gradual reduction of the priming effect both within and across sessions.

In this study we encouraged a number of volunteers from an

Alcoholism Treatment Unit to consume a priming does of alcohol in a safe environment and then resist consuming further available alcohol. All ten volunteers were severely dependent on alcohol. Figure 9.2 displays the combined ratings of desire to drink across six cue-exposure sessions, results which clearly indicate that a priming effect was produced, that desire for more alcohol decreased during each session, and that, after six sessions, the priming effect had almost completely disappeared. Furthermore, a similar decrease did not occur in a control condition involving only imaginal exposure.

We viewed this as a process study rather than a treatment study; nevertheless, we did demonstrate that alcoholics exposed to cues do respond in a very similar way to those who suffer from obsessive–compulsive problems.

These preliminary studies did not follow patients up after discharge from hospital and did not attempt cue exposure outside the safe environment of the hospital. Such an investigation is now a priority.

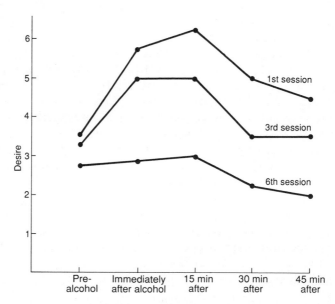

Fig. 9.2   Reduction in desire after 6 sessions of cue exposure.

4. Controlled drinking

During the 1970s there was a rapid increase in the number of research reports evaluating the effectiveness of controlled drinking as a treatment goal for problem drinkers. In general the early studies were very positive, with success rates at one year follow-up averaging between 60 and 70 per cent (Miller and Hester, 1986). However approaches typically used in these studies were very time-consuming. Later studies have used a less time-consuming approach, usually referred to as behavioural self-control training, with equal effectiveness.

Controlled evaluations of this approach have yielded rates of successful outcome comparable to those for the more extensive programmes. Average success rates of 70 per cent have been achieved at 12-month follow-up, with 97 per cent of clients located. One further development which emerges from the work of Miller and his colleagues is the effectiveness of a self-help manual instead of repeated therapist contact.

BRIEF INTERVENTIONS

There is growing evidence that a very brief intervention, when given at the right time, can provide a cue to action. A person in the contemplation stage might need just a little more information about harmful effects or perhaps a simple way of coping with temptation. For example, in one study the brief counselling was carried out by a nurse within a District General Hospital setting. In the months following discharge, patients receiving this intervention (one hour maximum) had fewer alcohol-related problems than a randomized control group. Other studies have confirmed these results.

Clinical psychologists have been at the forefront of these developments, since stages of change and motivational interviewing are key concepts relating to the development of brief interventions. Miller and Sanchez (in press) have reviewed a number of studies which have demonstrated the effectiveness of brief interventions in reducing alcohol consumption and problems. They summarized the common components of these studies using the acronym FRAMES, which stands for: Feedback, Responsibility, Advice, Menu, Empathy, and Self-Efficacy.

The assessment of health and social status followed by FEED-BACK of results is included as a key component in most brief interventions. The feedback might be of liver functioning or of the possible link between excessive drinking and sexual, marital, social, or work problems. Personal RESPONSIBILITY for change is emphasized. The aim is to promote internal attributions of responsibility for change rather than encouraging a reliance on doctors or psychologists. ADVICE to change is a third common element. Advice given sensitively by a high-status or respected person can be 'a cue to action' and move a person from one stage of change to the next. Sometimes, advice to change is accompanied by a MENU of specific recommendations from which to choose. The counsellor or change agent's ability to EMPATHIZE with a problem drinker has been shown to influence outcome; and the development of confidence in ability to cope (i.e. SELF-EFFICACY expectations) is also important.

The proven effectiveness of brief interventions is an important finding which changes the way in which we view a comprehensive drug and alcohol treatment service. Instead of using scarce resources to proliferate hospital treatment units, the first priority must be to ensure that each community has a widespread network of low-cost interventions. These could be based within a primary care setting, a community, or a District General Hospital out-patient department. Training and advising health and social workers about low-cost psychological interventions is a key role for clinical psychologists. Pamphlets and manuals should be easily available from health centres, social services, pharmacists, and other centres involved in providing help. One main objective should be to ensure that it is relatively easy to get some advice and support directed towards changing outcome and efficacy expectancies. Higher-cost alternatives would then be developed only for clients who require more intensive help, and only when there is good evidence that such approaches are likely to be effective.

PREVENTING ALCOHOL AND DRUG MISUSE

Clinical psychologists working on drug or alcohol problems will, more often than not, be involved in advisory committees, or community teams which have a wider remit than treatment and rehabilitation. District Health Authorities should be looking at the best way of using resources in order to produce maximum health gain for their resident population. Obtaining the correct balance between prevention, early interventions, treatment, and rehabilitation is a difficult task, but one that is attracting the interest of clinical psychologists. Undoubtedly more could be done to prevent drug and alcohol problems. In the previous section it has already been noted that early identification and the provision of brief interventions should be one component of a community response. But early interventions are not applicable or acceptable to every excessive drinker or drug user. Health promotion or prevention strategies must also be directed towards the wider community in an attempt to prevent problems occurring in the first place. Just one investigation will be described, which demonstrates how clinical psychologists sometimes link up with other services in order to develop and evaluate new approaches.

This investigation was carried out by a clinical psychologist and a police officer, and is based upon the hypothesis that the police can have a powerful preventive influence on drink-related problems simply by reminding both the publican and the drinker that excessive drinking can be illegal. They were able to evaluate the effectiveness of a community policing strategy which was implemented in an English seaside resort during the summer of 1978 and then withdrawn the following year. Public houses in the harbourside area of the town were visited by two policemen, and the first step was to remind licensees of their responsibilities under the licensing legislation. The licensees and the police agreed to co-operate fully in an attempt to ensure that the law was observed, particularly as it relates to under-age drinking and serving alcohol to those who are already intoxicated. During the summer months the selected premises were then visited regularly. Two or three uniformed officers amicably, but very conspicuously, checked for under-age drinking or the presence of persons who were the worse for drink. The checking was very thorough, and was designed to bring home to both staff and patrons the seriousness of their intention to enforce the licensing laws.

In order to test the effectiveness of this preventive exercise the rates of recorded crime and public order offences for the summer of 1978 were compared with those for the year before as well as the year after. Such an analysis did indeed suggest that crime in 1978 was 20 per cent less than would be expected from an extrapolation of the figures for 1977 and 1979. The implication that this change resulted from the alteration in police practice is supported by two additional pieces of evidence. First, this result was not apparent in a control town within the same tourist region. Second, the reduction in 1978 was greater for alcohol-related crimes than for those, such as burglary and theft, which are not strongly related to alcohol consumption.

This study suggests that a comparatively minor change in police practice, albeit a major change in policy, produced results which would be quite dramatic if they could be replicated throughout the world.

Of course, clinical psychologists are not employed by the NHS in order to spend all of their time influencing organizations outside the NHS. Nevertheless, enlightened NHS managers are beginning to realize that it is the responsibility of the health services to work together with other organizations in order to prevent accidents, illness, and disease. Clinical psychologists and other health professionals working on drug and alcohol problems have formed alliances with the police, probation officers, magistrates, licensees, education departments, trade unions, social services, and the voluntary sector in order to prevent alcohol and drug misuse.

NEUROPSYCHOLOGICAL IMPAIRMENT

Clinical psychologists have specific skills in psychometric testing and have, therefore, been closely involved in studying the relationships between substance misuse and cognitive impairment. More specifically, research on the effects of excessive alcohol consumption has developed very rapidly during the last ten years.

In alcoholics, the characteristic pattern of cognitive impairment relates to tests of abstraction, memory, visuo-spatial ability, verbal fluency, planning and organization, and shift of set. Several groups of workers have also found impairments in social drinkers; but there is still some debate about the exact type of impairment and the cause. The continuity hypothesis is that the alcoholic Korsakoff patient, the severe alcoholic, and the heavy social drinker all suffer from similar deficits along a single continuum of alcohol-related cognitive impairment. In a recent study investigators administered a range of neuropsychological tests that are sensitive to impairments in alcoholics to three groups of healthy male social drinkers. The subjects were divided into three groups according to their daily alcohol consumption (40 g or less, 41–80 g, 82–130 g). Subjects consuming more than

80 g per day (about 5 pints of beer) were found to be performing at a significantly lower level than the other two groups on these tests. The pattern of deficits found in these heavy social drinkers is less severe, but otherwise similar to that found in alcoholics. These impairments are also similar to those which occur during alcohol intoxication. Clinical psychologists are now paying much more attention to these cognitive deficits. In both prevention and treatment it is important to consider these impairments.

CONCLUSION

The role of a clinical psychologist in the alcohol and drug services is both varied and interesting. Most psychologists will be involved in assessment, psychological treatments, community interventions, prevention, teaching, and management as well as research and development. It should be added that other types of psychologist also provide a service within this field (for example, research psychologists, health psychologists, counselling psychologists). Furthermore, a great deal of psychological work is carried out by other professions. What is certain is that a clinical psychologist can bring useful skills to bear upon addictive behaviour. If we consider only the treatment of alcohol problems, the effectiveness of a psychological approach is supported by the available evidence. For example, a recent review of the treatment-outcome literature for alcohol problems concluded that the following interventions have reasonable scientific support for their effectiveness: antidepressant medication, behavioural contracting, brief interventions, behavioural marital therapy, self-control training, community reinforcement, covert sensitization, disulfiram, social skills training, and stress-management training. The majority of these treatments are psychological, and were originally developed by clinical psychologists.

Finally, it should be added that work in this field is sometimes difficult and frustrating. Relapse is the norm, and, to quote Mark Twain, 'You can't throw a habit out of the upstairs window. You have to lead it gently down the staircase step by step.'

REFERENCES

Baldwin, S. (1991). Helping the unsure. In *Counselling problem drinkers* (ed. R. Davidson *et al.*), pp. 39–57. Tavistock/Routledge, London.

Hodgson, R. J. (1988). Alcohol and drug dependence. In *Adult abnormal psychology* (ed. E. Miller and P. J. Cooper), pp. 299–317. Churchill Livingstone, Edinburgh.

Miller, W. R. and Hester, R. K. (1986). The effectiveness of alcoholism treatment: What research reveals. In *Treating addictive behaviours: processes of change* (eds W. R. Milller and N. Heather), pp. 121–74. Plenum, New York.

Miller, W. R. and Rollnick, S. (1991). *Motivational interviewing: preparing people for changing addictive behaviours*. Guilford, New York.

Miller, W. R. and Sanchez, V. C. (in press). Motivating young adults for treatment and life-style change. In *Issues in alcohol use and misuse by young adults* (ed. G. Howard). University of Notre Dame Press, Notre Dame, Indiana.

Prochaska, J. O. and DiClimente, C. C. (1986). Towards a comprehensive model of change. In *Treating addictive behaviours: processes of change* (eds W. R. Miller and N. Heather), pp. 3–27. Plenum, New York.

Van Bilsen, H. and Van Emst, A. (1989). Motivating heroin users for change. In *Treating drug abusers* (ed. G. Bennett), pp. 29–47. Tavistock/Routledge, London.

Watts, F. N. (1990). *The efficacy of clinical applications of psychology*. Shadowfax, Cardiff, Wales.

FURTHER READING

Bennett, G. (ed.) (1989). *Treating drug abusers*. Tavistock/Routledge, London.

Hester, R. and Miller, W. R. (eds) (1989). *Handbook of alcoholism treatment approaches: effective approaches*. Pergamon, Oxford.

Hodgson, R. J. (1982). *Drug dependence*. Encyclopaedia Britannica, Health Supplement.

Heather, N. and Robertson, I. (1981). *Controlled drinking*. Methuen, London.

Marlatt, G. A. and Gordon, J. R. (1985). *Relapse prevention*. Guilford Press, New York.

Orford, J. (1985). *Excessive appetites*. Wiley, Chichester.

10

Clinical psychology and physical health

Louise Wallace and Paul Bennett

Physical illness

Modern concepts of diseases such as cancer and heart disease are described in somatic terms, which imply that the cause can be traced to a lesion or breakdown of the structure and functioning of an organ system. The distinction between physical and mental disorder, between somatic and psychological diseases, is readily accepted by health care practitioners and lay people alike. However, it is also recognized that entirely somatic models of disease, to the exclusion of psychological processes, provide an inadequate picture of how illnesses develop. Shirreff (1982), for example, attributes perhaps half of present premature mortality to unhealthy behaviour, 20 per cent to environmental factors, 10 per cent to inadequacies of health care, and only 20 per cent to human biological factors. An under-standing of patients' experiences of illness, their response to any treatment, and their ultimate adjustment to illness are also critical to effective health care. Equally, a service should make some provision for those patients who need help in coping with the stresses involved at each of these stages, in order to alleviate both distress and undue use of health services. Collectively, these considerations provide a rationale for the contribution of psychologists to the care of people with physical health problems.

Clinical psychological services and physical health

People of all ages suffer physical health problems, and it is not surprising that psychologists working in mental health and disability services should also be concerned with those patients who have both mental and physical problems. For example, within child and adolescent services, clinical psychologists have developed expertise in managing patients' behavioural problems. These skills are applicable not only to children who present behaviour problems at home as a result of family problems, but also to the patient who becomes disturbed when faced with the prospect of repeated hospitalization as part of the treatment of a physical disorder. In Britain, the establishment of District Psychological Services, which provide psychological services to a given geographical population rather than to a specific hospital or ward, has enabled psychologists to respond to the demand for psychological advice from patients and from staff caring for the physically ill patient. The value of such a service, and equally its relative scarcity, has been recently recognized by the MAS Report which recommended the establishment of physical health specialities in all health districts. This growing demand for psychology services may also result in the employment of graduate or postgraduate health psychologists as an adjunct or alternative to established clinical psychological services. Although they have no formally recognized competence in clinical skills they have research, teaching, and change-management skills that complement the skills of clinically trained psychologists.

Similar assessment and therapy skills may be called upon to help the patient who is depressed as a result of a recent bereavement or the diagnosis of a potentially fatal illness. Not only are psychologists concerned with improving patients' psychological adjustment to physical disorder, they are increasingly concerned to modify the psychological factors which may contribute to the development of physical disorders and to the exacerbation of the symptoms of a chronic physical illness. It is perhaps expected, for example, that the occurrence of a heart attack in a young fit person can cause considerable anxiety, which may require psychological intervention. Further, whether the patient carries out the instructions of his or her doctor to change his or her diet, alcohol intake, exercise, and smoking behaviour may well influence that patient's subsequent morbidity and mortality. Psychological factors are clearly at work in the development of health attitudes and behaviour which can become a focus of intervention with an individual patient, health promotion activities such as Look After Yourself or antenatal classes in a health centre.

The recognition that all health care staff use psychological skills, and that their interactions with patients can greatly influence the patients' well-being and physical recovery and response to treatment, has created demand for psychologists' teaching and research skills. For example, through direct clinical work with individual cases, as well as research into the quality of care of all patients on the unit or ward, the psychologist can show that specific types of information are required by the patients about their illness and treatment. The psychologist may then teach the nursing, medical, or other staff how to use communication and counselling skills to overcome regularly occurring problems and to improve the overall quality of care.

For example, in a coronary care unit, patients are particularly concerned about their immediate survival, and yet the nursing and medical procedures which are designed to save life may endanger the patient's life by causing additional fear. In a patient with a compromised cardiovascular system, the occurrence of an acute anxiety state may influence the electrical activity of the heart. The importance of clear and reassuring communication with the patient is, therefore, paramount. Wallace and Joshi (1987) reported that the staff of the coronary care unit in Dudley in the West Midlands were interested in learning from the psychologist how to detect which patients were most anxious and in learning how to reassure them effectively. In this case, the clinical psychologist carried out some systematic observation of nurse–patient interaction to determine the degree to which staff were able to detect and manage patients' fears. One particularly effective method of changing these interactions was to provide a counselling course for newly qualified staff, which incorporated role-played demonstrations of accurate and reassuring communication by the most competent nurses.

The research skills of a clinical psychologist are employed in many ways within this speciality. For example, new medical treatments are typically tested in clinical trials by assessing whether the patients given the treatment show improved health or remission of disease compared with patients given a placebo or standard treatment regime. Psychological treatments can also be tested in this way. For example, the first author of this chapter, Christine Bundy, health psychologist, and Robert Nagle, cardiologist, have tested their clinical impression that angina patients who suffer more stress and have more difficulty controlling anger and frustration tend to have the more severe and frequent symptoms. Using a standard, medically supervised, exercise test, they found that patients who practised stress management had fewer angina attacks, took less medication, and were able to exercise longer. Moreover, stress management combined with exercise training produced even more beneficial results, suggesting that psychological and physical treatments can have complementary effects (Bundy *et al*, in press).

Psychological problems presenting as physical disease

Somatic symptoms are usually perceived by people as a sign of physical rather than mental ill health, and yet psychological problems can be confused with physical disorders where they produce similar symptoms, as is illustrated in the following case study.

Mrs Hartfield is a deputy headteacher in a large comprehensive school. She had been experiencing some slight but sharp pains in her chest at irregular intervals. One day she collapsed at school after experiencing a pain in the middle of her chest while giving a lesson. She was taken by ambulance to the coronary care unit of the District General Hospital. However, after two days, when all investigations were complete, the doctor told her she had not had a heart attack, 'it was just nerves'. She felt foolish that she had caused so much fuss. However, she was not convinced that there was nothing wrong, particularly as her father had been taken ill suddenly and it had been too late before anyone could get medical help to him. The clinical psychologist working in the District General Hospital was asked to see her. Discussion revealed that the patient had been experiencing many symptoms of anxiety, including feelings of physical tension, agitation, breathlessness, and poor sleep; and she reported being troubled by quite small problems which she found difficult to put into perspective. In addition to the periodic chest pain, she was also troubled by tension headaches. In a joint session with the clinical psychologist and cardiologist the nature of the physical symptoms, including the muscle-tension problem, causing sensations of tightness and ischaemic pain in the muscle of the chest, were discussed with her. It was further explained that these symptoms were not indicative of an underlying heart condition, and that she had now had a complete medical check-up. She was prepared to accept psychological treatment for her problem of anxiety.

This case serves to show how patients can present with a problem which may not ultimately be explained by the presence of a disease process. In this case, chronic work stress produced a state of chronic arousal which manifested in a number of minor unpleasant physical sensations. There are other situations where the clinical psychologist may be called upon to help determine whether a problem is a result of an organic disease process or non-organic causes. For example, elderly people who are depressed are very often more restrained in expressing their feelings than younger people. Sometimes people who are depressed are not aware of this, and may believe their forgetfulness, lack of concentration, poor appetite, lethargy, and sleeplessness are a result of physical disease. Here, the training of a clinical psychologist can be useful in helping staff to detect those elderly patients whose physical problems are a result of an emotional rather than a physical problem.

Similarly, a nurse who sustains a back injury lifting patients will learn to avoid activities that cause pain until the injury has recovered. If the nurse fails to take exercise to build up strength, the back may be weak, leading to further pain, which the nurse may seek to avoid out of fear of injury. The condition may also become a way of avoiding resuming a stressful job.

The skills of the clinical psychologist in detecting the presence of mental health problems in people presenting the symptoms commonly associated with physical disease processes are similar to those employed by the clinical psychologist in community and mental health services (see Chapters 2 and 3).

Psychological problems secondary to physical disease

Physical diseases usually involve discomfort and disruption of current activities and plans at best, and protracted pain, perhaps disfigurement, loss, and death at worst. Research into the causes of mental illness, life-threatening illness, and long-term disability gives examples of the kinds of stressful life events that are associated with the development of mental illness problems such as anxiety and depression. It is therefore to be expected that people with physical illnesses will have more psychological problems than physically well relations. Studies of patients consulting their general practitioner, or undergoing hospital treatment for heart attack, ulcer, and a variety of disorders such as asthma, diabetes, and stroke, showed that approximately one-third of the patients had detectable mental illness problems severe enough to warrant psychological treatment. However, very few of those patients are referred for psychological or psychiatric help, as Maguire has shown in his study of depression in women receiving surgical treatment for breast cancer in an Oxford hospital (Maguire *et al.* 1974). He believes that this neglect of the psychological consequences of severe physical illness may reflect the limited skill of the staff, who are trained to treat physical disorder. It may also reflect the lack of psychological services available in general hospitals, and also the reluctance of staff and patients to assign a 'psychological' label to people who are already in the unenviable position of having severe physical disorders.

Similarly, high levels of depression and anxiety are widely prevalent amongst AIDS patients and those with AIDS-Related Complex. Indeed, owing to the ambiguity of their diagnosis, this latter group may show higher levels of distress than AIDS patients. However, only a minority of those who are HIV-positive report prolonged emotional distress requiring psychological intervention. Perhaps as a result of fear-provoking messages in the media about AIDS, there is another group who seek help. These are the 'worried well', who perceive themselves at risk of HIV infection irrespective of their actual risk status, and often present with high levels of anxiety and frequent panic attacks.

The case of Mrs Jago provides an example of the type of psychological problem that may accompany physical disease, and how the two may interact to further exacerbate both physical symptoms and psychological distress.

Mrs Jago was a 32-year-old housewife referred to the District Clinical Psychology Department by a local gastroenterologist. Her main physical complaint was of daily diarrhoea, often occurring three or more times a day, accompanied by mild abdominal pain and discomfort. She was diagnosed as having irritable bowel syndrome. Her problems had begun about six months previously on a holiday trip to the United States of America. She had been nervous about the flight, but had coped well with the outward flight. However, once there she had been troubled by diarrhoea throughout her stay, and had problems on the flight back.

During the following six months her GP had prescribed various medications, but she was free of diarrhoea only occasionally. In addition, she had developed high levels of anxiety and fear of incontinence when away from easy access to a toilet. By the time of her referral she rarely ventured more than half a mile from her house—and then, only where she knew toilets were close by. This presented immediate problems, as her four-year-old son attended infant school in a residential area where there were no public toilets, and her mother had by this time begun to take him to and from school. Other difficulties included restricted shopping and travel by car, and a fear of going to parties and other social functions in case the toilet was in use when she needed it. Her anxieties, and the high levels of physiological arousal accompanying them, almost certainly contributed to an exacerbatory cycle (anxiety–(arousal)–diarrhoea–anxiety) which, at least in part, contributed to the maintenance of both her physical symptoms and her psychological distress.

Some physical disorders not only affect how people feel emotionally and how well they carry out their normal activities; they may have direct effects on patients' cognitive functioning. Chronic renal failure is associated with high rates of depression, which may be attributable to the very realistic fear of imminent death and long-term disability, but also to neuropsychological processes. The symptoms of fatigue, apathy, drowsiness, irritability, anorexia, and dysphoric mood can in some circumstances be attributable to uraemia. Occasionally, salt depletion or hypertension can lead to symptoms typical of dementia. Other symptoms of hallucinations and delusions can occur as a result of the cerebral effects of uraemia. In practice, although in some patients the symptoms will remit when the uraemic condition is controlled, in many circumstances the patient continues to feel depressed, and psychological intervention is warranted.

Major illness may not only influence patients' moods and ability to cope, but also influence activities that are important to them, such as achieving satisfactory sexual relations. It is accepted now that people develop difficulties in achieving satisfactory sexual relations for many reasons, including lack of sex education, unpleasant early sexual experiences, and concurrent family and marital problems. However, even couples with many years of satisfactory sexual relations can find that difficulties arise when one partner becomes physically ill. As physical appearance can be particularly important in maintaining sexual attractiveness, it is predictable that people who receive treatment which results in a disfigurement to the face, hands, and genital areas may experience self-revulsion and also rejection by their partners. Illnesses that result in disfigurement as well as disrupting normal functioning can be expected to produced sexual problems.

Mrs Hatton was referred to the clinical psychologist working in the gynaecology department when it was discovered that she had a severe form of cancer to her internal and external genitals which required urgent surgery. In this case, as the gynaecologist knew that most if not all women experience difficulties in sexual relationships after this mutilating surgery, and that there is also a high rate of suicide, the couple were referred for preventive sexual counselling.

Psychological problems exacerbating existing disease processes

There are many disorders where the patient's lifestyle and methods of coping with stress lead to an exacerbation of the disorder or a delay in remission of symptoms. The occurrence of one or more stressful events can be associated with the occurrence of symptoms of disorders such as psoriasis, eczema, allergies including asthma, cardiovascular diseases such as essential hypertension and angina pectoris, vascular disorders such as migraine headache, and even endocrine disorders such as diabetes, which can be exacerbated by stress.

Generally, the occurrence of recent stressful events is said to have a triggering effect on people with undetected early signs of disease. For example, although myocardial infarctions (heart attacks) can occur out of the blue, if the patient dies there is usually evidence of atherosclerosis or 'furring up' of the coronary arteries. There is evidence that chronic life stress is associated with increased occurrence of cardiovascular diseases. Stress-related disorders have many causes, but some people may be more susceptible than others.

For example, young people who show larger than average increases in blood-pressure in response to stress are at particular risk of developing hypertension. If they also encounter significant or prolonged life stresses, this will speed up the development of cardio-vascular disease. There is strong evidence that teaching hypertensive patients relaxation techniques and how to manage stress more effectively can lead to significant reductions in blood-pressure, and may reduce risk of angina and stroke (Bennett and Carroll 1990). These findings are important for people with mildly raised blood-pressure, who form the majority of those at risk of heart disease and stroke, as stress management training may lower their blood-pressure below the hypertensive range. This in turn will avoid the need for medication, with its risk of adverse side-effects.

Not only can patients' habitual ways of coping with stress influence their symptoms, but patients' moods, health beliefs, and health behaviours can dramatically influence how people seek and respond to medical treatment. Faulty health beliefs and the expected value of health-promoting actions when balanced against expected risk of not following advice or of maintaining unhealthy habits, contribute to the decisions which people make as to whether they will follow their doctor's advice. Several models of patients' health beliefs and attitudes have been researched, the best known of which is the Health Belief Model as proposed by Becker and Maiman (1975). The patients' beliefs about the course of their illness and the likely effectiveness of treatment, their assessment of the cost/benefits of health action and inaction are very useful in understanding why patients often fail to seek health care, and why they do not follow advice which is, according to accepted medical wisdom, apparently in their best interests.

Gary Adams was badly burned on his legs, face, chest, arms, and hands as the result of an accident. He and two other teenage friends had been drinking and smoking marijuana in a disused house in which one of the teenagers was living. The gas fire exploded, and they were unable to react quickly enough to save themselves. All three teenagers were burned, and one died subsequently in hospital. Gary was admitted to the regional burns unit. He received intensive treatment, including several surgical procedures to clean and cover his burns and to graft new skin into place. While in shock he was provided with the necessary fluids and nutrients, and after this phase he was required to eat up to twice his normal daily calorie intake, as burn injury raises the body's metabolism and results in the loss of protein and calories through the burns. He was required to remain in bed, with restricted movement of some body parts to avoid damage to his grafts, and to follow the physiotherapist's exercises to stretch other areas to prevent the skin from contracting. He experienced pain from these exercises and soreness from bed rest, and pain from the burned areas and from where his own skin had been removed to cover the burned areas.

However, when he was beyond the critical state, 14 days after the burn, his wounds became badly infected. His new grafts failed to 'take'. This meant that he would need to have more operations, as the surgeon would need to 'harvest' some new skin to cover the old wounds. After one month he was losing weight; he was refusing to eat, and pulled out his nasogastric feeding tube. He refused to exercise, and his grafts were not 'taking'. He also wanted to know about the fate of his friend; but the staff were avoiding telling him that he had died several weeks ago, as they felt he would become further depressed and would also no longer trust them.

When the clinical psychologist interviewed Gary she discovered that he had been depressed from the moment he began to suspect that his friend had died. He suspected that staff were not telling him the truth about his own future. He was terrified of looking at his disfigured face, and believed the future was hopeless for him. He believed, as his grafts were not taking and he was losing his appetite, that he was slowly dying. As he had been the ringleader of the gang he felt that the staff were sadistic and blamed him for the accident and the fate of his friend. He did not see why he should eat or follow the physiotherapist's advice when all of these things made him feel more discomfort. Discussion of the patient's feelings about his responsibility for the accident and his responsibility for his own future, discussion of his health beliefs concerning his prognosis and the likely costs and benefits of following medical advice were the starting-point of the clinical psychologist's psychological treatment of this case.

Psychological factors as causal of physical disease

Behavioural factors (including diet and smoking) have long been implicated in the development of heart disease. However, the work of two American cardiologists, Ray Rosenman and Meyer Friedman, emphasized a more direct link between behaviour and disease. They identified a behavioural style, characterized by excessive competitive striving, time-urgency, and aggressiveness, which they called Type A behaviour. Carefully conducted research studies showed that those with Type A behaviour were shown to be more at risk of heart disease. Modifying the Type A pattern can also lead to a reduction in risk in those prone to coronary heart disease. The potential for change of these and other risk factors has given impetus to the work of psychologists in designing health promotion programmes aimed at producing behaviour change such as smoking cessation, improved diet, and reduced stress (see Bennett and Carroll 1990).

There are also psychological factors not immediately under the intentional control of the person which may lead to the worsening of symptoms. This in turn may lead the person to reject potentially life-saving treatments because of their unpleasant side-effects. Chemotherapeutic treatments for several types of cancer are toxic. That is, in order to kill off diseased cells, the drug also kills normal tisues. This can produce very unpleasant side-effects, such as hair loss, tiredness, pain and discomfort, poor appetite, nausea, and vomiting.

While most patients feel sick during treatment on drugs such as Adriamycin, several studies in the USA have shown that approximately 25 per cent of people felt sick at the *thought* of treatment. That is, the smell of the hospital ward, the hospital food, the sight of the hospital, the thought of the treatment can make some patients not only feel anxious but feel nauseous and vomit. In some cases this can lead to anorexia, debility, and fatigue. Psychologists believe that a conditioned aversion may account for this process: that is the patient's feelings of nausea have become conditioned to the hospital environment by the process of classical conditioning (see Fig. 10.1).

If untreated, many patients are unable to complete the chemo-therapy, and can be expected to suffer further physical consequences of their untreated disease. Psychological treatment involves using anxiety-management techniques, such as relaxation and systematic desensitization, developed in the treatment of phobias (Morrow and Morrell 1982).

Physical health problems are not only caused directly by disease processes, but also by trauma. The staff of a hospital casualty department, a head injury unit, or a burn unit, are usually aware that accidents are seldom random events. That is, there are accident-prone environments and accident-prone people, and the combination of the two puts some people more at risk of accidents than others. While it is possible to be burned in a truly accidental way, as in an earthquake, it is much more likely that a burned person will live or work in a hazardous environment. It is also more likely that they will be careless or ignorant of safety precautions. The case of Gary Adams above illustrates the combination of a hazardous environment and accident-prone behaviours. It is also well established that the commonest cause of death in children is through accidents, of which burns injuries are second only to road traffic accidents. Many of these occur in the home, and in pre-adolescent children the cause of the injury is often traced to a poor and hazardous physical environment, with evidence of social disruption and family tension at the time of the accident. Some accidents may be the result of neglect; others may be more directly attributed to intentional child abuse. While the causes of accidents are multifaceted, and involve an interaction between the individual and the environment, approximately 75 per cent of burn accidents are preventable through legislation and engineering to change physical environments, and

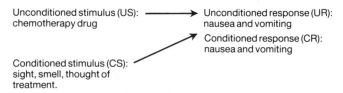

Fig. 10.1 A model of conditional anticipatory nausea to cancer chemo-therapy.

through social policy and health education to improve the psychological environment and the promotion of accident-prevention behaviour.

Assessment

Just as in other areas of clinical psychology, assessments are carried out to answer questions. Usually the questions involve determining if the particular patient needs psychological help, and what form of help is indicated. Assessments may also be made of groups of patients or of environments such as a ward, in order to determine if changes in services are required or if new changes are effective.

Cognitive–behavioural analysis

The aim of a cognitive–behavioural analysis is to determine the problem, enumerate the patient's responses, and evaluate the effect of the patient's methods of coping. The frequency and duration of symptoms, the antecedent conditions, and the responses and consequences are determined. There are many methods of carrying out such an analysis. In some cases information is gathered using a questionnaire in which patients identify situations that are associated with the occurrence of symptoms. This may be combined with a self-monitoring diary kept each day for several weeks, in which the patients record their activities and their symptoms and responses. From such a diary, it is often possible to determine whether there are predictable relationships between antecedent conditions and behaviour, and between behaviour and consequent conditions.

In order to assess fully Mrs Jago's irritable bowel syndrome, she was asked to keep a daily symptom diary, to record how tense she became at times of stress, and to write down the thoughts she was having when she became anxious. From her early diaries it became clear that not only did she suffer high levels of anxiety and physical tension when beyond her safe area; she was also tense and fearful of incontinence for some time before she left home. These data allowed us to plan an intervention in which Mrs Jago was first taught how to minimize her physical tension at times of stress by using relaxation techniques, and to modify her thoughts to give her rather more calming messages than previously ('You won't be incontinent now—you never have been before.') She then put these skills to work in a programme that involved her gradually extending her ventures beyond the previous safe area until she had achieved a number of her goals, including walking her child to school on her own and shopping in the city centre shops. During this time, her diaries were used to monitor her changing use of relaxation and mental coping strategies as well as her progress in achieving her goals and sub-goals.

A major feature of Mrs Jago's problems related to her thought (or cognitive) processes, and it is often important to encourage patients to record their thoughts as well as their behaviours. For example, where patients show a consistent pattern of undervaluing themselves and of their ability to control their symptoms, it may be important to ask them to record their thoughts, so that the therapist can teach them how to dispute these thoughts and substitute more appropriate coping self-statements. It can be helpful to provide patients with a list of typical thoughts that people have in response to stressful situations, as many people are reticent to record their thoughts verbatim. Other methods include encouraging patients to re-enact typical problems in imagination, and to verbalize their thoughts as they occur.

Behavioural observation

Observational methods are most often used where the clinician is concerned with the circumstances in which a behaviour occurs, rather than the patient's interpretation of the event. In the case of a young child in a burn unit where verbal communication is severely restricted by the patient's age and physical condition, behaviours such as excessive crying, self-destructive actions, or violence towards staff can be problematic. Systematic behavioural observation may be important in determining the frequency, antecedents, and consequences of these behaviours, and the alternative behaviours that the patient could be taught to substitute. In a burn unit where dressing changes and physiotherapy are painful, but non-compliant behaviour of patients only serves to prolong the treatment and exacerbates the painfulness of the procedure, the staff are often concerned to minimize excessive pain behaviour. Behavioural observations could include direct observation of the patient and recording the number of physiotherapy exercises completed in a given time-period. More indirect observation could be made after the exercises are completed by recording the mileage gauge on an

exercise cycle used by a burn patient instructed to increase movement of the lower limbs (Varni 1983).

Behavioural observations can be important in determining the
baseline of activities from which improvement in activity can be
negotiated as part of the treatment. For chronic pain patients the aim
of treatment is often to maximize activity, since many patients show
relatively stable patterns of pain irrespective of activity, and yet their
activity levels have often diminished since the onset of their pain
problem, as they believe that activity is necessarily limited by the
occurrence of pain. In an in-patient chronic pain treatment facility,
such as exists in the Walton Hospital in Liverpool, self-recording of
activity and staff observation of activity may be combined to get a
clear picture of the patient's activity level before setting appropriate
treatment goals. An operational definition of activities is usually
made, with categories such as sitting, reading, talking, and so forth.
Where a patient's problem consists of lying down too often, a
distinction may be made between 'up-time' (activities carried out
when patients are taking weight on their feet) and 'down-time' (when
the patients's weight is taken off their legs, as in sitting or lying). Clear
definitions of behaviour are necessary in order to enable reliable
observations to be made which can be used to monitor the effectiveness of the treatment.

Psychophysiological methods

Measurement of psychophysiological processes, such as parameters
of arousal level, can be particularly important where abnormal
functioning is believed to underlie the illness. For example, some
investigators believe that excessive muscle tension, which can be
measured by monitoring electrical activity of the muscles, may
underlie certain types of tension headache. Measurement from
various sites taken when the patient is at rest and under circumstances of psychological stress may help to locate the particular
muscle groups where abnormal tension is believed to occur. With
biofeedback techniques, where the level of muscle tension in specific
muscles is 'fed back' to the patient, it may be possible for the patient
to identify the physical sensations associated with build-up of muscle
tension, and to learn to apply preventive relaxation techniques prior
to the onset of problems. The importance of the identification of
specific muscle groups involved in causing tension and pain is
exemplifed by Turk's work on back pain patients. He found that

whilst most patients' pain was relieved by using general relaxation techniques, some patients had no relief from pain, or indeed reported a worsening of symptoms. These paradoxical results were only explained by more detailed measurements, which revealed that they had failed to relax the specific muscle groups involved in the pain process, despite having reduced their overall tension. When taught to relax these muscles using biofeedback techniques, most patients were able to reduce their pain significantly (Turk *et al.* 1983).

Recordings of other physiological processes, such as blood-pressure, respiratory rate, and heart rate, which along with muscle tension are all believed to be influenced by sympathetic nervous system arousal, can be used to determine if patients who are being taught relaxation training for stress-related diseases are achieving an adequate level of therapeutic response. In conjunction with these direct psychophysiological methods, an indirect method of assessing compliance with relaxation may be employed. For example, patients may be instructed to use a relaxation tape with a cassette recorder in which a device is fitted which records the number of times the cassette has been played. Such indirect methods may be useful where direct methods may have a reactive effect. That is, where patients believe that they are being recorded, social factors such as a will to please the therapist may produce a bias in the response under investigation.

Psychological tests

The standardized questionnaire method of assessment may be used for research purposes in order to describe a sample in a way that can be replicated by other researchers. When investigating a clinical problem, standardized questionnaires may be useful in order to cut down on the amount of therapist time, or in order to obtain information which may be biased by the presence of the therapist. For example, some therapists use standardized questionnaires in order to take a sexual history.

Standardized questionnaires can be particularly useful in providing methods of screening patients for psychological help, and to evaluate the effects of psychological treatment. Since much of the work of a clinical psychologist is concerned with detecting patients who are psychologically distressed, and the aims of many interventions are to improve their overall well-being and reduce symptoms of distress, a relatively well-researched area is the measurement of psychological disturbance. Unfortunately, most of the available measures have been developed for psychiatric populations, and it is difficult to interpret the meaning of these scores for other populations. This is particularly so when the patient's physical illnesses can cause them to have somatic symptoms such as fatigue or loss of appetite, which on some psychiatric inventories are automatically taken as indicators of psychiatric syndromes such as depression. One solution is to use questionnaires developed for use with physically ill populations, which exclude somatic items. The Hospital Anxiety Depression Scale was developed to screen patients for overall levels of disturbance, and problems of anxiety and depression in particular in the patients attending a mixed medical out-patient service (Zigmond and Snaith 1983). It is increasingly being used with patients suffering from psychologically traumatic illnesses such as cancer, and shows some promise.

Other methods of psychological assessment are used to determine degrees of disability, based on an assessment of the frequency with which patients carry out activities of daily living as determined by investigation of samples of disabled people living in the community. From such a measure it is possible to provide an overall score for a given patient which can be compared with their pre-morbid level of functioning and with scores typical of normal and disabled people in the community. This type of measure is useful in evaluating the effects of treatment. For example, many cancer patients are subject to noxious treatments for cancer, such as surgery, chemotherapy, and radiotherapy. Comparison of the relative effects of treatment on the patient's mood and his or her ability to return to normal activities in between courses of chemotherapy can be very important in helping clinicians to determine which form of therapy has the least deleterious effect on the patient's quality of life.

Treatment

Cognitive–behavioural treatments of physical disorders have a number of common elements (Turk *et al*. 1983). It is most important to conceptualize the problem and its treatment in a way that patients understand and that will motivate them to participate actively. Any physical problem is 'bad news' to some degree, and help-seeking usually involves much anguish and self-questioning. The first step, then, is to elicit the patient's perspective on the problem, its aetiology, and its likely treatment.

The second step is to carry out a full assessment, and, using this shared knowledge, to formulate an understanding of the problem. This 'translation' of the patient's knowledge into the working model of the therapist can reduce helplesness in the patient by explaining the unexplained. It also recasts the problems in a form that has feasible solutions. This step leads naturally to the third, which is the formulation of therapeutic goals and treatment strategies in a *collaborative* relationship.

This collaborative endeavour can be encouraged by having patients collect data on themselves (for example, using diaries or reporting anecdotes). Patients are encouraged to monitor their behaviour, emotions, and cognitions, and, using feedback from the therapist, to develop a more objective view of their problem and of their coping strategies. Patients are often taught to employ old strategies more effectively, and are taught new ones. Most therapies involve patients in changing their overt behaviour (for example, learning to be more assertive with the boss who overworks them) and their cognitions (such as learning to put their thoughts into perspective when under pressure).

A number of strategies are employed to help maintain therapeutic gains. A collaborative relationship helps ensure patients feel responsible for their improvements, particularly if the therapist is able to clarify how changes made are attributable to the patient's actions. Finally, unlike many medical treatments, which are assumed to be superfluous once the 'lesion' is 'healed', most psychological problems require continued effort. This effort is facilitated if patients are taught to monitor their problems and anticipate and plan for relapse.

Examples of the cognitive–behavioural treatment of a gynaeco-logical pain problem and of an acute burns injury illustrate some of the applications of this treatment perspective:

Cognitive–behavioural treatment for chronic pelvic pain

Pearce and Beard (1984) report the surprising finding that approxi-mately two-thirds of women presenting with pelvic pain to a gynaecology clinic proved to have no obvious organic pathology. Explanations for the cause of illness include as yet undetected physical pathology, such as infection in the fallopian tubes, and abnormal psychophysiological processes, such as stress-induced vascular congestion in the pelvic area. As with other chronic pain syndromes, such as low back pain, the longer the pain has been experienced the weaker the relationship between noxious stimulation and pain intensity. For a given patient the original cause of pelvic pain may have been resolved, but pain may still be experienced, even where there is little evidence of a pathological process. In a proportion of patients, however, physiological processes such as vascular congestion are implicated. Patients who have been trained in relaxation methods, which are known to influence vascular flow to the pelvic region, show improved pain control.

Social influences may also be important in the control of the subjective and behavioural components of chronic pain. Laboratory experiments have shown that instructing people to expect pain is associated with subjects' reporting a given level of stimulation as painful, whereas in other circumstances where no such expectation is given the same level of stimulation is not reported as painful. For chronic pain patients it may be expected that patients with prior experience of pain may be more attuned to physiological changes and may expect particular activities to be painful, and therefore they may more readily label sensations as painful. In a patient with a history of abdominal disease such processes may partially account for pain reporting in the absence of profound or continued pathology.

Experimental studies have shown that where subjects believe they are in control of the occurrence of painful events greater tolerance of pain is achieved. For the chronic pelvic pain patient repeated procedures and investigations may induce a sense of helplessness. A therapeutic goal, therefore, is to improve the patient's perceived control over pain. This may be achieved through preparing patients so that they are able to understand the likely effects of invasive investigations and physical treatments, and by helping patients to gain control over pain levels by reducing the anxiety component of pain through relaxation training. Control over the anxiety component may be particularly important, as anxiety is known to reduce the threshold for the detection of pain, and may also act by triggering abnormal blood flow to the pelvic region, hence influencing the physiological component of the condition.

Pain is a subjective experience, and the observer only knows a person is in pain by his or her behaviour. Even for acute pain induced in a laboratory or by medical/dental procedures, social influences affect pain expression and other pain behaviours, such as guarding movements, limping, and taking analgesics. Fordyce, a clinical psychologist in Seattle, USA, has shown that pain patients exhibit more pain behaviours when they believe their spouses are watching them through a one-way mirror than when told they are in the company of less sympathetic persons. The degree to which patients' normal activities are impeded by pain behaviours is also subject to psychological control. This is put to therapeutic effect where staff attention is switched from pain behaviours such as lying down and disengaging from physiotherapy exercises and switched to the achievement of therapeutic activity goals. Where systematic application of social reinforcement is carried out by the staff and the patient's spouse, patients can learn to improve their overall functional capacity. These techniques have been used to great effect with mixed chronic pain patients in in-patient facilities, and discussion of the relationship between patients' pain behaviours and social reinforcement are an integral part of the behavioural treatment of pain problems such as chronic pelvic pain (Fordyce 1976).

Pearce and colleagues (1982) compared relaxation training with behavioural counselling, non-directive psychotherapy, and a no-treatment control condition for 32 patients suffering from chronic pelvic pain with no obvious pathology of six or more months' duration. The patients kept a record of pain for one month before surgical investigation, throughout psychological treatment, and for three months afterwards. All patients were seen for four to six sessions over two to three months. Patients in the three treatment groups all showed some improvement in pain-free days; but relaxation training and non-directive psychotherapy showed the greatest improvement by one-year follow-up.

Additional techniques that have been effective with patients suffering other chronic pain syndromes such as headache include stress-management training similar to that described earlier in the treatment of stress disorders. Direct modification of the patient's experience of pain by hypnosis, similar to that described below for acute burns pain, can also be useful, particularly if patients are taught to induce a hypnotic state for themselves. This is particularly useful where the patient's pain diary shows that pain occurs at predictable times or in response to specific stimuli, such as stressful meeetings in work. In this way, patients can not only apply hypnosis once the pain has started, but it can be applied preventatively.

Psychological treatment of acute burns injury

Gary Adams's problems were discussed earlier, and were identified as:

1. Failure to comply with the medical regime of increased protein and calorie intake, leading to delayed healing, and failure to comply with physiotherapy exercises, leading to reduced movement and the development of contractures.
2. Depression.
3. Fear of repeated painful procedures.
4. Distress and fear for his own life and guilt associated with the accident and the prospect of long-term disability.

Initial discussions focused on explaining the interrelatedness of his problems, and how his own emotional behaviour could influence his recovery.

A behavioural contract was drawn up which specified the behavioural goals (i.e. the behaviours required of the patient) plus the rewards for achievement of the goals. The patient agreed that the main reward would be seeing his grafts 'take'. A short-term reward, such as being accompanied by a nurse he had befriended on trips in a wheelchair outside the hospital, would be useful. Staff were also instructed to comment on his progress.

The anaesthetist was reluctant to increase his medication, which could further reduce his appetite and could lead to the possibility of morphine addiction and of respiratory failure. Gary was instructed that he would have to tolerate the painful burn-dressing changes with only the help of mild analgesics such as paracetamol. In order to relieve the patient's fear, he was taught to identify fearful thoughts and substitute less fearful thoughts. For example, he was taught to substitute for 'I know it will hurt' more positive self-statements such as 'it will not be worse than before'. He was taught to practise using more positive thoughts, and also to reward himself when he coped well. He felt it was difficult to concentrate during the dressing changes, so a guided-imagery technique was used. He was taught to distract himself and dissociate his thoughts away from his body. He found he could concentrate on imagining himself walking along the bank of a river, which he used to do when he wanted to relax and unwind.

To reduce the muscle tension caused by involuntary tremors and involuntary muscle tension or guarding movements, he was taught behavioural relaxation techniques. As he was unable to tense up certain muscle groups he was taught a simple self-suggestion method focusing on increasing feelings of warmth and heaviness in each muscle group and deep-breathing exercises. Finally, a self-hypnosis procedure was taught in order to enable the patient to remain in a light trance. He was a responsive subject, and also learned not only how to dissociate himself from his body, but also develop feelings of numbness in the most painful parts of the body. The psychologist attended several burn-dressing changes in order to coach Gary and encourage him to use the techniques.

Finally, the patient was most fearful for his own safety. He began to discuss the fate of his friend with the clinical psychologist. Although he was shocked to learn that his friend had died, he had suspected this. Now the matter had been brought up he was able to grieve for his friend openly, and was encouraged to discuss his feelings. When it became apparent that his thoughts included a number of cognitive distortions typical of depression, a cognitive restructuring approach was initiated to help the patient learn to substitute more rational thoughts for irrational thoughts associated with his dysphoric mood. As much of his depression was associated with helplessness, the principle of behavioural contracting in order to encourage Gary to develop a feeling of control over his environment was extended to other activities. For example, where there was some particularly important social goal, such as having a visit from a friend who was only able to visit at certain irregular intervals, he was able to earn access outside the normal visiting arrangements provided that he had achieved the behaviour specified in the contract, such as wearing an uncomfortable pressure garment, eating, or attending to his personal hygiene as required.

Although many psychological hurdles remained for this patient at the time he was discharged from hospital, such as the problems of being disfigured, he reported that he no longer felt depressed, and he attributed most of his improvement to the feeling of self-control which was engendered by learning to control the fear of pain associated with the many painful procedures which he had repeatedly undergone for several months. He also resolved his feelings of guilt concerning the accident by 'trading off' his painful hospitalization against his past misdeeds.

The psychological assessment and treatment of Gary Adams illustrates some of the complexity of the relationship between psychological and physical problems and the multi-faceted nature of clinical intervention.

CONSULTATION

Where there is limited time available from the clinical psychologist, and where other staff are in more direct contact with patients on a regular basis, the clinical psychologist may choose not to accept individual referrals of patients, but to advise staff on the management of particular patients, or on strategies for preventing or managing frequently occurring psychological problems. The example noted earlier of the clinical psychologist looking at staff communication in the coronary care unit is one such example.

In some renal dialysis units, a clinical psychologist has provided support and advice to nursing and medical staff as an indirect means of providing a service to the patient. Nichols's work in a renal unit in Exeter provides such a service. A major concern of the staff who have regular contact with the patients while on dialysis is to find ways of helping the patients to cope with chronic illness and with the strain that this puts on the families of young and old patients alike. Making a determined effort to retain and regain ability to carry out normal activities rather than to sink into the role of a chronic invalid requires considerable motivation. Psychologists may counsel individual patients, but they also have a role to play in training staff to detect patients who are under severe stress and to develop and support their ability to counsel patients appropriately (Nichols 1987).

Staff may also request help in dealing with service problems. The first author was invited to investigate whether the trend towards shorter hospital stay for minor gynaecological surgery was harmful, and whether it was beneficial for some women (Wallace 1986). It was found that day-case patients were more anxious before surgery, and more often unable to be discharged on the evening surgery than expected. These unplanned overnight stays were costly to the hospital, and caused social disruption for the patients. Interviews with patients before and after the operation showed that anxious patients had a slower or more complicated recovery. The next stage was to find a way of reducing fear and increasing patients' ability to cope with post-operative pain and other minor complications. It became clear from interviews with the patients that much of the fear was the result of fear of the unknown. Most of the patients had little idea how much pain to expect, or of the effectiveness of post-operative medication or of other methods of relieving the post-operative pain, such as lying in particular positions or using relaxation tapes. The staff believed they were already giving adequate verbal information to the patients, and yet much of this information was not understood or remembered. The staff were willing to assess whether a booklet containing information about surgery, how to cope with fear and pain, and the particular ward routines associated with being a day case or an overnight-stay case would be effective in improving patients' adjustment to surgery and recovery. A subsequent study showed that patients who received the informative booklet, in comparison to patients receiving a minimally informative 'placebo' booklet or who received a routine verbal explanation only, were less anxious before the operation, experienced less pain after the operation, and recovered faster both while in hospital and during the first week after discharge home. Consultation with the staff in this way suggested several options for improving the service, such as providing information for day-case patients prior to their admission to hospital, in order to avoid unplanned overnight stays.

RESEARCH

The research skills of clinical psychologists may be used to investigate the causes of health problems, such as the role of stress in coronary heart disease, or the development of psychological treatment such as stress-management training, or the more effective medical management of ill patients by using psychological models of patients' understanding of their illness in order to tailor information to patients about their illness and the benefits of treatment. Research skills may be used to investigate service problems, such as the causes and some solutions to staff stress in particular medical environments, such as Intensive Care and Coronary Care units.

An example of theory-based clinical research is provided by Grossmarth-Maticek and colleagues (1984), who extrapolated from research which suggested that cancer-prone patients are characterized by a cognitive style which involves suppression of emotions (particularly aggression), low self-esteem, and lack of assertion. They examined whether psychotherapy aimed at changing these characteristics would alter the course of disease in a group of patients with advanced breast cancer. They found that chemotherapy improved the survival by an average of 2.8 months, while psychotherapy improved life expectancy by 3.6 months. However, the combination of both treatments results in a far more impressive improvement in survival time of 22.4 months. This work remains almost unique, and requires replication. However, stress has consistently been shown to impair the immune system's response to disease and its ability to control or prevent the progression of diseases such as cancer and the development of AIDS. One implication of such findings is that stress-management strategies may slow down the progression or development of these and other diseases. This remains somewhat speculative at present, although in the case of AIDS, where there is no effective medical treatment, such approaches may be particularly appropriate.

HEALTH PROMOTION AND HEALTH CARE SYSTEMS

As has been previously noted, as much as half of present premature mortality can be attributable to 'unhealthy' behaviours. As a result both politicians and health care providers have focused on health promotion as a means of improving public health. Health promotion operates at a number of levels, and any psychological contribution must vary accordingly.

Co-operation between a district psychology department and the health promotion department can occur at local level. For example, one of the authors (PB) worked as a clinical psychologist on a project involving screening and counselling for risk factors for heart disease. The primary clincial role involved running stress-management groups for hypertensives, combined with a staff training and consultancy role. In addition, the psychologist was involved in evaluating the effectiveness of the stress-management groups and the project as a whole. Finally, some time was given over to the development of health education literature—focusing on aspects of smoking cessation and stress management—to accompany similar output from the dietitian.

The potential for psychological output is not limited to the local or district level. Heart-disease prevention programmes have provided the major innovative thrust in health promotion both at a community and a national level. All the major European and American programmes have involved psychologists both in the planning and the evaluation of the programmes. For example, the Stanford Three Communities Project's attempt to reduce smoking prevalence utilized psychological methods, based upon social learning theory, to teach the necesary skills for behaviour change. Successful behaviour change was modelled by televising the progress of a group of people attending a smoking cessation group.

A number of health authorities now have psychologists in their health promotion teams. Their role might be to bring about change in the health authority policy, thereby facilitating changes in the behaviour of health care professionals as well as changes in the behaviour of individual people. Service-delivery problems can arise because the system of health care fails to deliver a service that meets the conflicting needs of its users. Out-patient departments are traditionally run as a series of 'production lines' for processing the maximum number of patients by each medical team, with the back-up of clinical therapy, diagnostic, and administrative services. In practice, this production line results in frustration for staff, who often experience problems of poor co-ordination of services, and patients, who either fail to attend, or seem to turn up repeatedly for treatment beyond the capacity of the service to provide it. Patients complain that they see different professionals each time, and do not get answers to questions of 'what is wrong with me, what can be done for me, and what can I do myself?'

A radical rethinking of the way the service is delivered is being developed by the first author. This idea designs the service around the needs of the patients, and is called the 'Patient Centred Approach'. This collaborative project between management, psychology, and clinical staff brings health care staff together to assess jointly patients with complex needs and to provide multidisciplinary care, with the emphasis on building a partnership between staff and patients. For example, chronic patients are assessed by the anaesthetist, psychologist, specially trained nurse, occupational therapist, and physiotherapist, and given individual treatment or referred to a pain self-management group. The expertise of the psychologist is used not only to treat patients, but also to reorganize the service around the needs of the patients, to train other staff, and to set up methods of evaluating the effectiveness of the service.

SPECIAL ISSUES

A recurrent theme in this chapter is the extent to which patients should be involved in their health care. This includes whether they should be informed in order to take decisions affecting their treatment, their rights to refuse treatment, their responsibility to accept and comply with treatment, and the extent to which information about patients' prognosis or treatment will adversely or positively affect their health. Such issues involve complex physical, legal, and psychosocial factors, and are not solved by putting the responsibility entirely on the staff or on the patients. However, some of the issues are capable of clarification by systematic clinical observation and by clinical research. For example, an extension of the concern of doctors about the effect of cancer treatments on patients' quality of life is to investigate the patients' judgements of the overall worthwhileness of treatments. Some clinical trials have shown that most patients did not judge as worthwhile a treatment which promised only a moderate improvement in survival of a few weeks when they underwent chemotherapy that caused considerable side-effects.

An intriguing study of patients in Liverpool by Jennifer Ashcroft (Ashcroft *et al*. 1985) sought to establish whether patients who were given the choice between two apparently equally effective treatments for breast cancer had better psychological adjustment than patients who were not given such a choice. Interestingly, she found that initially the patients experienced considerable difficulty in taking this decision. A form of structured decision-making analysis, including analysis of the individual's perceived costs and benefits of the two treatments, which formed the basis of a counselling interview, enabled all patients to make an informed decision. Those women who were more concerned about their body image chose the less radical surgery (lumpectomy and radiotherapy). The results showed that patients were more satisfied and showed fewer signs of depression than would have been expected from previous studies of patients where no such choice has been given (Owens *et al*. 1987).

The importance of feeling that they have participated in the decision is confirmed by the equally positive psychological effects on women who, if required on medical grounds to have a mastectomy, are offered the choice of reconstructive surgery; they also feel more in control and able to cope (Owen *et al*. 1987).

It could be argued that the responsibility for such an important decision as which of two equally effective surgeries one undergoes could provoke additional stress and guilt if the disease recurs and the 'wrong' decision taken. In a later study by the same team, women were given the same choice between surgeries, or allocated to a group in which they believed the surgeon had chosen for them (when in fact the surgeon chose the patient's preference). The results supported the hypothesis that, over and above the benefits of having their preferred treatment, women can further benefit from taking explicit responsibility for their treatment choice (Deadman *et al.* in press). These studies show how ethical dilemmas such as these can benefit from empirical analysis.

CONCLUSION

The clinical psychologist as a member of the health care team for physical diseases is a new development. The development of psychological services will depend on continued research into the processes of psychological factors in illness and health behaviour and the quality of life of physically ill patients, particularly those suffering from chronic disease, which are so seldom completely remedied by medical treatment.

REFERENCES

Ashcroft, J. J., Leinster, S., and Slade, P. D. (1985). Breast cancer—patient choice of treatment. Preliminary communication. *J. R. Soc. Med.*, **78**, 43–6.

Becker, M. H. and Maiman, L. H. (1975). Sociobehavioural determinants of compliance with health and medical care recommendations. *Med. Care*, **13**(1), 10–14.

Bennett, P. and Carroll, D. (1990). Stress management approaches to the prevention of coronary disease. *Brit. J. Clin. Psychol.*, **29**, 1–12.

Bundy, E. C., Wallace, L. M., and Nagle, R. E. Stress management training in chronic stable angina. *Int. J. Physol. and Health*. (In press.)

Deadman, J., Owens, R. G., Leinster, S., Dewey, M. E., and Slade, P. D. Responsibility for choice in the treatment of breast cancer: preliminary communication. *Soc. Sci. Med.* (In press.)

Fordyce, W. E. (1976). *Behavioural method in chronic pain and illness*. Mosby, St Louis.

Grossmarth-Maticek, R., Schmidt, P., Vetter, H., and Arndt, S. (1984). Psychotherapy research in oncology. In *Health care and human behaviour* (ed. A. Steptoe and A. Mathews). Academic Press, London.

Maguire, G. P., Julier, D. L., Hawton, K. E., and Bancroft, J. H. J. (1974). Psychiatric morbidity and referral on two general medical wards. *Br. Med. J.*, **I**, 268–70.

Morrow, G. R. and Morrell, C. (1982). Behavioural treatment for the anticipatory nausea and vomiting induced by cancer chemotherapy. *New Engl. J. Med.*, **307**, 1476–80.

Nichols, K. A. (1987). Teaching nurses psychological care. In *Teaching nurses psychological skills* (ed. D. Miller), British Psychological Society, Leicester.

Owens, R. G., Ashcroft, J. J., Leinster, S. J., and Slade, P. D. (1987). Informed decision analysis with breast cancer patients: an aid to psychological preparation for surgery. *J. Psychosoc. Oncol.*, 5, 23–33.

Pearce, S. and Beard, R. W. (1984). Chronic pelvic pain. In *Psychology and gynaecological problems* (ed. A. K. Broome and L. M. Wallace), pp. 95–117. Tavistock, London.

Peace, S., Knight, C., and Beard, R. W. (1982). Pelvic pain—a common gynaecological problem. *J. Psychosom. Obstet. Gynaecol.*, **1**, 12.

Shirreff, J. H. (1982). *Community health: contemporary perspectives*. Prentice Hall, Englewood Cliffs, New Jersey.

Turk, D. C., Meichenbaum, D., and Genest, M. (1983). *Pain and behavioural medicine: a cognitive behavioural perspective*. Guilford Press, New York.

Varni, J. N. (1983). *Clinical behavioural paediatrics: an interdisciplinary biobehavioural approach*. Pergamon Press, Oxford.

Wallace, L. M. (1986). Day-case laparoscopy: patient preferences, adjustment and recovery. *Eur. J. Psychosom. Obstet. Gynaecol.*, **5**, 207–16.

Wallace, L. M. and Joshi, M. (1987). Video-tape modelling of communication skills in a coronary care unit. *Intensive Care Nursing*, **2**, 107–11.

Zigmond, A. S. and Snaith, P. P. (1983). The Hospital Anxiety Depression Scale. *Acta Psychiat. Scand.*, **67**, 361–70.

FURTHER READING

Bernstein, N. R. (1976). *Emotional care of the facially burned and disfigured*. Little, Brown and Company, Boston.

Broome, A. K. (ed.) (1989). *Health psychology: process and applications*. Chapman and Hall, London.

Broome, A. K. and Wallace, L. M. (eds) (1984). *Psychology and gynaecological problems*. Tavistock, London.

Gatchel, R. J., Baum, A., and Krantz, D. S. (1989). *An introduction to health psychology* (2nd edn). Random House, New York.

Pearce, S. and Wardle, J. (1989). *The practice of behavioural medicine.* Oxford University Press.

Roskies, E. (1987). *Stress management for the healthy Type A. Theory and practice.* Guilford Press, New York.

Russell, E. (ed.) (1988). *Stress management for chronic disease.* Pergamon Press, New York.

Wallace, L. M. and Graham, J. A. (1990). *The complete mind and body book: total body care.* Simon and Schuster, New York.

11

Clinical psychology and primary health care
John Marzillier

Clinical psychologists have traditionally worked as specialists in health care. They have been attached to hospitals, special units, or other institutions, and have applied their psychological knowledge and principles to the problems of the particular client group. In the field of mental illness, for example, clinical psychologists have often been attached to psychiatric teams, carrying out specialized assessment, and treatments (see Chapters 2 and 3). Hospitals for those with learning difficulties, neurology departments, adolescent units, Regional Secure Units, Special Hospitals, physical rehabilitation centres, paediatric departments, are all specialist services to which clinical psychologists have contributed a specialized service. Their work is illustrated in various chapters of this book.

However, the people seen by the various specialist services constitute only a small percentage of those who experience similar problems in the community at large. This relationship is aptly illustrated in the notion of different *levels* of care (see Fig. 11.1).

Goldberg and Huxley (1980), from whom the idea of levels of care is derived, suggest that of 250 people with psychiatric disorders found in the community (level 1) only 17 will in fact reach the specialist psychiatric services (level 4). Of these 17 only a certain indeterminate percentage will come to the attention of clinical psychologists. Goldberg and Huxley describe how between each level of care certain filters come into operation. For example, between the presentation of a psychiatric disorder in primary care (level 2) and its recognition (level 3) is a 'detection filter', indicating that a substantial number of psychiatric disorders remain undetected. Equally, of those detected (level 3) only a very small number are in fact referred on to psychiatrists (level 4), indicating the operation of a 'referral filter'. Clinical psychologists can receive direct referrals of patients from GPs, and so be subject to a similar filtering system to that which affects psychiatrists, or may receive many of their referrals from specialist physicians (for example,

	the community		primary medical care			specialist psychiatric services		
	level 1	1st filter	level 2	2nd filter	level 3	3rd filter	level 4	4th filter	level 5
	morbidity in random community samples		total psychiatric morbidity, primary care		conspicuous psychiatric morbidity		total psychiatric patients		psychiatric in-patients only
one-year period prevalence, median estimates	250 →		230 →		140 →		17 →		6 (per 1000 at risk per year)
characteristics of the four filters		illness behaviour		detection of disorder		referral of psychiatrist		admission to psychiatric beds	
key individual		the patient		primary care physician		primary care physician		psychiatrist	
factors operating on key individual		severity and type of symptoms psycho-social stress learned patterns of illness behaviour		interview techniques personality factors training and attitudes		confidence in own ability to manage availability and quality of psychiatric services attitudes towards psychiatrists		availability of beds availability of adequate community psychiatric services	
other factors		attitudes of relatives availability of medical services ability to pay for treatment		presenting symptom pattern socio-demographic characteristics of patient		symptom pattern of patient attitudes of patient and family		symptom pattern of patient, attitudes of patient and family delay in social worker arriving	

Fig. 11.1. The pathway to psychiatric care. (Reprinted with permission, from Goldberg and Huxley 1980.)

neurologists, psychiatrists), and in the latter instance be subject to yet another filter. Operating as specialists in the health care system means that clinical psychologists will only see a fraction of the psychological problems presented by people at large. To a certain extent this protects the psychologist from being subjected to a larger volume of clients that she or he can cope with. But in other respects it results in a selective and at times idiosyncratic service to clients which is dependent more on the nature of the 'filters' than on the applicability of the service to particular problems or clients.

A recent development in clinical psychology has been one of establishing closer and more direct links with primary care staff. Some psychologists have carried out treatment sessions on general practice premises. Others have forged close links with health visitors and community nurses. There have also been occasional examples of a psychologist working full-time in primary care serving the needs of one or more teams (see, for example, Johnston 1978). This 'move into the community' has also been seen in the work of other mental health professionals, psychiatrists, and nurses in particular. It reflects a general climate of change in mental health in which the traditional reliance on specialized care, particularly in terms of large mental hospitals, is giving way to the idea of 'care in the community'.

PRIMARY HEALTH CARE

Primary health care describes the nearest contact that individuals have with their local health service. It is one of a number of levels of care, as Table 11.1 indicates.

Primary health care is concerned with the delivery of services to a small local community of up to 50 000 people. In developed countries this is achieved through doctors, who act as 'gatekeepers' to the specialist hospital services, diagnosing and treating the vast majority of patients themselves and referring on those who need a specialist assessment or treatment.

The organization of primary health care differs from country to country. For example, in some countries such as France the vast majority of doctors work single-handedly, whereas in the UK the majority of general practitioners collaborate in partnerships (i.e. groups of doctors co-operating together) or interdisciplinary teams. The funding of primary health care differs too. In a few countries

Table 11.1 Population size, level of care, and professional service

Population	Level of care	Professional/premises providing care
Family unit (1–10)	Self-care	Friends; non-professional helpers; (only one in four of all symptoms are taken to professional medical worker)
50–50 000	Primary	Single-handed general practitioner; group practice; health centre practice; polyclinic
50 000–500 000	Specialist	General hospital and specialist clinic
500 000–5 000 000	Super-specialist	Regional or super-specialist hospital or clinic

such as Denmark, New Zealand, and Britain, the service is centrally funded by government taxation. However, the majority of countries operate under a pluralist system of compulsory health insurance, private insurance schemes, and direct payment to doctors. In the UK the primary care doctor is a generalist (hence the term general practitioner) who provides personal and medical care to individuals and families within his practice irrespective of their age, sex, and illness. But in other countries patients may call directly on specialists such as paediatricians or gynaecologists, who will have a specific responsibility for the category of patients within their area of expertise.

Primary health care team

There has been a trend in some countries for primary care physicians to work in collaboration with other professionals in the form of a primary health care team. This development has been seen in particular in the UK, and an example of a primary health care team is given in Fig. 11.2.

The core of the team is a group of GPs, who directly employ the practice manager, secretaries, receptionists, and practice nurses. In the UK 70 per cent of the salaries of these professionals can be claimed back by the general practitioner from central government. In addition, health visitors and, occasionally, 'attached' social

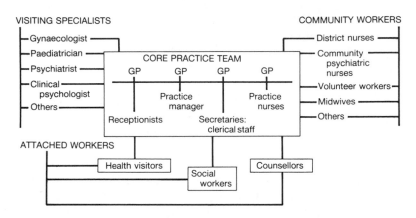

Fig. 11.2   The primary health care team (UK).

workers and counsellors work directly on the practice premises, providing a service to their particular client groups. For the most part they do not come under the direct employment of the general practitioners, but are responsible to their own managers. However, in a recent development, some counsellors have been directly employed by GPs in a similar way to practice nurses. District nurses, community psychiatric nurses, and others operate in the local catchment area of the practice and will liaise with the various team members. Finally, consultants and specialists from local hospitals may occasionally visit the practice and hold clinics on the premises. It is here that clinical psychologists come in. They are one of a number of specialist professional groups who have deliberately set out to extend their services into primary health care.

PSYCHOLOGICAL PROBLEMS IN PRIMARY HEALTH CARE

What psychological problems present in primary care? This is a difficult question to answer, because the term 'psychological problems' is vague and open to many different interpretations. The range of psychological problems that people have is considerable, from everyday problems of life such as marital discord, stresses at work, worries about bringing up a family, etc., to major psychiatric disorders such as depression or schizophrenia. In addition, many purely physical illnesses can have psychological consequences, for example, the need to adjust to a permanent disability, the impact of a chronic illness on family and friends, or the effect of surgical disfigurement on feelings of self-esteem and acceptance by others. Fortunately, people do not perceive most psychological concerns as problems for which they seek professional help. Most people cope with their psychological problems themselves, and, as far as we can tell, they cope reasonably well. This is an important point for health care professionals to remember, since many of the minor worries and concerns that people experience will 'resolve themselves' without the need for intervention. There is some risk that professional help can have a negative effect, crystallizing ordinary worries as 'illness' or 'disorders', with the implication that remedies need to be sought in order for these apparent 'illnesses' to be treated. For example, there is now a growing recognition that the prescription of minor tranquillizers, benzodiazepines, for anxiety has in many instances been unnecessary and potentially harmful, creating a state of psychological and physical dependency and reinforcing the view that emotional states are chronic disorders requiring treatment.

Prevalence of psychological problems

Because of the vagueness of the term 'psychological problems', it is difficult to get a clear picture of their prevalence in primary care. In a questionnaire survey, over 1000 general practitioners in the Oxford Region were asked the following question: 'Roughly what percentage of your consultations include psychological problems?' (Marzillier and Fowler, unpublished findings, 1986). On average, the GPs rated about 28 per cent of their consultations as including psychological problems, and, of these, 30 per cent were rated as severe enough to warrant specific treatment—about 8 per cent of all consultations. The range of estimates was large, however, varying from 0 to 100 per cent! In another study, a clinical psychologist sat in on 366 consultations, and he and the doctors separately rated consultations for 'psychological relevance' (McPherson and Feldman 1977). The psychologist rated 12 per cent of all consultations as 'quite' or 'highly relevant', whereas the GPs rated 18 per cent. The correlation between the psychologist's and the doctor's ratings was very low, indicating substantial disagreement about which consultations were the psychologically relevant ones.

These subjective estimates may say more about the 'psychological mindedness' of the GP rather than being a reliable or accurate assessment of psychological disturbance in primary care. Not only will GPs differ in their readiness to perceive psychological problems, but patients will vary in their readiness to present such problems to particular GPs. In this way some doctors may genuinely never be presented openly with a psychological problem, while others will be inundated with them. An alternative approach to the assessment of prevalence is to concentrate upon specific and discriminable categories of disorder, such as psychiatric illnesses.

Prevalence of psychiatric illness

A distinction can be made between 'formal psychiatric illnesses' such as neurosis, schizophrenia, manic-depressive psychosis, and those physical disorders or social problems with a psychological or psychiatric component. Even with regard to formal psychiatric diagnoses, estimates of their prevalence in primary care are quite variable. It has been estimated that between a quarter and a third of all illnesses treated by GPs are psychiatric illnesses, and that in one year about 14 per cent of a GP's patients will consult for psychiatric disorders. By far the most common disorders are the minor affective illnesses, that is, anxiety, depression, and mixed anxiety-depressive states. Many psychiatric disorders that present in primary care will not be detected by the GP: this has been termed 'hidden psychiatric morbidity'. For example, Goldberg and Bridges (1987) found that, while almost one-third of all consecutive new illnesses presenting in general practice were classifiable as psychiatric according to established diagnostic criteria, GPs rated just over half of these as 'entirely physical'. Moreover, pure psychiatric illness (i.e. without physical concomitants) was uncommon. Most psychiatric symptomatology is masked by somatic and physical complaints. Thus, although exact estimates of the prevalence of psychiatric illnesses are difficult to achieve, research has shown that these illnesses—particularly the minor affective disorders—are very common and that, further, a substantial number of them are not detected by the GP.

An example of 'hidden psychiatric morbidity'

Mrs Barnes is an example of 'hidden psychiatric morbidity'. She consulted her GP because of persistent insomnia, and after a brief chat was prescribed sleeping tablets. However, Mrs Barnes's presenting complaint masked a more deep-rooted anxiety. She had been experiencing intrusive fantasies of harming her children, and was terrified that she might be driven, against her will, to kill them. These fantasies kept her awake at night. Her anxiety was beginning to develop an obsessional quality; she hid away knives and sharp objects, and would recite ritualistic phrases to forestall the possibility of harm occurring.

Mrs Barnes was eventually referred to a clinical psychologist, and successfully helped to deal with her anxieties. Many patients present with a physical complaint (for example, headaches, physical tension, skin problems, tiredness) which, on further analysis, reflects underlying psychological problems. These physical symptoms have been described as the patient's 'ticket of entry' to the consultation.

An alternative approach to attempts at assessing prevalence of psychological problems is to ask what sorts of problems would be most effectively dealt with by clinical psychologists. It is these problems that will then tend to be more usefully referred. Several clinical psychologists have sought to categorize psychological problems from this perspective. One of the most influential attempts has been that of Kincey (1974) (Table 11.2).

Kincey's five categories describe the broad problem areas that clinical psychologists come across in their specialist work. The role of the psychologist is essentially that of therapist, and in a sense they are simply transferring their normal professional skills to a different context (for example, from psychiatric clinic to GP clinic). Surveys of GPs' attitudes to clinical psychologists suggest that these are by and large the problems that they would tend to refer. Thus, in a survey of GPs in Oxfordshire and Buckinghamshire the seven most common problems deemed particularly suitable by a sample of GPs for referral to a clinical psychologist were (in order): Phobias, Chronic Anxiety, Obsessional Disorders, Smoking Problems, Drinking Problems, Psychosexual Problems, and Interpersonal Problems (Marzillier and Fowler, unpublished findings, 1986). The GPs also rated a therapeutic service as by far the most useful role for

Table 11.2 Five categories of psychological problem amenable to clinical psychological intervention. (Adapted from Kincey 1974.)

Category	Description
(a) Problems of anxiety and stress	Generalized anxiety, panic attacks, phobias, obsessional ideas or rituals, psychosomatic or stress-induced ill-nesses, e.g. migraine, asthma
(b) Habit disorders	Various habitual behaviours that lead to personal distress, ill-health or social problems, e.g. smoking, obesity, bulimia, problem drinking, enuresis, encopresis, drug addiction
(c) Educational, occupational difficulties or decisions	Choice or transition points throughout life-span, e.g. leaving school, change of job, retirement. Problems that arise in the educational–occupational context, e.g. study problems, lack of confidence and social skills
(c) Interpersonal–social–marital problems	Problems arising out of relationships with others, e.g. shyness, unassertive-ness, marital discord, psychosexual problems, antisocial and aggressive behaviour
(e) Psychological adjustment to physcial illness and other significant life events	Adjustment to psychological trauma of illness and hospitalization. Adjust-ment to chronic disability. Childbirth. Accident. Terminal illness. Death

clinical psychologists. However, important as the therapeutic service is, it represents only one of a number of ways that clinical psychologists may work in primary care.

General practice has been the most fruitful ground for the work of clinical psychologists in primary care. Over the years GPs have begun referring many more patients directly to specialist psychological services, rather than through the medium of psychiatric clinics, and this has resulted in a better knowledge of what the service can provide. Closer collaboration has been achieved when clinical psychologists have worked directly in general practices. One early example was the work of Johnston (1978). Johnston worked full-time as a clinical psychologist in a health centre attached to a Community Hospital, where she took referrals from the GPs. Johnston saw about five patients per day for appointments that lasted on average just over 40 minutes, using a behavioural approach to treatment. The majority of patients seen were female, with a ratio of female to male of 3:1. About 15 per cent of the appointments were quite short, between 5 and 15 minutes, and quite a few patients were seen in their homes. Johnston reported favourably on the results of her work, commenting upon the greater flexibility that arose from being sited in the general practice, the easier access for patients, the greater opportunity to see relatives, the avoidance of the stigma of attendance at a psychiatric clinic, and the reduction in waiting times. These advantages of working directly in a general practice have been noted by other psychologists too.

THE WORK OF CLINICAL PSYCHOLOGISTS IN GENERAL PRACTICE

There are four main ways in which clinical psychologists can work in general practice. These are:

(a) providing a specialist treatment service;
(b) acting as consultants and teachers to other profesions;
(c) carrying out research;
(d) prevention and health promotion.

Specialist treatment service

Most clinical psychologists working in primary health care have worked in an essentially similar way to their traditional role in a clinic setting, that is, they have carried out specialist psychological assessment and treatment on the patients referred to them by GPs. Johnston's work falls into this category. Specialist assessment consists in the main of the assessment of cognitive abilities by means of psychometric tests, for example, the assessment of intelligence and memory. This is much less common than a therapeutic service, but it can be useful in physically handicapped or impaired patients, where a formal assessment will reveal the pattern of their intellectual abilities and disabilities. Assessment of intelligence and attainments (reading, spelling, arithmetic) can also be of value in gaining a picture of the all-round abilities of schoolchildren. (Educational psychologists, who are attached to schools, are usually the more appropriate professional group for this type of service.)

Specialist treatment has been predominantly in the form of cognitive behavioural methods for people with emotional problems such as anxiety, depression, obsessions, and phobias, and for those with habit disorders, relationship problems, or problems in living (see Table 11.2 earlier). This approach consists of short-term treatments using psychological principles to achieve clearly defined and agreed goals. For example, for an agoraphobic patient with anxieties about going out on her own, the goal might be to go to the local shopping centre on her own with the minimum of anxiety. For a patient with an eating disorder such as anorexia or bulimia, the goal might be to establish a more normal eating pattern and to modify abnormal attitudes to eating (for a fuller description of this approach see Chapter 2). Clinical psychologists working directly on general practice premises tend to spend rather less time in treatment sessions than when working in specialist clinics. In a careful study of clinical psychologists' work in general practices, it was found that, on average, a patient received 3.7 treatment sessions or about $2\frac{1}{2}$ hours treatment time (Robson *et al.* 1984). This was about half the time spent per patient in a local specialist clinic. An additional benefit of a treatment service on general practice premises is therefore that less time is spent with each patient. On the other hand, it is likely that the psychologist will see a wider range of patients, particularly those whose problems are less severe. The economics of a specialist therapy service in general practice are discussed below.

The effectiveness of psychological treatment

How successful has this move to general practice been? In the UK there have been several reports of both patient and doctor satisfaction with a clinical psychologist service in primary care. Studies such as that by Johnston have suggested that patients are significantly improved as a result of receiving psychological treatment. However, it is only recently that properly controlled evaluations of the work of clinical psychologists in general practice have been carried out. Two controlled trials have been carried out in the UK. In both studies patients were randomly assigned to either treatment by a clinical psychologist or 'normal' GP treatment.

In the first study (Earll and Kincey 1982), 50 consecutive referrals by the GPs to the clinical psychologist were randomly assigned to either treatment or control groups. Apart from patients' needing to be 15 years of age or older, with no evidence of psychosis or organic brain disease, and not to be involved in any treatment elsewhere, no specific criteria for patient suitability were used. Kincey's guidelines were given to the GPs, and the majority of patients had anxiety-based problems. Patients in the treatment group were seen by one clinical psychologist, who followed a behavioural self-control approach. On average patients received 7.7 sessions of treatment over 16.3 weeks. Patients in the control group were treated in whatever ways the GP felt appropriate.

The results of this study showed that during their treatment with the psychologist, the patients took significantly less psychotropic medication than the control patients, but that there were no other statistically significant differences between the two groups (for example, in terms of prescription for other medications, consultation rates or number of out-patient attendances). At 7-month follow-up, 85 per cent of the treated patients reported that they had been helped to some extent or a great deal by the clinical psychologist. However, there were no statistically significant differences between the treated and control patients on psychological measures of emotional distress, life satisfaction, and personal control. Moreover, the differences between the groups in terms of prescription of psychotropic medication had disappeared, with the patients in the treated group tending to increase their medication during the follow-up period.

This study therefore failed to show that referral to a clinical psychologist was of clear benefit to patients. Although 85 per cent of the patients treated were satisfied with the service, and there was a reduction in the prescription of psychotropic medication during treatment, there were no significant differences between treated and control groups at follow-up. A major problem in interpreting the study is the fact that one psychologist carried out all the treatment, confounding the evaluation of a clinical psychology service with that of a particular clinical psychologist. The small numbers of patients in each group also made statistical significance between the groups difficult to achieve.

The second controlled study (Robson *et al*. 1984) avoided the methodological shortcomings of the Earll and Kincey study while following an essentially similar design. Four hundred and twenty-nine patients were randomly assigned to either a treatment group consisting of psychological treatment from one of four clinical psychologists working in the general practice, or a control group, which consisted of management by the GP. Treatment was up to a maximum of 10 weeks, and, as reported earlier, averaged 3.7 sessions or $2\frac{1}{2}$ hours of psychologist time. Patients were assessed on psychological measures, prescription costs, consultations, and hospital appointments at various stages after the end of treatment up to one-year follow-up. Kincey's categorization was used, with the majority of patients having anxiety problems (47.9 per cent), inter-personal problems (17.4 per cent), and habit disorders (16.2 per cent). In addition, 13.7 per cent of patients were referred because of depression.

The results of this study were more favourable to psychological treatment. Patients treated by the clinical psychologists showed significantly greater improvement in their presenting problems than control patients immediately after treatment and up to 34 weeks' follow-up. They made significantly fewer visits to the GPs during treatment and up to 24 weeks' follow-up, and received significantly less psychotropic medication during treatment and up to 1 year follow-up. Control patients improved steadily over time, but at a lesser rate than those treated by the psychologists; at one-year follow-up the control did not differ significantly from the treated group on most measures except for the cost of psychotropic medication (higher for controls). Robson *et al*. (1984) concluded that the patients treated by clinical psychologists in this study showed an accelerated improvement compared to controls, with less frequent consultations and less expenditure on medication. Results, therefore, supported the value of a clinical psychologist service in a general practice setting.

The research described above suggests that, for the most part, psychological problems resolve themselves over time, albeit more slowly than with psychological help. This may well be true for the milder types of problems, but is not necessarily true for others. In evaluating their clinical psychology service Milne and Souter (1988) found that, while on a waiting-list, patients showed little or no improvement, but made significant gains during and after cognitive-behavioural treatment. They suggested that for more chronic and difficult problems psychological treatment is necessary.

Further research is needed to establish how beneficial a therapeutic service is. GPs and patients appear to value the service and many psychologists are prepared to offer it. The Robson *et al.* study gives some indication of the likely benefit to patients and to the practice. Economically is such a service viable? Robson *et al.* assessed the savings from reduced prescribing and translated this into a percentage of a psychologist's salary. They estimated that savings from reduced prescribing would pay for about 28 per cent of a senior clinical psychologist's salary (at 1981 rates). Other economies can arise, such as earlier return to work and reduced consultation time. A major obstacle to such a service, however, is the shortage of clinical psychologists in the UK and most other countries. There are too few psychologists for them to be attached to all general practices in this way, so that the current pattern in the UK is of a few practices being well served by clinical psychologists and many more not being served at all. Without a sudden and rapid increase in clinical psychologists, a specialized therapy service in general practice will remain a luxury for a few rather than a routine service for all.

A consultancy service

A clinical psychologist may work collaboratively with GPs and other members of the primary health care team either by working together with them on individual cases or by carrying out specific projects. There are some obvious advantages to a collaborative approach, not least of which is the fact that it makes more efficient use of clinical psychologists' time and skills. Consultation between clinical psychologists and primary care workers can be at various levels. At its simplest there may be informal meetings over coffee and lunch in which cases are discussed, possible referrals mooted, and information about treatment (medical and psychological) shared. A step up from this is joint work on individual cases (for example, marital disorders, sex therapy), in running a group, or in family therapy. Deys *et al.* (1989) described a collaborative project between clinical psychologists and a GP, taking a family systems perspective and team approach to treatment. As part of ongoing therapeutic work with families, the therapist (sometimes the GP, at other times the psychologist) was observed by other team members through a one-way screen. Immediate consultation was available when the therapist desired it. Team consultation of this sort is standard practice in a family systems approach, and has the advantage of immediate and specific clinical relevance. At another level clinical psychologists have run training courses or workshops for GPs and other primary care workers with the aim of teaching specific skills. One example is the teaching of anxiety-management skills (relaxation; target-setting; planned practice) to primary care workers with the aim of their using these skills as an alternative to medication or simple advice. Care must be taken to evaluate how effective primary care workers are in the use of such skills.

Behavioural group treatment for sleep-disordered children: a collaborative project between health visitors and clinical psychologists

The health visitors attached to a practice in a small market town reported that a large proportion of their time was taken up with sleep problems in the pre-school child, and that although they could offer support to parents, they did not know what constructive advice to give on management. Could clinical psychologists help? This request led to a collaborative project evaluating the effectiveness of a group-based behavioural management programme run by health visitors and psychologists.

Sleep problems in pre-school children are quite common, and consist of difficulties in settling, frequent waking, and disturbances to sleep routines, for example being taken into the parents' bed. While many parents will cope without help, others find the disturbance to their own sleep and the child's sleep distressing and emotionally draining. Health visitors, because they routinely visit parents with young children, are often the recipients of the parents' worries, and are frequently asked if they can help in any way.

Behavioural management of sleeping problems involves careful record-keeping, analysis of the individual's problem in terms of contingencies maintaining the behaviour, and establishing agreed goals and working gradually towards their attainment—an approach which has proved helpful when carried out by psychologists (Douglas and Richman 1984). There is evidence that this approach is effective when carried out on an individual basis. In this project a group approach was developed and assessed.

The behavioural management groups

Since three health visitors were attached to the Health Centre, it was decided to run three groups in each of which the clinical psychologist worked in collaboration with a health visitor. Parents and children were assigned to the group run by their own health visitor. The groups were held on a weekday morning in the Health Education Room at the Health Centre. Between five and six mothers and their children attended each group. At the first meeting the parents were informed about the project, and information was systematically collected on each child's sleeping problem. Various assessment measures were completed, in which the parent recorded in detail her child's sleeping pattern in the form of a diary. This group met weekly over the next six weeks, during which time the principles of behavioural management were introduced, and parents were advised how to apply them to their children's problems. Five weeks after the final session the group met again for a follow-up session.

An example of the behavioural management was a $4\frac{1}{2}$-year-old girl, Linda, who refused to go to bed in the evenings and fell asleep on the settee in front of the television each evening, after which she would be taken up to bed. She then woke between 12.00 and 1.00 a.m. and wandered as if sleepwalking into her parents' room. Linda would then get into her parent's bed and sleep the rest of the night without waking. If her parents attempted to put her to bed in the evening or at night she screamed, and if left alone would come and find them. The main goal established was that Linda should go to sleep in her own bed. The advice on management involved:

1. Bathtime to precede bedtime immediately;
2. Linda to have a story read to her in bed for about 20 minutes; and
3. the parent reading the story was then to stay in the room until Linda was asleep, but was to have minimal interaction with her— for example they could read a book, knit, etc.

Later advice involved the parent gradually withdrawing from the room before Linda was asleep, for instance sitting outside the room, then on the landing, and finally downstairs. These procedures successfully led to the resolution of the settling problem.

Outcome of the project

Parents in all three groups attended consistently, and all bar one rated the groups as useful. The main criterion of success was an increase in the number of 'clear nights', i.e. nights without any form of disturbance from their child. Parents in all groups reported an increase in clear nights over the course of the treatment, from an average of between 0 and 1 night per week prior to the groups, to an average of 2.5 to 4.1 nights per week at the end of the group. Follow-up at one month showed that progress had been maintained and improved upon.

The positive effects achieved in this project encouraged the health visitors to apply behavioural management principles themselves in the course of their normal work (Mercier, unpublished findings, 1984).

Research in primary health care

An important part of the training of clinical psychologists is in research skills and methodology. In their undergraduate degree psychologists are taught experimental methods of inquiry, and are required to carry out and report a research project using appropriate statistical analysis. In their postgraduate training they are taught to apply these research skills to clinical problems and are required to carry out a major research study (see Chapter 1). Carrying out clinical research may be part of a clinical psychologist's job description (though not in all cases), and up to one day per week may be made available for research. For various reasons—the presssure of clinical commitments, competing interests, awareness of the snags and pitfalls of research work—the majority of trained clinical psychologists are not actively involved in research. Yet their contribution as researchers may well be of particular value in primary care. Some ways in which clinical psychologists could carry out collaborative clinical research are now considered.

Detection and identification of psychological problems

Knowledge about what psychological problems present in primary care is still only rudimentary. The problems of definition and categorization of psychological problems were noted earlier. By focusing on discrete and widely identifiable categories of disorder such as anxiety, depression, and obsessions, where standardized assessments have been developed, there is scope for psychologists to uncover the extent to which such problems present in the community and to primary care workers such as health visitors, district nurses, and GPs. It is also of interest to find out more about the 'natural history' of psychological problems, since, as was mentioned earlier, many problems will be resolved without any professional intervention. Clinical psychologists, with their knowledge of psychological problems and ways of assessing them, could fruitfully collaborate with other specialists, particularly those with experience in epidemiology such as public health doctors. The knowledge gained from this type of inquiry will be of practical use in, for example, helping to determine what problems need intervention.

Psychological aspects of the work of primary care professionals

It has been increasingly recognized that a large part of the work of doctors, nurses, receptionists, health visitors, and others who work in primary care is 'psychological'. At its crudest this refers to the importance of interpersonal skills and behaviour in professional work—which, of course, would also apply to medicine in general. But a singularly important feature of primary care is the frequency of contact with people, over 95 per cent of whom will visit their GP at least once in five years. A large part of primary care work entails dealing effectively with people, whether it is in making appointments, in changing dressings, in one-to-one consultations, or in clinics. Psychologists and other social scientists have become interested in the process of communication in primary care, and in particular in what factors aid and what impede effective communication (Pendleton and Hasler 1983).

The failure of many patients to adhere to the treatment regimens suggested by doctors and others is in part due to deficiences in communication. While most patients report being satisfied with the communication they receive from their doctors, a substantial minority (between 35 and 40 per cent) report dissatisfaction. Psychological studies of doctor–patient communication have highlighted some of the factors that affect satisfaction. For example, many communications from doctors are too complex for patients to understand and too long to be adequately recalled, and are delivered in a way that fails to take into account the patient's existing knowledge and beliefs. Psychological studies of the processes of remembering and forgetting can be useful in designing more effective communications. People tend to remember information presented at the beginning of a message (the primacy effect) and at the end of a message (the recency effect); whereas the bit in the middle—which often contains important information about treatment and its effects—is less well remembered. Equally, information that is concrete, emphasized as important, and repeated will be more easily remembered. It is obvious that well-established psychological knowledge such as this can be practically applied, as indeed it has begun to be. For example, a collaborative project between a social psychologist and a group of GPs has led to a training programme focusing on teaching key interpersonal skills in the consultation (Pendleton *et al.* 1984).

Prevention and health promotion

There has been an increasing awareness that primary health care is one of the most fruitful fields for the prevention of illness and the promotion of health. The GP in particular has been seen as potentially a major agent of change, although other primary care workers such as practice nurses and health visitors are also important. About two-thirds of patients consult their doctors in one year, and the availability and accessibility of the GP creates many opportunities for health education and promotion. The doctor too is generally a respected and trusted figure whose advice is taken seriously. For example, studies of GPs giving advice to smokers to quit smoking have clearly demonstrated that a small but significant number of smokers successfully give up directly as a result of that advice. In recent years, doctors and other primary care workers have become more and more involved in promoting health, from straightforward activities such as immunization and screening to education and advice on aspects of lifestyle.

Clinical psychologists have also begun to direct their attention to prevention and health promotion. This makes sense, since it is primarily psychological change that is necessary to achieve a healthier lifestyle. For example, there is an accumulating body of evidence linking diet, particularly one high in saturated fat and low in fibre, with coronary heart disease and certain cancers. If people can shift their eating habits, then they will reduce the risk of these very common diseases. What is required is a change in attitude (i.e. being prepared to recognize that a change in diet is important for health) and in behaviour (viz, to adopting a healthier pattern of eating). The GP, practice nurse, or health visitor may well be the best means of seeking to instigate change, but how should his/her advice be given? Clinical psychologists, whose daily business is seeking to change attitudes and behaviour, could work closely with primary care workers to maximize the effectiveness of their interventions.

While there has been most emphasis on prevention and health promotion in physical health, some attention is beginning to be paid to mental health promotion. Newton (1988) has analysed the research into major psychological disorders such as depression and schizophrenia and suggested a number of psychological preventive measures. These range from practical help to ensure greater security for infants and young children, thereby hopefully reducing the risk of depression and anxiety in later life, to better means of identifying and helping those at most risk of serious breakdown. As Newton points out, there is a growing body of knowledge about psychological conditions which could form the basis of much needed research into prevention and mental health promotion.

COMMUNITY SERVICES

The work of clinical psychologists in primary care has predominantly been with the general practice team. This is not surprising, since clinical psychologists are health care professionals with already established links to GPs, nurses, and other health care staff. In the transition to primary care clinical psychologists have extended their customary ways of working, and general practice has been a most fertile ground. However, as was illustrated earlier in Fig. 11.1, many more psychological problems exist in the community than actually present or are recognized in general practice. Awareness of this has led some clinical psychologists to work directly 'in the community'.

Community teams

The slow transition from the institutionalized care of the mentally ill and mentally handicapped to 'care in the community' has been accompanied in some instances by the setting up of community teams. Community mental handicap teams (CMHTs) are a good example of this development. A CMHT consists of personnel from both the NHS and from local authorities, whose main role is to provide specialized advice and help with problems related to mental handicap. The team consists of a core of two or three full-time professional staff, usually a community nurse and social worker, with back-up support from clinical psychologists, consultants in mental handicap, and other specialist professional staff (for example, occupational therapists, physiotherapists). The CMHT functions are (i) to act as the first point of contact for parents and families of people with learning difficulties providing direct help and advice; (ii) to co-ordinate access to services; and (iii) to establish close working relationships with relevant local voluntary organizations. CMHTs deal directly with problems in the community as they arise, and in addition act as intermediaries between the primary care teams (who can refer patients) and the specialist services (to whom the team can refer people for longer-term and more specialized work).

The major role taken by clinical psychologists on CMHTs has been to provide psychological advice and training to the core members of the team in their work with people with learning difficulties and their families. This is acting in a consultant–teacher role as outlined above. Occasionally, psychologists may also act as 'key workers' in CMHTs, and work directly with clients on skills training or behavioural programmes. CMHTs have the virtue of being community-based rather than institution- or hospital-based and, in theory at least, can be more responsive to the needs of the community. For clinical psychologists, it has meant the opportunity to work outside the umbrella of a medical bureaucratic system and deal directly with psychological problems in the community. Other examples of community teams are community alcohol teams and community drug abuse teams, which, although differently organized to CMHTs, have similar aims of a greater involvement in the community and a move away from an excessively medical perspective on psychological and social problems.

Community mental health centres (CMHCs)

CMHCs were first established in the USA in the 1960s in response to widespread dissatisfaction with the then existing methods of care and treatment of mentally ill people, particularly the large state mental hospitals, and out of an awareness that many of the most needy people (the poor, the disadvantaged, ethnic minorities) were simply not gaining access to any form of professional treatment. CMHCs served a small catchment area (between 75 000 and 200 000 people) in which professional staff worked alongside non-professionals providing a psychological service that was designed to be accessible, flexible, primarily educational, short-term, and open to all members of the community. CMHCs worked most effectively in small, compact communities. They were not so effective in either very large urban conurbations or sparsely populated rural areas. Moreover, doubts have been cast on their accessibility to those most in need. A decline in CMHCs occurred during the Reagan era, when direct federal funding was withdrawn.

In the UK the development of CMHCs has been a sporadic one, and largely dependent on local initiatives. In some health authorities CMHCs have been seen as a direct alternative to institutional psychiatric care; in others, as a development taking place alongside the traditional services. The latter development is the most common, and follows a similar pattern to the Community Mental Handicap Teams described earlier. A clinical psychologist works in close conjunction with other health care professionals either directly as a member of a team or as a consultant to a team. Referrals come from GPs and other local sources. The team offers a range of therapeutic interventions—usually short-term pragmatic treatments. Groups are often run, such as stress-management, assertiveness-training, or a group for the bereaved. The aim of the community team is to be more responsive to local needs, although it remains uncertain whether or not that is achieved.

The advantages of CMHCs are their greater accessibility to people, the reduction of stigma associated with psychiatric services, the benefits of a multidisciplinary approach, and their ability to offer psychological interventions that are pragmatic, brief, and effective. However, CMHCs also have their problems. Some clinical psychologists report that working in 'democratic' teams can lead to a loss of professional identity and a diminution of specialist skills—the philosophy can be that 'everyone can do everything' (Anciano and Kirkpatrick 1990). Others report being overwhelmed by the number of referrals, and that allocation to team members can be arbitrary rather than based upon matching client needs to professional skill.

Clinical psychologists can find themselves torn between being a core team member working directly with clients and a consultant advising other professionals. As CMHCs proliferate, these issues need to be discussed and resolved. It remains to be seen, however, to what extent CMHCs provide a radical alternative to traditional medically based systems of care, for example, by taking in people 'off the streets' rather than through referral, by being able to respond to the needs of all the people in the community and not just a select few, and by focusing on mental health education and promotion rather than conventional treatment. These activities demand a different role for clinical psychologists and other professional staff: one which looks more to social and environmental change, rather than to the treatment of the individual.

Community psychologists

Community psychology is a term that first appeared in the USA to describe a radical shift in applied psychology away from individual psychotherapy in a professional health care context to an approach that views psychological problems from an ecological viewpoint. Community psychology emphasizes the critical importance of social and environmental forces in the determination of human behaviour problems, and favours what is loosely described as a 'systems-oriented' approach to intervention. There is also the recognition that many mental health problems are the product of social and political conditions such as poverty, unemployment, racism, and urban deprivation, and that changes in these social conditions are required in order to make much impact on these psychological problems. Community psychology, therefore, seeks to embrace a broader perspective on mental health and illness than is currently adopted by most clinical psychologists. Homelessness is a prime example. Lack of employment and family difficulties can force young people to move to large cities in search of work. However, without resources, friends, or other support, they find themselves living rough, unable to find either work or accommodation. The problems that ensue—hopelessness, depression, alcohol and drug abuse—are as much a product of the social system as the individual.

There are in fact few community psychologists *per se* outside the USA, probably because there does not exist a career structure in the health and social services. Some clinical psychologists have sought to take more of a community psychology perspective in their work. This entails a deliberate move away from individual treatments to attempts to produce or provoke changes in social systems, for example, by working closely with voluntary groups seeking social and political change, by taking an advocacy role in the pursuit of the rights of the mentally ill and handicapped, by working in or with Social Services Departments, and by helping to establish and support self-help groups. To date this community role has been relatively little developed; but as political and financial constraints directly affect the health care system, this is a role that may become increasingly important.

SUMMARY

Clinical psychologists have only recently begun working in primary health care. There are four main ways in which they have worked. Firstly, a treatment service is offered similar to that provided in out-patient clinics. This has been the commonest and most preferred service. Recent research has provided some support for the effectiveness and efficacy of such a service. Secondly, a consultant–teacher service can be provided. An example of this has been described in which a clinical psychologist worked closely with health visitors to teach behavioural methods for managing sleep disorders in pre-school children. Thirdly, research can be carried out into various aspects of primary care work; doctor–patient communication is one example. Finally, clinical psychologists can participate in health promotion and prevention programmes, many of which are carried out in primary care settings. Advice on diet and smoking are two examples. While clinical psychologists have on the whole worked in primary care through the medium of general practice, this is not the only way of working. Some clinical psychologists have begun to work directly in the community either as community psychologists or as part of community teams.

REFERENCES

Anciano, D. and Kirkpatrick, A. (1990). CMHTs and clinical psychology: the death of the profession? *Clin. Psych. Forum*, **26**, 9–12.

298   *Clinical psychology and primary health care*

Deys, C., Dowling, E., and Golding, V. (1989). Clinical psychology: a consultative approach in general practice. *J. R. Coll. Gen. Pract.*, **39**, 342–4.

Douglas, J. and Richman, N. (1984). *My child won't sleep*. Penguin, London.

Earll, L. and Kincey, J. (1982). Clinical psychology in general practice: a controlled trial evaluation. *J. R. Coll. Gen. Pract.*, **32**, 32–7.

Goldberg, D. and Bridges, K. (1987). Screening for psychiatric illness in general practice: the general practitioner versus the screening questionnaire. *J. R. Coll. Gen. Pract.*, **37**, 15–18.

Goldberg, D. P. and Huxley, P. (1980). See 'Further reading'.

Johnston, M. (1978). The work of a clinical psychologist in primary care. *J. R. Coll. Gen. Pract.*, **28**, 661–7.

Kincey, J. A. (1974). General practice and clinical psychology—some arguments for a closer liaison. *J. R. Coll. Gen. Pract.*, **24**, 882–8.

McPherson, I. and Feldman, M. P. (1977). A preliminary investigation of the role of the clinical psychologist in the primary care setting. *Bull. Br. Psychol. Soc.*, **30**, 342–6.

Milne, D. and Souter, K. (1988). A re-evaluation of the clinical psychologist in general practice. *J. R. Coll. Gen. Pract.*, **38**, 457–60.

Newton, J. (1988). *Preventing mental illness*. Routledge & Kegan Paul, London.

Pendleton, D. and Hasler, J. (eds) (1983). See 'Further reading'.

Pendleton, D., Schofield, T., Tate, P., and Havelock, P. (1984). *The consultation. An approach to learning*. Oxford General Practice Series No. 6. Oxford University Press.

Robson, M. H., France, R., and Bland, M. (1984). Clinical psychologists in primary care; controlled clinical and economic evaluation. *Br. Med. J.*, **288**, 1805–8.

FURTHER READING

France, R. and Robson, M. H. (1986). *Behaviour therapy in primary care*. Croom Helm, London.

Goldberg, D. P. and Huxley, P. (1980). *Mental illness in the community. The pathway to psychiatric care*. Tavistock, London.

McPherson, I. G. (1989). General practice: the contribution of clinical psychology. In *Health psychology, processes and applications* (ed. A. K. Broome), pp. 277–94. Chapman and Hall, London.

Markus, A. C., Murray Parkes, C., Tomson, P., and Johnston, M. (1989). *Psychological problems in general practice*. Oxford University Press, Oxford.

Pendleton, D. and Hasler, J. (eds.) (1983). *Doctor–patient communication*. Academic Press, London.

12

Working with others
John Hall

It is just about possible to imagine a clinical psychologist practising in isolation, seeing patients who refer themselves directly, with minimal contact with other health care staff. However, in most settings a psychologist will be involved with members of other professional groups from the very moment that a referral is made. As well as working with members of professional groups, clinical psychologists are likely to be working with staff of voluntary organizations, to be in contact with officers of local authorities, and to be responding to groups representing the consumers of health care. This last group of people will normally have no professional training, may know little of the shared assumptions of health care workers, and may be actively challenging some of those assumptions. A clinical psychologist in these circumstances needs to be able to build therapeutic alliances with all who can contribute to better health care. Apart from a psychologist's concern with identified patients and their families, many psychologists will be concerned with other aspects of the local health care system, such as helping to run a day centre, or planning a new service for people dependent on drugs. If a doctor makes a referral, or a manager makes a request, this suggests they have some knowledge of the contribution that psychologists can make to the care of that patient. How was that knowledge acquired?

WHO ARE THE OTHER PROFESSIONALS?

Professions and professional boundaries relate mainly to particular diagnostic or therapeutic skills, they may also relate to pay and status, or to patterns of authority. They have arisen because the amount of technical information on health care is so great, and the range of clinical skills so varied, that no one person could possibly be expected to be conversant with them all.

These boundaries are not fixed, nor are they impermeable. New demands upon the health care system, for example the demand for better information on the delivery of services and for better evaluation or audit of existing services, lead to the demand for new skills which may not reside in existing health care professions, and which may have to be imported from those without a conventional professional membership.

Some people may be trained in more than one health care profession. Indeed, a proportion of clinical psychologists have previously been nurses or therapists of some sort (such as occupational therapists) before retraining.

But these boundaries do exist, and an important part of a clinical psychologist's job is to recognize the boundaries, and to work with people on the other side, maybe changing the boundary in the process. This suggests identifying the main other professional groups with which a clinical psychologist will work, and the main ways in wihch collaboration can and does occur.

The concept of 'profession'

The latter part of the nineteenth century saw the emergence of groups such as engineers and architects, complete with their own institutions. As striving for 'professional' status has been a constant theme in this century, sociologists have tried to identify the characteristics of a profession, suggesting that a profession is defined by possession of a body of specialized knowledge; a monopoly of practice in a field of work; an acceptance that fellow members of a profession are adjudged competent to assess the work of a member; and an ideology of service to clients.

The two major professional groups in health care, doctors and nurses, developed gradually from the middle of the last century, in England dating from the establishment of the General Medical Council for doctors in 1858. However, the development of a profession's standards has to take account of external pressures, the realities of finance, and availability of people able to do the job. An examination of the variation in length and type of training of clinical psychologists in different European countries shows how these pressures and realities continue to operate today. Even now, the length and standard of training of some professionals is changing, as some therapist groups have moved to a graduate-level degree training course.

The introduction of the term 'semi-professions' by Etzioni indicates that some professions may be more professional than others! Certainly within health care professions, medicine has achieved an ascendancy over most other clinical care groups, to the extent that they may control, or 'prescribe' the therapeutic actions taken by members of other groups. Where the medical profession does not have prescriptive or legal control over another group, and where it cannot be seen to possess knowledge which encompasses that of the other group, then negotiation has to take place on how members of each profession relate to doctors, and negotiation has to take place between members of each of those professions generally. The rapid development of counselling as a profession or 'semi-profession' is a particular challenge to medical ascendancy, and the issues to be negotiated between doctors and counsellors parallel in some ways the negotiations which have taken place between doctors and clinical psychologists.

Professional views and standards thus have a range of functions. They clarify the nature of the task each group can perform; they provide a set of guidelines of inter-professional conduct; they can protect both professional and client. Conversely, professional differences can be over-rigid, and can fail to cope with changing patterns of health need and professional skill; they can hamper collaboration in helping individual patients; and they can lead to confused communication. Understanding the ethos of other professions is a prerequisite for working with them.

Working with doctors

Doctors are, in virtually every country, the most influential professional group in health care. Because of the central position of doctors in any health care system, it is essential that as a group they are aware of the clinical implications of developments in psychological theory and practice, and aware how psychologists both can provide a service and can assist them to modify their own practice accordingly. Chapter 10 gives examples of the relevance of psychological procedures for some clinical problems in general medicine.

In most countries there is a clear separation between the 'general practice', 'family medicine', or 'primary care' type of practice, and the specialist practice of a particular branch of medicine, such as neurology. While in Britain these two areas of practice are highly, but not totally, separated, in many European countries a family doctor will also have an associated specialist practice. The relationship between these two branches of practice has changed in recent years, but the family doctor usually occupies a key position in the care of the individual patient. Chapter 11 describes Goldberg and Huxley's 'Filter model' of referral by family doctors, indicating the pivotal role of family doctors in steering patients to specialized treatments.

Patterns of training for doctors are also changing: although different countries have a differing emphasis on pre-clinical experience, traditionally the neophyte doctor spends a period of two to three years studying 'pre-clinical' subjects, such as anatomy and biochemistry, before being exposed to 'clinical' subjects by direct contact with patients who are attending clinics and wards associated with the medical school. This separation means that the trainee doctor cannot be expected to integrate easily his medical 'clinical' knowledge with his pre-clinical knowledge. There have thus been attempts to introduce some clinical contact much earlier in the basic 'scientific' training, and correspondingly to introduce scientific topics at a time when they can be related to clinical phenomena. All of these developments have prompted a growth of interest in the process of professional acculturation by medical students and in the process of acquisition of the relevant skills, and thus promoted a development of behavioural science teaching from the very beginning of the medical course. From a psychological viewpoint, the more that relevant teaching of topics such as doctor–patient communication can be integrated with early clinical experience, the more trainee doctors are likely to absorb a psychological perspective to their work.

Following basic training, doctors usually follow some course of specialized training. Some medical specialities have a high proportion of psychological content in their future training, the best examples being paediatricians and psychiatrists. In these specialities some knowledge of developmental psychology (for example, parent–child bonding and normal language develompment) and normal psychology (for example, psychology of small groups) respectively is essential, so that clinical psychologists come to have a specialized teaching role for these specialities. This implies that psychologists with the relevant professional knowledge are themselves available, not only to become familiar with the clinical practice of the speciality, but to make the trainee doctors aware of some of the conceptual difficulties in their fields. Public health, or community, medicine is also of special interest to psychologists, with the growing interest in health promotion and illness prevention and the accompanying emphasis on understanding the impact of the total environment on health status.

Working with nurses

Nurses constitute the largest staff group in a health care system. They are the people who will have the closest day-to-day contact with patients in hospital, and who both in hospital and in the community have to carry out the most personal tasks for people who cannot look after themselves. A group of nurses on a ward often have to provide a 24-hour service every day, so that at any time of the night they may have to deal with medical—or psychological—emergencies or sudden outbursts of disturbed behaviour. While a particular doctor will have medical responsibility for a patient, many of the minor—and indeed major—worries of the patient will be shared with and solved by the first available nurse, who may be relatively junior and inexperienced.

Because nursing is the key caring health profession, continued recruitment of nurses is essential to a health care system. A lot of psychological attention has accordingly focused on the way in which interest develops in potential nurses, and why nurses withdraw from training. It has been suggested that a third of all 18-year-old girls in Britain, for example, have been interested in nursing at some time in their lives. Yet the young nursing student is confronted with illness, suffering, and dying in a way that young people starting other jobs are not, exposing student nurses to considerable personal stress. Perhaps as a result, voluntary withdrawal from training is much more common for nurses than for other health care groups. Another study suggested that many nurses who smoke may start to smoke during their nursing training: together these findings suggest that day-to-day contact with patients is personally demanding, and those nurses should be helped to develop support mechanisms for coping with this stress.

One of the appeals of working as a doctor or a nurse is the idea of 'working with people'. Many texts on psychology and nursing, for example, focus on the interpersonal elements of nursing, often described as nurse–patient interaction. From the patient's point of view, the quality of human relationship with those looking after him or her is extremely important, as is evidenced by such phrases as 'a good bedside manner'. Qualities such as warmth, sensitivity, and respect for the patient are encouraged in all sorts of care situations, quite apart from their value in more intense one-to-one therapeutic relationships.

However, while patients may want such qualities in the staff about them, it is not easy for those staff always to display them. Particular types of setting are associated with higher levels of stress, so that nurses on medical wards show higher levels of stress than nurses on surgical wards. Wards with high rates of death on them, such as intensive care units and terminal care units, are also associated with high stress levels. The end result of this type of stress has been called 'burn-out'. Burn-out describes a range of responses to increased emotional demands, such as emotional detachment, cynicism, and an unwillingness to admit to having emotional needs. Burn-out can be seen, of course, in a number of other professional groups where there are high personal and emotional demands, and where there may be a lack of support from others, such as clergymen and policemen.

What can be done about this? From a psychological point of view, it may be possible to offer a psychological analysis of burn-out, and then do something to relieve the problem. Llewellyn (1984) describes an approach to helping cope with burn-out based on Personal Construct Theory, a theory put forward by Kelly which proposes that people are essentially trying to make sense of the world around them, and relate events according to their own constellation of 'constructs', which are based on each individual's own life history and beliefs. A valuable part of this theory is the way in which it has yielded a technique known as a Repertory Grid, which is a graphical way of representing the construct system of an individual. The relevance of this to coping with the burn-out is that it helps to explain what is happening to both patient and nurse in what may be a very confusing situation. For the patient, all sorts of strange things will be happening, with threatening medical procedures and an endless stream of strange new people, each anxious to ask about this or take a drop of blood for that. A general approach to the patient which accepts that they will all interpret these events differently, and positively need help to make sense of their experiences, will offer more support to the patient. For the nurse, it emphasizes the value of exposing hidden anxieties: a hidden anxiety cannot be tested or rejected. The nurse in the front line then needs to be supported by others alive to these anxieties and stresses, and with some skills in resolving them.

Parry (1990) points out the major role of social support in times of stress; that social support consists of information and practical components, as well as emotional ones; and that social support does not just happen, but has to be obtained or elicited from those about us. People who feel unsupported in a stressful professional situation may therefore have help potentially available to them, but be unsure how to elicit that help. The literature concerning patterns of social interaction in lonely and depressed people suggests how to help people elicit help. If some people in a situation feel support, and others do not, what can we observe about the supported people that differentiates them from the others? 'Remedial help' for unsupported people would, for example, focus on social norms of intimacy and its reciprocation, knowing when and how to complain. This type of analysis, applicable to patient and staff alike, could give an added dimension to more straightforward advice usually given to staff feeling under pressure.

The demands made on nurses vary widely from one setting to another, so that some nursing, such as that in operating theatres, is highly technical, while other fields of nursing, such as work with mentally handicapped people, are primarily interpersonal and social. Some nurses work entirely within a specialist unit, such as a coronary care unit, and others, such as community psychiatric nurses, work entirely in the community. If there is pressure for patients to be discharged early from in-patient care, then community nurses will take on some tasks that would otherwise be the responsibility of hospital-based nurses. In some European countries, such as Belgium, community psychiatric nurses do not exist, so those tasks may simply not be carried out. Some countries train nurses as polyvalent; some specialize from the start of basic training; some specialize after a common basic training. Basic standards of training vary greatly, ranging in Europe from completion of primary studies to university admission level, although those countries who are members of the EEC have signed an agreement which will lead to more consistency in standards of training. In Britain 'project 2000' describes a national effort to reconstruct nurse training to be both more student-centred, and more relevant to the health needs of people at the turn of the century.

For all these reasons, the assumptions that can be made about the level of psychological knowledge and skill in nurses vary greatly. Yet there are an increasing number of reputable nursing journals and texts that demonstrate an increasing psychological sophistication among at least a proportion of nurses. As more nurses become psychologically informed—partly as a product of a number of people's being doubly qualified as nurses and psychologists—this sophistication, and demand for more psychological orientated training and support, is likely to grow.

Nurses are the people who potentially have the greatest knowledge of a patient's day-to-day behaviour. They also often have the closest, if not the only, knowledge of patient's relatives. Equally important is the fact that careful observation of ward interaction between nurses and patients shows that it is the more junior or less well-trained staff who usually interact more with patients. From a psychologist viewpoint perhaps the less well-trained staff actually have more potential to change patient's attitudes and behaviour than the better trained senior staff who are necessarily involved in other tasks. If that view is correct, it carries major implications for the design of staff training programmes, both for who should be trained and for the level of knowledge and literacy that can be assumed of trainees.

Working with remedial therapists

After doctors and nurses, the members of the various therapeutic professions are the most numerous, dignified by such catch-all phrases as 'paramedics' or 'ancillary professions'! The diversity and differentiation already noted in nurse training is even greater with this group. While in Britain the two major professions in this group are called physiotherapy and occupational therapy, kinesitherapy and ergotherapy are parallel titles used in other countries. Since the professions use complementary techniques, despite the differences in attitude already noted, they are often grouped together as the 'physical therapies'.

The importance of these professions is that, for many patients, they provide the main rehabilitative daytime activity for patients in hospital. Many of the activities are highly intensive, and may involve much physical contact between therapist and patient. Apart from the technical nature of the therapy offered, physical therapists also potentially offer a strongly supportive relationship to their patients, this being particularly apparent when patients are recovering from traumatic accidents. People—often active young men—who have, for example, had a severe spinal injury will spend several months having regular physiotherapy with usually young women therapists. In this setting, as in others, physical therapists need to know how to use the relationships they become involved in, and how to cope with the problems that arise.

There are many specific issues in different branches of physical therapy that can be analysed in psychological terms. Measurement of progress in rehabilitation requires careful assessment of such subjective or complex phenomena as pain and gait. Just as many people do not comply with a prescribed medical regime, so some people do not use a prosthesis or physical aid as prescribed, and need instruction and guidance to use it properly. Should activity regimes provide a relatively modest level of stimulation for, say, two or three hours, or provide a more demanding level of stimulation for half an hour?

Speech therapists are a particular group of therapists concerned to alleviate defective speech patterns, and to correct acquired speech defects after, for example, a stroke. They have a special training in speech development and linguistics, and thus necessarily need to be familiar with a number of psychological concepts. For all these therapists, and others such as audiologists, their significance to psychologists lies in the length of time they are in contact with the patient, and the significance of a particular skill they offer to the patient.

Working with social workers

The boundary between health care and social care has always been loose and movable, yet people's needs often require that the two systems of care work closely together. Different countries organize the two sets of services differently, so that even within the UK there are major differences between England, where the health and social services agencies are separated, and Northern Ireland, where one agency organizes both services. Depending on differences between the organization of the health services and social services, issues such as differing degrees of responsiveness to local political opinion, the load of statutory duties (such as the procedures for taking children who are 'at risk' into residential or alternative foster care), differing methods and time-scales of financial budgeting, and differing styles of professional accountability, may loom large as matters requiring resolution.

This suggests that a certain degree of political sophistication is required from a clinical psychologist working with both health and social care agencies.

To the extent that the organization of services dictates the training and roles, there is thus a huge diversity in the range of work undertaken by 'social workers'. There may be generic field workers providing a comprehensive service to a population, including everything from arranging adoptions to supporting the families of people currently in prison; there may be specialist field workers funded by religious or voluntary bodies providing services to a particular client group such as alcoholics; there may be specialist workers attached to day or residential units, such as a day care centre for elderly people.

In some of these functions, a social services department may lack staff with skills to provide the best sort of help. Indeed, it is noticeable in Britain that one of the greatest uses made by social services departments of clinical psychologists is in providing advice on day care, or in special residential settings for children. It is likely that a social services department will be presented with other highly specific demands; such as improving the selection of foster parents, or developing a community programme for substance abusers—glue-sniffers—which a clinical psychologist may be best equipped to manage. These two examples give an indication of the type of advice that a wide range of voluntary agencies may also seek from clinical psychologists, so that the psychologist's role with respect to these agencies becomes that of a true 'consultant'.

Other professions associated with clinical psychology

The main professional groups with which clinical psychologists work are doctors, nurses, remedial therapists, and social workers. In addition, they work with a number of other professions, or people working in health care who do not readily fit into existing professional 'slots'. This is due to the appearance of totally new techniques, the realization that a specific established technique does not require more than a specific range of skills to apply it, or the wish to utilize existing skills outside the conventional health care system.

Chapter 4 indicates some of the work done by educational psychologists with children; depending on the way in which countries organize their health and education services, there may be an integrated profession of child psychology, seeing children with problems irrespective of how the problems present, or two separate professions. In a similar way, clinical psychologists may often have very close links with teachers, particularly if the psychologists are working in a special day or residential unit (for example, for disturbed adolescents, for children who have committed serious offences and are in special units, or for multiply-handicapped children). The recent increased attention paid to child abuse has lead to new groupings of workers in this field, so psychologists may be more closely involved with foster parents and health visitors (known in other countries as public health nurses).

Another allied profession is that of 'health educator'. Until the last twenty years or so, positive public education in health promotion was very limited, and in Britain often carried out by health visitors, a group of community nurses often known as public health nurses in other countries. A positive decision was made to encourage health promotion, and many people now working as health educators have a background in nursing, teaching, and increasingly in psychology. Their concerns with 'health care routines' and 'health beliefs' can be seen as highly psychological, and there is plenty of scope for collaboration between psychologists and such workers. Indeed, members of many professions may have a mutual concern for health-education, disease-prevention, or health-promotion—perhaps relating to a common problem such as smoking—which overrides their profession of origin.

For a number of reasons, partly perhaps a greater willingness to admit to psychological difficulties, itself a product of better public awareness in this field, the training of counsellors has increased substantially. In a number of European countries counselling psychology is a major field of applied psychology; but in Britain counselling has largely developed outside the discipline of psychology, but informed by it. Counsellors may be generically trained, often in essentially a Rogerian approach, or they may be working within a particular problem area, such as substance abuse. A number of psychologists now work in this way, having a training specific to the work they do, and sometimes as part of a team which may be led by a clinical psychologist.

TEAMWORK

Good teamwork has been mentioned in several other chapters in this book, such as the chapter dealing with work with physically handicapped people. Teamwork obviously assumes the existence of a team—a group of people who work co-operatively with each other. Teams in health care vary in their composition, and fall into three categories. They may be made up of groups of people of the same profession, who usually are of varying levels of expertise and experience within that profession. Thus nursing teams will consist of one or more ward charge nurses or head nurses who clearly organize the work of registered or qualified nurses, and a number of assistant or learner nurses. Secondly teams may be made up of members of different professions, where a member of one specified profession—usually medical—specifies the work of the whole team: an excellent example is the group of staff in an operating theatre, where the operating surgeon is very clearly in charge of the operation.

A third option exists: where members of different professions are in the team, but where no one profession inevitably carries prime responsibilty for all the work done by a team. Such multidisciplinary teams may have either a management function or a clinical function—sometimes both. Where clinical psychologists work as team members it is very often in teams of this third and last type. A team of workers at Brunel University in Britain have been working to clarify some of the organizational and structural concepts implicit in team working, and a series of publications by them illuminate a number of difficulties inherent in team working (Øvretveit 1984).

Multidisciplinary teamwork is seen by some as impeding clear executive action, and by others as the only acceptable way for members of different professions to work together. In either case the issues it raises are central to the way in which psychologists relate to members of other professions, and work with them.

As far as management teams are concerned, any health authority will lay down clear lines of authority, and should establish clearly where, in the last resort, responsibilty for action lies. Management needs to be constantly reviewing services priorities, and interpreting data on the efficacy of different types of treatment, for example. Clinical psychologists obviously have a role in contributing to management in this way, and if they possess the confidence of their employers or colleagues can appropriately be the chairpersons of such teams in, for example, planning a new type of service for mentally handicapped people, or can become managers of the range of services for mentally ill people.

More typically, however, a clinical psychologist will be contributing to a multidisciplinary clinical team, where staff are appointed to or seconded to the team for all or part of their work. The activities of this type of team include the acceptance, diagnosis, and assessment of new cases; the discussion of cases as a group; the determination of appropriate treatment; and the organization of follow-up after treatment. The key questions which immediately arise in such groups are: Who does what? Who is the leader? and Who is responsible for what? The allocation of tasks among members of a team is determined by a number of factors. Usually members of a team will contribute specific skills and knowledge derived from their particular professional training, and will have other more personal knowledge, such as knowledge of a particular locality or of a particular local voluntary group, which may be highly relevant to who does what with a particular patient. A psychologist working in a community mental handicap team, for example, might be expected to contribute particularly to decisions on individual care programmes, and to the design of treatment programmes for specific behavioural problems. The British Psychological Society (1988) has produced some very helpful guidelines on methods of team working.

The concept of a 'key worker' is becoming increasingly widely accepted, so that one person is designated as the main link or liaison with an identified patient, so that specific professional skills are seen as secondary to the development of a positive one-to-one relationship between key worker and patient. The 'practice assumptions' of a profession also dictate how work is allocated. Some professions, of which medicine and clinical psychology are examples, organize their work on the assumption that a patient expects to see one individual member of that profession exercising their professional skills during their episode of illness. Nurses, on the other hand, are organized on an 'agency' assumption, so that nurses will change shifts and even wards during the course of a patient's illness.

Leadership of teams may be vested in a member of any professional group who possesses the relevant experience and knowledge. Sometimes leadership in such groups rotates among members according to a set pattern. Sometimes the appropriate leadership of a team may apparently be settled by appeal to the purpose of the team. The example of a child guidance teams—teams of child psychiatrists, psychologists, psychotherapists, and social workers—in Britain illustrates how different professional orientations may then impose their own pressure on leadership questions. A health-centred orientation, stressing the child's health, suggests medical leadership; an educational orientation, suggesting classroom adjustment and attainment, might favour psychological leadership; a social orientation, emphasizing the effects of family and social conditions, might indicate social work leadership. Yet the nature of child guidance work is such that for any group of children seen, some children will have presenting problems mainly in one sphere, others problems in other spheres. There is no uniform solution to leadership in such teams; what is certain is that as professions other than medicine—not only psychology—offer an increasing proportion of experienced and competent staff, so their claims for the leadership of teams are bound to increase.

The title of teamwork is often applied to what is in reality a different style of joint working, which is described by the Brunel workers as a network. In a number of settings, a professional will be a regular contact with members of other professions, but contact will be primarily by telephone or by letter. It is vitally important that communication is good between members of a network, as in a team; but in networks, the team as a whole need not, and often do not, meet face to face. With the move to community services, as opposed to hospital services, health care staff inevitably move away from patterns of joint working, produced by working on a common site, to patterns of working more resembling a network than a team. If this shift is not recognized, staff may be left working with little personal support, with the associated risk of work dissatisfaction and loss of morale.

Since teams are groups of people, a number of findings of social psychology, particularly of the psychology of small groups, help to explain why teams do what they do. Leadership styles, as already implied, are important in inducing members of the group to adopt a unified approach to problems. In any group there needs to be a balance between activities aimed at achieving the group's common objectives, and activities aimed at meeting the social and inter-personal needs of group members. Different group tasks require different levels of thinking and working, so that some group members will then be satisfied with one type of activity, while other group members will be satisfied by others. Team loyalties can become so strong that they supersede other loyalties or responsib-ilities that individual members should at least be bearing in mind, so that group tasks become subtlely modified, and a team heads off in a direction different to that which was intended (Øvretveit 1984).

TEACHING AND TRAINING HEALTH CARE PROFESSIONS

A major issue in meeting rising expectations of health care is the limited supply of teachers, not only for training the major health care professions, but also for training auxiliary workers. Traditionally teachers at the highest levels of the education system in most countries have not been trained as teachers: whatever skills as teach-ers they may possess have been obtained by apprenticeship, or by trial and error. However, limited skills obtained in this way are often not adequate to design an educational programme that may be trying to produce a range of specific skills from a student body highly heterogeneous in ability and prior experience.

A World Health Organization report, published in 1973, paid particular attention to the training of teachers in the health care field. The report pointed out the need for teachers, for example, to be able to plan objectives relevant to local needs and to plan instructional strategies to provide varied routes for achieving these objectives. They must also be able to evaluate their own teaching and consider such issues as teacher effectiveness. All of these activities presuppose some knowledge of the extensive educational and psychological literature on these topics. Thus clinical psychologists are often closely concerned with curriculum design and course evaluation, together with members of other professions, to increase the effectiveness of teaching. To take but one example, knowledge of educational evaluation techniques is important to any health care professional who has to do any teaching. Evaluation of a teaching course is usually limited to some assessment of how much knowledge the student has acquired, largely because this type of assessment, involving some sort of set essay or factual questions, is easy to set up and use. In many situations, of course, some sort of skill is the desired outcome, whether it be a specific clinical skill, such as learning how to take blood-pressure with a mercury sphygmomanometer, or a more interpersonal skill, such as knowing how to comfort mothers who have just been delivered of a stillborn child.

Both these types of assessment focus on the gains of skill the student has made: they do not focus on the educational methods used to produce those gains, and thus would not be helpful in designing an improved teaching method. In the example of comforting a mother, a clinical psychologist would explore the range of teaching procedures that could be used: observing an experienced clinician carry out this difficult task; formal teaching on typical reactions of mothers in those circumstances,; talking with mothers, or seeing videotapes of mothers, who have been through this painful experience and who can now look back on it and reflect on their feelings; asking students to role-play with a 'stooge' mother and videotaping the attempt; or any combination of these. Finding out which combination of methods works best, and working out how to design a practicable training module from the results, requires some evaluation of the methods used, not just of the student.

Psychological knowledge is thus relevant to a wide range of teaching and training situations in a health care system. More specifically, we can consider teaching and training members of other professions in psychological knowledge and skills—not forgetting the training of psychologists by members of other professions in *their* skills.

Teaching psychology to other professions

The demand for teaching of psychological topics from other professions is growing: the statutory training syllabuses for many health care professions now require what may be dozens of hours of psychological teaching. Some such syllabuses still imply that the best way to introduce psychology is by teaching a watered-down academic course on general psychology. This approach is nearly always inappropriate: the trainee comes to psychology expecting it to provide the answer to questions his discipline prompts, so a more appropriate introduction is to explore immediately, from a psychological viewpoint, practical problems the trainee encounters. These might include the problem of compliance with medication; or how to prepare someone for surgery; or why people respond to placebos; or how to control pain. Most of these topics can be presented in a way that integrates theory with practice, and presents psychology as relevant to the trainee.

The boundary between psychology and related disciplines such as ethology or anthropology is sometimes unclear, and increasingly psychology is taught as one component in a 'behavioural sciences' course embracing these related disciplines, especially medical sociology. It is usually important that a clinically experienced psychologist is involved in both planning and teaching such a course. There may be an excellent teacher locally available, not technically a clinical psychologist, who can cover some of the teaching; but an increasing number of colleges and training schools for health care professions now employ clinical psychologists for this purpose.

Psychology does pose some problems, when deciding how to teach it. Many students come to the subject ignorant of the experimental nature of the subject; ask almost any group of students of psychology to name a well known psychologist, and Freud will come top of the list every time. Some students come with what almost amount to fantasies about the subject, and imagine the subject has a mystery and power that is quite unrealistic. As with any discipline, the subject has its own vocabulary; but the need to define terms carefully can be overlooked by students used to everyday concepts of 'emotion', or 'learning', or 'reward'. The importance of animal experimentation in some fields of psychology can be off-putting to some students, who see reference to animal studies as a reductionist account of human behaviour. For all these reasons, careful thought has to be given in planning the teaching of psychology to other professions, especially at the beginning of the course.

Training in psychological treatment skills

One important consequence of the development of treatment procedures by clinical psychologists is the realization that members of
other professions can, and in some circumstances should, themselves learn to use those procedures. There will be heavy demands
upon the limited numbers of skilled staff, both to see the maximum
number of patients and to train others. Skilled staff are thus a scarce
resource, to be used strategically. A comprehensive review of
clinical psychology practice in Britain (MAS 1988) suggested a
three-tier model of psychological skills, which translates into a training strategy. Level 1 psychological skills are those which need to be
possessed by all health care workers; level 2 skills are specific but
limited skills, as for example those used in a particular mode of
psychological treatment; level 3 skills imply a comprehensive
psychological knowledge, and will normally only be possessed by a
qualified psychologist. Thus any staff capable of working at level 3
should concentrate their clinical work at that level, and should not be
doing level 2 or level 1 work if another can be found to do it.

Psychologists are also involved in training other groups of staff or
would-be therapists in other types of skills. The range of skills is
considerable, including basic counselling skills; treatment of sexual
dysfunction; psychological care of children in hospital; and educational techniques for severely handicapped children at home. The
range of people so trained is also wide: family doctors, community
nurses, clergy and church workers, parents, marriage guidance
counsellors, and voluntary workers in day centres.

When a psychologist becomes involved in direct skill training a
number of practical issues become important. Very often the
learners have never read a psychological book in their lives, and
need to acquire some sort of general psychological perspective along
with the particular skills they are acquiring. Scheduling teaching or
training sessions into the lives of often very busy learners means that
considerable flexibility in fitting in the sessions may be needed—
including sessions at 10 or 11 p.m. for night staff. Some learners
become over-enthusiastic, so that they do not appreciate the limitations of some techniques, and have to be restrained from over-
zealous application of the techniques. Despite these demands and
problems, many psychologists find this form of training to be one of
the most stimulating areas of their work.

A good illustration of how this essentially simple idea has been developed is given by a series of studies by Milne (1986) in a book also concerned with the training of parents and teachers. He carried out a series of carefully planned experiments aimed at producing an effective training package for ward-level staff. He considered the level of sophistication and skill which the nurse needed to acquire: some nurses might only need to become 'applicators' of behavioural techniques, so they could dispense tokens in a highly structured token economy programme. At the other end of the scale, some nurses could become 'nurse therapists', able to assess and treat a wide range of complaints without supervision.

Milne examined in detail several components of training nurses in behavioural skills. A five-day training package was developed, which covered 16 main topics in the general areas of assessment of behaviour, learning theory, and techniques of therapy. The training package was designed to use a range of educational techniques, and to be acceptable to nurses who had little or no prior experience of these techniques.

In evaluating the effectiveness of such a training course, it is necessary to use a range of measures of the skills the nurses acquired during the course—obviously a pen-and-paper test could assess knowledge, but a different approach is required to assess skills. Milne used a range of measures, three of which were: a simulated proficiency test, consisting of 10 videotaped nurse–patient inter-actions, to which the nurse students had to respond; a functional analysis test, which required the nurses to select a behaviour of their choice from a short videotape, and then to note the frequency of that behaviour and what happened immediately before or after the selected behaviour; and a formulation and treatment plan which had to be prepared, again following observation of a videotaped vignette.

Milne found that a first version of his training course did not produce the desired change in the behaviour of the nurses when they returned to their wards; the benefits of training had not spread, or generalized, from the teaching setting to the ordinary ward setting. He therefore increased the attention paid to a special project, carried out on the ward by the student, to make sure that these projects were carried out; and then found that the benefits of training were found in the ward.

This series of studies demonstrates very well the detailed attention to content, teaching method, and evaluation which is necessary to make sure that a staff training programme achieves what is intended. The lessons learned from this type of experimentation are of course relevant to the training of direct-care staff in *any* treatment modality, and to the training of staff working with the elderly and mentally handicapped, as well as with psychiatric patients.

There is a continuing debate within clinical psychology on the advisability of training other professions in psychological techniques. However, most psychologists in Britain take the view that psychological skills can be usefully acquired by others. In view of the relatively small number of psychologists compared to doctors, nurses, and other therapists (let alone parents and spouses!) perhaps most clinical psychologists should be actively engaged in 'giving away' or sharing their skills.

EVALUATING THE SERVICES PROVIDED

Other chapters have described some of the ways in which psychologists have evaluated their services they themselves provide. For most psychologists, such an evaluation of their own effectiveness, or the effectiveness of the particular unit or team with which they work, will be relatively limited in scope, and often concerned with outcome for the patient. There is now an increasing pressure for health care services to demonstrate their effectiveness on a much broader scale, often under circumstances where close experimental control or manipulation of the service is impossible. A range of terms is used to describe this concern about effectiveness, including quality assurance, audit, and setting standards. While some of these terms may differentially emphasize the views of users of the service, or the views of professional providers, they are all concerned with the effective and efficient application of resources, and the term evaluation is as good an umbrella term as any.

This pressure to evaluate effectiveness derives from a number of sources. There is public concern about the extent to which widespread discharge of institutionalized patients has not been accompanied by proper community provision. Government may be concerned that public money is used in the most cost-effective manner. Professions may themselves be aware that new patterns of service cannot be convincingly demonstrated to be superior to the old. A spreading interest in some so-called 'fringe' therapies and in the use of non-statutory charities or service-providing agencies is generating new techniques and services that also need appraisal.

Clinical psychologists have a number of contributions to make to evaluating the work of other professions in concert with them. One accepted definition of evaluation is 'the formal determination of the effectiveness, efficiency, and acceptability of a planned intervention in achieving stated objectives' (Holland 1983). Those objectives should be a set of desired outcomes which are attainable, measurable, and sufficient to justify a programme. These definitions indicate the areas where a psychological perspective is most relevant.

First of all, can clear objectives or desired outcomes be stated, and stated in advance in such a way that relevant baseline or pre-intervention measures can be obtained? A psychologist can work with other colleagues to identify and clarify specific goals, which are shared by all—or most—of those concerned with a project.

The evaluation approach also turns attention away from what one profession alone might see as a desirable outcome, to those outcomes which might be desired by patients and by others, such as direct-care staff. This requires that all those groups contribute to the evaluation procedure, and that the results of the evaluation are comprehensible to all those who contribute. Evaluation reports then have to be readable by direct-care staff, not just published in scientific journals, and they have to be readable by the planners and managers who may have to make difficult decisions of resource allocation on the basis of those results.

One matter of continuing debate that is central to many evaluation projects is what constitutes 'quality of life'. Quality of life is a concept used to supplement the usually simple but essentially rather arid measures of survival or cure-rate relevant to some conditions or operations, such as stroke or coronary bypass surgery, where the patient may still encounter significant limitations of everyday activity. Any clinical intervention will, of course, only affect the function or behaviour to which it is directed, and while the 'quality of care' may be improved, it may be rather grandiose to suggest that 'quality of life' will be affected by possibly a rather limited intervention. The concept of quality of life may thus need to be heavily qualified if in any particular study it is to be a valid and useful measure.

In some fields of physical rehabilitation indices of Activities of

Daily Living (ADL) have been used as global outcome measures. These are less relevant for people with a primarily non-medical disability, where more comprehensive indices, including information on social activity, are required, such as the Index of Well-Being (IWB) suggested by one team of workers. All of these more comprehensive measures raise issues of reliability, validity, sensitivity to bias, and utility under service conditions with which psychologists are likely to be familiar.

Communicating with others

Some forms of health care can be given without any spoken or written communication, such as emergency resuscitation or the giving of an injection. However, most care or treatment involves some spoken communication, even if it is only to require some simply response such as opening your mouth or rolling over. For most patients, there will at some stage be a complex series of communications, intended to establish a diagnosis or to advise on treatment, which may include detailed questioning about symptoms, the issuing of detailed guidance on, for example, diet, or giving instructions to direct-care staff on what they have to do.

Psychologists have been interested in several aspects of this information-exchange system, not least because many health care staff do not appreciate how difficult many patients find it both to provide and to retain the relevant information. Some patients may have defective senses, so that some artificial communication aid— such as an electronic aid to give a visual display of what is required— or artificial language may be needed. A substantial proportion of patients, certainly 10 to 15 per cent, will not be highly literate, and will simply not understand high-level vocabulary words. This suggests the use of various indices of 'readability' to make sure that instructions are generally comprehensible, although the simplistic application of such formulae is open to criticism.

Another approach is to look at the amount and type of information conveyed to the patient, examining, for example, whether fear-arousing messages to patients work—in other words, do they lead to more compliance with prescribed treatment by patients? Some studies suggest that fear-arousal cannot be strongly advocated on present evidence. However, an approach which examines just the way in which the doctor or patient evaluates that information is criticized by Tuckett and Williams (1984). Their social-psychological or sociological analysis also draws attention to the social setting within which information is exchanged, particularly examining the degree of control exerted by doctors in their communication with patients.

There is now a wealth of useful psychological guidance on many aspects of communication with patients, relevant not only to highly qualified staff but to portering or domestic staff who may have to deal with a violent patient or visitor. The guidance may relate communication with compliance—how to improve the often 50 per cent rates at which out-patients take oral medication as prescribed. The guidance may make sure that the huge range of forms used in any hospital are comprehensible to the wide range of both staff and patients who must use them (Wright 1983).

SUMMARY

Clinical psychologists work closely with a wide range of other professions and people. The significance of these other people to the life of the individual patient varies considerably—they may be making a highly sophisticated diagnostic decision, or they may be engaged in practical 'hands-on' care. There is a psychological component to all these tasks. How does the diagnostician obtain the fullest possible information from the patient? How can direct-care staff be helped to maintain an individualized and relevant ward regime month in, month out?

Current practice suggests that clinical psychologists have a number of key functions with respect to other staff. They can facilitate team working. They can disseminate psychological knowledge and skills. They can help to ensure that the most effective treatments are chosen. Lastly, they can help to promote clear and uncluttered communication between everyone concerned with the individual patient.

REFERENCES

British Psychological Society (1988). *Responsibility issues in clinical psychiatry and multi-disciplinary teamwork*. British Psychological Society, Leicester.

322 *Working with others*

Holland, W. W. (1983). *Evaluation of health care*. Oxford University Press.
Llewellyn, S. P. (1984). The cost of giving: emotional growth and emotional stress. In *Understanding nurses: the social psychology of nursing* (ed. S. Skevington), pp. 49–65. Wiley, Chichester.
MAS (Management Advisory Service) (1988). *Review of Clinical Psychology Services*. Management Advisory Service, Cheltenham.
Milne, D. (1986). *Training behaviour therapists: methods, evaluation, and implementation with parents, nurses and teachers*. Croom Helm, London.
Øvretveit, J. (1984). *Organising psychology in the NHS*. Brunel Institute of Organisation and Social Studies, Uxbridge.
Parry, G. (1990). *Coping with crises*. British Psychological Society, Leicester.
Tuckett, D. and Williams, A. (1984). Approaches to the measurement of explanation and information-giving in medical consultations: a review of empirical studies. *Social Sci. Med.*, **18**, 571–80.
WHO (World Health Organization) (1973). Training and preparation of teachers for schools of medicine and of allied health services, WHO Technical Report Series NO. 521. WHO, Geneva.
Wright, P. (1983). Informed design for forms. In *Information design—the design and evaluation of signs and printed material* (ed. R. Easterby and H. Zwaga), pp. 545–77. Wiley, Chichester.

FURTHER READING

Davis, H. and Butcher, P. (1985). Sharing psychological skills: training non-psychologists in the use of psychological techniques. *Br. J. Med. Psychol.*, **58** (3) (special issue).
Ham, C. (1991). *The new National Health Service*. Radcliffe Medical Press, Oxford.
Jaques, E. (1978). *Health services: their nature and organisation, and the role of patients, doctors, nurses, and the complementary professions*. Heinemann, London.

13

Overview and implications

John Marzillier and John Hall

In Britain forty years ago there were only a handful of clinical psychologists, working as technician scientists in psychiatric hospitals. Like physicists and biochemists they were 'backroom boys', whose contribution to health care consisted of highly specialized scientific investigations, mainly in the form of psychometric tests and investigations. In many other countries in Western Europe clinical psychologists did not exist. Only in the USA had clinical psychology any appreciable history and a developing professional identity. In the 1990s the picture is very different. Clinical psychology has become an established profession in many European countries and in the English-speaking areas of Australia, New Zealand, and South Africa. Some countries such as Britain have seen a rapid increase in the number of clinical psychologists, particularly over the last decade. Most importantly, as is illustrated in the chapters of this book, clinical psychologists have shed their backroom image and have become front-line workers in many spheres of health care. Clinical psychologists have had a practical impact in such diverse fields as child health and working with older people, in drug addiction and physical handicap, in psychotherapy, and in staff training. There has been a recognition amongst health care workers, sometimes slowly and painfully gained, that psychology is important and sometimes vital to health care, and that psychologists can and do have a direct and useful influence on health in diverse fields.

The preceding chapters of this book have provided illustrative accounts of the practical working of clinical psychologists in various settings. In this chapter we describe some of the common themes that emerge from those working practices and tentatively discuss their implications for both clinical psychology and health care in general.

THEORY AND PRACTICE

Clinical psychologists see themselves as 'scientist–practitioners' whether their work is in teaching basic skills to people with learning difficulties, in carrying out intensive psychotherapy with disturbed adolescents, or in evaluating the success of a new environmental programme for institutionalized elderly residents. What does the term 'scientist–practitioner' mean? In Chapter 1 we describe how the profession of clinical psychology is based upon a growing knowledge base (the science of psychology), and how the training of clinical psychologists entails using that knowledge for beneficial ends. The application of scientific knowledge is therefore a fundamental feature of clinical psychology, which distinguishes it from the practical 'common-sense psychology' that all of us use in everyday life. For example, in Chapter 4 we can see how knowledge of normal child development is essential to understanding when a particular behaviour such as encopresis becomes a significant problem. Understanding of the stages and processes of developmental change in young children enables the psychologist to assess a problem in its appropriate context and to tailor interventions to suit the developing child. The same point may be made for adults too, though the process of development takes place over a longer period of time and reflects social and cultural influences, as in the transition from young adult to parent or from worker to retired person. Models of 'science' too are changing, so that psychology has itself grown by, for example, the adoption of ethological concepts and the development of more qualitative, as opposed to quantitative methods of assessment.

Scientific knowledge consists of facts embedded within theory, and psychology is driven by various often competing theories about human behaviour. Theories are vital. They are the lifeblood of our attempts to make sense of our behaviour. Clinical psychology has been influenced by several theories, notably theories about learning processes, and many have directly guided clinical practice. Cullen and Tennant in Chapter 5, for example, describe how as psychologists they use learning principles to teach a person with learning difficulties to tie a bow successfully. The behavioural treatment of anxiety illustrated in Chapter 2 arose directly from experimental studies of conditioning in the laboratory. Theories about the way memory operates in terms of different stores and processes directly influence the memory retaining programmes that Wilson and Staples use for the head-injured patients (see Chapter 6). The interplay between theory and practice is not simply a one-way relationship, but a reciprocal one. Studies of the way memory is disturbed in head-injury patients help psychologists understand more about the way memory normally works.

The plethora of different theories can sometimes be confusing. This is evident in the field of psychotherapy, where Freudian theories sit side by side with behavioural theories, humanistic theories, cognitive theories, and many other variants. This is partly a reflection of our ignorance about the complexities of human experience and the real difficulties in testing theory in the complicated world of clinical practice. Yet, despite the confusion, theories are essential in order that scientific progress can be made. In recent years there has been a growing recognition of the central importance of cognitive processes, notably disturbances of thinking, in various emotional disorders such as anxiety and depression (Brewin 1988). This had led to new theories about therapeutic change and a rethinking of established psychoanalytic and behavioural theories. We are beginning to see a synthesis of different psychological theories in the area of psychotherapy, which may help dispel some of the current confusions.

The scientist–practitioner model also entails the application of *scientific principles* in clinical practice. The development of behavioural assessment batteries such as REHAB in the assessment of psychiatric disability (see Chapter 3) involves the scientific procedures of item analysis, scaling, correlation, and factor analysis in order to produce an assessment tool that is scientifically reliable and valid. Many other psychometric instruments or tests have been developed using similar scientific principles, such as the British Ability Scales used in assessing the intellectual abilities of children. Attention to these scientific principles enables the psychologist to develop an assessment measure that is free from gross errors such as bias, poor reliability, or invalid inferences, so that greater confidence can be placed in the results of the assessment.

The use of scientific principles is also evident in the systematic evaluation of treatment methods. This can take the form of clinical research trials, such as the evaluation of a clinical psychology service in primary care reported in Chapter 11, or the careful assessment of individual cases. Data on the problem in question are collected by means of a self-monitoring record (by observation, or by other means), before, during, and after treatment, thereby providing evidence on the extent to which change occurred. Wilson and Staples in Chapter 6 provide several examples of systematic evaluation applied to single cases. In recent years research strategies suitable for the single case have been developed which give the clinician–researcher greater confidence in the validity of the treatment outcome (see, for example, Barlow and Hersen 1984).

The 'practitioner' component of the scientist–practitioner model should not be overlooked. Working with clinical cases demands many practical skills. These range from the subtle, interpersonal skills involved in psychotherapy to diplomatic skills required for working with other staff. These skills are acquired not so much from scientific principles and procedures, but as a result of practical experience. Clinical psychologists, like other professionals, can only be scientists to a degree. They must also learn to be creative and sensitive practitioners, and while some skills training occurs in professional courses, many skills are learnt from personal experience.

Psychology is about people

Underpinning the work of clinical psychologists in various settings is a fundamental concern with the rights and values of patients as people. As Garland states in his account of work with older people in Chapter 7: 'While old people do have some unique concerns, they are basically just people who have been around longer than us.' Cullen and Tennant in Chapter 5 describe the 'normalization' philosophy which has come to influence work with mentally handicapped people. It is strongly asserted that people with learning difficulties should not be segregated from the community, but treated as equal members with equal rights and privileges. This is all too rarely achieved. A similar argument can be made with respect to the care of psychiatric patients (see Chapter 3).

Concern about the rights and values of people can be found in different aspects of the work of clinical psychologists. It can be seen in the respect for the dignity and worth of the client in psychotherapy, where an open and non-judgemental attitude is adopted by the therapist and the client is able to discuss painful, personal concerns in an atmosphere of acceptance and trust. It is very much a part of the advocacy role suggested by Wilson and Staples with regard to the rights of the disabled and physically handicapped and by Blackburn with regard to offenders, in Chapters 6 and 8 respectively. It underlies the concern expressed by Wallace and Bennett in Chapter 10 that hospitalization and medical treatments should take into account the personal concerns of patients as well as their medical needs (see, for example, the case of Gary). It can be found in the need to protect children and young people from abuse and exploitation by parents and other adults.

This essentially ethical statement is also reflected in the view that most psychological problems are not different *in kind* from the problems all of us experience. For example, problems of anxiety, depression, sexual difficulties, addictive behaviours, are part of a continuum, and are experienced by most of us. Professional help may be sought when the problems become too intense or severe to be managed on their own, or cause too great a disruption to normal life. Even in cases where there is clear evidence of a biological deficiency (for example, in some mentally handicapping conditions), the psychological approach is to emphasize the communalities with normal experience. People with learning difficulties have to learn skills like other people, following the same principles of learning. People with physical illnesses experience the normal psychological reactions to pain, trauma, and isolation that all of us experience from time to time. This is not to say that there are not unique or peculiar features to having learning difficulties, or being severely depressed, or in undergoing major surgery. But it is with the experiences and behaviour of *people* that psychology is ultimately concerned, and there is much to be gained from recognizing the continuity of such experiences across all conditions and problems.

ASSESSMENT, INTERVENTION, AND EVALUATION

The common clinical strategies of assessment, intervention, and evaluation are exemplified again and again in the various chapters of this book. Whatever the setting or whatever the population worked with, clinical psychologists are concerned to provide a thorough assessment of the problem, a psychologically based method of intervention, and a systematic evaluation of the outcome.

(a) Assessment

Three important characteristics of assessment stand out. Firstly, assessment is always in response to a significant clinical question. In the past clinical psychologists were sometimes asked to assess the patient's 'IQ' or 'personality', often without any real consideration of the value of such information. These essentially descriptive assessments have been replaced by more practical and specific questions, the results of which will have a direct bearing upon the patient's clinical state. In the case of learning difficulties, for example, Cullen and Tennant in Chapter 5 contrast an IQ assessment, which is of little practical use, with an assessment that seeks to understand why a child with learning difficulties might giggle and run away whenever she is asked a question. This type of information is of practical use, since the information can be used to help the child improve her communication skills. In the field of physical health Wallace and Bennett in Chapter 10 illustrate how a simple diary record sheet can be used to assess what factors provoke a woman's anxiety about chest pains and headache. Understanding the factors that lead to such anxiety (antecedents) can not only help us to understand it better but to plan methods of change.

This leads to the second major characteristic of assessment, which is that it contributes to an analysis of the factors that cause and maintain problems. This is known generally as a *functional analysis*, since it is concerned not merely with the description of the problem, but with the function it has for the patient in question and for the patient's family. This type of analysis can be applied to very precise patterns of behaviour, such as the triggering of an aggressive outburst in a psychiatric resident, or to more complex psychological relationships. The successful treatment of problems such as depression, anxiety, and eating disorders depends upon a sensitive and careful assessment of how these problems relate to other important aspects of people's lives. If a person's self-worth is strongly determined by believing herself to be slim and attractive, as it was in the case of Susan, illustrated in Chapter 2, then understanding that relationship is necessary for successful therapy.

It is precisely because a functional analysis provides information about the causes and consequences of a problem that it leads on to the third major characteristic of assessment, which is that it provides the basis for intervention. The information provided is useful precisely because it suggests ways of achieving change. Fielding illustrates this well in Chapter 4 with respect to parental reactions to John's encopresis (see pp. 96–102).

Assessment is not simply confined to an individual and his problems. There are various levels of assessment, for example, intrapsychic, interpersonal, social, institutional, familial, etc. In Chapter 3 Hall illustrates how assessment can be concerned with the characteristics of the institution (in this case a psychiatric hospital), taking into account the behaviour of ward staff, administrators, and doctors, as well as the residents. Such an approach has sometimes been called a *systems* approach, since the assessment is concerned with the interaction between various systems. Thus a child's anti-social behaviour can be seen in terms of the relationships between him and his various family members or between him and his peers at school, each of which describes a particular system of interactions. Whether assessment is concerned with problems at an individual level or at a systems level, similar strategies will be found, namely the concern with a specific practical question, a systematic analysis of the various maintaining and causative factors, and the generation of specific treatment objectives.

(b) Intervention

Psychological interventions are concerned with promoting bene-ficial change using psychological procedures and principles. Much of this book is about change, which ranges from reducing confusion in elderly residents by means of reality orientation, to applying hypnosis to acute burn injury to reduce trauma and tissue damage. Although the specifics of treatment vary according to the type of problem and the population concerned, it is possible to identify several common features.

Firstly, clinical psychologists are very much concerned with teaching specific skills. It requires skills for a person with learning difficulties to learn to tie his or her shoelaces, and equally it requires skill for a haemophiliac child to carry out factor replacement therapy or a brain-damaged soldier to recognize the sounds and names of letters. Skills training draws upon some well-established procedures such as modelling or demonstration of the skill in question, repeated practice, informational feedback, reinforcement or incentives, and homework tasks.

A second common feature of interventions is the reduction of fear or anxiety. Cognitive–behavioural treatments of phobias and anxieties are described in detail in Chapter 2. Similar methods can be found in the treatment of school-phobic children (Chapter 4), in reducing understandable anxieties about hospitalization and surgery (Chapter 10), and in the direct treatment of a fear of falling in an elderly amputee (Chapter 6). Anxiety is a characteristic not only of psychological problems but also of many physical problems, where it can exacerbate the problem and delay treatment. Wallace and Bennett, for example, make a strong case in Chapter 10 for greater attention to the reduction of fear and anxiety in physical medicine, where there is evidence of both physical and psychological benefit.

The third aspect of treatment that is worth noting is the emphasis on the role played by cognitive processes such as thoughts, attitudes, and beliefs. This is particularly evident in the treatment of depression by cognitive therapy (see Chapter 2), but is applicable in other problem areas too. For example, the motivation to overcome physical disability will be directly influenced by the extent to which the patient's attitude is positive and his or her expectations are realistic. Wallace and Bennett's description of the case of Gary illustrates how negative attitudes and unrealistic expectations can hinder progress.

Many patients are strongly motivated to seek change. They desperately want to overcome their disabilities. In other cases motivation is itself a problem, as is seen in the apathetic institutionalized behaviour of many chronic psychiatric patients. Some psychological treatments are directly concerned with increasing the patient's motivation for change, as in the token economy programmes described in Chapter 3. In psychological terms motivation is not some predetermined state or personality trait, but a product of the various factors that maintain and cause behaviour. The successful treatment of addictions will in part depend upon the person's ability to create and sustain strong incentives for change to counteract those of the addiction in question, as Hodgson shows in Chapter 9.

In psychological terms interventions are concerned with four major processes: the change in *behaviour*, such as the acquisition of certain skills; the change in *emotions*, such as the reduction of fear or anxiety and the elevation of depressive mood; changes in *cognition*, such as the modification of attitudes and beliefs; and *environmental* change. In the latter category more attention is paid to the controlling factors in the person's environment and the specific description of the individual's problems. Garland illustrates this with respect to room management in Chapter 7 and Hall in Chapter 3 in discussing the institutional changes in psychiatric hospitals.

(c) Evaluation and quality

The functional analysis of problems and the specification of treatment objectives makes evaluation a logical component of any intervention programme. By specifying in advance the goals of treatment, and by then monitoring the attainment of those goals, it is possible to see directly whether treatment has or has not been successful. It is also possible to see if aspects of evaluation other than outcomes— such as the efficiency and acceptability of planned interventions— have been determined. While the concept of service evaluation is well established, a number of other terms—such as quality assurance, audit, standard setting, peer-review, and consumer-satisfaction—are used with varying degrees of precision to describe related ideas and procedures.

Evaluation can occur at different levels, and with respect to different criteria and measures. Hadley and Strupp (1977) outline a tripartite model for evaluating psychotherapies that embraces the interests of the client, of the professional, and of society. Clients are primarily interested in personal changes, such as reduced distress and increased happiness. Professional staff will view change in terms of the theoretical model underlying their interventions—so that some therapists would regard changes in specific symptoms as of less value than changes in beliefs. From society's viewpoint, therapies are valued in terms of social norms and standards, to the extent that they reduce 'problems' that are socially visible, such as people who are both homeless and mentally ill. Public concern may also focus on the cost of treatments, to the extent that these costs are seen as being carried by taxation of one form or another.

Ideas of quality—quality-assurance, quality of care, quality of life—are perhaps the most important after ideas of service evaluation. Definitions of components of quality look rather similar to the components of an evaluation study—referring to effectiveness and efficiency, for example—but in addition components such as accessibility and equity tend to be added. Accessibility describes the ease of access to a service—this is determined not just by the distance from home to clinic, but by the cost of travel (including parking charges) and by the average waiting-time at the clinic. Equity describes the extent to which a service is available to a population in need of a service, irrespective of age, sex, income, or employment status. Quality assessment also takes account of the passage of the client through the total episode of care, in the course of which the client will be seen by members of different professions, may be seen on several different sites, and may require fundamentally different types of service—a diagnostic service, a rehabilitative service, and perhaps terminal care. The emphasis on quality essentially takes the view of the consumer of the service more seriously, and assumes a more multidimensional perspective towards effectiveness.

The different levels of evaluation are important, since not only do they contain different perspectives and values, but the type of evaluation determines what measures are used. Financial considerations can result in a concern with gross measures of change, such as how many people are admitted and discharged from a hospital, or assessing the efficiency of a treatment service in terms of numbers of people treated in relation to staffing. The problem with these measures is that they do not reflect either the client's perspective (being discharged from hospital need not result from psychological improvement) or the professional's perspective. Knowing the logistics of a therapeutic service tells us nothing about its quality and aims. Concern with evaluation therefore is not simply with cost, effectiveness, and efficiency, although these will be important, but with psychological change from the perspective of both client and therapist.

WORKING WITH OTHERS

Day-to-day practice of clinical psychology inevitably results in close contact with other people. This is illustrated in the many examples of collaborative work in the various chapters of this book. In

Chapter 12 Hall discusses the different forms such collaboration can take and some of the issues arising out of it.

The most common form of collaboration is that of joint work on clinical cases, in which the specialist skills of psychologists combine with those of nurses, health visitors, physiotherapists, doctors, and other professionals. Wilson and Staples, for example, in Chapter 6 describe how psychological assessments and interventions combine with the work of physiotherapists and occupational therapists with brain-damaged patients. Mercier's work, described in Chapter 11, indicates how health visitors and psychologists can effectively combine in group treatment for parents of sleep-disordered pre-school children. In these and other examples successful collaboration depends upon mutual sharing of specialist skills and knowledge. This is of benefit not only to the patient but also to the different professionals, who in this way will learn about each other's particular contribution. Collaborative work is particularly valuable, since so many problems are multidimensional. Wallace and Bennett's description of their work in intensive care units in Chapter 10 indicates the value of monitoring and treating patients' psychological states—in particular their anxieties, which may inhibit their response to prescribed medical treatment such as exercise. There are also ways in which various aspects of physical treatment may have adverse psychological effects, as when the technology of modern obstetric medicine can interfere with the mother's emotional response to her new baby.

In addition to collaborative work, there is a clear role for psychologists in training and supervising others in procedures informed by psychological principles. Recently a distinction has been made between training and 'consultancy'. Training implies an explicit objective of the transfer of knowledge and skills, and the systematic creation of a training programme or regime to attain those objectives. Many psychologists are already involved in training others in psychological skills, such as counselling and cognitive therapy. In doing this it is important that those being trained are not only given a thorough training in practical skills, but also become familiar with the psychological perspectives and theories that underlie those skills. The best training courses involve fairly lengthy and thorough training in both theory and practice.

Consultancy, on the other hand, implies a structured response to a particular presented problem, where the psychologist formulates the problem psychologically, and then guides and supports the people in direct contact with the person-with-the-problem, offering them the psychological knowledge and skills necessary for that particular presented problem. Consultancy is usually time-limited, and does not lead to another trained person, but is a time-efficient way to make the best use of limited psychological time.

A consultancy model of working is advantageous in its own right—a substantial proportion of the problems encountered by, say, a community psychiatric nurse will not need the specialized skills of a clinical psychologist or psychiatrist; but nurses will be better able to help their clients by the availability of consultancy. However, it is undeniable that this model of working has been stimulated by the continuing shortage of clinical psychologists.

In the first edition of this book, a national vacancy rate for clinical psychologists of 14 per cent for England was given. A more recent survey, published in 1990 by the British Government Manpower Planning Advisory Group (MPAG), indicated a 22 per cent vacancy rate, despite a growth in overall numbers of psychologists working. The MPAG report also made it clear that the period of training for clinical psychologists, and the limitation on training numbers imposed by the number of available supervisors, together mean that rapid expansion of numbers is not possible. There is in fact a shortage in Britain of several health care professions, including occupational therapists and psychiatrists, and similar constraints upon rapid expansion apply to them, so that making the most effective use of limited human resources is a concern shared with other professions.

FUTURE PRACTICE

It is possible to discern several trends in practice that give some hint as to how clinical psychology is developing. We have already referred to some of these, notably the increasing application of psychological methods in various health fields and the increasing emphasis on collaborative work with other professional groups. Three other features are also evident: the move to community care, changing models of health and medicine, and the challenge of long-term disability.

(a) Community care

There is currently a strong trend towards provision of community care for the mentally ill and people with learning difficulties. This has arisen partly from laudable concern about the low standard of accommodation in large mental hospitals and the documented concerns about the effects of institutionalization on the patients resident there; and partly out of financial reasons, since the run-down of such hospitals can lead to immediate savings in terms of both labour and capital costs, even if these savings will have to be offset by the necessary increased costs of a community service. In several areas clinical psychology services have already moved 'into the community', as is described in examples of their work in primary care in Chapter 11, with the elderly in Chapter 7, and with people with learning difficulties in Chapter 5. One immediate question arises—what constitutes appropriate community care?

One important element of the community care system is that treatment facilities should be as accessible as possible for the person in need. In this way existing community support such as family and friends can remain in contact, especially during crisis periods. A second element is that there should be organizational collaboration between different professional and voluntary agencies. This permits greater continuity of care and the possibility of preventing minor problems turning into major ones. Thus a vital feature of community care is the establishment of close links between specialists, such as psychologists, and primary care staff. There is a need too for the various specialist groups to work together to avoid duplication of skills and contradictory advice and practices. The setting up of Community Mental Handicap Teams, in which specialists take a consultancy role in relation to the activities of front-line workers such as social workers and nurses, is one example of how a community service can be developed. Similar models for the mentally ill have been developed.

In addition to providing psychological advice and supervision, a clinical psychologist can contribute to a community care programme by working closely with the different groups or teams. This might entail, for example, the setting up of staff support groups or training groups whose function would be to improve communication and provide a forum for the sorting out of interprofessional problems.

There has as yet been relatively little attention paid to the psychological problems and stresses of a transition to community care for staff who have acquired specialist skills in other settings. Not only does it involve the acquisition of new skills, but also changes in working practices that may have significant psychological effects, for example the relative isolation of community-based nurses from their own professional group.

The ideal of care in the community, however, needs to be tempered with the realities and limitations of both local receptivity and health service practice. The closure of large mental hospitals in Britain, Italy, and other parts of Europe had led in some instances to many seriously ill and vulnerable patients being left without any form of proper care; many end up wandering the streets or languishing in prison cells. The community does not always care, as is shown in the opposition of local people to the establishment of psychiatric hostels and homes for mentally handicapped people in their neighbourhood. The NIMBY phenomenon ('not in my back yard') does not only apply to the dumping of nuclear waste.

In Britain community services are on the whole funded from a different budget from that of the health service. It is therefore financially beneficial to hard-pressed health service managers to close down expensive hospitals, releasing much-needed cash from the sale of often valuable land, and to transfer the care of the long-term mentally ill to the local authority. Local authorities, however, are also severely cash-limited, particularly as the money they raise from local taxes is increasingly 'capped' by central government. The costs of community care, which are far from insignificant, will have to compete with the costs of education and general services out of resources which are insufficient to meet the needs of all. The result is an inevitable failure to provide the hostels and staff to care for those who are mentally ill or in need of long-term support.

Another cause of concern arises out of the recent changes to the management of the health service in the UK, whereby services are split between *purchasers* on the one hand, whose role is to buy health care from hospitals and other resources, and *providers* on the other, who contract to provide the services. This 'internal market' highlights the costs of the various services, and, in theory, brings in an element of competitiveness between different service-providers. However, in practice, because resources are finite and opportunities for generating further income limited, the internal market is likely to lead to a squeeze on services; once again, community provision may be curtailed as managers desperately strive to maintain basic health care out of inadequate budgets.

For clinical psychologists community care is a more satisfactory way of delivering psychological services to many groups of people: the service is brought closer to the individual; the model of care is less medical; there is opportunity for local communities to take on more responsibility for the care of their members; professionals can work closely with local groups and thereby disseminate their skills and expertise more widely; preventive and educational measures can be implemented more easily. But if resources are not adequate, and the appropriate structures not put in place, community care will not be successful, and those most in need will suffer enormous deprivation.

Movement to a community care model is by implication a move away from an institutional care model, so that it can be simplistically seen as a pendulum slowly swinging on a uni-dimensional axis. In that sense, the pendulum in many parts of Europe has swung as near to the community-care end as is practicable. Community care is multifaceted, and is defined not only by care in the community, but by closer links between primary and secondary care services, and by an emphasis on early intervention. A need remains for some centralized resources, especially for the most disabled, and to offer respite for families for whom care is a heavy burden. A recent publication on the concept of 'asylum' (Kings Fund 1987) reasserts the need for places of safety and haven, while very clearly condemning the poor standards of institutional care which have stigmatized the essentially positive meaning of 'asylum'.

(b) Changing models of health and medicine

A traditional view of the health service is one in which doctors assisted by nurses apply their skills and expert knowledge to treat illnesses. While this is a large part of modern medicine, it has become increasingly obvious that illness and disease will never be eradicated by technological medicine alone, that much of ill health is a product of the social and environmental conditions in which people live, and that many of the most notable improvements in health have come about as a result of societal change. Diseases such as typhoid fever, cholera, and rickets were virtually eliminated in Western countries by changes to sanitation and improvements in material conditions. Poverty is still a major determinant of ill-health, as a glance at the disparities in health between First and Third World countries will confirm. Even in the relatively affluent United Kingdom those who live at or below the poverty line are much more vulnerable to illness and premature death. Illness therefore cannot be seen simply as an individual's misfortune; health is in a large part a social and economic concept.

The socio-economic dimension of health and disease has mostly bypassed the attention of health professionals, including clinical psychologists. This may be because it is seen as a 'political' issue, and therefore touches uncomfortably upon the many inequities that govern our lives in general. However, this situation is rapidly changing. The spiralling costs of health care have resulted in a radical restructuring of the health care system in Britain, introducing an 'internal market' whereby different sections compete for often scarce resources. One result has been to make the disparities in health much more visible, as well as forcing professionals to confront the socio-economic issues that underly clinical practice at all levels. How can comparisons be made between better care for long-term mentally ill patients, on the one hand, and the care of AIDs sufferers on the other? Should resources be directed to more sophisticated (and expensive) technology for cardiovascular surgery or to a programme of health promotion to prevent the onset of coronary heart disease? These decisions—which had always been implicitly made—are now openly debated, because their economic basis is manifest. Clinical psychologists, like other health care professionals, cannot afford to ignore the debate: their very existence is threatened by the implications of the decisions taken by managers and others. It will not be long, for example, before a clinical psychology service is privatized in an effort to reduce health care costs. The politicization of the professions is an inevitable result of increasing social and economic pressures on health care.

Another area of fast-growing awareness is that of environmental factors in health and illness. Over the last decade media attention has been focused on world-wide disasters such as famine, earthquakes, political oppression, war, enforced migration, flooding, oil spills, and nuclear accidents. It is impossible to ignore the massive effects that are produced by such disasters, not only at the point of impact but across the globe. At a related level there is growing concern about the damage inflicted on our environment by the consequences of our industrially-fuelled, consumer-led way of life. There are direct and indirect effects on health of acid rain, nuclear waste, urban decay, and motorway expansion programmes amongst other things. The 'greening' of our society is only a small beginning in the process of social change that is necessary not only for improved health but for the continued existence of the planet. A model of health that ignores the environment is just not possible.

There is a growing public interest in health and medicine. Scepticism about the value of many medical treatments has been fuelled by well-publicized examples of apparently effective treatments proving to be ineffective and sometimes harmful. The consumer of health care is forced more and more to follow the old legal adage, *caveat emptor* ('let the buyer beware'). The use of tranquillizers for the treatment of anxiety is a good example. Recognition that barbiturates were highly addictive drugs led to their replacement by benzodiazepines, which were hailed as revolutionary, non-addictive, and harmless. However, in the 1980s it was belatedly acknowledged that benzodiazepines were also capable of producing dependency, and moreover could, with chronic use, lead to permanent effects on the brain (Catalan and Gath 1985). Tens of thousands of people who have become dependent on these drugs felt betrayed by their doctors; some have initiated legal action against the drug companies that made the tranquillizers. In this climate of scepticism and uncertainty consumers have been turning more to 'alternative medicine'—alternative to conventional medicine—and to 'complementary medicine', which co-exists with conventional medicine. Perhaps mistakenly, there is a belief that such medicine is safer, more environmentally friendly, and less likely to be subject to economic pressures. The emphasis on a *holistic* model (i.e. one that sees mind and body as inextricably linked) is also attractive: too often modern medicine has concentrated on physical change at the expense of psychological care.

Models of health and medicine are therefore in flux. Social, environmental, and economic factors on the one hand underline the importance of large, external, world-wide influences on health, which are difficult for the individual to control. On the other hand, the consumer is anxiously seeking greater knowledge and control over his or her own health, being aware of the need to take active steps to avoid illness and ensure good health; the continued emphasis on a healthy 'lifestyle' is an example of this concern. The conflict can produce its own problems. Anxieties about potential hazards to health are increasing. Worries about HIV infection, for example, are just beginning to make an impact on Western societies; we are likely to see more psychological problems as a consequence.

Where does clinical psychology fit into this picture? In their chapter on physical health (Chapter 10) Wallace and Bennett stress the importance and value of taking psychological factors into account, not only in terms of a holistic approach to the individual, but in the planning and management of the health system as a whole. Some clinical psychologists have taken the step into management, and thereby taken the opportunity to apply directly psychological concepts and principles to health care. It remains to be seen what impact they may make. At a more specific level the contribution of clinical psychology to health could take a number of forms. Firstly, more individual assessment and treatment programmes could be developed, for example, for stress-management for those at risk for coronary heart disease, for counselling services for actual and potential AIDS sufferers, and for psychological help for the terminally ill and their relatives. Secondly, there could be an expansion in the numbers of psychologists able to offer counselling and consultation services in general hospitals, and thereby to begin to influence the way health care is delivered in those settings. This would conform to the wider role for clinical psychologists envisaged in the MPAG report on clinical psychology in Britain. Thirdly, local services could draw on psychological expertise when, for example, planning health care for the elderly or looking to ensuring good community care for the mentally ill. Fourthly, there is a powerful role for psychology in the promotion of health, advising on the strengths and limitations of strategies for changing lifestyle, for example. Fifthly, there is still a paucity of good research on psychology and health; too many gimmicky ideas are put forward without attention to proper understanding or careful evaluation. Finally, clinical psychologists, like other health care professionals, will need to be much more active in lobbying governments to take a broader view of health and to recognize that resources are essential at all levels of health care.

(c) The challenge of long-term disability

The application of psychology to health care should reflect the health problems and needs of a population. If that population and those needs change, then the priorities of the health care system should also change. Kaprio (1979) pointed out a decade ago that

Europe is becoming healthier, death rates are falling, and patterns of need are changing ... Pathological conditions determined by a combination of genetic, environmental, and behavioural factors are beginning to dominate the health scene and intrude into family and community life.

This places great emphasis on the notion of need for care, a topic that has only recently attracted the attention of psychologists. A key article by Bradshaw (1972) differentiates between normative need—as expressed by a professional; felt need—where need equals want; expressed need—felt need turned into action; and comparative need—where need is perceived to exist in members of a population because others with equal need receive a service. Need is often expressed as someone X needs Y for purpose Z, when the nature of Z is itself often obscure. The related concept of dependency draws attention to the person's life-span experience of receiving support and help as a determinant of care elicitation. Developing formal means of need analysis may be a major psychological contribution to long-term care.

Clearly increasing attention needs to be paid to the health care needs of the increasing numbers of people of all ages who have a disability. There is a growing population of young adults with non-degenerative but irreversible handicaps with considerable expectation of life, who require specialized help to adapt to their disabilities. The development by the WHO of a classification of Impairment, Disability, and Handicap, to match the classification of disease, is indicative of the growing significance of chronic disability in health care. Psychological adaptation to disability, both by the person with the disability as well as by families and carers, is thus of increasing importance.

Changed patterns of family life also have an effect on the care of those with chronic conditions. The increasing proportion of single-parent families, and of families where children have had successive different parents through divorce and remarriage, is likely to reduce the amount of support available to a child within such families. The greater availability of work outside the home for women, and the greater proportion of older people with fewer children to look after them means that care for older people within their own families is less likely to be available. This suggests an increased need for information and guidance to families with a handicapped member, to enable them to cope better and longer with the relative.

Clinical psychologists have not traditionally been concerned with care—as opposed to cure. Recently there have been a number of comments on the need for psychologists to adopt a more ameliorative or rehabilitative model of intervention, accepting in so doing that positive treatment does not always work—and may be viewed as a failure. Care consists of at least four elements: a set of explicit or implicit beliefs which guide care; a set of goals or objectives; a set of care practices, such as alertness to the needs of the cared-for, and appropriate use of touch for its own sake; and the emotions and feelings which accompany care (Hall 1990).

Several aspects of care stand out as demanding attention from psychologists. What psychological processes are involved in the vigilance, risk-taking, and decision-making of care? How is care elicited and terminated, and what features of the cared-for elicit care? Why do people want to care when there is no pre-existing emotional or social attachment to the other? Since one in four of the readers of this book are likely to require care at some time in their lives, simple self-interest alone suggests we look at some of these questions.

INTERNATIONAL TRENDS IN THE DEVELOPMENT OF CLINICAL PSYCHOLOGY

Clinical psychology as a discipline varies in some aspects of orientation and structure from country to country. It is instructive to compare developments within Europe to the present position within the USA, traditionally seen as the 'market leader' in clinical psychology. In those European countries where a number of psychologists are available for employment, the main areas of employment tend to be in the areas of health, education, correction, and employment/ vocational guidance. Psychologists may also be employed as such in research, and by the public services and armed forces (such as the police and army) to assist with training, support at times of stress, and equipment design. The contribution of psychologists to public service in different countries has been outlined by Gilgen and Gilgen (1987).

There are a number of organizational changes affecting British and European health and professional psychological services, including changing United Kingdom policies on the funding and structure of health care agencies, and EC changes in the acceptability of professional qualifications. Jansen (1986), in reviewing common trends in five European countries regarding mental health and social welfare policy, points out the shared emphasis in the countries studied on adequate social support systems, on integrated health care systems, and on support of the co-ordinated care system by a social welfare system which allows for community-based care. Thus there are a number of political assumptions shared by European countries relevant to the delivery of publicly-funded psychological services.

The broad similarity within Europe is likely to increase after 1991 with the implementation of article 27 of the Treaty of Rome of 1957 (by EC Directive 89/48/EEC), which provides for the mutual recognition of professional qualifications in member states. The existence of the EC directive will give a powerful thrust towards increasingly common procedures in licensing and certification of psychologists in public services, perhaps based on the American Examination for the Professional Practice of Psychology (EPPP, described by Hill and Reaves 1990), which is built on a formal role-delineation study which is already accepted in most American states as the standard test of relevant knowledge.

The impact of the vast American psychological establishment upon psychology elsewhere in the world has been substantial. Moghaddam (1987) has suggested that there are three worlds of psychological research and practice: the first consists of the USA alone, the second comprises the 'other developed nations', and the third the developing nations. Moghaddam goes on to suggest that the traffic of psychological knowledge has mostly been one way—from the First World to the Second, and from the First and Second to the Third, even though 'there are few important ideas of contemporary psychology that are North American in origin'. This analysis suggests that European countries may have imported psychological ideas from the First—American—World of psychology, which are not necessarily those most relevant to their needs, or consistent with their political and social values and institutions.

The EC regulations will both force and encourage clinical psychologists in Europe together more, and there is likely to be more interchange of psychological knowledge within the EC. This has the capacity to create a professional psychological community potentially large enough to challenge some of the implicit assumptions of the American psychological community, which ever since the 'Boulder' Conference of 1948 has guided clinical psychology internationally. We may need to re-examine what psychology is best suited to the needs of public services.

SUMMARY

Clinical psychology has developed very rapidly as a profession, both numerically and in the range of client problems that are now presented for treatment. A continuing interplay between theory and clinical practice has meant that new areas of psychological research and theory have become of practical significance. The continuing concern of psychologists with assessment has been modified to emphasize those aspects of behaviour and experience more directly related to client problems and treatment. The growing range of effective psychological interventions has increased the interest of both clients and other professionals in them, leading to an important growth in collaboration with and training of other professionals.

Public views of health and illness are changing, and the health needs of that public are changing. Part of that change is a readiness to look at non-medical forms of help, and to take more personal responsibility for health care. The practice of clinical psychology supports both of these changes, and offers many useful concepts and procedures to assist them.

REFERENCES

Barlow, D. N. and Hersen, M. (1984). *Single-case experimental designs. Strategies for studying behavior change* (2nd edn). Pergamon Press, New York.

Bradshaw, J. (1972). A taxonomy of social need. In *Problems and progress in medical care* (ed. G. McLachlan), pp. 71–82. Oxford University Press

Brewin, C. (1988). *Cognitive foundations of clinical psychology*. Erlbaum, London.

Catalan, J. and Gath, D. (1985). Benzodiazepines in general practice: a time for decision. *Br. Med. J.*, **290**, 1374–6.

Gilgen, A. R. and Gilgen, C. K. (1987). *International handbook of psychology.* Greenwood Press, New York.

Hadley, S. W. and Strupp, M. H. (1977). Evaluations of treatment in psychotherapy: naïveté or necessity? *Professional Psychologist*, **8**, 80–92.

Hall, J. N. (1990). Towards a psychology of caring. *British Journal of Clinical Psychology*, **29**, 129–44.

Hill, D. S. and Reaves, R. P. (1990). Licensure/certification of psychologists in North America. *News from European Federation of Professional Psychologists' Associations*, **IV** (No. 2), 23–9.

Jansen, M. A. (1986). Mental health policy: observations from Europe. *American Psychologist*, **41**, 1273–8.

Kaprio, L. A. (1979). *Primary health care in Europe*, WHO Regional Office for Europe, EURO Reports and Studies No. 14. Copenhagen.

King's Fund (1987). *The need for asylum in society for the mentally ill or infirm*. King Edward's Hospital Fund for London, London.

Manpower Planning Advisory Group (1990). *Clinical Psychology Project: full report*. HMSO, London.

Moghaddam, F. M. (1987). Psychology in the Three Worlds. *American Psychologist*, **42**, 912–20.

Glossary

Advocacy. Pleading, defending, or interceding on behalf of another. In psychological usage refers to advocacy on behalf of handicapped or disabled people (such as people with learning difficulties) to enable them to have access to a range of benefits within the complex welfare, social care, and health care systems, and to improve the quality of those systems as used by them.

Agoraphobia. From the Greek 'fear of the market place'. Characterized by fear of being away from a place of safety, usually the home. Low self-esteem and excessive dependence on others are features.

Alternative and complementary medicine and psychologies. Non-traditional theories and techniques of disease and treatment, such as osteopathy and aromatherapy. The terms are often used interchangeably, although strictly alternative medicine refers to medical practices which are not acceptable to conventional medicine, while complementary medicine refers to practices which are compatible with [and not infrequently themselves practised by] conventional medicine. Alternative psychologies are based on a variety of doctrines and philosophies, often including elements from psychodynamic schemes of thought, neurophysiological studies, mystical or esoteric philosophies, and so-called 'unexplained' phenomena.

Anorexia nervosa. Loss of weight usually due to persistent fasting or excessive dieting. Amenorrhoea is also common, as are fear of fatness and disturbed body-image. Almost entirely found in girls and younger women.

Anxiety. Feelings of apprehension and unease in response to real or imagined threat. Anxiety consists of *physiological reactions*, such as increased heart rate, sweating, and trembling; *behavioural responses*, such as avoidance; and *cognitive disturbance*, such as worrying thoughts or frightening fantasies. There are a variety of clinical anxiety states, for example, generalized anxiety and phobic anxiety.

Anxiety-management training. The use of behavioural treatments of anxiety in the form of a skills training approach. Anxious patients are directly taught methods of managing their anxiety such as relaxation and planned practice, either individually or in a group.

Applied behaviour analysis. Applied behaviour analysis is the application to problems of social importance of the concepts and methods associated with the philosophy of science known as radical or operant behaviourism. Behaviour itself is its fundamental subject-matter, and is not an indirect means of studying something else, such as cognition or mind or brain.

Assessment

Behavioural: psychological measurement procedures which focus on the behaviour which is to be treated, or which is likely to change, at the time it occurs and without making any assumptions about underlying causes or variables.

Psychometric: psychological measurement procedures which measure assumed traits or characteristics, typically involving comparison of the patient with appropriate norms, and often conducted in a face-to-face assessment setting.

Backward chaining. Backward chaining is a process whereby a task is broken down into its components and the final link in the chain of components is taught first. This is then followed by reinforcement. When the person is able fully to complete the final component the penultimate component is taught, and so on back to the beginning of the chain.

Baseline. An assessment, or the results of an assessment, carried out before treatment has started and normally continued until the measure is stable or steady.

Behaviour therapy. Method of psychological treatment developed in the 1950s, derived from experimental studies of conditioning and learning. The focus of treatment is on overt behaviour, using psychological principles to achieve specific behavioural goals. Often contrasted with **psychodynamic** psychotherapies (see below), where the focus is more on achieving insight or personality change.

Between-groups design. An experimental design where two or more different groups are studied, one receiving the experimental treatment and the other(s) receiving control or comparison treatments. In some such designs all groups receive all treatments, but in a different order.

Biofeedback. Use of electronic equipment to monitor bodily reactions (for example heart rate, EEG) to enable individuals to modify and control these reactions. Usually achieved by the feedback of the response in terms of a visual or auditory signal that varies in intensity according to the subject's control. Clinical applications are in anxiety states, headaches, high blood-pressure, and some musculo-skeletal disorders.

Bulimia. Disturbance of eating characterized by excessive preoccupation with food—a pattern of binge eating and self-induced vomiting or laxative abuse. Occurs mainly in young women of slightly older age-range than anorexics. See **anorexia nervosa**.

Case-management. The provision of a single person or team to assume responsibility for long-term care and support to a client, regardless of where the client lives or which agencies are involved. The case manager must work in the community, sometimes intensively, and serves as a helper, service broker, and advocate (see **Advocacy**).

Child abuse. Serious physical, mental, or sexual assault, neglect, or exploitation of a child, by implication referring particularly to that initiated by someone [well] known to the child. Includes intentional acts of omission as well as repeated excessive violence and incest; being subject to abuse may lead to profound disturbance in later adulthood.

Client-centred therapy. Developed by Carl Rogers in 1940s, CCT aims to help clients explore their feelings in the context of a warm, empathic, and trusting relationship. Therapy is seen as personal growth rather than 'treatment', and the approach eschews specific techniques or procedures.

Clinical psychology. The application of psychological theory and practice to a broad range of problems—mental and physical—for which people seek treatment.

Cognition. A general term to cover all aspects of knowledge—perceiving, thinking, imagining, reasoning, etc. Contrasted with affect or feeling. It is maintained by some that all emotions are cognitively processed and by others that emotions are at times directly experienced.

Cognitive–behavioural therapy. Describes the combination of behaviour therapy and cognitive therapy in which, generally, behavioural procedures are used to change cognitive processes. It is a more liberal form of behaviour therapy in the recognition paid to thoughts and beliefs in understanding and changing psychological problems.

Cognitive therapy. The prime focus is on patients' thinking processes, with the goal of changing distorted or unrealistic thoughts and beliefs. Methods vary from Socratic argument to behavioural procedures. Beck's cognitive therapy, developed in the 1970s, is a promising treatment for depression.

Community psychology. The application of psychological theory and practice to people living in natural communities, and to the problems encountered by people in that setting.

Conditioning. The process by which a particular response comes to be elicited by a stimulus, event, or object other than that to which it is the natural or reflexive response.
Classical conditioning: the association in time of a neutral stimulus (for example, a bell) with a reflexive stimulus (for example, food) so that a conditioned response (for example, salivation) occurs to the neutral stimulus.
Operant conditioning: the process by which behaviour is modified by systematically varying its consequences (rewards and punishments).

Constructional approach. A constructional approach is one which deals with a person's problems by establishing new behaviours or by re-establishing behaviours which have been lost. It avoids focusing on the removal of behaviour by whatever means. The 'constructional question' would be 'if you didn't have this problem, what would you be *doing*, what would you be like?' A constructional approach gives particular recognition to how a problem first occurred or developed or is maintained.

Control group. A group of patients or people in all respects similar to the main group, except that they are not subjected to the treatment or condition that is being experimentally investigated.

Coping skills training. A problem-solving approach which first identifies cues and high-risk situations leading to temptation or relapse. Then alternative ways of dealing with these high-risk situations are systematically explored.

Counselling. A helping relationship in which the counsellor seeks to enable the client to explore his or her concerns and to find ways of resolving them. Counselling is a form of psychological treatment, although generally its focus is on less disturbed clients and it often takes place in non-medical settings, for example, student counselling.

Cue exposure. An approach to psychological treatment which involves deliberate exposure to those cues or high-risk situations which provoke desire or compulsion. Prolonged repeated exposure, whilst at the same time resisting temptation, leads to a gradual reduction in desire.

Depression. Feelings of sadness and hopelessness, and lowered bodily activity. Clinical depression is characterized by a reduction or increase in appetite, disturbances of thought and movement (these usually being slowed down or occasionally agitated), lethargy, poor concentration, feelings of guilt and self-blame, and general loss of interest in previously enjoyed activities.

Educational psychology. The application of psychological theory and practice to educational methods, and to problems encountered by people in the educational process.

Evaluation. The process of finding the value of a treatment, by formally determining whether it is effective, efficient, and acceptable, in achieving predetermined objectives.

Event-sampling. A behavioural assessment technique where only a proportion of the key events are observed thoroughly, although all events are recorded; this technique is particularly appropriate for complex key events demanding very detailed observation.

Forensic psychology. Psychology as applied to the legal process; sometimes also used generally to describe the application of psychological theory to the assessment and treatment of offenders.

Functional analysis. The analysis of the relationship between a key event, and the preceding, concurrent, and following events, to see if there is any association between them. If such an association is found this functional relationship can be used to develop a treatment strategy.

Health psychology. The application of psychological theory and practice to the beliefs, behaviour, and experience of people relating to their health, both when they are well and when they are ill.

Hypnosis. A state in which the hypnotized person responds to external suggestions allowing events to be experienced as if they were actually occurring. Successfully used as an anaesthetic and analgesic in selected subjects. Used as a form of psychotherapy, and it has been closely studied by experimental psychologists.

Intelligence. General mental ability and specialized abilities such as numeracy, verbal reasoning, and perceptual skills. There is a long-standing controversy over the extent to which general intelligence (called G) exists over and above a variety of specialized abilities. The Intelligence Quotient (IQ) describes a way of measuring intelligence using psychological tests.

Learning. The process by which knowledge and behaviour are acquired and understood. *The laws of learning* refer to basic principles formulated by psychologists in the scientific study of learned behaviour. *Learning theory* describes the body of theoretical knowledge on the processes involved in learning.

Learning disability/mental handicap. The following definition has been proposed by the American Association on Mental Retardation in December 1990. These terms are essentially synonymous, and refer to 'substantial deficits in certain aspects of personal competence. [Learning disability] is manifested as significantly sub-average abilities in cognitive functioning, accompanied by deficits in adaptive skills. These deficits in adaptive skills may occur in one or more of the following areas: communication, self-care, social skills, functional academics, practical skills, leisure, use of community, self-direction, work, and independent living.

Specific adaptive deficits often co-exist with strengths in other adaptive skills or other areas of personal competence.

The existence of deficits in adaptive skills must be documented within the context of community environments typical of the individual's age peers, and indexed to the person's individualised needs for support.

[Mental handicap/learning disability] begins prior to age 18, but may not always be of lifelong duration. With appropriate services over a sustained period of time, the life functioning of the person with a mental handicap/ learning disability will generally improve.'

Millieu therapy. A method of psychotherapy that arose in the context of institutional care of psychiatric patients. The total environment or milieu, including staff and patients, is designed to be a 'therapeutic community', conducive to the patients' psychological welfare and recovery.

Morbidity. The nature and frequency of specific mental or physical conditions in the population, often expressed as the number of contacts or notified cases for every 1000, say, of the population.

Motivational counselling. An approach to counselling which emphasizes a supportive empathic relationship, a non-confrontational approach, exploration of the benefits of behavioural change, and helping a client to make choices about coping strategies and alternative activities.

Needs, and need analysis. In experimental psychology a need refers to a deficiency or lack in terms of a postulated goal, which may be physiological. It has acquired a secondary meaning in clinical psychology practice, referring to a lack of appropriate clinical service for a person with a health-care problem. Need-analysis consists of formally establishing the needs for psychological and health care of a population or an individual, examining normative, felt, expressed, comparative, and met and unmet need.

Neuropsychology. The study of the relationship between brain structure and pathology, and behaviour and experience.

Normalization. A complex philosophy of care advocated by Wolfensberger, which essentially stresses that the objectives and practices of caring institutions or regimes should be socially valued: the philosophy has many detailed implications, and although mainly applied to the care of people with learning difficulties has potential applications for other clinical groups.

Obsession. Irrational idea or thought that persists against one's will. Often accompanied by ritualistic, compulsive behaviour. Common obsessions are of checking, contamination, and harm to oneself or others.

Personality. The integrated organization of the physical and psychological characteristics of an individual, including intelligence, emotionality, and social behaviour, in the way that the individual presents himself to others. *Personality traits* describe general characteristics of the individual, for example impulsive, social, taciturn, etc. *Personality types* describe major patterns of personality, for example introvert, neurotic.

Personality disorder. A catch-all psychiatric term used to describe individuals with relatively intractable personality problems such as anti-social behaviour, egocentricity, inability to form or sustain close relationships with others, or impulsivity. *Borderline p.d.* is a label attached to individuals whose personality problems are more severe and, as the name implies, are regarded as on the borderline with overtly psychotic states.

Phobia. Intense fear and avoidance of harmless events or objects. There are a variety of specific phobias, for example of insects and animals, and also social phobias and **agoraphobia**.

Post-traumatic stress disorder (PTSD). A syndrome or set of presenting problems arising as a consequence of the experience of an unusual, sudden, and major threat or distressing event, such as serious harm to oneself or one's close family, or sudden destruction of one's home. The consequences may include intrusive distressing recollections of the event, recurrent distressing dreams, persistent avoidance of places and stimuli associated with the event, and persistent symptoms of increased arousal, such as disturbed sleep.

Processes of change. These are the processes which are often involved in successful behavioural change. *Raising awareness* can encourage movement from precontemplation to contemplation. *Self-liberation* is involved in the movement from precontemplation to action, and other processes are linked to the action and maintenance stages.

Prompts, physical and verbal. A prompt is help given to a person so that they may complete a task. A verbal prompt is essentially an instruction or some spoken help; a physical prompt is manual guidance.

Psychoanalysis. A method of psychological treatment, developed from the work of Freud, which focuses on the uncovering of unconscious conflicts by predominantly verbal means. Significant features of psychoanalysis include free association, interpretation, and the development of transference, whereby strong emotional feelings experienced in other relationships are 'transferred' to the therapist. Classically a lengthy and intensive therapy lasting several years, although briefer and less intensive forms have also been developed.

Psychodynamic. A term derived from psychoanalytic theory, describing the interplay of mental and emotional forces and the way these affect behaviour and mental state.

Psychopathic disorder. A psychiatric term used to describe abnormally aggressive individuals whose conduct can lead to violent and criminal acts. A controversy exists as to whether or not such individuals are impervious to the moral and ethical consequences of their actions.

Psychotherapy. General term for any treatment by psychological means designed to reduce personal distress, raise morale, or help solve personal or social problems. Sometimes used to describe verbal methods of therapy in contrast to **Behaviour therapy**, although this distinction is not consistently used.

Psychotropic. A term used of drugs with an effect on psychological function, behaviour, or experience. The term can cover a wide range of substances, but is usually taken to refer to those drugs most frequently used in psychiatry (for example major tranquillizers or antidepressants).

Punishment. Describes the way the probability of a response is reduced by the presentation of an aversive consequence.

Questionnaire. A list of questions seeking information about a person's attitudes, knowledge, or traits, often self-administered, and thus easy to use, and often used for surveys. Some questionnaires contain an anti-faking scale.

Rating scale. A list of questions or statements about a person which are judged or rated, typically by another person (the rater) about the extent to which they occur. The observation or rating procedure is usually well-defined.

Regional secure unit (RSU). A medium-secure health service facility for disruptive psychiatric patients and mentally disordered offenders. RSUs were set up in the English and Welsh regions following the recommendations of the Butler Committee in 1975 as a complementary facility to **Special Hospitals**.

Rehabilitation. Procedures for helping disabled patients to return to society after illness and to maximize their general functioning. It is applied both to institutionalized psychiatric patients being returned to community settings and to physically handicapped people being helped to recover from or adapt to their disability.

Reinforcement. Describes the process in **operant conditioning** by which a response is strengthened by its consequences.
Positive reinforcement describes the strengthening of a response by presenting a stimulus (for example a reward). *Negative reinforcement* describes the process of strengthening a response by taking away an aversive or unpleasant stimulus (for example by the removal of loud noise or shock). The latter is not to be confused with **punishment**.

Reliability. The extent to which a measurement procedure gives consistent or closely similar results when applied more than once, under similar conditions, to the same person or group. When the measure is applied by two or more different users (or raters or testers) the degree of consistency or similiarity is a measure of inter-user (or -tester) reliability.

Room management. Room management is a system whereby the behaviour of a number of clients may be influenced by 2 or 3 staff members. The system involves designating specific roles for the room manager (such as ensuring that materials are available for all clients and that crises are dealt with) and an individual helper (whose job is to move around the room systematically prompting clients to work with materials).

Schizophrenia. A major psychiatric disorder characterized by disturbances of thought, flattened or inappropriate emotions, delusions, and hallucinations, usually in the form of imagined voices. Tends to occur in young adults in acute form, and can become chronic.

Self-monitoring. Assessment procedures that involve people in recording their own behaviour by suitable charts or diaries, or by suitable physiological devices.

Single-case designs. An experimental design where one person receives a series of treatments or conditions in a carefully planned sequence, with some conditions possibly repeated (but where the sequence minimizes the effect of early conditions on later conditions).

Social skills training. The use of didactic procedures of modelling, role-playing, and feedback, to train people in 'social skills'. 'Social skills' refer to specific features of social behaviour that result in successful interaction. These range from specific non-verbal behaviours, such as eye-contact or gesture, to complex patterns of interaction.

Special Hospital. A maximum-security hospital for patients whose violent or criminal behaviour is deemed to require treatment under conditions of special security. Broadmoor hospital is probably the best known Special Hospital in the UK.

Stages of change. A number of stages are involved in behavioural change. In the precontemplation stage no changes are planned in the near future. The contemplation stage covers that period when costs, benefits, and ability to cope are being reappraised. In the action stage positive steps are being taken. During the maintenance stage vigilance is still relatively high, in an attempt to prevent relapse.

Statistical analysis. The process of subjecting a number of figures to a particular manipulation (which may include correlation, analysis of variance, calculation of means) essentially to condense the figures to show some central characteristics of the data. *The statistical significance* of the results is the probability that that result could have been achieved by chance, or by random allocation, and is conventionally expressed at probability levels of 5, 1, or 0.1 per cent (or as 0.05, 0.01, or 0.001).

Stimulus control. Stimulus control is the extent to which an antecedent event influences the subsequent occurrence of a particular behaviour. It is measured as a change in response probability that results from a change in stimulus value. The greater the change in response probability the greater the degree of stimulus control with respect to the continuum being studied.

Stress. *Either* unpleasant aspects of the external social and physical environment *or* the subjective response of the individual to threats and challenges arising from that environment.

Tests
Attainment: sets of standard questions or items designed to measure specific achievements or attainments, such as reading, and distinguished from the measurement of more general abilities.
Intelligence: sets of standard problems and materials designed to measure maximum general mental ability, or power of learning and understanding, and typically yielding an intelligence quotient (IQ).
Personality: *either* sets of standard questions relating to a person's own distinctive character, or normal mode of functioning, scored to yield measures of different personality traits; *or* sets of *projective* materials which

are essentially ambiguous or neutral in meaning, the responses to which are assumed to reveal underlying traits or characteristics.

Time out. Withdrawal of positive reinforcement for a particular behaviour (for example shouting, fighting) by taking the individual out of the environment where such behaviour is being reinforced. Often used in managing aggressive behaviour in children and adolescents.

Time-sampling. A behavioural assessment technique involving observation of the patient or setting for only a proportion of the total time possible, by observing according to a predetermined schedule of random or systematically chosen times, thus giving a representative sample of observations.

Validity. The extent to which a measurement procedure assesses what it is supposed to assess. This somewhat circular definition may be clarified by distinguishing between face or content validity—the extent to which inspection of the form or content of the procedure shows it is appropriate; and empirical validity—the extent to which the procedure is consistent with the scores derived from another totally independent measure of the same phenomenon.

Index